Modern Critical Views

Modern Critical Views

Modern Critical Views

PABLO NERUDA

Edited and with an introduction by
Harold Bloom
Sterling Professor of the Humanities
Yale University

CHELSEA HOUSE PUBLISHERS
New York ◊ Philadelphia

© 1989 by Chelsea House Publishers, a division
of Main Line Book Co.

Introduction © 1988 by Harold Bloom

Printed and bound in the United States of America

10   9   8   7   6   5   4   3   2   1

∞ The paper used in this publication meets the minimum
requirements of the American National Standard for
Permanence of Paper for Printed Library Materials, Z39.48-
1984

Library of Congress Cataloging-in-Publication Data

Pablo Neruda / edited and with an introduction by Harold
Bloom.
    p.   cm.—(Modern critical views)
  Bibliography: p.
  Includes index.
  Summary: A collection of nineteen critical essays on the
Chilean writer and his work, arranged chronologically in the
order of their original publication.
  ISBN 1-555-46298-7
  1. Neruda, Pablo, 1904-1973—Criticism and interpretation.
[1. Neruda, Pablo, 1904-1973—Criticism and interpretation.
2. Chilean literature—History and criticism.]   I. Bloom,
Harold. II. Series.
PQ8097.N4Z719 1988   87-27686
861—dc19   CIP
                                              AC

Contents

Editor's Note

This book brings together a representative selection of the best criticism available in English on the work of the great Chilean poet, Pablo Neruda. The critical essays are reprinted here in the chronological order of their original publication.

Essentially this is Frank Menchaca's book, a young poet's labor of love for the poetry of Pablo Neruda. Menchaca, the true editor of this volume, researched it, translated several of the critical pieces into English, contributed his own appreciative essay, here published for the first time, and advised me on my introduction. I express my profound gratitude, as I believe this to be the first book that gathers criticism of Neruda in English.

My introduction addresses itself to Neruda's assertion of sonship to Walt Whitman, a beautiful though problematical idea on Neruda's part. Neruda's friend, the most extraordinary of modern Spanish poets, Federico García Lorca, begins the chronological sequence with his introduction of Neruda to a Madrid audience in 1935, translated here for the first time. Lorca prophecies what proved to be true, that Neruda was the first authentic Latin American poet, even as Whitman began a new poetry in English in the New World.

The *Odas elementales* are analyzed by Walter Holzinger as a learned and very personal Marxist revision of Pindaric form and vision. Neruda's American epic, *Canto general*, receives a thorough structural study from Frank Riess, which perhaps underestimates the erotic poignance of the work. The poet's compatriot, Fernando Alegría, follows with a personal reminiscence.

Residence on Earth, the culmination of the earlier Neruda, is examined both by Amado Alonso and Alexander Coleman. Alonso traces the poet's development from the unhappy eroticism of the *Twenty Love Poems* to the High Romantic visions of the first two volumes of *Residence on Earth,* while Coleman centers upon the extraordinarily depersonalizing imagery of these books.

Two essays follow, each translated into English by Menchaca for the first time. Julio Cortázar, eminent novelist and intellectual, provides a fresh perspective upon the place of Neruda in Hispanic American letters. The late E. Rodríguez Monegal, probably Neruda's most thorough exegete, centers upon *Estravagario,* the poet's most splendidly outrageous self-revelation.

We return to *Canto general* with Gordon Brotherston's reading of the epic as having its necessarily equivocal aspects, particularly in regard to the exploitation and enslavement of the continent's original inhabitants. Neruda's moving final phase, lyrics of the self, are read by Jaime Alazraki as a sequence of conversations with the abyss, as the poet confronts mortality on the Chilean sea coast.

Ben Belitt, American poet in the mode of both Hart Crane and Neruda, has translated Neruda for many decades, and contributes a poignant overview arguing for the ultimate unity of Neruda's amazingly diverse canon. The maligned and neglected *Tentativa del hombre infinito* is defended by René de Costa as an essential preparation for the complex and difficult poetry of *Residence upon Earth.*

Neruda's place in the romantic-symbolist line of Blake, Shelley, and Baudelaire is examined by Manuel Durán. *The Heights of Macchu Picchu,* generally regarded as Neruda's masterwork, is illuminated by John Felstiner, the poem's translator, as he turns translation into an explicit mode of poetic interpretation.

España en el corazón, the true inauguration of Neruda's political poetry, is explored here by the English critic Robin Warner. The visionary and prophetic stances of Neruda's poetry are the concern of Enrico Mario Santí, after which Florence L. Yudin responsibly analyzes the vexed matter of the ambiguous role of women in Neruda's poetry. The crucial transition that Spain in 1937 constituted for Neruda is described by Alfred J. MacAdam.

The volume concludes fittingly with Frank Menchaca's intense appreciation of Neruda's poetic achievement, in an essay published here for the first time. Menchaca offers the provoking speculation that Communism attracted Neruda as a way out of the dangerous poetic solipsism of the first two volumes of *Residence upon Earth,* a speculation tempered by Menchaca's precise sense of what is and is not Whitmanian about Neruda's poetry of the self.

Introduction

In 1930, the year that Hart Crane published *The Bridge*, Federico García Lorca completed the composition of his *Poet in New York,* which includes his "Ode to Walt Whitman." The "Ode to Walt Whitman" of Pablo Neruda was written much later, in 1956, and has very little in common with Lorca's poem, a difference surely deliberate on Neruda's part. Lorca's English, at least in 1930, was nonexistent, and his Walt Whitman was a marvelous phantasmagoria. Neruda translated Whitman, and in some ways knew Whitman, and how Whitman influenced other poets, better than some of Neruda's best exegetes have known. Not that Neruda's "Ode to Walt Whitman" is a good poem, but then paradoxically it is one of his least Whitmanian poems. Insofar as I can judge, Neruda is not only a poet of extraordinarily diverse styles, but of very mixed achievement, ranging from bathos to the high Sublime. Whatever the reader's political sympathies, the last phases of Neruda's life, personal and political, and of his poetry, possess a noble pathos, constantly augmented for us by the hideous survival of the barbaric regime that came into power by murdering Allende, and sacking the home and possessions of the dying national poet. Neruda's directly political poetry, even in much of his *Canto general* (1950), some day may be judged as a generous error, human and humane, but aesthetically inadequate. His later political poetry seems to me scarcely readable, but that is the usual fate of nearly all political poetry of any century. Very little American poetry written in English, and that is overtly political, has survived, or is likely still to join the canon. There is Emerson's fine Channing Ode, written against the Mexican War, and William Vaughn Moody's "An Ode in Time of Hesitation," concerning our landgrab in the Spanish-American War. The poems inspired by our Vietnamese debacle are themselves an aesthetic debacle, as is so much current verse of an ideological kind, reflecting the various passions of our composite School of Resentment. No Victor Hugo has come out of us in North, South, or

Central America, or the islands of the Caribbean. American political poetry is perhaps too belated, and Neruda is hardly an exception, nor ought he to have been.

Walt Whitman, despite the ways all too many lame verse writers attempt to see him, was not the ancestor of Allen Ginsberg and other contemporary shamans. Whitman, at his most Sublime, is an immensely difficult and hermetic poet: subtle, evasive, ineluctable, withdrawn, defensive, shy, and endlessly metamorphic. His truest poetic descendants were Wallace Stevens and T. S. Eliot, each of whom repressed him, but the return of the repressed poetic father, partly in the son's own colors, produced their finest poetry. True, deep, poetic influence, a matter I have studied obsessively all my life and attempted to think through as that one thought each of us can hope to think, seems to me to depend upon unconscious or purposive forgetting. As such, it tends to take place in the language in which the poet actually writes his own mature poems. America is not Europe, but American English is also not American Spanish, and Whitman therefore is not the actual precursor of Neruda or Borges, Vallejo or Paz. Whitman is the strongest American poet, and the major figure in American Romanticism, but his language is the language of Shakespeare and of the English Bible. Hispanic poetry, like French, came to Romanticism belatedly, and until our century rather weakly. That must be anyone's impression, but I rely here upon *Children of the Mire* by Octavio Paz, and upon the recent criticism of Roberto González Echevarría, particularly his essay on Nicolás Guillén and the Baroque. The strong Spanish poets before our century were Quevedo, Góngora, and Calderón, a very different grouping from the English line of Chaucer, Spenser, Shakespeare, and Milton, and the descendants of that great fourfold in the High Romantics: Blake, Wordsworth, Shelley and Keats in England, Whitman and Dickinson in America. Neruda's crucial turn, to Blake and Whitman, was clearly an almost desperate effort to find what the Spanish tradition could not give him. Yet Quevedo and not Whitman is clearly his true ancestor, just as his near precursor, who caused him some discomfort, was Vicente Huidobro. T. S. Eliot tried to find ancestors in Dante, Baudelaire, even the rather minor Laforgue, yet remained always the child of Whitman and Tennyson. Neruda's case of poetic influence was not wholly dissimilar.

Neruda, excessive and expressionistic, overtly rhetorical, necessarily delighted in Quevedo, a poet neither Blakean nor Whitmanian. González Echevarría catches the precise dilemma of Neruda's poetic stance, as the critic sets the background for his own investigation into the poetics of Afro-Antilleanism in Nicolás Guillén:

A central feature of that revision is a return to the Baroque, that is to say, to the work of the major poets of the language, Góngora, Quevedo, and Calderón, and to the Baroque aesthetics formulated by Baltasar Gracián. The inversion of the concept of representation from mimesis to expression envisioned by the Romantics was already implicit in the Spanish Baroque. As the Spanish and Spanish-American Romantics were a mere echo of their European counterparts, the great Hispanic poets of the avant-garde had to search for their poetic foundation not in the Romantics, as their English and German counterparts did, but in the Baroque. While it is a commonplace of Spanish literary history to say that the Generation of '27 in Spain looked to Góngora for inspiration, the fact is that the revision which brought about Góngora's rediscovery began in Spanish America with the *modernistas*—José Martí and Rubén Darío in particular—and continued in the writings of the Mexican Alfonso Reyes during the teens. It also has not been made sufficiently clear that both the Spanish-American and the Spanish writers looked to the Baroque poets because there were no Spanish language romantics worthy of rediscovery or rejection: no Goethe, no Coleridge, no Wordsworth, no Schiller, no Leopardi, only Espronceda, Bécquer, and in Spanish America Heredia, Echeverría, all minor poets, no matter how much we strain to find traces of originality in their works. The great Spanish-language poetic tradition that begins with the *modernistas* and makes yet another start in the twenties with the Generation of '27 has as foundation a rewriting of the Baroques.

Implicit here is a realization that runs counter to the overt assumptions of Formalist, Anglo-American literary Modernism: productively accepted contingency must come out of the poetic traditions of one's own language. We cannot choose those whom we are free to love, and poets cannot choose their own precursors. Overdetermination may be much the same process in the erotic and the literary realms. We demand liberty in both, and yet we must compound with the past in both. And in neither past do we confront the universal, but always what is closest at or to home. In Neruda, the place to discover what was closest is in his *Memoirs* (posthumously published, 1974; translated into English by Hardie St. Martin, 1977).

An aspiring poet by the age of six, if we are to credit his account, Neruda had a memory (or a fantasy) of his first poem that is a very dark version of the Enlightenment myth of the birth of what then was called the Poetic Character:

> I have often been asked when I wrote my first poem, when poetry was born in me.
>
> I'll try to remember. Once, far back in my childhood, when I had barely learned to read, I felt an intense emotion and set down a few words, half rhymed but strange to me, different from everyday language. Overcome by a deep anxiety, something I had not experienced before, a kind of anguish and sadness, I wrote them neatly on a piece of paper. It was a poem to my mother, that is, to the one I knew, the angelic stepmother whose gentle shadow watched over my childhood. I had no way at all of judging my first composition, which I took to my parents.
>
> They were in the dining room, immersed in one of those hushed conversations that, more than a river, separate the world of children and the world of grownups. Still trembling after this first visit from the muse, I held out to them the paper with the lines of verse. My father took it absentmindedly, read it absentmindedly, and returned it to me absentmindedly, saying: "Where did you copy this from?" Then he went on talking to my mother in a lowered voice about his important and remote affairs.
>
> That, I seem to remember, was how my first poem was born, and that was how I had my first sample of irresponsible literary criticism.

Like Whitman before him, Neruda came to associate the genesis of his poetry with the death of the father. Lincoln, particularly in the magnificent elegy, "When Lilacs Last in the Dooryard Bloom'd," became a surrogate father for Whitman, as Neruda understood, and that was Neruda's own placement of Walt Whitman, a knowing substitution of the greatest poet of the Western Hemisphere for José del Carmen Reyes, the trainman, the first and most important of Neruda's irresponsible literary critics. The "deep anxiety . . . a kind of anguish and sadness" testifies to what might be called a Primal Scene of Instruction, in which the poem to the mother meets the father's indifference, and a second narcissistic scar is formed.

Neruda's poem, "The Father," hardly can be termed an elegy, and its fiercely effective conclusion chills the reader:

Mi pobre padre duro
allí estaba, en el eje de la vida,
la viril amistad, la copa llena.
Su vida fue una rápida milicia
y entre su madrugar y sus caminos,
entre llegar para salir corriendo,
un día con más lluvia que otros días
el conductor José del Carmen Reyes
subió al tren de la muerte y hasta ahora no ha vuelto.

(My poor, hard father,
there he was at the axis of existence,
virile in friendship, his glass full.
His life was a running campaign,
and between his early risings and his traveling,
between arriving and rushing off,
one day, rainier than other days,
the railwayman, José del Carmen Reyes,
climbed aboard the train of death, and so far has not come
    back.)

                                    (tr. Alastair Reid)

The irony, as Neruda must have known, is that the hard father was
the best gift that the poet's genius could have received, just as the substitution of the figure of Whitman as idealized father must be a knowing irony
also. Frank Menchaca shrewdly observes that: "Neruda also must have
understood that the self which claims to be everywhere freely available in
Whitman's poetry is nowhere to be found." The sublime evasions that constitute *Song of Myself* offer Whitman to everyone, and on what do not
seem to be Whitman's own terms, though they are. This is the phenomenon that Doris Sommer wittily terms "supplying demand" in her essay on
the fatherhood of Whitman in Neruda, Borges, and Paz. She argues that:
"Neruda's admiration for the master may have displaced Whitman's narcissism with love for others; but . . . ironically, by re-placing self-love with
the hierarchy-producing secondary narcissism of hero worship." I think
Sommer describes part of the normal process of poetic influence, and I myself would suggest that Borges and Paz, lesser poets than Neruda (though
Borges is of similar eminence in his fictions, and Paz as a man-of-letters),
actually benefited more from Whitman because they understood him far
less well than Neruda did. An idealized father is best misunderstood.
    Neruda's misreadings (in what I think I can call the Bloomian sense)

of Whitman were creative only when they were deliberate, a process that Sommer again depicts accurately:

> Ironically, an heir such as Pablo Neruda seems indifferent to the problem; he will destroy his teacher by resuscitating older models that never even tempted the reader with a promise of equality and the like of whom Whitman had kissed off in the Preface to his poems. Neruda's colossal *Canto general* (1950) writes in and closes off the spaces for the poet's interlocutor by returning the model of America's new fragmented "epic" to a familiar tradition of apparently seamless romantic narrative. It sets Whitman's rawness right; it tames the earlier and more revolutionary aesthetic until what is left of Whitman is the figure of the father, something Whitman claimed he never wanted to be. Neruda thus reaffirms the political usefulness of representative romance over a poetry of "pure possibility" and reestablishes the hierarchy of poet over people that Whitman had managed (however briefly) to level.

I disagree only with "Whitman's rawness," since that is merely Whitman's deception of his reader; no poetry could be more delicate and finished, while pretending to be tough and raw, and *Canto general* is far rawer than Whitman even pretends to be. Compare to the end of *Song of Myself* the conclusion of *The Heights of Macchu Picchu*, the crown of *Canto general:*

> contadme todo, cadena a cadena,
> eslabón a eslabón, y paso a paso,
> afilad los cuchillos que guardasteis,
> ponedlos en mi pecho y en mi mano,
> como un río de rayos amarillos,
> como un río de tigres enterrados,
> y dejadme llorar, horas, días, años,
> edades ciegas, siglos estelares.
>
> Dadme el silencio, el agua, la esperanza.
>
> Dadme la lucha, el hierro, los volcanes.
>
> Apegadme los cuerpos como imanes.
>
> Acudid a mis venas y a mi boca.
>
> Hablad por mis palabras y mi sangre.

(tell me everything, chain by chain,
link by link, and step by step,
file the knives you kept by you,
drive them into my chest and my hand
like a river of riving yellow light,
like a river where buried jaguars lie,
and let me weep, hours, days, years,
blind ages, stellar centuries.

Give me silence, water, hope.

Give me struggle, iron, volcanoes.

Fasten your bodies to me like magnets.

Hasten to my veins to my mouth.

Speak through my words and my blood.)
(tr. John Felstiner)

Like Whitman, Neruda addresses the multitudes, multitudes in the valley of decision. His expressionistic tropes are true to the High Baroque: river of light, buried jaguars, "struggle, iron, volcanoes," and the dead workmen magnetizing Neruda's language and the very drives within him. This is intensely moving, but perhaps rather strenuous when juxtaposed to the quiet authority of our father, Walt Whitman:

I depart as air. . . . I shake my white locks at the runaway
       sun,
I effuse my flesh in eddies and drift it in lacy jags.

I bequeath myself to the dirt to grow from the grass I love,
If you want me again look for me under your bootsoles.

You will hardly know who I am or what I mean,
But I shall be good health to you nevertheless,
And filter and fibre your blood.

Failing to fetch me at first keep encouraged,
Missing me one place search another,
I stop some where waiting for you.

Walt is out there, up ahead of us, but patiently waiting, somewhere. The reader is anxious to catch up, but Walt is beyond anxiety, since he is early, while the reader is belated: "Will you speak before I am gone? Will

you prove already too late?" At the close of *Heights of Macchu Picchu,*
we wonder if the poet is not oppressed by belatedness, even as he urges
the dead workers to speak through him. But Neruda, who meditated upon
Whitman throughout a lifetime, learned the lesson beautifully, in the su-
perb Whitmanian conclusion of his justly famous poem, "The People":

> Por eso nadie se moleste cuando
> parece que estoy solo y no estoy solo,
> no estoy con nadie y hablo para todos:

> Alguien me está escuchando y no lo saben,
> pero aquellos que canto y que lo saben
> siguen naciendo y llenarán el mundo.

> (So let no one be perturbed when
> I seem to be alone and am not alone;
> I am not without company and I speak for all.

> Someone is hearing me without knowing it,
> but those I sing of, those who know,
> go on being born and will overflow the world.)
>   (tr. Alastair Reid)

The direct model is clearly the two uncanny tercets that end *Song of
Myself.* I might not have believed anyone could come so close to Whitman's splendor as Neruda does here, in a poetic act at once bold and
generous. Whitman's grand closure is superbly interpreted by Neruda's
self-valediction. Neruda and Whitman together seem to be alone and are
not alone; they keep each other company and each speaks for all. Someone
among us, or within us, is hearing Neruda and Whitman without knowing
it, without knowing who they are, but they are good health to us nevertheless. Here, at least, Neruda too stops somewhere waiting for us.

FEDERICO GARCÍA LORCA

Introduction of Pablo Neruda to the School of Philosophy and Letters, Madrid

W hat I am going to do now is called an introduction in the conventional protocol of conferences and lectures. But I do not introduce, because a poet of the quality of the Chilean Pablo Neruda cannot be introduced. Rather, in all earnestness and giving my own brief account of the poet, I will single him out, turning my attention to him quietly, but looking deeply.

I tell you that you are about to hear an authentic poet, one of those who has tuned his senses to a world which is not ours, and which few people perceive. A poet closer to death than to philosophy, a poet closer to pain than to the intellect, closer to blood than to ink. A poet full of mysterious voices which, fortunately, he himself does not know how to decipher, a poet of man as he truly is, knowing that the bulrush and the swallow are more eternal than the hard stone cheek of the statue.

Latin America constantly sends us poets of a different muse, of varying capacities and techniques. Gentle poets of the tropics, of the flatland, of the mountain: distinct rhythms and tones which add to the Spanish language a unique richness, a new language that is already somehow familiar for describing the drunken laziness of the snake, or the penguin delighting in play. But not all of these poets possess the tone of America. Many strike one as peninsular and others accentuate with their own voices the bluster of foreign poets, above all the French. But among the great ones, no. In the great ones there is the flash of a light that is full, romantic, cruel, wild, mysterious, American. Like blocks in space waiting to be plunged downward, their poems are suspended above the abyss by a spiderweb. They are like smiles with the light shadings of a jaguar, like a huge hand covered with hair playing delicately with a small lace handkerchief. These poets give the brazen tone of the great Spanish language of the Americas, tying it directly into the sources of our classics, creating poetry which does not regret breaking molds, which does not fear the ridiculous, and which breaks down sobbing in the middle of the street.

Close to the prodigious voice of the always masterful Ruben Darío, to the extravagant, loving, recklessly coarse and glowing voice of Herrera y Reissig, and to the lament of Lautréamont (more Uruguayan than he is French), whose song is filled with horror at the dawn of the adolescent, the poetry of Pablo Neruda rises with a tone never equalled in America, of passion, tenderness and sincerity.

It stands before the world filled with true astonishment and lacks the two elements that have kept so many false poets alive: hatred and irony. When he goes to punish and raises his sword, he suddenly finds a dove, wounded, in his hands.

I advise you to listen attentively to this great poet and to try to be moved with him, each in your own way. Poetry requires a long period of initiation as does any activity, but there is in true poetry a scent, an accent, a luminous streak which all creatures recognize. I hope that it serves as nourishment for that kernel of madness that each of us carries within, and which many murder to earn the hateful monocle of bookish pedantry. Without it, it would be unwise to live.

WALTER HOLZINGER

Poetic Subject and Form in the Odas elementales

Pablo Neruda's *Odas elementales* are particularly interesting for their fusion of a considerable amount of social doctrine and of many subjects traditionally considered "unpoetic" into very effective poetry. I wish here briefly to attempt to establish by a close analysis of one poem, and a more cursory look at several others, that Neruda's choice of poetic subject has made certain poetic techniques particularly apt. For it is evident that personification, catalogues, and the creation of foil relations between large parts of poems (frequently structured dialectically) are techniques common to most of these poems.

Nevertheless, a hasty equation of the dialectic structure common in Neruda's poetry with the dialectic form of his Marxist social doctrine (generally progressing from past to present to a more or less hortatory future) would certainly be an oversimplification. For these poems are odes, and their dialectic structure also corresponds to the traditional division of the Pindaric ode into strophe, antistrophe, and epode. The two influences would appear to compliment and reinforce each other, the form of the ode perhaps supplying the tripartite structure, the Marxist doctrine the tendency toward the temporal division into past, present, and future.

Such a structure is readily apparent in "Oda a las Américas," where the epode, while not typographically marked, nevertheless begins with the change of tone in "Américas heridas" (l. 76). The strophe and antistrophe correspond to the typographical division between stanzas one and two, and their temporal division into past and present. But Neruda's dialectic

From *Revista Hispánica Moderna* 36, nos. 1 & 2 (1970–71). © 1971 by the Hispanic Institute.

here is somewhat complicated by his concern with universalizing his poem. This concern causes him to call upon America primarily in terms of the beauties of its nature, especially at the beginning, and only to present a more explicit and direct vision of its people in the middle section, between the images of the "mandón . . . con su sable," (35) and the "sanguinarios loros" (73). For America as a continent with its natural beauties has a greater direct appeal for the reader, regardless of national, class, or ideological affiliations, than a more partisan class or historical approach, say exclusively through the pre-Columbian Indians, could possibly have. At the same time, specific historical, class, and even certain chauvinistic appeals to a Pan-Latin Americanism, must be and are made in the poem to fill both doctrinal and exemplary needs. This results in some tension and ambivalence between the two directions, finally united at the end.

It is evident from the prominent place nature has in this poem, and from its first lines, where the oceans are said to have kept the continent pure and intact in a more or less military metaphor ("guardaron"), that we are here in a world similar to the beginning of the *Canto general*, where nature is called upon to resist the Spanish conquerors and to act as one with the Indian defenders. A different emphasis, however, is apparent in this poem. Whereas in the *Canto general* nature's purpose was primarily to protect the largely helpless Indian civilizations, here it is clearly the other way around, and in the latter part of the poem there is a fairly explicit reproach to the Latin Americans for allowing their beautiful continent to be plundered by the new conquerors ("Cómo puede continuar el silencio," 70–71).

Much of the ambivalence evident in the second part of the poem over just where the real value of the Americas lies, whether in the unspoiled beauty of its nature, or in its people, is undoubtedly due to the poet's personal sense of outrage and disappointment at what he feels to be the complete failure of Latin Americans to achieve viable and independent political and economic institutions. A resolution of all ambivalence finally occurs when the speaker makes clear in the last section of the poem that the continent's treasure includes both the land and its people (especially in line 103 wherein people and nature are fused by the figurative labeling of the inhabitants of America as "espigas"). The dialectic between nature's purity and man's misery and corruption finally resolved in a new man in harmony with nature also presents a specific Latin American formulation of the general Marxist dialectic of past versus present to synthesize in an ideal future.

The translation of "Américas," itself ambivalent and readily used in either a political or a geographic context, into terms more explicitly geographic in the next three lines, sets the tone for the entire first stanza. The rest of the stanza takes the form of a six-part nature catalogue that serves to emphasize the unity of the Indians with nature. The distribution of the members of this catalogue is as follows: the first member is from nature, the next two are from the Indians, followed by another two from nature. Then the Indians themselves are presented, and described in two subordinate verses. The "pirámides, vasijas," the objects created by the Indians, are separated from their creators and surrounded by the creations of nature. Besides stressing the harmony between the Indians and nature, this association also raises pathetic images of the state of these pre-Columbian creations which, with the destruction of their creators, have until recently, at least, faded back into nature.

The first member of the catalogue—"siglos de colmenares silenciosos"—is particularly significant. For the beehive is especially important as a ready microcosm for human society, suggesting a community of maximum collective effort and cooperation. In addition, the implicit association of the Indians with the bees shows the oneness with nature of these "razas" which are "silenciosas," and in complete harmony with nature like the "colmenares." "Pirámides, vasijas" correspond chiasmatically to "cántaros" and "piedra," and thus help to link the artifact with the artisan, but at the same time make more apparent the separation of the two by the intervening nature images.

The next stanza stands in a foil relation of present to past to the previous one. The earlier emphasis upon nature becomes more ambivalent in the naming of Paraguay and the other three countries, since as countries, they conjure up political rather than geographical associations. But the nature imagery continues.

A closer examination of the figurative character of much of this nature imagery is now required. In the first four lines of the poem, the words "purísimas" and "intactas" were prominent, and as rather weighty moral terms in a nature context, had no more specific tenor in the poem than the reader's knowledge that this is an image of a paradisiacal America before the European invasions. Now, in "rosa enterrada," and "cárcel," we at least begin to see specific political foils to "purísima," and "intactas." "Purpúreas" is part of the string of images that includes "turquesa fluvial," "corona," "coro de plata," "antigua vestitura," "diadema," "esmeralda," and finally culminates in the "tesoro" (36) sold by the "mandón." All of these images of jewelry and royalty applied to nature suggest that the true treasure to be protected is the land, not its inhabitants.

The countries named are personified to a considerable extent, and, as already suggested, it remains unclear as to whether their tenor is geographic or political. Paraguay provides the transition as it is closest to the previous rather idyllic description of what the continent was before, and thus still carries the emotional burden of those images. These are continued through "turquesa fluvial," until we see them destroyed, first by a nature image in "rosa enterrada," and then by the first explicitly political image, "cárcel." The other three countries are now already viewed in a different light, the essentially political one of the nation as the prison of its inhabitants.

There follows, then, a painful contrast between Peru in nature—"pecho del mundo, / corona de las águilas"—and Peru as a political entity, whose very independence is a matter of debate. The personification, in the case of the remaining two countries becomes rather remote and appears to reflect a certain abstruseness behind the kind of dialectic Neruda has chosen to create. He seems here to be opting for the sentimental view of the pre-Columbian Indian as the noble savage living in a largely paradisiacal environment, who is now come to woe at the hands of foreign invaders, rather than for a more orthodox Marxist dialectic, which would see pre-Columbian America in a more objective and perhaps less rosy light. Neruda then runs into difficulties, for the "no se oyen / vuestras bocas felices" (20–21) has neither a foil nor even a clear subject in the first stanza, where emphasis was placed upon the Indians as "razas de silencio." If not the pre-Columbian Indians, who, then, are these "bocas felices?" Neither the *Canto general* nor most histories would suggest that the Indians under Spanish rule, or any considerable part of the population of these countries since independence has been much better off than they are now. The cause of this logical inconsistency, apart from what is perhaps some simple carelessness in the poem's elaboration, appears to lie in Neruda's political beliefs. These seem to have dictated the creation of an earlier, golden age, to act as a foil to the present state of affairs, and so to portray that state as negatively as possible. That golden age is conveniently not specified. The resulting lack of a clear subject to make possible the creation of a dramatic antithesis or foil considerably reduces the effectiveness of this last image, and leads to the simplistic visualization of these countries in terms of editorial page cartoon images as caricatures of mouths, rather than of their suffering inhabitants.

After a mournful *ubi sunt* in "Dónde ha partido el coro . . . ," we see that only nature has managed to keep some of its old majesty—"antigua vestidura" and "diadema." But the prison has grown, and even among its remaining splendors "en el húmedo reino" a "mandón" carves up and auctions away nature's "tesoro." The insistence upon the growing "cárcel" just before "en el húmedo reino," generalizes the plight of Paraguay to the idyllic nature of the whole continent that is now threatened with destruction by the political forces of the "cárcel" and the "mandón." "Tesoro" has considerable emotive weight, as it sums up all the sensuous images nature has been endowed with. These associations are aptly juxtaposed to the prosaic "hipoteca y remata," with their craven commercial connotations.

Only now the imagery from "sable" and the commercial terms continues to "cacería del hermano" ("cacería" in the previous commercial context implies not the aristocratic sport of a Nimrod, but the hunting down and selling of man for profit). The verses, from "sube un mandón" (35) to "los dólares resbalan" (49) are connected both imagistically and syntactically. Imagistically, the progression is from "cacería" to "tiros," from "tiros" to "nuevos conquistadores," to "sangre," and, perhaps, to "resbalan" (which points back to "sangre"). A separate group of images connects "tiros-puertos" with "llegan," "Pennsylvania," "expertos," "conquistadores," "plantaciones," and fuses with the first group in "dólares." Syntactically, "sube," "se abre," "suenan," and "llegan," are all antepositions of the verb into a larger anaphoric parallelism.

The "mandón" begins a series of images, directly presenting the human reality of the continent. "Mandón con su sable" is a caricature of the "gorila." The indeterminate article "un" here suggests their nondescript interchangeability; the only characteristic which they all share is indicated by the augmentative "ón," and the "sable," both suggestive of the brute force they incarnate. The meaning of "sube" ranges from "subir al poder," to "alzarse en un golpe de estado." "Carcería del hermano," itself a rather abstract and perhaps overly melodramatic image, can represent practically any form of violence possible in such conditions. The next, very specific image, "suenan tiros perdidos," is left open-ended for lack of a particular context. Most readily, it conjures up nocturnal political assassinations, but really stands in a metonymic relation to the complete range of violence present in these regimes. From "puertos" the progression to "llegan" is direct and significant.

In "los expertos de Pennsylvania," both "expertos" and "Pennsylvania" are very particular terms, synecdoches for all the accessories to such neocolonial takeovers. "Expertos" probably takes on an added significance with Neruda by its ready association with numbers, which he rather constantly equates with death and sterility. "Nuestra sangre" is a synecdoche for something like "nuestros hermanos, nuestra raza." In addition, it also suggests the literal feeding of the earth by the shedding of blood. This is a reversal of the more common view of the land itself being plundered for its natural wealth, particularly for its minerals. We are presented instead with a vision of labor as the decisive factor in the land's exploitation. This is indeed close to the orthodox Marxist view, but appears somewhat at odds with the stress placed upon nature previously in the poem, and anticipates the final synthesis. Such an unexpected reversal also serves to heighten the force of the expression. "Pútridas plantaciones o minas subterráneas" (only the most negative aspects of nature are associated with these new conquerors in contrast to the previous harmony with a benevolent nature), are in a chiasmatic relation, and there is a progression of negative *estrújula* adjectives that climaxes on the *esdrújula* noun, "dólares." "Resbalan" conjures up the "dólares" flowing in from these enterprises, but also forces a literalization of "sangre," as if the dollars, vaguely personified, slipped upon the blood with which these enterprises were cultivated.

The "y" serves as a marked pause, both rhythmically, by stopping the flow of verse, and visually, because of the typographical arrangement. The pause calls attention to itself and to what is to follow: the cultural and moral consequences of the new invasion. "Locas" and "descaderan" especially connote prostitution, but "aprendiendo el baile de los orangutanes," whose obvious tenor are various kinds of not very graceful, popular North American dances, suggests the kind of upside-down world where men learn from apes, or a civilization with a rich cultural heritage as distinct from one with a lesser one. "Orangutanes" also suggests "gorilas," and thereby gives a grotesque political tint to the image. Most significant, however, is the paratactic juxtaposition of this image of moral and cultural degeneracy into a direct antithesis with the previous one of economic exploitation and suffering, separated only by one letter—"y"—whose meagerness is emphasized by its typographic isolation.

This image of the girls is once more in contrast with the brief vision of nature in the next three lines, particularly with "purísimas" and "sagrados." The following line is a specification of the earlier "un mandón" into more historical and particular terms. Three dictators are named, but the indefinite article "un" depersonalizes and abstracts them into a class. The chiasmatic construction here adds to the seeming inevitability of the progression from one dictator to another, presenting as it does, a closed process within a strongly end-stopped line, and emphasizes the interchangeability of the names. Trujillo, on the other hand, stands out in contrast as immobile and enduring as a part of the very landscape.

Juxtaposed to this abject human reality are some more lines of nature description, with the especially significant "libertad" of nature in contrast to the previous tyrants. The nature images are also contrasted with the "minúsculos negociantes de sangre," which include both the "mandones" who sell and the "expertos" who buy, and recalls the earlier mention of "sangre." The brunt of the vast nature description in these images is born by "minúsculos," and the disproportion between the two creates an effect of caricature. Two rhetorical questions follow. The "silencio" of the second question now serves as a foil to the earlier silence of the Indians, a silence then of harmony with nature, which is now one of guilt and shame. "Entrecortado" recalls the earlier "sable corta." "Encaramados," the previous "sube," for which it is a synonym, and "sanguinarios loros" are related to "minúsculos negociantes de sangre," both in their common caricature and in the mention of blood. "Loros" are trained to speak by people, their masters. This suggests the puppet nature of these tyrants and their relations with the "expertos." The metaphor is sustained in very specific terms through "encaramados" and "enramadas," until the next line throws it open both in meaning and in levels of diction. From the specific we go to an abstraction, "codicia," and then to another term, "panamericana," with rather particular, unpleasant associations of official hypocrisy and bureaucratic grandiloquence. These images from such disparate fields and levels combine to form an almost allegorical picture of greed, much like that of poverty in "Oda a la pobreza."

Then the poem turns, proceeds into a synthesis or epode, a vision of the immediate future. Again there is rich nature imagery, "ancha" and "felices" in particular contrast with the previous degeneration. The Americas are seen as "oscuras" in their present state, but their day, their "estrella," approaches; other roads appear to lead out of the present state. "Existen otra vez naciones viejas" seems specifically to refer to the rebirth of countries with long histories but recent western domination, such as China. But "existen" is significant as it recalls the earlier rhetorical question "Perú . . . existe?" Peru was, of course, the center of the greatest of the pre-Columbian empires. This passage, therefore, seems to suggest a return to some mythic Indian civilization. Fortunately, this is not developed and difficulties such as those with "bocas felices" are avoided. Instead, the focus again shifts upon the new, clear light which is to enable America to overcome its present wane or "otoño." Then, in a forceful reversal of nature, the new flags are said to move the wind: this new human force impresses itself, finally and significantly, upon nature.

The poem then closes with the narrative voice calling upon America to let its voice be heard, its deeds seen. The alienation of the inhabitants from the continent, present in the previous part of the poem, is here replaced by a reuniting of the two. In the first image, America, now clearly referring to both the land and its people, is to bring forth, almost to give birth to, its own "voz" and "hechos," which are finally to rise out of the earlier shameful silence. In the following images, the stress falls more obviously upon the unity of the continent and its inhabitants. "El decoro" clearly refers to the original state of purity of the continent where neither nature nor man was subject to predatory exploitation (the same tenor in much the same kind of vehicle may be seen in the earlier "antiguas vestiduras," and "diadema," the only remaining signs of the past).

More important, however, is "te dio nacimiento." On one level, this refers to a restoration of the liberty the Indians enjoyed in the past. But more than that, "decoro" seems to suggest the earlier harmonious relation between nature and man, where neither was exploited nor exploiter. This interpretation is supported by the next image where America is called upon to support by means of its "espigas" (its offspring, its people), along with other peoples, the "irrestible aurora." The previous suggestion of a dichotomy between the continent and its inhabitants is thus resolved into a new unity in the future society. The poem has taken us through a dialectic with three kinds of relations between man and nature. The first presents the two in a primeval harmony, in which nature plays the more important part. Next, man is enslaved and used by his fellow man to exploit nature's riches. Finally, nature cooperates with man ("eleves tus espigas sosteniendo . . . la irrestible aurora"), though it is now man who is clearly in command ("el viento se estremece con las nuevas banderas") to form the new society.

The narrative voice in this poem, while not personalized into a full rhetorical "I", nevertheless creates a pseudo-dramatic situation and dramatic tension by apostrophes (e.g. to the personified America at the poem's end, and the four countries at its beginning), and by emotional rhetorical questions ("Qué pasa?" / "Cómo puede?"), which suggest shame in the speaker and are clearly meant as a rebuke to the whole continent. In addition, then, to the structural use of foils for the creation of the dialectic and the general polemic and extra-literary foils of exploited-exploiter which pervade the poem ideologically, Neruda manages to create another, a very emotional foil relation between the polemic eloquence of his narrative voice which reproaches and contrasts with the shameful silence of the Latin American reader. This final foil relation reaches out beyond the poem itself, seeking to resolve the poem-reader dichotomy in the synthesis of the reader's direct action against the postulated common enemy.

In "Oda a la pobreza," Neruda uses similar techniques, but structures his poem about a central dichotomy between himself, the poor of the world, and a poverty personified much like the figure of a medieval vice. The poem is divided into the past of the poet, when he himself was perse-cuted by poverty, and the present, when he relentlessly hounds poverty wherever he can find it. The foil relation is thus dramatized into a personal confrontation between the narrative voice and a personified enemy. The explicit appearance of the narrative voice as the rhetorical "I" in the poem greatly increases the vigor and force of the poem, adds to the effectiveness of the contrast, and serves as a sincerity ploy to capture the sympathy of the reader for the speaker and his cause.

Catalogues serve an important function in the poem. The enumeration of the objects which he first associates with poverty ("tablas podridas," "las goteras," etc.) is essentially metonymic, but the more extended cata-logue of his persecution of poverty toward the end of the poem, beginning with "te sigo," is so amplified as to create its own world, a world of the future where poverty is already substantially defeated. There is apparent a clear progression from "hospital imposible," corresponding to the present, through the agon of the verbs of action, to climax in "que te quedan," which seems to mark an emasculation of poverty, so that the tremendous sense of action and the images of positive, constructive work seem already to represent the desired millennia. The last three lines, with the subjunctive "se levanten" seem to suggest that they are no longer standing anywhere, though they could possibly rise up again. The structure of the poem, then, while essentially a dichotomy between the poet pursued by poverty in the past, and the poet now pursuing it in the present, nevertheless manages to arrive at the suggestion of a synthesis, where poet and people together con-struct a world without poverty.

In "Oda al caldillo de congrio," a poem much lighter in tone, Neruda is presented with a problem which is roughly the opposite of that in "Oda a las Américas." There he had to make specific a very general subject, along with a good deal of potentially unacceptable social doctrine. Ne-ruda's program in these poems includes subjects considered inherently un-poetic. This is implied in the title *Odas elementales,* and here takes him into that area of the expository presentation of cognitive material which is usually avoided by most good poets. This poem is a poetic recipe.

Besides the able creation and manipulation of images and rhythms, Neruda manages to generalize the subject by certain specific poetic tech-niques in combination with the humorous tone. Thus we progress by syn-tactic association and juxtaposition from "En el mar / tormentoso / de

Chile" to "y en las ollas / chilenas" which approaches bathos. The dynamic force of the verbs directing the process, the vaguely dramatic quality aroused by the use of the "tu" form in these verbs, the somewhat ironic climax at "entonces," and the equally ambivalent images of conception (e.g. "impregna," "entregar el tesoro," "recién casados"), all these are more than sufficient to bring us to the climax of the poem, where the hyperbolic summary catalogue "mar y tierra" leads us to the quaint cap of the poem in "cielo." To insure that the reader has not been completely swept away, and that he remembers the tenor of these witty hyperboles, the poem's subject appears again in "ese plato" for a final juxtaposition.

But this poem is not typical of the manner in which Neruda handles such a problem in these poems, just as the lack of polemic content and social doctrine is not typical. The link between polemic content and the combination of foil, personification, and catalogue is therefore made more apparent in this poem by a prominent diminution of both foils and personification. Catalogue structure is, of course, inherent in a recipe. Much more common is the solution in "Oda al átomo," where he strongly personifies and dramatizes a specific, scientific concept, the atom, puts it into a social setting, and creates foils into a dialectic structure, all through amplification and catalogues of pathetic, emotion-arousing imagery with exemplary value ("alcanzando / a la madre dormida / con su niño, / al pescador del río / . . . todo fue polvo / que mordía, / . . . fueron súbitos leprosos, / . . . la mano de sus hijos / . . . se quedaba en sus manos.").

Whatever focus Neruda uses in these poems, in nearly all of them foil, personification, and catalogue are key structural elements. This is undoubtedly in part due to the epic mode of most of the poems, which calls for generous amplifications and broad, emotive contrasts. More specifically, personification allows Neruda to bring into a specific dramatic framework both the abstractions of his social doctrine (as in "Oda a la pobreza"), and very specific, somewhat unpoetic subjects (as in "Oda al átomo"). Foils are used to organize his material into the dialectic perspective of his doctrine. And the catalogues serve mainly to universalize by amplification and thus to create the distinctly epic mode of these poems.

Neruda's ideology also creates some interesting similarities between these poems and much medieval doctrinal poetry, especially the *Everyman* morality play, where foil, personification, and catalogue were also key structural elements for the exposition of an ideology whose dichotomy between good and evil was even more absolute than that of Neruda, and which supplied no synthesis as it refused to countenance any true dialectic between good and evil. It is indicative of Neruda's talent as a poet, however, that whereas in the plays the resolution of the dichotomy always occurs within the character of Everyman himself, and the audience remains largely passive, Neruda often manages to focus his dialectic upon the reader himself, who is then called upon to provide the synthesis by direct action.

FRANK RIESS

The Poet and the Collectivity

Taken as a whole, the *Canto general* constitutes the definitive description of Pablo Neruda, both as a man, and in his relation to nature and to other men. These relationships can be discerned in the poem by drawing up various "instrumental sets." These are structures which link the poet as an individual to larger entities such as *pueblo* and *tierra*. Several self-contained sets can be enumerated which are the "instrumental" ones, i.e. in the major structures which define the connections between man and nature, nature and the poet, at the most general level in the *Canto general*. The first requirement, therefore, would be to show how the poet as an individual becomes the spokesman of, and is identified with, the continent as a whole, through the essential equation *Hombre-Tierra,* and any others that may be found to exist.

The second requirement would be to point out how there arise from these instrumental sets smaller patterns which are a part of them, but which are used in various contexts of the poem, while they continually imply their general level of reference. Once a reader knows and understands these general, over-all instrumental sets, the *Canto general*'s precise field of reference becomes easier to examine. To take two examples: first—

> Aquí encontré el amor. Nació en la arena,
> creció sin voz, tocó los pedernales
> de la dureza y resistió a la muerte.
> Aquí el hombre era vida que juntaba

From *The Word and the Stone: Language and Imagery in Neruda's* Canto general.
© 1972 by Oxford University Press.

> la intacta luz, el mar sobreviviente,
> y atacaba y cantab y combatía
> con la misma unidad de los metales.

What interests the poet here is the quality of group action, taken by men
in a particular environment. The manner of these men is compared to the
manner of metals, sea, and light. The lines imply a set and a system of
relationships existing between man and nature. The second example will
further illustrate this, and introduce another point in more detail:

> Patria, nave de nieve,
> follaje endurecido:
> allí naciste, cuando el hombre tuyo
> pidió a la tierra su estandarte
> y cuando tierra y aire y piedra y lluvia,
> hoja, raíz, perfume, aullido,
> cubrieron como un manto al hijo,
> lo amaron o lo defendieron.
> Así nació la patria unánime
> la unidad antes del combate.

Here the natural phenomena are taken to pieces and reconstructed into
cultural concepts such as *patria;* the coming together of these is compared
to the coming together of men, and when the two are put together there
arises:

> la patria unánime
> la unidad antes del combate.

What do these connections imply? Is there perhaps a set of general
principles or relationships behind the *Canto general,* made up of the images used in differing contexts, which give it more form and unity than
have hitherto been supposed? Do these relationships also stand for a coherent perspective of the poet himself and the world around him?

The opening sections of the *Canto general,* for example, state in great
detail the nature and extent of the poet's relationship with other men and
the world of matter and nature. The two sections *La lámpara en la tierra*
and *Alturas de Macchu Picchu* are both crucial to an understanding of the
themes of the whole poem, working from the personal and private emotion
of the poet as individual, to a general and integral vision of men and the
continent as a whole, of which the poet is a part. In this [essay] our first

purpose is to catalogue these instrumental sets, and to observe how their presence is made manifest in any part of the poem, by the use of images that are from a part of one or another of the sets.

The first and most important instrumental set is the one which outlines and defines the connection that exists between *Hombre* and *Tierra,* a basic equation in the *Canto general.* The manner of equivalence of these two entities is the main source of connections and comparisons, and the intermediate parts of nature are the material itself of Neruda's vision. Beginning very simply, we could build the following set (fig. 1). In this set the place of man in nature is defined as the climax of all the forms of nature. As man synthesizes all these, so equally does *Tierra,* the source of all life. This instrumental set is really the most general, because any part of nature can be fitted into it, and equally any reference in the poem can be worked back to it. Apart from placing man in some kind of scheme of creation, it works right through to the poet himself, who can then work outward on planes of increasing generality to the whole continent itself. The nature of the set is that one can refer both ways, i.e. *Hombre-Tierra.* Furthermore, the system can be isolated at any point, thus:

This, as we hope to show later on, is worked out very thoroughly throughout the *Canto general.*

The second instrumental set effects a comparison between *Hombre* and his parts and *Continente* and its parts. This is implied right at the beginning of the introductory poem:

> Antes de la peluca y la casaca
> fueron los ríos, ríos arteriales:

Man as a sum of parts is merged into, and emerges out of, the continent, which is also a sum of parts coming together to form a unit (fig. 2). This instrumental set connects with a related one, namely the comparison effected between America as a named continent and the female form. In *La lámpara en la tierra* and *Alturas de Macchu Picchu* America is referred to by the following names:

> Útero verde, americana . . .
>
> Amada de los ríos, combatida
> por agua azul y gotas transparentes,
> como un árbol de venas es tu espectro . . .
>
> Madre de los metales, . . .
>
> Madre de las piedras . . .
>
> Antigua América, novia sumergida . . .

The implications of this are better discussed when we come to consider the various planes of reference, but there can be no doubt that the fertility of the woman and the fertility of the soil are equated, especially since Neruda views past time in accumulated layers buried in the soil, and since later on the fertility of the soil serves to give a historical continuity to the recurring *libertadores*. Moreover, the woman-earth equation serves to round off very neatly the notion that *Hombre* springs from the soil, and is made up of the earth itself.

When Neruda addresses the rivers of America he works geographically from north to south, just as he works from the head to the feet of the woman. A glance at the rivers shows this, where he moves down: Orinoco, Amazonas, Tequendama, Bío-Bío, the river of his own homeland. This parallels a similar movement when he describes the pre-Columbian peoples in *Los hombres:* Tarahumara, Tarasco, Azteca, Maya, Inca, Araucano. Again, the last-named are the people with whom the poet feels most links, since he is one of their descendants. This movement describes the general framework, and the gradual and systematic movement down the continent to the particular place and tribe, which are (a) a part of the poet, and (b) a part of the continent as a whole, of which the poet is also a part. These dimensions of the poet's "place" are important, and normally they are effectively combined, so that in practice it is difficult to separate these two levels, as the following extract shows:

> Pero háblame, Bío-Bío,
> son tus palabras en mi boca
> las que resbalan, tú me diste
> el lenguaje, el canto nocturno
> mezclado con lluvia y follaje.
>
> .   .   .   .   .   .
>
> y luego te vi entregarte al mar
> dividido en bocas y senos,

ancho y florido, murmurando
una historia color de sangre.

The conscious mingling of the parts of the body and the parts of the continent is systematically carried out, and the intention of the poet is to
"place" himself as the recipient of the river itself. The body of the continent and the body of the poet become as if they were a single entity. Note,
however, that through the parts of nature the poet always works through
to man. The essential idea that these instrumental sets illustrate is the importance of man individually and collectively, both as a whole made up of
parts, and as the most important entity in the poem. However varied and
detailed the elements of nature, they exist in the scheme of the poem, as
the example quoted shows, to illustrate man. These sets serve to outline
the relationship of the poet with the continent and nature, since he is
on the one hand a part of it, and on the other a microcosm of the whole.
He is able by the connections outlined to become infinitely large or infinitely small, to identify himself systematically with anything and everything, to be a part and a whole, to be all men, or a man among many.
Such is the meaning of the final sentences in *Alturas de Macchu Picchu*:

> Apegadme los cuerpos como imanes.
> Acudid a mis venas y a mi boca.
> Hablad por mis palabras y mi sangre.

Here *por* is used in a double sense, meaning "on behalf of," and
"through." The poet has become a poet-spokesman and he does not speak
himself, but others from the past and the present speak through him. The
past yields up its forgotten words from the soil. The quotation illustrates
now the relevance of the sets that have been discussed.

Another instrumental set that exists to define *Hombre* is the relationship between *hombre* and *océano*. In the section *El gran océano* the poet
addresses the ocean as a whole, and also in its parts, especially in his classification of the creatures and plants that inhabit it. It is not the business of
this chapter to examine in detail the meaning that *océano* embodies, but it
is necessary to classify the elements or parts that Neruda uses when speaking of the whole body Ocean, since he uses them frequently to illustrate
descriptions in different parts of the poem. The programme of *El gran
océano* suggests that it might have been intended as a "creation" piece for
the *Canto general*, although it is very different from *La lámpara en la
tierra*. In this section of the *Canto general* a vast scheme of creation and
natural phenomena is categorized. The programme of this section is not so

cumulative as *La lámpara en la tierra,* but in *El gran océano* Neruda seems
to have worked backwards in time from *hombre* to the sea, the stones, and
the molluscs of the sea. The section ends with the birds of the coast, *Phala-
crocorax* and the albatross, and a final evocation of the sea as a whole *La
noche marina,* where the dominant image is again the female form, which
appears in great detail and is very particularly described.

Taking the equation *Hombre-Océano* (see fig. 3) the same process of
isolation can be put into effect, which parallels the one described [earlier]:

Further on it will be possible to show not only how each of these breaks
down into further subdivisions, but how in many cases the separate
Océano and *Tierra* sets are merged into one overall cosmology.

A further instrumental set would be that which describes the ocean in
terms of a woman (see fig. 4). This is particularly evident in the final poem
of *El gran océano* entitled *La noche marina,* which forms a résumé of the
section as a whole. The poet reiterates a desire to become merged as a
whole with the whole of the sea:

> Quiero tener tu frente simultánea,
> abrirla en mi interior para nacer
> en todas tus orillas, ir ahora
> con todos los secretos respirados,
> con tus oscuras líneas resguardadas
> en mí como la sangre o las banderas,
> llevando estas secretas proporciones
> al mar de cada día, a los combates
> que en cada puerta—amores y amenazas—
> viven dormidos.

These constitute the sum total of the instrumental sets in the *Canto
general;* but they are so general that every plant, creature, or mineral can
be fitted into them. It remains now to show how the poet operates within
this over-all framework, how he implies reference to these in any particular
part of the poem, and how, as we move into particular focus, the technique becomes increasingly complex. This can be said to be analogous to
languages whose basic structures are relatively simple, but difficult to arrive at. The multiplicity of elements and their combinations obscure the

clear and simple general structures. In any case general frameworks of reference, or instrumental sets as they are called here, are so large that they could invite criticism for the following reasons: (a) they must be related to the specific working of the poem; and (b) they do not "structure" the elements inside them sufficiently; or, to put it in another manner, they are not committed to any particular explanation. Only when it can be shown how they are contained in particular and specific instances in the poem will they acquire any meaning or validity.

The instrumental sets outlined so far bring together the shape of man and the shape of natural forms. In the *Canto general* the poet observes in the forms that nature takes a device for comparing the form that man and society take. Furthermore, the substance of matter in nature itself is compared and seen as a part of the essence of man himself. This last statement should be evident if the two main instrumental sets outlined are observed. They show *Océano* and *Tierra* at the other end of an equation with *Hombre*. Between these two poles all the objects of nature, both in form and substance, are fed into *Hombre* or *Océano / Tierra* (see figs. 1, 3). The movement can be taken both ways. In the initial poem of the *Canto general* man made up of mud is paralleled by objects formed of earth and substances of the earth, so that a double equation ensues:

A. Objects made up of elements of the earth;
B. Man made up of elements of the earth.

Both A and B comprise definite forms: *hombre, vasija, forma de la arcilla, copa imperial*. Man is a unity, therefore, a "whole" or self-contained system made up of parts (figs. 5, 6). Nature, too, is populated with animal, vegetable, and mineral forms which can be viewed as "wholes," but also as parts of the "whole" of man. From the instrumental sets that have so far been classified the shape of man and the shape of the sea and continent can be carefully compared. In this case, it should be noted that a man (as a member of a species) has to be viewed quite apart from any biological connotations, in a double sense. It is a question of considering his organism as a self-contained system, and his membership of a species which is in turn a system, i.e. *pueblo*. Man's form then is a conceptual tool, so to speak, which can be referred to as a whole or in parts, and in this manner compared to other "wholes" and "parts" on related planes of reference. This is equally applicable to any other parts of the instrumental set, such as *árbol* or *ola*. In this respect the following cluster of concepts are extremely important in the *Canto general: estatua, forma, sistema, organización, unidad, extensión*, and such verbs as *construir, elevar, organizar,* where the action brought about by the joining up of people to form units such as *pueblo* and *patria* is paralleled or compared with the organization and structure of *árbol* or *ola*. To take an example, the opening poem of *Los libertadores* has an immense theme on several planes, which is clearly defined by the shape and parts of the tree. The constant renewal of the tree, through the roots in the soil, on a natural plane is parallel to the continuity of *libertadores* on a historical plane, whose bodies feed the blood of the continent (see fig. 2); and it also gives rise to organized resistance in the shape of people coming together to form *pueblo:*

> Asómate a su cabellera:
> toca sus rayos renovados:
> hunde la mano en las usinas
> donde su fruto palpitante
> propaga su luz cada día.

The identification of the poet with people, and people as a whole with *árbol,* is incomprehensible without having the *Hombre-Tierra* (fig. 1) equation clearly defined. Here, the poet isolates one branch of the instrumental set:

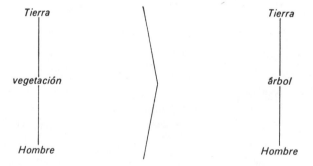

As *pueblo* signifies unity, organization, and a positive system, so, in this particular case, does the tree:

> Aquí viene el árbol, el árbol
> cuyas raíces están vivas,
> sacó salitre del martirio,
> sus raíces comieron sangre
> y extrajo lágrimas del suelo:
> las elevó por sus ramajes,
> las repartió en su arquitectura.

The men that emerge from the earth organize themselves in the same way as the growth of the tree, and take on the shape and architecture of *árbol*. In this context the tree is the largest image that refers outwards, but it involves the instrumental set *Hombre–Tierra* (see fig. 1). The poet uses the tree as a conceptual device to define the limits of the poem's field of reference:

> monta guardia en la frontera,
> en el límite de sus hojas.

The tree has several meanings in the one poem, as for instance when it illustrates some important historical and social themes which are constantly occurring in the *Canto general*, and which will be examined separately elsewhere. Another important example of the isolation of one part of an instrumental set is the following, taken from *Hombre–Océano* (fig. 3):

Looking at *ola*, the poet is seen to break it down to:

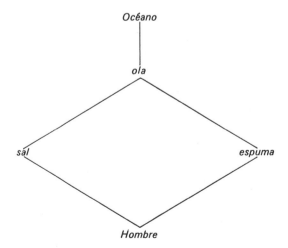

These aspects of a wave are the ones that are constantly selected for *ola*; moreover, either *sal* or *espuma* can be taken sometimes to imply the parts or elements of the set, and refer back to *océano* as a whole. *Ola* embodies all the visible and endless energy of the sea, which is bringer of both life and death. *Ola,* therefore, has retained the essential characteristics of the sea:

> el mar cayó como una gota ardiendo
> de distancia en distancia, de hora en hora:
> su fuego azul se convirtió en esfera,
> el aire de sus ruedas fue campana,
> su interior esencial tembló en la espuma,
> y en la luz de la sal fue levantada
> la flor de su espaciosa autonomía.

The particular shape that the *espaciosa autonomía* takes is compared to *flor,* here used in the same sense as *árbol* to express the form and organization of the sea as an independent "whole." When Neruda has occasion to address *ola* directly, he uses the same set of associations:

> La escuela de la sal abrió las puertas,
> voló toda la luz golpeando el cielo,
> creció desde la noche hasta la aurora
> la levadura del metal mojado,
> toda la claridad se hizo *corola,*
> creció *la flor* hasta gastar la piedra.

The movement of the wave crashing on the rocks is a fragment of *océano* as a whole delivering a measure of its total energy, force, and unity, and the movement is arrested in the substance of *espuma* and *sal,* the shape and organization of the wave, in the shape and organization of a flower. The ambiguous role of the wave and its function as a part of the whole of the sea are stated in this manner:

> es la unidad del mar que se construye:
> la columna del mar que se levanta:
> todos sus nacimientos y derrotas.

This illustration is included to clarify observations about the instrumental sets, rather than to explain the meaning of the ocean in Neruda's cosmology; but it can be usefully taken as an introduction to later remarks.

   Sal and *espuma* are sometimes used on their own and in connection with other instrumental sets whilst implying their original frames of reference. For example, in an otherwise obscure section, knowledge of the instrumental sets makes the following reference clearer:

> Madre de piedra, espuma de los cóndores.

Where the shape of a wave over the sea is like a range of mountains over land, the positions of *nieve* and *espuma* by association become interchangeable. Hence the high situation of the city of Machu Picchu in the peaks of the *cordillera* is likened to the tip of the waves. Furthermore, the *cóndor* is a bird of prey that flies very high, a fact that is particularly important in Neruda's cosmology.

> y sobre las plumas carnívoras
> volaba encima del mundo
> el cóndor . . .
> . . . .
> talismán negro de la nieve.

Taking the connections still further, in the opening lines of the *Canto general*, the *cordillera* is described as the shape of the waves:

> fueron las cordilleras, en cuya onda raída
> el cóndor o la nieve parecían inmóviles:

Here *cóndor* is again associated with "wave" through its original connection with mountain peaks and snow; the circle is closed if we come back to the poem *La ola*, where a description of the wave finishes with the following comparison:

> hasta que de las ramas en la fuerza
> despegó su nevado poderío.

These connections matter, for they enable the poet to choose within a definable framework and to make comparisons which may appear as random ones, but which betray a coherent set of general principles.

If any of these elements (see fig. 7) can be associated, it becomes of some importance to clarify the instrumental set, in order to comprehend the meaning fully in a particular case. A passage from *Alturas de Macchu Picchu* brings into relief the process under discussion:

> Pero una permanencia de piedra y de palabra:
> la ciudad como un vaso se levantó en las manos
> de todos, vivos, muertos, callados, sostenidos
> de tanta muerte, un muro, de tanta vida un golpe

de pétalos de piedra: la rosa permanente, la morada:
este arrecife andino de colonias glaciales.
Cuando la mano de color de arcilla
se convirtió en arcilla, y cuando los pequeños párpados se
     cerraron
llenos de ásperos muros, poblados de castillos,
y cuando todo el hombre se enredó en su agujero,
quedó la exactidud enarbolada:
el alto sitio de la aurora humana:
la más alta vasija que contuvo el silencio:
una vida de piedra después de tantas vidas.

These lines illustrate the point that the instrumental sets bring together the shape and substance of man and those of nature or man-made objects. In this extract there is a contrast between the life of men and the life of the city, a continual movement between the form and substance of the city and the form and substance of man. The final line shows how so many lives become one in the shape of the stone that makes up the essential matter of the city. The city of Machu Picchu as a whole synthesizes all the different strands of Neruda's cosmology, as for example the address to the city in section 9 clearly demonstrates. There, all the forms and substances of the instrumental sets come together; stone, metal, earth, sea, beasts, and birds (both as species and particular named ones). Especially emphasized is the position of the city, and this fact illustrates the point made earlier in connection with the relationship between *cordillera / ola* (see fig 7).

Cordillera esencial, techo marino.
Arquitectura de águilas perdidas.

Here, the city's position and construction are brought out. It is the city as a unit, and the city as a single pattern of interconnected shapes (*arquitectura*), that seize the poet's imagination. Through these two concepts the poet arrives at a definition of man both as a unit or whole in himself and as a part of a larger whole; this is just like the city, which is made up of autonomous stones which come together to form a single construction. The stone of the city is the crucial element isolated from *Hombre ⇌ Tierra,* but the movement between man and matter is expressed conceptually through the shape of *vaso,* which enables the poet to abstract logically and connect both the city and man as shapes or quantities that are linked. The unity and organization of the city are compared to the organization and unity of the *vaso.*

The movement from lines 1 to 6 is:

>permanencia de piedra y palabra:
>ciudad como un vaso . . .
>muro, . . .
>pétalos de piedra: . . .
>rosa permanente . . .
>arrecife . . .

Both the "wholeness" and the permanence strike the poet, but it is a permanence attributable only to man who formed it, so the movement cannot end there. The death of man is seen as part of the existence of stone itself, which also makes the different deaths of the builders into one collective death, just as they made the different stones into one unity or whole; i.e. the city with its *arquitectura*. The death of the builders is seen as part of the existence of the stone itself, its very exactitude and perfection is the exactitude and perfection of men as both separate individual units and collective units shaping the stone into an outline whose organization and beauty has a form and an essence parallel to those of natural forms. Thus there is a movement from the form of man to man-made forms to natural forms.

Vaso is a form which not only indicates a shape made by man, but is itself a comparison with man (see figs. 5, 6). Therefore we have *hombre, vaso, ciudad* all connected through form and substance; and this relationship implies or leads through to the *Hombre* ⇌ *Tierra* instrumental set. Note how the collective death becomes transformed into an image that survives, i.e. *vaso* (see l. 2), which refers to the city or the collectivity that built the city. The whole city is perched upon mountain peaks (l. 2), which are like the human fingers of the continent, or the waves of the sea. In both cases it rises above the surface of the earth and sea (see "Madre de piedra, espuma de los cóndores"), so that it does not lose its shape and identity by becoming submerged. In line 4 the *muro*, whose organization and perfection are like a flower that endures in the constant cycle of nature, is made up of stones whose function as parts of the wall is likened to the petals of a rose as parts of a flower. It is also, of course, the walls of *vaso*, which, like the whole of the city, can be broken up into parts for the city to be examined in parts. But above all, this line and the following emphasize how the concept of the life and the death of the builders has been discerned or caught in the substance and the shape of the stone, thus:

>la ciudad como un vaso se levantó en las manos
>de todos, vivos, muertos, callados, sostenidos

de tanta muerte, un muro, de tanta vida un golpe
de pétalos de piedra: la rosa permanente.

The death of all is as present as the wall, and yet its permanence and life
are like a rose which never died. Here, *golpe* can mean either the work and
energy involved in the building of the wall, or more particularly the *golpe*
or crowd of people, here referring to the anonymous mass that built the
wall, i.e. *pueblo*. Neruda uses the rose here as a conceptual device to bring
across the idea of life, organization, and beauty.

Finally, the city as a reef rising above the sea, *arrecife* (l. 6), continues
the idea of stones or rocks as matter that endures the constant action of
the waves, which, like time, are constantly eroding the natural forms. This
comparison is permissible if earlier remarks are cogent.

The position of the city is a quality which explains its permanence: it
is above the waves which would bury it. More important for our purpose,
however, is the fact that it implies the instrumental sets in the background
and explains apparently emotional or illogical juxtapositions. Lines 7–14
take one through from the life of man himself to his death and existence
in the substance and shape of the stone. Neruda works from the parts of
man in lines 7 and 8 to *todo el hombre* in line 10. This movement is a
development of lines 1–6, since now man is described as *vaso* and, by implication, as the city as well. Man returns in his death to his original substances, into the shape and substance of *vaso:* so, in line 10,

y cuando todo el hombre se enredó en su agujero,

the *vaso, hombre, ciudad* network linked by form and substance is abstracted successively, and what remains is a substance and a shape which
embodies the collective whole of man, and man as an individual. Thus the
movement of the images develops in the following manner where the city
begins to lead through to the growth and dawn of a new life which was
buried but potentially obtainable all the time:

exactitud enarbolada . . .
alto sitio de la aurora humana . . .
la más alta vasija que contuvo el silencio . . .
una vida de piedra después de tantas vidas.

Here the position of the city, and the city as a shape which implies man
and life, both similar to man and a part of him (*vasija*), lead the poet
through to the man himself, who is an entity apart from all these substances, i.e. *piedra arcilla*, but linked in his origins to them (see fig. 8). The

men of Machu Picchu are dead, but their death has assumed a shape and
a meaning which will live on in the present. This is evident if we look at
the last line,

> una vida de piedra después de tantas vidas.

The function of this commentary is to bring into relief the technique
which operates in the *Canto general*, and which in every case implies the
instrumental sets that define and describe *hombre* in the most general
terms. The movement in the above piece is the same in section 11 of *Alturas de Macchu Picchu*, where the measure and proportion of the stone
are related to the activity of *hombre*. Nor is it a question of the stone's
disappearing; the movement of the poetry shows that there exists a coherent set of general relationships logically centred upon *hombre*, which enables the poet to move within and about natural forms and substances, so
that he can build cultural concepts such as *patria* and *pueblo*. Hence the
remarks earlier, about the anatomical shape of man and his parts relate
here to the shape and parts of the city. But this same man is a member of
a collectivity or species, so that the collectivity can be defined equally by
the shape and parts of the city, of man, and of *vaso*. Nor is the process
limited just to *hombre*; the exactitude of the city perched on the mountain
peaks is compared to the shape and outline of a tree (l. 11), and the penultimate line has the same *vaso* image as line 2:

> la más alta vasija que contuvo el silencio.

The approach from particular context to general frames of reference in this
piece shows how the main image of *vaso* brings together both *hombre* and
Macchu Picchu, in its substance and form. Nor is it merely the stone of
the *vaso*; a further possibility is the clay of *vaso* and *hombre*, as shown in
lines 7 and 8. This reinforces the notion of *vaso* as a substance and a form
which indicates man: man has already been referred to as *forma de la arcilla* in the preceding section of the *Canto general*. This, however, illustrates the role the instrumental sets play in any particular context of the
poem—the pieces being taken out and recast in the heat of the poem, but
their original reference back to the general scheme remaining unchanged.
The parts can be rearranged according to what axis of reference one cares
to adopt; so that the various networks of comparison in this passage are:

1. A comparison between the parts of the city and the parts of
   man, leading to a comparison between the city and man as a
   unified whole.

2. A tracing backwards to the common substance of *hombre,*
   ciudad, and *vaso* in *Tierra,* through *piedra* and also *arcilla,*
   which links *hombre, vaso,* and *Tierra.*
3. A comparison between the form of the city and the form of
   man, and the shape that their collective effort embodies in the
   work they poured into the shaping of the city (see fig. 8).

The various groups and patterns of relationships that can be discerned always relate back to the major relationship of the instrumental sets.

A similar organization could be deduced from any part of the *Canto*
general, where the movement of the poetry links the various elements of
any instrumental set through to the shape and substance of man and to
that of matter. Why is this possible? Because the poet has in the background the sets that connect man up with *Tierra* and *Océano* (figs. 1, 3),
and these two subdivide into the forms that inhabit both these different
natural domains. Furthermore, by connecting these wholes up to *hombre,*
it is possible to consider any concept, however large, in terms of the human scale. The poetry of the *Canto general* is, therefore, an attempt to
classify and systematize the human form, not out of any erotic curiosity,
but by the idea that all proportions and harmony begin there.

Another poem, *Los constructores de estatuas (Rapa Nui)* from *El gran*
océano, illustrates the last point. The poem is about the men who built the
statues on Easter Island; it is also a comparison between the men who built
them and the statues themselves, a comparison which links the survival of
man and the survival of the statue, the origins of man and the origins of
the statue, and the substance and form of both. The movement is much
the same as in the previous extract, for the statue remains, but the substance and shape of man are contained in it as well.

> La estatua que creció sobre nuestra estatura.

Here, too, the shape moves outward to confront the shape of the sea, itself
referred to as *estatua* in the final poem in the section *La noche marina.*
The movement of time shapes matter just as the waves do the rocks of the
coast, but the shape of the stone carved by man remains and retains the
life and activity of the man who formed it.

> Miradlas hoy, tocad esta materia, estos labios
> tienen el mismo idioma silencioso que duerme
> en nuestra muerte, y esta cicatriz arenosa,
> que el mar y el tiempo como lobos han lamido,
> eran parte de un rostro que no fue derribado,
> punto de un ser, racimo que derrotó cenizas.

The shape and substance of man can be discerned and touched on the worn-out surface of the stone which bears the marks of his work on it. The connection between matter and man in relation to the poet who discerns it is seen as *idioma silencioso*. What does *idioma* mean in this context? How does it refer outwards?

In the *Canto general* there are the following images for language:

> idioma——————palabra, sílaba.
> alfabeto——————letras, iniciales.

The concept of *idioma* is a device in the poem that enables the poet to organize and build unities such as *pueblo* and *patria;* it enables him to refer to parts and wholes in the manner outlined. This scheme is also used throughout the *Canto general* to illustrate the kind of language which is revealed to the poet, and also to show how any particular object comes across as a structural whole, i.e., as *idioma* which is meaningful and intelligible to the poet. Describing the *hombre* in the opening lines of the *Canto general,*

> en la empuñadura
> de su arma de cristal humedecida,
> las *iniciales de la tierra* estaban
> escritas.

This set of images pertaining to *alfabeto* establishes a connection between the shapes and substances of the earth and sea and the cultural forms of man, which leads to the language of *hombre* and finishes with the words of the poet himself. By means of linking *hombre* to *Tierra* and *Océano* the poet has another conceptual device which enables him to identify himself with the continent itself and the collective aspect of *pueblo:*

> Tierra mía sin nombre, sin América,
>
> · · · · · · · · · · · · · · · ·
>
> tu aroma me trepó por las raíces
> hasta la copa que bebía, hasta la más delgada
> palabra aún no nacida de mi boca.

The impression is of a movement from *Tierra* to *raíces* to *cuerpo* and finally to *boca;* and *palabra* links up with *iniciales de la tierra* earlier in the same poem. In the description of the city of Machu Picchu the poet concentrates on linking the form of the city to the men who built it; consequently one of the crucial images is that of language, which survives to tell of other men's achievements to the poet, who then communicates this to us through the medium of the poem:

> Pero una permanencia de piedra y de palabra.

This permanence, which survives, contrasts with the disappearance of the fragments of the everyday life of the inhabitants of the city.

> porque todo, ropaje, piel, vasijas,
> palabras, vino, panes,
> se fue, cayó a la tierra.

This is repeated again in the following section:

> cuanto fuisteis cayó: costumbres, sílabas
> raídas, máscaras de luz deslumbradora.

Later on the movement of the poem begins to emphasize the coming to-gether of these parts (*sílabas, palabras*) to form a recognizable pattern with meaning for the poet. In section 8 there are the following examples:

> Sube conmigo, amor americano.
> . . . .
> Oh, Wilkamayu de sonoros hilos,
> . . . .
> qué *idioma* traes a la oreja apenas
> desarraigada de tu espuma andina?
> . . . .
> Qué dicen tus destellos acosados?
> Tu secreto relámpago rebelde
> antes viajó poblado de *palabras?*
> Quién va rompiendo *sílabas* heladas
> *idiomas* negros, estandartes de oro,
> *bocas* profundas, *gritos* sometidos,
> en tus delgadas aguas arteriales?

The poet and his subject are moving closer together as he asks the river, the mountains, and the city to yield up their meaning, their past, the men who lived and died amongst these forms. Questions about the origin of the river should be viewed as questions related to *hombre,* as the last lines quoted demonstrate.

This language is the *idioma* whose pattern and meaning the poet is trying to discern. It is the story of the men of the city, which is revealed to him in the shape and substance of natural forms or those which have been made by man himself. The *idioma* is conclusively established when the poet's vision of man and his environment comes together as a meaningful pattern which can be compared to the meaningful pattern of language. Hence:

> Yo vengo a hablar por vuestra boca muerta.
>
> . . . .
>
> contadme todo, cadena a cädena,
>
> . . . .
>
> Acudid a mis venas y a mi boca.
> Hablad por mis palabras y mi sangre.

The whole of the *Canto general* is a story whose language the poet discerns, but which others speak for him. Language as an organized form is parallel to organized forms such as *piedra, metal,* which in turn are parts of a larger organization. Thus to return to the Easter Island statues:

> Miradlas hoy, tocad esta materia, estos labios
> tienen el mismo idioma silencioso que duerme
> en nuestra muerte.

What can be said of the use of *idioma* in this context is analogous to our points made earlier about the form and substance of matter. For here the poet is touching the statue of stone shaped by a man many centuries ago, and through the shape of the statue he arrives at the shape of the man; the process is similar if one thinks of the substance of the stone leading through to the substance of man. The overriding idea that is communicated, then, is that the death of the stone-carver has not been lost: of course he is dead, but his death has assumed a substance and a shape in the statue. This is exactly what the reference to *idioma* accomplishes. As a medium of communication it brings across to the poet the death of the man who carved the statue, and incorporates it into the meaning of our own existence. But it comes out of the stone statue, which is a unified structure like *idioma.* Therefore the parts of *idioma* are used as signs which imply and lead the poet to a larger over-all meaning, as the extracts from *Alturas de Macchu Picchu* show. *Idioma* is thus used metaphorically, with the effect that the image as a whole works by establishing a significant link between two fields of association. The above examples should show that it serves to reinforce the connection of *Hombre* to *Tierra* and *Océano* (see figs. 1, 3), by using the parts of the instrumental sets and establishing a comparison between these and the organization of language as a whole made up of parts which have meaning for the author. This should lead through to the other use of *idioma* in the *Canto general;* namely that it is a language with a meaning as well as a structure. *Idioma* can refer to the language of meaning that is communicated to the author, as well as to a structural comparison between parts and wholes.

The following examination of *A pesar de la ira* from *Los conquistadores* should lead the argument from a consideration of the above question through to a more detailed examination of the particular role of specific names and numbers in a language of reference, as well as a consideration of its organizational nature. We are trying here, in other words, to show the capacity that the images have to refer from the most general properties and elements of a system down to the individual name of a tree or a historical figure. But first we must examine how the relationships of *Hombre* ⇌ *Tierra* are set up.

> Roídos yelmos, herraduras muertas!
> Pero a través del fuego y la herradura
> como de un manantial iluminado
> por la sangre sombría,
> con el metal hundido en el tormento
> se derramó una luz sobre la tierra:
> número, nombre, línea y estructura.
> Páginas de agua, claro poderío
> de idiomas rumorosos, dulces gotas
> elaboradas como los racimos,
> sílabas de platino en la ternura
> de unos aljofarados pechos puros,
> y una clásica boca de diamantes
> dio su fulgor nevado al territorio.

In this passage the positive aspects of the Spanish Conquest are integrated into the relationship between *Hombre* and *Tierra / Océano,* and as history progresses the *conquista* becomes part of the enduring or structural order which persists beneath the order of events; it is itself a transient, changing, and conflicting order. By the poet's definition of *hombre* in relation to *Tierra* and *Océano,* the Spanish conquest is subsumed into a larger frame of reference. "A través del fuego y la herradura" recalls a similar movement in *Alturas de Macchu Picchu* "A través del confuso esplendor." This line is not unconnected, since it initiates the same movement of getting behind external shapes and structures into the internal or reconstituted ones. Whereas in *Alturas de Macchu Picchu* the line and proportion of the stone were a pleasure and a perfection in themselves, which had to be reassessed into a new relationship with *hombre,* here the externals of the *conquista* are violent and conflicting, and the whole pattern of relationships which is born out of it is difficult to discern. This passage shows, for example, how printing as communication, and the Spanish language as a unifying force, give rise to a unity expressed by the people and nations that will arise after the bloodshed and conflict have subsided. The emergence and growth of this structure are like the bubbling of water, the spreading of light, or the unfolding of a plant or a tree, which derive their nourishment from the soil; and like the image of the tree it opens out to reveal its autonomous organization and structure. The image of the tree in line 10 will be taken up in much greater detail in the following section of the poem, *Los libertadores.* Its growth in the final lines of *Los conquistadores* foreshadows the next section, which opens with *árbol.*

The death and the passing away of the *conquista* is evoked by the debris of objects which will be eaten away by time, but which can also lead through to a reconstituted *hombre* and his connection with *Tierra / Océano.* These objects (*yelmo, herradura*) betray the hand of man; they are shaped by man and made up of metal which is incorporated in the minerals of the earth. They imply and lead us through to the structural order beneath or behind the insignificant pile of the surface events. The re-emerging structure is like a light that spreads over the earth; this has come out of the blood and the torment of the *conquista* (l. 3–5). This parallels the movement of the blood of the dead spilled into the soil, and the objects of line 1, as *metal hundido.* This becomes the water of the *manantial* spreading light over the earth. The association between water and blood recalls earlier suggestions made of *Río–Agua—Arterias–Sangre* (see fig. 2), where the parts of the body and its elements become identified and intermingled with the parts and the elements of *Tierra.* But here these elements, *sangre, metal,* become reconstituted out of the soil into *luz,* and more specifically into the attributes of line 7, which are particularly important. For the poet, therefore, the organization and form, the name and the number of any structure are describable. Furthermore, it is crucial for him to use these attributes, so that he can work through to the same qualities in both social and man-made forms. There has been a movement in this poem from order of events to a structural order, from disorder to order, from death to life. The importance of the concepts in line 7 cannot be overemphasized, for these are mediators between the shape and parts of man and the shape and parts of nature. In other words, the poet is able to compare the proportions of any and every object to those of man, and such cultural forms as *pueblo,* by using *número, nombre, línea, estructura.*

Lines 8–14 take up *luz sobre la tierra* in more detail, leading us through to a comparable image, but now much more specific and clearly defined than in line 6:

> dio su fulgor nevado al territorio.

Thus, where we had *luz* and *tierra* in line 6, in the final line the poet has a comparable but more particular *fulgor, nevado,* and *territorio,* which refers to a more specific region that derives from the general *luz* and *tierra.* What has occurred? The process in between has shown in more detail the parts that go to make up line 6 and rendered them more particular and specific. Lines 8–14 show how the structure that unfolds is compared in *número, nombre, línea,* and *estructura* to the attributes of man and a language. Lines 6 and 7 describe the essential substance and shape of this light, lines 8–14 give it a more particular delineation.

The movement of water and the movement of language and learning are resolved in line 8, where the spring of water which is described as coming out of the soil, out of the blood and torment of the *conquista,* communicates a social as well as a natural sound, i.e. the sound of water and language, whose organization and beneficial effects are likened to the autonomous structure and architecture of the branches in a tree (*racimo*). This language, before only spoken, and now written, is made up of the parts that come out of the soil: hence *manantial* gives forth water composed of drops, compared in its form and organization to syllables and language. The organization and structure of language are linked to the natural organization and structure of *agua,* and ultimately *Tierra* (see fig. 9), from whence it springs. The importance of the concepts in line 7 brings us to a central problem in the poetry of the *Canto general.* Much has been said up till now about the comparisons effected between the form and the substance of nature and man. The relationships can be mapped out in the instrumental sets, as is evident in the words *línea* and *estructura;* but what about *número* and *nombre?* Can these in any way be seen as the names and numbers of people and other natural forms which imply at a more general level their *línea* and *estructura?*

For the poet, the importance of number and name and line and structure is that they enable him to classify and categorize the endless variety of nature, but also they permit him to discern the origins and the substance of man himself in particular named or classified forms and their own autonomous organization (see fig. 8c). The most important aspect of the American continent before the poet has established any connection with it is

> Tierra mía sin nombre, sin América.

This is reinforced in the following lines of the opening section, where the description of the continent before the poet builds his created world emphasizes that name and number are lacking. For Neruda, the name, the number of a man or a creature (i.e. quantity or size) place and define them in relation to larger schemes of classification:

> A las tierras sin nombres y sin números
> bajaba el viento desde otros dominios.

Thus trees, animals, minerals are named, but behind each name there is the species to which it belongs, which in turn refers outwards still further to the substance it comes from, leading ultimately to *Tierra* or *Océano*.

This subject can only be touched upon here for purposes of demonstrating how it affects the organization of the instrumental sets; but it offers a whole subject of inquiry into the botanical, geological, and zoological fields of reference in the *Canto general*. Here the interest is mainly in the particular use that the instrumental sets serve in illustrating the thematic content of the poem, i.e., the various levels of reference that such connections imply.

To take an example: *árbol* is treated as a conceptual device to link various associated fields, i.e. the natural and the social; but Neruda also has a naturalist's interest in naming and classifying all plants and creatures. Recalling the instrumental set *Hombre* ⇌ *Tierra* (see fig. 1), we see that a process of increasing particularization occurs:

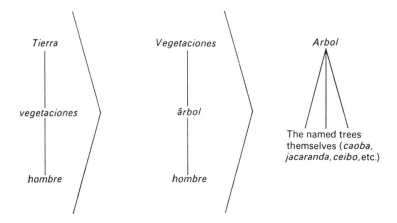

The progressive working from general instrumental set to particular named tree, and vice versa, is definitely linked, as is also the case with any particular beast, bird, or mineral, or named social unit such as a tribe and country.

In *Los libertadores* the named heroes are invoked for more than their
revered memory; they imply a whole structure behind them, from name to
hombre to *pueblo*, and from there to *árbol* as a conceptual device or to
tierra as a whole, which is compared to the action of the particular named
individual. Take for example the movement from general to particular,
and vice versa, in *San Martín (1810)*, where the name of the man itself
leads outwards to the earth itself:

> Eres la tierra que nos diste, un ramo
> de cedrón que golpea con su aroma,
> que no sabemos dónde está, de dónde
> llega su olor de patria a las praderas.
> Te galopamos, San Martín, salimos
> amaneciendo a recorrer tu cuerpo.

This evidently links up with the *Hombre–Tierra, Cuerpo–Continente* sets
(see figs. 1, 2); but in this context it illustrates the movement of classification from named man to man as species (*Cuerpo*) to *Tierra*. The connection established, the poet mingles the body of the named man with the
body of the continent in the now familiar fashion, ending with our death:

> Así sea, y que nos acompañe
> la paz hasta que entremos
> después de los combates, a tu cuerpo
> y duerma la medida que tuvimos
> en tu extensión de paz germinadora.

The shape of the man, the name of the man, the substance of the man are
conceptually broken up and re-formed in a comparison with the earth itself.
This can be viewed as a movement by the poet from the name of the man
to the man as a member of a species, to a dismembering of this man and
a progressive re-establishment of his form or totality on another plane, as
the above lines plainly show. The connections between *hombre* and *tierra*
in the background as an instrumental set make this possible. This example
should illustrate how the very name of a man, a creature, or an object implies a classificatory system designed to place somebody or something in
relation to other men, or in relation to species of the same order. However,
the systems of classification that refer out towards ever-increasing planes
of generality are of interest in so far as they help to explain the description
and definition of *hombre* and of the named *hombre* Pablo Neruda. The
possibility that there exists a parallel with the classification devised by Lin-
naeus is but a tentative suggestion; further research might reveal a different

type of system. However, in the *Canto general* it is no accident that the trees of *América* are named, that Neruda names in the *Canto general de Chile* trees, birds, plants. The instrumental sets establish how they are linked to man and to the poet, and how through their form and substance they suggest and explain man's relationship to nature and to other men. It must be made clear that there is no hierarchy implied in the classification of the *Canto general.* The instrumental sets show the parts of nature related to *hombre,* and man as a creature amongst other living beings, but for Neruda there is no naturally pre-ordained "chain of being" in which some men come above others. The naming of peoples and individuals is, then, a device to connect man to nature and to *Tierra,* to explain his origins by comparison with natural creatures and forms, whose continual existence around him implies his substance and origin. This enables the poet to work outwards from his own particular description and definition to the description and definition of man as a whole. The movement can be viewed as a passage from a species or group of species to a more general system of properties or categories. Frequently in the *Canto general* a device, like *árbol* or *mineral,* is used to take the movement from the level of species (be it man, or a bird, or a plant) upwards or outwards in the direction of *Tierra* or *Océano* (see figs. 1, 3). This movement upwards or outwards on to planes of increasing generality contrasts with the movement downwards or inwards in the direction of proper names. Take for example the poem *Hacia los minerales* in *Las flores de Punitaqui:* here the instrumental set *Hombre* ⇌ *Tierra* is isolated and progressively refined; then a mineral is named, and finally a man is named, giving us the final and most particular stage in this context:

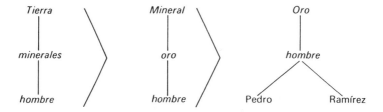

The shape of the man and the shape of metal are compared, and the shape of the continent as the ultimate general reference is compared (see fig. 10) to the body of the man. The mundane, everyday actions of work and labour are given a profound and resonant dimension far beyond the particular context of the event. Furthermore, the relationship of the body of the continent and the body of man is described in male-female terms:

ven,
Pedro, con tu paz de cuero,
ven, Ramírez, con tus abrasadas
manos que indagaron el útero
de las cerradas minerías.

The action of work and the action of producing gold from the interior
of the continent suggest themes that will be dealt with in a later chapter.
Here the point to be made is of the movement from the particular to the
general, the reference outwards to *Cuerpo–Continente* and *tierra* through
oro to *mineral* and finally to *tierra*. The natural organization and quality
of the minerals in the earth are compared and contrasted with the men or
pueblo who descend into the earth, back into their own origin and substance, to dig out the minerals. The walls of the mines recall the walls of
Macchu-Picchu:

eran los dulces muros en que una
piedra se amarra con otra,
con un beso de barro oscuro.

The unity of the walls contrasts with the condition of the worker: these are
social implications which relate back to *hombre*. The references attempt to
explain the miners in terms of their descent into the uterus of the continent, as a descent into a structure which contrasts in some manner with
that of their existence on the surface. In this piece the shape of the stones
and the metals is both positive and negative. The work is both hard and
painful for these men, but it is also ennobling and a symbol of their perpetual struggle. The work assumes a collective substance and shape, like the
work of the men who built the city of Machu Picchu. It is seen chiefly in
reference back to the poet, who identifies with their work through his relationship to *Hombre–Tierra* as these men come up to become part of him,
his *cuerpo,* his *palabra,* and his name.

Here the multiple devices operating show how the instrumental set in
its simplicity gives way to a far more complex picture, where various logical comparisons are exploited at the same time:

1. The form of man and the form of the continent.
2. The action of going down into the mines, and the male enter-
   ing the female form of the continent.
3. The common substance of *Hombre* and *Tierra* that is implied
   in *Oro* $\rightleftharpoons$ *Mineral.*

The movement of the piece shows remarkable affinities with *Alturas de Macchu Picchu;* indeed the whole of *Las flores de Punitaqui,* with its autobiographical look backwards, and its description of the poet's discovery of his vocation as poet-spokesman in relation to others, is like the pattern of the more famous poem. The comparison effected between the beauty and the form of the rose and the men themselves becomes fused into a form and substance which captures and retains in an image the collective agonies and aspirations of the men and the poet himself.

> Flores, flores de altura,
> flores de mina y piedra, flores (see fig. 8c)
> de Punitaqui, hijas
> del amargo subsuelo: en mí, nunca olvidadas,
> quedasteis vivas, construyendo
> la pureza immortal, una corola
> de piedra que no muere.

This recalls the same rose image in *Macchu Picchu:* indeed *Alturas de Macchu Picchu* and *Las flores de Punitaqui* can be fruitfully compared, in the way that Neruda gets behind matter to man, and in the survey of his life looking both backward and forward:

> Antes anduve por la vida, en medio
> de un amor doloroso: antes retuve
> una pequeña página de cuarzo
> clavándome los ojos en la vida.

But the movement of the section as a whole is even more striking, the movement up to the city and down into the earth, as in *Macchu Picchu,* behind the aspect of the mine and its metal to the essential substance of man, as it is revealed in the substance of the metal itself when it comes into contact with man. Furthermore, the labour in the mines is linked to the person of the poet whose task it is to speak for these men:

> Hermano de corazón quemado,
> junta en mi mano esta jornada,
> y bajemos una vez más a las capas dormidas
> en que tu mano como una tenaza
> agarró el oro que quería volar
> aún más profundo, aún más abajo, aún.

The coming together of men and metal is expressed in the shape and structure of the flower, and linked in substance to the enduring *piedra* which, as the stone of the Easter Island statue, and the stone of *Macchu Picchu,* is one of the key substances in the *Canto general* to define and describe man's relationship to his environment. Likewise *oro* plays its role in this section and in the *Canto general* as a whole, where the changing meaning and value of gold, as matter touched by men or used by exploiters for different functions, leads through to the various interconnected themes of the poem. This compares with the significance that the stone of Rapa Nui and Machu Picchu has on the social and historical level. Thus, all these substances and the forms they take in different parts of the *Canto general* can be referred back to the *Hombre–Tierra* instrumental set (fig. 1). The comparison between these sections underlines the stages of generalization in the *Canto general*'s frame of reference, and the fact that the poem has an enduring set of connections, in the background of which the internal dispositions and relations are constantly rearranged in different parts of the poem into new relationships that do not destroy the instrumental set to which they relate back.

In the *Canto general* as a whole there is an overriding feeling of tension between the poet's own private and personal description as an individual in relation to an environment, and the description of men, the continent, and the environment as a whole. Obviously the private and the public are linked systematically and logically, as this [essay] has already shown, but nevertheless, on any level of meaning, be it social or historical, there is a self-contained public and private relationship. Pablo Neruda the individual is related to *Tierra / Océano* (figs. 1, 3), but *hombre* in general is related to *Tierra / Océano* as well, and the poet as an individual is part of *hombre* (figs. 1 and 3). Therefore within the reference upwards to a general connection there is this dual quality, which has already been noted. In his use of *idioma,* for example, the poet's language becomes linked with the general language of the people for whom he speaks, but his own language is separate as well. Nevertheless, it is also true to say that the collective experiences are described and illuminated by virtue of the individual experience of the poet himself. Although the poet works neatly from the particular event to the general framework, and vice versa, it does not obviate this feeling of dualism or tension, i.e. the concept that two strands are intertwined in any reference in the poem. First, the poet as a man defines and describes himself; and second, other men are defined and described. The two strands are, of course, connected by virtue of the fact that the poet is an individual within a larger whole, a man amongst other men. Nevertheless it is important to distinguish the strands as they present themselves in the poem. The poet is always the particular *hombre* of any context of the *Canto general;* that is, when the poem moves to any particular man, in the foreground is the named man Pablo Neruda, a man and part of *pueblo* and made up of *metal* and *piedra.* It is this process which is crucial in *La lámpara en la tierra* and *Alturas de Macchu Picchu,* in *El gran océano,* and *Las flores de Punitaqui,* as this [essay] has demonstrated; and it is this process which operates in any part of the *Canto general.* By defining man as a whole, the poet defines and describes himself as well. It is important, however much one emphasizes the general and social framework, to remember the degree of personal and emotional involvement, and therefore in every case how the context of any part of the poem relates back to *hombre* and to the poet's poem in particular. However, *hombre* and Pablo Neruda are two distinct, though related, entities. The poet is an individual whose anatomical form is a self-contained system of parts, but he is a member of a species who collectively make up *pueblo* or *hombre* in general. This species as a collectivity is in turn a system connected with *Tierra / Océano* (figs. 1, 3). The form of the body can be used as a conceptual device to link up all these entities, but that does not eradicate this dualism. Neruda can describe himself, he can talk about himself, whilst all the time implying his connection with *Hombre* $\rightleftharpoons$ *Tierra / Océano* and men in general. Conversely, he can speak about nature and men in general whilst implying himself. Thus in every case Neruda is defining himself as well as others, but the two strands are related, in the sense that he is one of the others as well as himself. It is the existence of other people, and their experiences as human beings, that enrich the life of Pablo Neruda and consequently materially affect his poetry. When this relates back to the parts in the instrumental sets it can be seen that the poet's form receives and synthesizes all the elements that are classified, flowing from *Tierra* and *Océano* in every case; therefore, the parts of a whole are regrouped within the poet's form. The poet's relation to the collectivity is now clearly defined in the light of these two main devices that operate throughout the *Canto general.*

First, there are the instrumental sets, which are finite. Their structure is simple, but the number of elements that can be incorporated into them is limitless, although in practice it is defined by the structure of the poem itself. With these classificatory schemes Neruda is able to classify and relate to man the whole framework of nature, so that all the parts of the natural order are used to describe and define man.

Second, within the poem he isolates an instrumental set at a particular connection, in order to utilize it to make interconnected references about man on a social and historical level. When Neruda moves up the instrumental set, this merely implies that he moves from the individual or particular event on to planes of increasing generality, which are implied by the isolated part of any instrumental set. The part that is isolated is used to compare man with a natural or man-made form, in both its shape and substance, moving from the particular context to a general proposition (such as the death of men in the shape and substance of the stone). This Neruda is able to do by virtue of the fact that he can use the instrumental set as a framework of reference to appeal to in any context.

This [essay] has shown, first, that it is a question of placing the stone, tree, or wave in some natural context, and defining its relationship to man in terms of a general system; and that, furthermore, this general system moves down on to the most particular category, to the very names of plants and minerals in the poem. Second, it has demonstrated in detail the use of stone, tree, or wave as images that logically work out the themes of the poem on various levels of meaning, or on general interconnected planes of reference. Therefore the first question deals with a classification of nature into some kind of order or pattern, and the second has to do with the use made of these natural forms, in a logical and conceptual way, as images to illustrate the themes of the poem. Because of the two points examined here certain substances in the *Canto general,* such, for example, as *piedra* and *oro,* are important both for their place in the natural scheme of things, and also as devices, once their place has been defined, to illustrate some aspect of *hombre:* the relationship between man-made forms and forms found in nature, and the emphasis on natural substances used by man, take the *Canto general* into a well-defined set of comparisons between nature and culture. The movement from nature to culture explains the origin of man and his make-up, and this fact is implied in any reference back, right through to *Tierra / Océano.* Furthermore, in his social organization, in explaining and understanding himself, man builds social systems which are made up of comparisons effected between plants, metals, and creatures which are both natural and logical. They are natural because they occupy a preordained place in nature, and they are logical because men structure them into concepts which are of their own making, but which are based on the parts of nature. The imagery in the *Canto general* does two things: (a) In the instrumental sets it defines and describes in the most general terms the place of man in relation to nature. (b) In any particular context of the poem, the images used are parts of these sets, and they link man and nature in a logical way. The poetry of the *Canto general* celebrates this connection between man's cultural forms, which are man-made, and the natural forms, there long before men. But the images are now used to convey facts which are not natural but logical in relation to the instrumental sets. This distinction might be taken by some to beg the question that the organization of a poem's imagery must be logical in some way, but the point here is that, when talking about the connections between nature and culture (culture in the sense of men's work and activity, both physical and spiritual), the connections established in the instrumental set are natural, in that they describe and place plants and metals in their context of reality, whereas to talk about these forms when they are used as images in a poem implies that they are being used logically, as part of the organization of the poem's structure.

The word "natural" implies the place of an object or creature in the poet's scheme of things, in which he aims to name it and to relate it to a species. Once this has been achieved, the poet can use it as a conceptual device with multiple possibilities to define and describe man. It is these possibilities which constitute the poet's themes in the *Canto general*. Although it is proposed to divide them into interconnected planes of reference, within each plane, say the social or historical plane, there is a self-contained movement from the particular to the general. The key factor in Pablo Neruda's poetry is the way that some of these images, used long before the *Canto general,* have taken on additional levels of meaning or reference outside the poet's own personal situation. This is what makes the *Canto general* a poem at the same time so personal and so epic in its view of men.

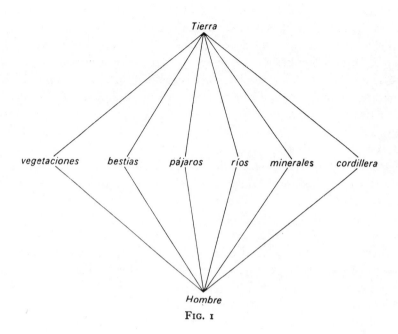

Fig. 1

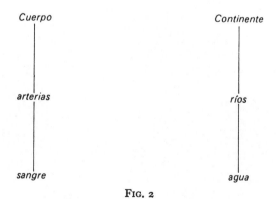

Fig. 2

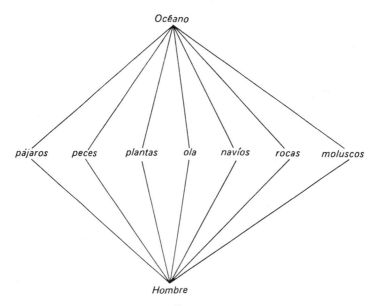

FIG. 3

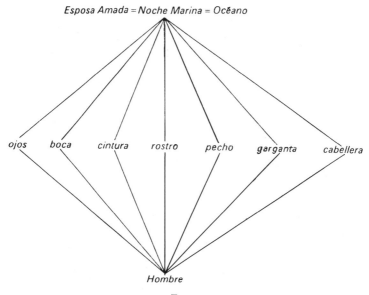

FIG. 4

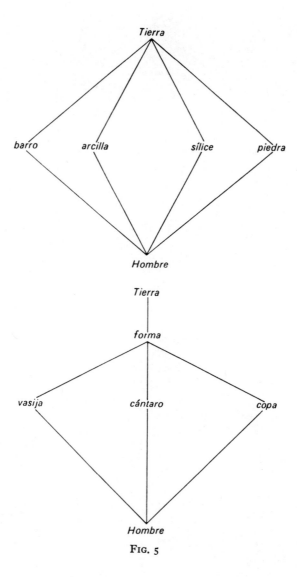

FIG. 5

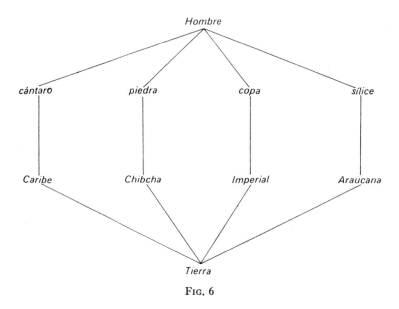

FIG. 6

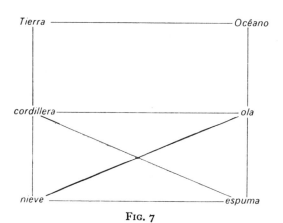

FIG. 7

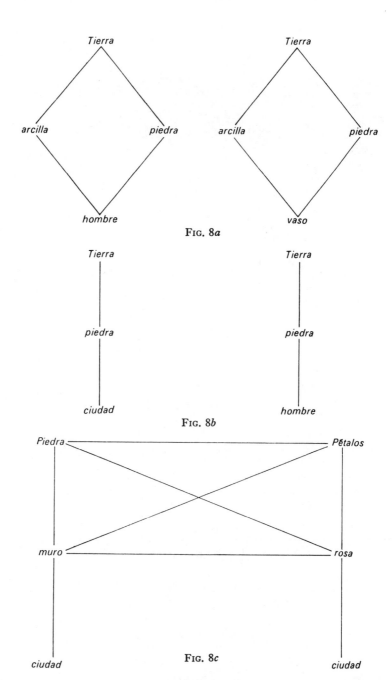

FIG. 8a

FIG. 8b

FIG. 8c

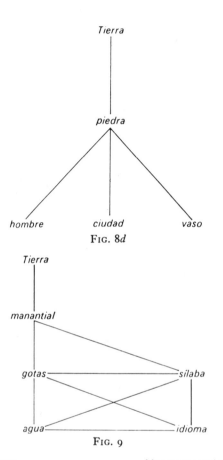

Fig. 8d

Fig. 9

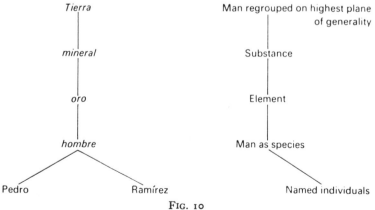

Fig. 10

FERNANDO   ALEGRÍA

Reminiscences and Critical Reflections

As I write about Pablo Neruda I find it hard to dispel a certain sadness,
a heaviness of heart; I worry about creating a melancholy impression, but
at the same time I am reassured, believing that people ought to understand
my uneasiness and discover in it not just mourning for a death, but also
the vision of a unique battle from which death emerges the loser. The other
day, in the sunlit, sea-blown open air of Santa Barbara, I took part in a
beautiful and dignified homage to Neruda. It was presided over by Ken-
neth Rexroth, who spoke in a serene and stentorian voice, accentuating his
word concert with the ocean and a small string accompaniment whose
sounds seemed to blaze up and down in the snatching gusts of wind. I
thought of what I was going to say to these students and professors who
were being enveloped by the musical waves of Neruda's poetry, filled with
his jubilant passion for Chile and his intimate love for Matilde.

I said simply that Neruda was there right then, that I saw him peaceful and smiling as he ambled, or at times soared, among them, lending an
ear to wind and words, to the insistent cry of a sea-gull, an eye to the passing of a runner in shorts who went jogging by at the back of the amphi-
theater, paused, looked at us in shocked surprise, and continued on his
way. It's true. Neruda, like the deceased in Vallejo's poem, is not fully
dead. He will keep on dying with the movement of our century and with
us: a vast and profound death of incalculable significance, dying first here,
later there, and then beyond; now in me and then in other men and
women, without obvious rhythm, but really with the rhythm of the seasons, of the sea, the stars and the trees, through which he keeps growing,

From *Modern Poetry Studies* 5, no. 1 (Spring 1974). © 1974 by Jerome Mazzaro.

stretching, resting from his life, breathing at last all the atmosphere and all the earth, all of time, the components of his death.

So, before it gets any later, I want to write a few things down about the friend I loved and the poet, who at the end faced up to the fact of his death, clothed as always in a magical complexity and simplicity. To my mind what is significant is how Neruda, dying so quickly, transformed this moment of truth into a fascinating and delicate balancing act of reserve, allusion, boldness, shyness, vertigo and tranquility. My evidence is two fold: the ten poems which Neruda published in *Crisis* in August 1973, and the encounters I had with him between April 1972, up through September 9, 1973, dates that saw him travel from Paris to New York and from New York, with several stops, to Santiago, Isla Negra, and back to Santiago. The change from a smile to a death mask.

The first thing to be noted is the ordering of these ten poems: Neruda begins with "Integraciones," ends with "Una canción de amor" and sends special instructions to the publisher that both poems should be printed in italics. His death testimony is thus supported by two love songs, like a medal where the front and the back, the face and its shadow, sustain an affirmation of life. Second, I'm in New York with Neruda, along with Matilde and my wife, Carmen. We are in adjoining rooms in the Hotel Algonquin. I know that Neruda is gravely ill, that he has been operated on already in Paris, but he refuses to talk about any of that; nevertheless, his true condition shows through, revealed by insignificant details. We eat and drink with a knowledge bestowed by our native land and the penchant for consuming the world with still and silently violent actions. Matilde looks after him gently but firmly.

Soon we are all looking after him. An end is put to the "one more for the road" in the Algonquin bar. Neruda says nothing. There is a horrendous session at a dentist's, afterward we take a taxi to go buy shells. The developing conversation takes an unexpected turn. One grows older. Of course, one grows older. People don't have to remind you; one look is enough, one word, one gesture. Neruda says "death begins in the legs." I look at him and he looks at me. We both know that this death doesn't begin in the legs. I don't really know why Neruda claimed later, in Isla Negra, that what was wrong with him was a pesky, persistent rheumatism, clinging to his legs like fog, without ever alluding to the incurable disease which was creeping up his spine. One morning, Sunday, September 9, Delia Domínguez advised him that this rheumatism would now go away with the coming of the September sun, and Neruda answered that another sun was burning him, that he wouldn't see the sun of this spring. He didn't say cobalt, he said sun.

He handles the delicate shells like a sage, not seeming to pick them up; they seem to cling to his fingers as he turns them over, examines them, puts them to his ear, weighs them in his hand, where they become stars, caves, skies, stamens, thorns, rings, ears and lips, taking on the moody denseness of his dark skin. He selects and classifies them with precise references, afterwards leaving out on the glass an ocean floor that intrigues and belongs to him, returning the rest to the cotton-lined cardboard box.

The third thing: we're waiting for his North American publisher in the lobby of the hotel. Neruda holds a glass up in the air as if it were transparent onion and says that only in the U. S. A. would he try martinis, that they would be incongruous anywhere else. We sit and watch the silvered poison, pure and powerful, in the light from the old lamps and the red curtains; our heads turn icy and our chests become lemon armor; we breathe slowly and a glance at our mouths and we've become fire belching dragons, still lucid, but soon to be extinguished. He gives a talk at the PEN Club in New York. Too many crowd around him. I see how Neruda turns grey and there are already ashes clinging to his black suit. They besiege him, press against him, corner him, until they make him disappear. Now he is in an elegant little velvet salon where an intimate group has gathered to give him air and draughts of champagne, as if he were a boxer exhausted by the final rounds. Arthur Miller has said that Neruda was a tree, and this tree heads back toward the bathroom with slow, tired steps. He says in passing that he isn't well, that he will return to Chile in November and that no one must know. But everyone did know.

But to get back to the poems, there are two that refer directly to the theme of death, clearly reflecting his secret speculation: "Animal de luz" is a recognition of his solitude, of the closed circle, and of those who can no longer touch him in his innermost being. The poet has retired, followed by his escort of ocean waves and stars, an escort determined by time. What is left is at once small and vast. Terribly weary, cities resting on his shoulders and strings of countries around his neck, he flees, but not from the others who have already said and done all, but from his own interminable inner dialogue. "There is no more deciphering to do." It's clear. "Nothing more to say." Alone, surrounded by silence but also by the sound of the ocean, he concludes simply: That's all. The enormity of this conclusion falls at the end of the poem like a stone curtain. Neruda unhesitatingly turns out the lights. Great doer that he was in life, he prepares himself to work in the great inactivity that will be his death.

"Triste canción para aburrir a cualquiera" is a solitary game, a balancing of achievement against absurdity, of hours against emptiness, the waverings of man divided, the eternal rhythm of life and death. The simple force of the *leitmotiv* slips through his fingers like the beads of a rosary, a wise and melancholy litany which can nevermore arrive at conclusions.

In "Preguntas" there are four clues to man's initial and ultimate curiosity: the butterfly which doesn't know the signs of its wings, the bee unaware of its path, the ant ignorant of the number of casualties in its army, and the cyclone unable to remember its name while it is quiescent. Neither love nor knowledge offers answers to man who remains "looking at buried time." Only in doubt, at the edge of death, can man sustain certain hope: "Or is it that what I see from afar / Is that which I have yet to live?"

In summing up his poetic experience Neruda becomes aware of the personal dimension he gave to words, but without forgetting what effect words had on him. At first he names things, then he delves beyond into their essences, searching for the sound and the echo, that is, the secret action which reveals the meaning of matter. A virgin sound, a name seemingly chosen at random, "Oregano," is launched as the symbol of his battle against rhetoric, against the irrationality of rationalism, the vehement search for the magic word which will "not speak to anyone," but which will bring him to his destiny, an inner recess, substance in a sownfield, a flower blooming-decaying, oregano-defense, oregano-elation, oregano-revolver, a green and aromatic word brandished like a sword.

We seem to be approaching inescapable ends, affirmations that echo through a world in which old symbols open up and let their fruits fall to the ground. Both "El héroe" and "La situación insostenible" are images which represent the implacable assault of death. The hero is a man who passes through life stripped naked, an intransigent philosopher, unchanging before the claims of society, covered with black scales, civilization's last great nudist, reflecting in his nakedness the passage of history "like an old editorial—in a defunct newspaper," dead on his terrace due to the harshness of winter.

The second poem, "La situación insostenible," refers to a family, a household, a world, methodically appropriated and invaded by its dead, thrown off-kilter by likenesses of man, cheeky and intrusive deceased, who first enter the living room, filling the chairs, the tables, the family larders, break into the bathrooms where they polish skulls, push the kindly and patient Ostrogodos into the farthest reaches of the garden under the shade of an orange tree, there climbing into its branches and diligently proliferating, until the Ostrogodos have no choice but to submit and deliver themselves benignly and complacently to the cemetery.

Another fact: operations are useless scalpel strokes. Sickness spreads like spilled mercury. And another: Neruda, tall, solid, slow, at the same time distant and accessible, made of great love and enveloping tenderness, creator of the sky and the earth, makes water and from on high, indifferent, confirms the passage of blood through his urine. "El gran orinador" is the recognition, both direct and cosmic, of the sickness into whose custody death has placed him: a creeping cancer of the prostate.

Months pass and now time must be counted in days, in hours. Bedridden in Isla Negra, Neruda works intensely. The sea becomes rough and closes in on him, his winter quarters are soon his campaign quarters. A fascist conspiracy coils around the body of Chile, air-tight and elastic as a boa. Everyone knows what is going to happen. The rhythm of life is suspended mid-beat. People look at one another distrustfully. A few well-known reactionaries go around with smiles a mile wide. International agents come and go from Pudahuel airport with mysterious suitcases. Neruda writes an appeal to his friends in Europe, the Americas, Africa and beyond, to come to the aid of Chile, stop the coup and save the small socialist nation which is about to be sacrificed. Neruda's voice is clear and firm.

September 9, a desolate Sunday, calm before the storm, I know Neruda has asked for me. He doesn't know I am in Santiago; he suggests to Delia Domínguez that she call me in California. I pick up the phone. Matilde answers in Isla Negra. I hear Neruda saying loudly: tell him to come today, it would be best if he comes right now, today. He is in bed, and judging by his tone of voice, he seems to be busy with his work, his papers. We leave it that I'll come Tuesday, the 11th. I'll go by way of Casablanca, not by the road to San Antonio because it is controlled by fascist truckers. Tuesday the insurrection by the Armed Forces breaks out.

And this last thing: Neruda is very ill, his doctor gives him a few months to live. I don't know if Neruda knows it. Hawker-Hunter planes bomb La Moneda. Allende falls riddled with bullets. Workers are machine-gunned down the length of the country. The SUMAR factory falls, the

State Technical University falls, La Legua and Lo Hermida. The bleeding cadre of the Unidad Popular come down out of the hills of Valparaíso. There are summary trials and executions in Temuco, Valdivia, Concepción, Pisagua, Antofagasta. Neruda, wide-eyed, bearded now, wants to see all this death, and pulling himself half-way up, suddenly knows that at last he is "face to face with truth." The world he made, verse by verse, step by step, the country he built out of sand and stone, of coal, copper, and salt-peter, the country he worked from clay, foam, grain, rock, snow, that he named and sang over the years, the peasant and workers' country, falls in on him with all the dust and clatter of an old beamed ceiling and cracked adobe walls. Nothing is left but silence, the sea at his feet, a distant shore and a boat.

Seeing him feverish, gravely ill, Matilde calls an ambulance to take him to Santiago. Soldiers block the road several times. They arrive at the clinic. Neruda dies of a heart attack. His funeral turns into a passionate political demonstration. The mourners sing and shout the International. Behind the coffin, on the streets to the General Cemetery, people are hurrying, disheveled, pale, trembling. Meanwhile, a mob attacks Neruda's house, his Chascona, on San Cristóbal Hill. They ransack, rob, destroy. Someone photographs Neruda in his black boat. There is something in the dead poet's face like a suppressed laugh, a real laugh, that will persist there, ready to burst out, but motionless. Scarcely visible, glimpsed in the corner of his left eye, there is also a consuming rage, blind and final.

The eight poems in *Crísis* dealing with death bear no direct relation to two of Neruda's fundamental books: *Residencia en la tierra* and *Canto general*. In the first two volumes of *Residencia,* Neruda faces a death which is an essential part of the eternal movement of life, an implacable and progressive wearing-down, a seed destroying itself in a vague search, blind, constant, for an atmosphere not to be found again, for a stalk already cut; the image of a world in the present which carries in it the dead burden of a future mirroring past destructions. Neruda sees the world disintegrate before his eyes and knows himself to be part of this ruin that grows and envelops him from without and from within.

Hernán Loyola describes this conception of death in *Residencia en la tierra* when he says:

> The mention of Time in *El fantasma del buque de carga* (the freighter *Forafric*, 1932) is associated with the notion of wearing-away, disintegration, of the slow ship-wreck of things

in the sea of death. With comparable precision the same device is used in *Ausencia de Joaquín*. But *Residencia* doesn't offer us the image of attrition and ruin through the use of allusions to Time, Forgetfulness, or to Death. So the repetition of such allusions does not explain why this book is able to communicate the sense of ever-present collapse. Neruda achieves this effect through an incessant shooting of corrosive images and representations.

Loyola refers as well to the theme of death in the poetry of the young Neruda: not just to the rhetorical pain, but also to the affirmation of life against death rooted in the dynamic eroticism of *Crepusculario* and *Veinte poemas de amor y una canción desesperada*.

What we are dealing with is a mature conception of death, not as a unique, individualized event, but as a process gauged by its material consequences and metaphysical projections: destruction and emptiness. Neruda manages two powerful symbols: the sea and time. He submits them to collective experiences of the phenomenon of alienation and to a personal state of anguish. He will search incessantly the answer to this anguish, drawing himself closer to the peaceful nature of things that remain unconscious of their attrition and their voyage toward death: stones, sacks, trees, mirrors, papers, shackles.

In *Canto general* Neruda considers death historically, not as boundless history, but a daily chronicle of the deaths in which he is routinely clothed: an autumnal tree, demises which cover him like patches, a collective death speaking to him from the fortress of Macchu Picchu or slowly spanning the abysses of the Great Ocean. His testament is a literary document with political content, the balance sheet of a life's struggle, testimony of his faith in the Communist Party.

Death in the poems in *Crisis* is his own death, with his name on it, the integral experience of a man who saved up days for his big night, treasures, plaster statues and tin stars to decorate his grave. This mended sick man, a clever, stubborn warrior, awaits death with firm determination. Death actually begins in the legs, arriving quickly like a powerful emptiness in the stomach and a bloody darkness in the throat, in short, the death that Dr. Orrego is going to certify. I've said that Neruda died of a heart attack overcome by the September 11th tragedy of Chile. At his side is Matilde Urrutia, his wife and companion, who presides at his violent funeral.

I think Neruda confronted the final enigma with total consciousness and solved it in terms of love and surrender to the materialistic dynamic of the world as he conceived it. What I want to emphasize is something very simple: Neruda was, above all, a love poet and, more than anyone, an unwavering, powerful, joyous, conqueror of death. That is why he asked the editor of *Crísis* to italicize his two love poems. What does he say in them? What didn't Neruda say about love in his poetic works?

> Because without going beyond the present
> which is a fragile ring
> we touch yesterday's sand
> and in the sea love teaches us
> repeated raptures.

Time has not been, nor shall it be, anything but a fragile ring; duration through tenderness has its own will and logic, that of the sea in its wise and constant motion. He will remain in what he calls "integrations," the most important of which is Matilde and all that is within her. "Canción de amor" is a ballad, a tender *ritornello,* a song to the youthful glory of tenderness, music and possession.

Home, your family and mine, you and I, the world, Pablo, throw death at us like the wind scattering our papers, yours and mine: our land "one day was left without anyone—without doors, without a home, without light—without oranges—and without dead ones," at the foot of the hill, at the edge of the river, next to the sea, the sewers open, and, in the darkness watching over you, seeing us, everything inundated, an indestructible red shadow, hours passing from one gun to another, and the black coffin in the air. They'll say it is a familiar story, the simple order of old-fashioned hearths, the cortege awaiting us at the door. I prefer another, slightly different, version: The simple story of humanity and its immediate destinies, no ritual, just the order of our families and the plea for delayed caskets. The poem shows confidence in the only possible direction of time: toward us, against us, like a stubborn wind, taking from us the only space which, in truth, never even belonged to us.

AMADO ALONSO

From Melancholy to Anguish

Upon reading, in the order of their publication, *Crepusculario* (1919), *El hondero entusiasta* (1923–24), *Twenty Love Poems and a Desperate Song* (1924), and *Residence on Earth* (I, 1925–31; II, 1931–35), we discover that the poetic evolution of Pablo Neruda consists of a progressive condensation of emotions by self-absorption and an ever deeper rooting in feeling, in the depths of his being, as well as an ever greater detachment from objective structures. The poet's extreme introspection demands a new method of relating his feelings to their appropriate expressions and his technique of representation increasingly approaches the extremes of obscurity. Along with the advancing introspection, emotional condensation and obscurity in technique, the very heart of Pablo Neruda's poetic sentiment undergoes a progressive intensification from melancholy to anguish.

All of Neruda's poetry prior to his *Residence on Earth* unveils a beautiful sadness that revels in itself. Often this melancholy speaks of an infinite pain but only in *Residence* are we offered, without its being explicit, truly infinite pain. The melancholy of his early poetry is overlaid with nostalgia: sorrow over the loss of something valuable which is retained only in memory. There, the waters of feeling lurch with threatening rushes of anguish, but they are still transformed into melancholy, a form of happiness after all, because suffering contemplates itself, enveloped in beauty and turned into song:

From *Review* 74 (Spring 1974). © 1974 by the Center for Inter-American Relations.

> Tonight I can write the saddest lines.
> To think that I do not have her. To feel
>   that I have lost her.
>
> (poem 20, tr. W. S. Merwin)

Thus he writes in *Twenty Love Poems*. The melancholy of an everlasting farewell to things past is still a way of holding on to them; it is the tribute to sorrow, through which we relive in our souls those joyful moments that are already gone. In the poetic works of Neruda, we find, first of all, biographical sources of melancholy which pierce through the soul like clouds; subsequently, it is no longer a state of the soul, it is its way of being: fog permeates the air and even the sunlight of today's love shines gloomily with a halo of melancholy; happiness carries sorrow with it. It is a feeling which at times, cleaved with flashes of anguish, loses its blandness, its abandonment, its resignation. In *Residence on Earth,* the tornado of fury will no longer pass without lingering, because it will be identified with his heart. In *Twenty Love Poems,* he still attempts to seek refuge in melancholy while fleeing from anguish.

In *Residence on Earth* he no longer finds a shelter to rest from anguish because anguish is everywhere. The fallen pangs embitter the waters in the depths of his heart. The songs have become hoarse cries, and the thick waters will overflow and stagnate. When anguish first becomes manifest in Neruda's early poems, it is intermittent and due to something that has come to pass. It is an acute anguish which diminishes slowly.

A PERFECT AND BEAUTIFUL SORROW

In order to better understand the manner in which the poet's emotional state has changed, let us compare the way in which his images depict the same objective material during the two periods. Let us focus on the sound of the wind. He writes in his Poem 17:

> Hour of nostalgia, hour of happiness, hour of solitude,
> hour that is mine from among them all!
> Megaphone in which the wind passes singing.
> Such a passion of weeping tied to my body.
>
> (tr. W. S. Merwin)

The passion of tears is a way of searching for happiness in a perfect and beautiful sorrow, in the transposition of suffering to a level of esthetic perfection, if you will. Suffering has its fascination. Solitude, nostalgia and delight, together in this singular moment, become beauty like the song of the wind blowing through a trumpet. The wind's voice sings a sad but beautiful song. Now, let us look at "Barcarola," from *Residence on Earth:*

> If you were to come into being, suddenly, on some sad coast,
> surrounded by the stuff of the dead day,
> face to face with a new night
> full of waves,
> and were to blow on my cold, fearful heart,
> on its lonesome blood,
> on its flames like a flight of doves,
> its black blood syllables would sound,
> its unquenchable red water swell
> and it would sound and sound in the shadows,
> it would sound like death itself,
> calling like a pipe full of wind and crying
> or a bottle gushing fright.
>
> (tr. Nathaniel Tarn)

Here, also, the wind and cries are associated but now they are painfully equivalent. The desire to endow the symbols with beauty, in order to mold the significant elements into a pleasurable substance, no longer predominates. He now utilizes the hideous, the ugly: the wind no longer blows through a trumpet, but through a tube. It no longer blows singing but howling with a cry; it is no longer even certain that what passes is that movement without body which we call the wind; it is no longer a sound magnified into a song and a secret zest for life; now it is as uncontrollable as the sound of a hemorrhage, deadfully emptying itself. Then the nostalgia and melancholy, deeply rooted in memory, and the misery because of estrangement (a way of longing for, searching and finding one's self in moments past, a form of loving and of possessing); now, the loneliness, the anxiety of despair, the anguished affliction of a total shipwreck. If up to now, his feelings poured forth the painful songs of melancholy, now he cries, choking with ominous tremors:

> like fierce and self-devouring waters.

THE SHAPING OF THE WORLD

Accordingly, what astonishes us in this poetry is the certainty that the horror of its form is not a posture adopted at will and valid only for the creation of beautiful poetry, but that it is entirely valid because it corresponds to a unique—distinct and desolate—vision of the world and of life.

The poet's eyes, ceaselessly open as if they never closed ("Like eyelids held forcefully and horrifyingly open"), see the slow decomposition of all existence in a sweeping and instantaneous gesture, like a motion picture camera which shows us in a few short seconds the slow development of plants. They see the never-ending task of death's scythe in a static flash of lightning, the suicidal tendency of all things to lose their identity, the tumbling of the erect, the decomposition of forms, the fire's ashes. The anarchy that is life and death, with its secret and terrible control. The thawing of the world. The anguish of observing all life incessantly dying: man and his works, the stars, the waves, the plants in the midst of their organic movements, the clouds through their whirling, love, machines, the wear and tear of furniture, and chemical corrosion; in short the crumbling of the physical world, all that moves and gives expression to life is dying.

The living lives because of its will to live, to move, to flee from death, but each footstep of life is a lethal step, not only a step towards a certain death in time, but already an act of death, a dying, a prey that death has clutched and does not release, since each movement, each act of life engenders a change in the living being which kills something within him and, consequently, destroys his identity in him. Pablo Neruda sees everything in the world as a part of an irrepressible disintegration.

There is not a single page of *Residence on Earth* where this terrible vision of decay is missing. It is what is invincibly and intuitively felt by the poet, both seen and contemplated. This is not known or comprehended through reason; it is felt, it is lived, and it is suffered in the very bloodstream. Pablo Neruda's eyes are the only ones in this world meant to sense with such concreteness the invisible and ceaseless work of autodisintegration, underneath or within its movement or stillness, to which all living beings and inert things surrender. His eyes are the only ones condemned to observe the drama of

the river ruined in its own duration,

a splendid verse which encompasses the definitive image of this painful vision of reality. All of his verses are filled with images of deformity, dispossession and destruction, very frequently in a dreamlike structure, images in which some objects are deformed and disintegrated by means of processes existing only in others, and where objects and their images appear to shove one another, to penetrate one another, and to compress and deform with a chaotic mutual influence, just as in dreams where the principle of contradiction does not prevail. It is the hallucinated vision of destruction, of disintegration and of lost forms; it is a holographic vision that expresses itself like a crowded thunderstorm which recurs again and again over all those things that are in the process of disintegration and deformation to redeform and redisintegrate them again. The apparently extravagant, disjoined wave, extinguished homes, leafless sky, voice decomposed by time, are the expression of a vision of reality concretely perceived through intuition, and of its corresponding emotions. Unlike King Midas, everything that Pablo Neruda touches dilapidates, turns into dust, because he touches the root of endless destruction. "Ashes and dust; dusty and ashy" are persistent words in his poetry: "and I smell ashes and destruction in the air." There are dusty glances, dusty hearts, dusty dreams, dusty shadows; there is decayed dust as well as walls and cups of ashes, and at each turn ashes and ashes, and ashen horses, ashen rivers, ashen destinies and ashen dancers, "in a nation of ashen rubber and ashes."

THE SALT OF DESTRUCTION

Our poet, whose vocabulary is filled with words that suggest states of loss, dispossession or decomposition, sees the never-ending work of the mills where forms and entities are ground: the disintegrated, the faded, the moth-eaten, the consumed, the pale, the wilted, the dissolved, the widowed, the extinguished, the used, the rotten, the spent, the decayed, the destroyed, the shredded, the fallen, the disjoined, the befallen, the tumbled, the old, the corroded, the corrupt, the poisoned, the molten, the degraded, the dead . . . And so many broken things: broken rivers, broken ships, broken waters, broken roses, broken cruets, broken glass, broken steps, broken candelabra, broken lips, broken fish, broken fans, broken things, broken armatures, broken corners, broken objections, and then, cracked steps, crushed arrows, and bitten suits and bitten walls, and shredded cups, and severed feet, the befallen, the demolished, the spilled, the tumbled. The persistent image of the work of disintegration and self destructiveness of the salts is the most characteristic: the brine sword, "the touch of the dead among the lost salts," and the salt which shreds, the salt strikes, the demolished salt, the destitute salt, the consumed salt, the multitude of salt, "and there is the taste in the mouth, the salt of sleep," its drop of trembling salt, dry airborne salt, its certain nitrate, forlorn salt, fragile salt, and the acids and the strike of sulphur, and the fallen sulphur.

This process of distintegration is a physionomical aspect of our times. It is like a trunkful of odds and ends, an accumulation of objects both separate and disintegrated in their totality, but set up as a sentimental symbol of a state of mind, for example the twilight state, or fear, or erotic anxiety.

The poetry of Pablo Neruda also unmasks this manner of disintegrating, which is one of the most significant features with which our times are
etched. In his poems we see severed hands and feet, braids, hair, nails, machines and parts of machines, loose utensils, debris, so many things and
more things pulled from their place and tumbling down his tumultuous
river of verse.

This disintegration is a violent sectioning of reality. Thus all of reality
is contemplated in its fragmented manner by Pablo Neruda. Disintegration
in the arts of our times consists, above all, in the manner of treating reality.
With Pablo Neruda, it is the way reality is. While for many modern masters, disintegration consists of partitioning reality, for Pablo Neruda it is a
total process. The life of all that is alive is a progression towards death;
the existence of everything that stands firmly is a constant act of decay.
Not even psychic experiences escape from this destiny:

> Like a wreck, we die to the very core
> as if drowning at the heart
> or collapsing inwards from skin to soul.
> ("Death Stone," tr. Nathaniel Tarn)

This is how Pablo Neruda sees existence: not an isolated episode of
existence but existence itself. His eyes contemplate with unerring concreteness the ceaseless ruin of all that exists,

> and whatever among leaves falls to the ground:
> the dark of a day gone by
> grown fat on our grieving blood.
> ("There's No Forgetting [Sonata],"
> tr. Nathaniel Tarn)

Here lies the very crux of Pablo Neruda's anguish. If only this disintegration were but a Heraclitian vision of reality! If only it were the darkness
of a bygone day! But it is above all a way of being affected by reality, the
fact that past days have fed on our very blood. A death of a day is no less
than the death of that which we have lived through and been during that
day. The death of objects is identified with our own death. And the poet
is anguished.

ALEXANDER COLEMAN

Neruda: Vox Dei

QUESTION: *Why* did *Neruda* go to *Rangoon?*
ANSWER: "My friend gave to the minister (of Foreign Relations)
the names of available cities all over the world, but I only
caught the name of a city that I had never read nor heard
of before: Rangoon. The minister said to me, "Where do
you want to go, Pablo?' 'To Rangoon.' I answered in a
flash. 'Put his name in,' said the minister. My friend left the
office and came back in a minute with the nomination."

("Memoirs")

Neruda's "decision" to go to Rangoon, seemingly reminiscent in its total hazard of a Babylonian Lottery, or, in circus terms, of a roll of the
raffle wheel of Life itself, finally might be seen as something less than pure
fluke; I suspect that the sound of "Rangoon," a few glimpses of the East
in an encyclopedia, a taste for exotic literary texts might have prepared
Neruda's soul for that fateful question posed by the Minister of Foreign
Relations. Mr. David Gallagher, in his recent *Modern Latin American Literature,* makes the good point that the experience of the East represented
no liberation for Neruda, no factitious acquisition of cosmic Wisdom, no
dabbling at all among the bereft in the now sanctified manner of our own
hippie movement. For him, it was a living cosmorama of rapaciousness,
oppressive colonialism, solitude. This last should be given its due emphasis, since Neruda himself remembers those days and his solitude as "not
only a theme for literary invocation, but rather something hard as a wall

From *Review* 74 (Spring 1974). © 1974 by the Center for Inter-American Relations.

of a prison which you bang your head against, without anyone coming though you shout and weep. The worst of it is that this wall that surrounded me was a wall of sun." This experience is at least a part of an explanation for Neruda's heroic discontent with satisfaction and finality in the poems of *Residencia en la tierra,* his sense of the glory of the imperfect, of what is in the process of becoming and decaying. Neruda's East is a Hell of boredom, halting English, Burmese lolitas, diplomatic teas and boiled dinners. And then there are those millions he cannot touch nor reach, cannot speak to—as he says in one of the letters, "How can I approach this palpitating world without being considered an enemy?" Encased in this brand of solitude, these poems *do* make up a book of "claustrophobic rooms, of stifling Asian cities made all the more squalid by the tropical Asian heat that envelops them."

One of many anguished souls between the wars, then. But among those visions of grand apocalypse in poetry published in Europe during the twenties and early thirties, *Residencia en la tierra* owes the least apparent debt to literature itself. It is not a bookish book of poems. If that preoccupation for source hunting has any practitioners left these days, they will have a hard time with the *Residencia en la tierra* and Neruda himself, no matter how hard they pore through their copies of *The Waste Land, Songs of Experience, The Book of Thel,* or *Song of Myself.* It just won't do.

But this doesn't at all suggest a divine ignorance on the part of the poet, a spirit unsullied by a literate idea or the impression made by another poet. Neruda has often been considered by mischievous readers as an exemplar of the *ingenio lego,* that is to say, a genius all right, but still a child, a divinely gifted imagination wherein the reading of other poetry and other literatures has no functional place. And all this in spite of the fact that Neruda's critical observations, while few, show a canny perception of what might irrationally be of use to him. And he was, after all, a fanatic bibliophile. The greatest debt in the *Residencia en la tierra* is not to literature *prima facie,* but rather to the protean assimilative powers of the poet, where all sensations, intuitions, experiences, readings (yes, these are experiences, too) fell not into a void, but rather onto a broad and rich field— imaginative osmosis did the rest.

I would argue that this organic sense in Neruda relates to the quality and caliber of his imaginative response to the world, and *that* has nothing of the infantile about it, although it is (I'm repeating myself) sub- or super- literary at its source. In Rita Guibert's fine interview with Neruda, she extracted from him the following telling remark about the transfiguration of the written word: "Just as the action of natural elements pulverizes our deepest feelings and transforms them into an intimate reflective substance, whether emotional or factual, which we call literature, so also it is the writer's duty to contribute his own work to the development of the cultural heritage, by pulverizing, purifying, and constantly transforming it. It is the same effect nutrition has on the blood, on the circulation. Culture has its roots in culture, but also in life and nature."

A GUEST ON EARTH

I wonder if there isn't a hidden irony in that title, *Residencia en la tierra*. Poets have been guests elsewhere, Neruda seems to be saying to us, but not on earth, and this is going to be a book of poems about being on earth for a while. So it might be read as a poetic diary, but with a reek and stench of a life lived well at a distance from Mallarmé, Juan Ramón Jiménez, Abbé Bremond and the whole argument about "Pure Poetry." In his essay "On Impure Poetry," Neruda contemplates not essences, but used, worn-out or exhausted objects; from them, he says, one senses "the contact of man and earth as a lesson for the tortured lyric poet." He speaks glowingly of worn surfaces, the wearing away that hands have inflicted upon things, the sometimes tragic and always melancholy atmosphere around those objects. A century-old wooden plow, a rocker worn smooth, a carpenter's favorite hammer. These objects, caught in time and showing the passage of time in their very exhaustion, will suggest to Neruda the thankfully impure nature of our world, so that poetry should be "ravaged by the labor of our hands as by an acid, saturated with sweat and smoke, a poetry that smells of urine and of white lilies, a poetry on which every human activity, permitted or forbidden, has imprinted its mark. A poetry impure as a suit of clothes, as a body."

This is one aspect of the unchanging Neruda, and all this in spite of the radical transformations of style, tone, politics and themes evident throughout his work. As he said to Rita Guibert, "A writer is always moving house; he must change his furniture but not his soul." Neruda's cosmovision, so energetically celebrated by critics who laud the apparently more "humanitarian" Neruda evident in the third book of *Residencia en la tierra* and of course the *Canto general,* is not radically different in stance from the so-called "hermetic" Neruda found in the earlier books of the Residencia ... and the still earlier books: *El hondero entusiasta 1923-1924* published in 1933, and the later *Tentativa del hombre infinito* (1926). As a matter of fact, there is a moment in the *Tentativa* ... (*Obras completas,* 1.1113) where the poet intentionally abandons the ordinary celebration of night and day, ceding his self to universe, the sky now being seen as an "inverse well" into which the eyes of the poet *fall,* falling into an ascension to a sacred place where mutability, flux, and the ever-shifting phantasmagoria resolve under the scrutiny of this newly cosmic poetic "I." This may be a key moment in the poetry before *Residencia en la tierra,* as Rodríguez Monegal first saw in his definitive study of Neruda, *El viajero inmóvil.* It suggests the dissolution of the vainly narcissistic lover-self that seemed to reign over the atmosphere of *Veinte poemas de amor y una canción desesperada.* Let it be said at the same time that Neruda, in expanding the possibilities of the poetic self, under the possible tutelage of his beloved Walt Whitman, is not about to transform his voice into an impassive, timeless, incorporeal unmoved mover of poetry and sensibility. No, this moment in the *Tentativa* . . . simply signals a displacement of self to another plane, not at all Olympian, and where the poet gains a deeper optical perspective. It's a question of removal to see the whole of things. This brings up, I hope not too pedantically, the necessity for the poet's ascension *from* things that Schiller speaks of in his *Philosophical Letters;* there he reminds us that "our vision covers too small a part of the universe; and the harmonious fusion of the vast multiplicity of discords cannot reach our ears." Urging the poet thereby to take a step up the "scale of being," he argues for the protean in the poem—the diverse, the fullness of all reality and, miracle of miracles, both a noumenal and a temporal ego within the poet—"Since the world is spread out in time, since it is change, the complete realization of that potentiality which relates man to the world must consist in the greatest possible variability and extension." This surely must be a portion of Neruda's secret—the fabrication and creation of a broad poetic voice born of the contemplation of objects in flux and wearing away, the ephemerality of sex and love, the world as a carnivorous beast. All the while, these objects contemplated remain in their fullness, neither expanded nor shrunk, without ever spinning off into the realm of symbolic essence or vain strivings for "meaning." The poet can sense the power lines of an epoch from such a contemplation, but things have their rights too, they mean what they mean, in total quietude. "I don't believe in symbols. The sea, fish and birds have material existence for me. I depend on them just as I depend on daylight. The word "symbol" doesn't express my thought exactly. Some themes persist in my poetry, are constantly reappearing, but they are material entities. We live with flames, wine, and fire. Fire is a part of our life in this world. A dove means a dove and a guitar is a musical instrument called a guitar."

A JEREMIAH FOR OUR TIMES

Much has been made of the diction of *Residencia en la tierra,* with its extraordinary probe into the bleakest kind of quotidian experience. It's not that this is new in Spanish American or any other poetry, but, as Eliot said of Baudelaire, what is new is the "elevation of such imagery to the first intensity." This *is* new. Later, Neruda will carry out a massive attack against the use of metaphor and image, considering these poetic elements to be bourgeois indulgences, a plot to lull us all into esthetic resignation, *dolce far niente,* social conformity and, of course, anti-progressive attitudes. But that later militant Neruda hides a heart laid bare more than once, and one of those unique moments consists of the first two books of *Residencia en la tierra,* and so to be treasured. The hypnotic quality of the book, then, is not due to that daily, sordid diction, but rather to the tone behind the words—the poems seem to be dictated by a demiurge, while the words are very much of this world. This tonal "problem" lies at the heart of the mystery of *Residencia en la tierra,* and yet it is a tone that can be intermittently found before in Neruda, as I mentioned above. It is also to be found in the later "Alturas de Macchu Picchu." That tone is measured, impassive, horrified by misery and finding the essence of existence only in misery—an artificial Jehovah, a Jeremiah for our times. Perhaps the most striking kind of poetic witness available to us now and to Neruda then during those anguished years in the East was the tonal quality to be found in Eliot's *The Waste Land* (1922). Although we are sure that Neruda read the poem soon after its publication, I myself wonder if Neruda ever bothered to read Eliot's footnote to the poem concerning the visionary function of Tiresias. It is worth quoting in full:

> Tiresias, although a mere spectator and not indeed a "character," is yet the most important personage in the poem, uniting all the rest. Just as the one-eyed merchant, seller of currants, melts into the Phoenician Sailor, and the latter is not wholly distinct from Ferdinand Prince of Naples, so all the women are one woman, and the two sexes meet in Tiresias. What Tiresias *sees,* in fact, is the substance of the poem.

Tiresias, then, is the name given to an accretion of selves, an artificial consciousness, a God-figure. The power of this figure speaking with such tonal majesty lies not in his actions, not in his participation, but rather in his role as chorus-witness to his own observational consciousness. Tiresias is an attempt to get out of a fixed point of view, an avowal that personal perspective is not at all primary. *Residencia en la tierra* is the script for this brand of scrutiny of the processes of this world and the alterations of love embodied in those processes. The sensibility that wrote *The Waste Land* and Neruda's are not at all similar in any other respect. Both poets were to continue on their way toward a widely diverging set of allegiances. If, in the *Four Quartets,* Eliot's Heraclitean *Logos* is transformed into the Word Made Flesh and the seraphically Christian vision of "Little Gidding," Neruda's resolution of his spiritual claustrophobia was to lie inevitably in the political realm, but with a fervor not without a good tinge of religious salvation and justification. In any case, both poets would agree that, insofar as whatever powers there might be above us, "humility is endless."

Now, is there any evidence in Neruda's own work or letters concerning this purposeful obfuscation of the self? After all, we are well within the epoch of European poetry in which poetry, as Eliot would have it, "is not a turning loose of the emotion, but an escape from emotion; it is not the expression of personality, but an escape from personality." (Let us keep in mind the extraordinary importance of the theory of the mask in Yeats, the massive conjunction of cultures brought together by that greatest fabricator, Ezra Pound, in his *Cantos*.) In his harrowing letters to Hector Eandi, Neruda seems to delineate just such a depersonalization. A letter from Rangoon dated January 16, 1928 mentions that "in the periodicals you've been sending me, there's so much agitation, so much life, but little altitude . . . they need superhuman tones, a few solemn and disinterested choirs. True?" In later letters, he proclaims that "the poet shouldn't have to agitate himself, there's only one command for him and that is to penetrate life and make it prophetic: the poet should be a superstition, a mythic being" (November 21, 1928). And later, "I am so happy to have finished and sent off my book, but I also don't know what to think of it. Is it too lugubrious perhaps? Perhaps monotonous? But this is where I disagree with this century: the old books are all monotonous, but that doesn't prevent them from having other qualities." Still later, "*Residencia en la tierra* is a mountain of poems of great monotony, almost ritual, with the mystery and anguish done the way the old poets did. It is something very uniform, like one thing begun and then begun again, as if it were eternally rehearsed without success. I'll make copy for you one of these days and send it along" (April 24, 1929).

One senses here some elements of a post-symbolist ethic—the avoidance of the dialect of the tribe, the innate assumption that naming is destroying, and that words must be lifted out of usage, liberating associations and affinities, permitting unthought-of combinations. One also senses a quest for purity, but this time we have an altogether different meaning, since this quest for purity is associated with a connection with everything that has gone on before in the most traditionalist sense, and this in turn includes a profoundly messianic view of the origins and role of poetry. The poetry of *Residencia en la tierra* lies within the kind of poetry that Eliot spoke of in his essay on Matthew Arnold, where he defines an "auditory imagination," describing it as "the feeling for syllable and rhythm, penetrating far below the conscious levels of thought and feeling, invigorating every word; sinking to the most primitive and forgotten, returning to the origin and bringing something back, seeking the beginning and the end." It is, in this sense, that Neruda participated by ESP with the whole thrust of poetic practice during the period between the wars. The Nerudian antennae could not possibly have picked up more had he been an inhabitant or visitor of select circles at Coole, Granada, London, or even Vice-President of The Hartford Accident and Indemnity Company, sometime poet and sometime prologuist to translations of the dialogues of Paul Valéry.

JULIO CORTÁZAR

Neruda among Us

> My eyes did not come only to eat away at oblivion.
> —*Canto general*, "Hacia Recabarren"

> I love you, pure earth, as I loved so many contrary things: the
> flower, the street, abundance, ritual.
> —*Canto general*, "La arena traicionada"

As close in death as he was in life, every attempt to *fix* an image of him from his writing runs the same risk as any photograph of him or any generality: it shows Neruda from only one side, or Neruda as the social poet. It is one of the usual approximations and almost always wrong. History, archaeology, and biography come together in the same awful task—that of trying to pin the butterfly to the cardboard. The only redeeming factor that justifies any of it comes from the imaginative side of intelligence, from its ability to see in full flight those wings which now are covered with dust in every little museum display case. When I walked into his bedroom in Isla Negra for the last time in February of 1973, Pablo Neruda was in bed and perhaps even then totally immobilized. And yet I know that afternoon and that night we walked together on the beach and along the trail, that we went even further than we had two years before, when he had come to wait for me by the door of his house, wanting to show me the land he was thinking of donating so that a residence for young writers might be built at his death.

So, as if I were walking alongside him and listening to him, I would like to have a word here as a Latin American who now is also old. Many times in the whirlwind of this century's almost unbelievably accelerated history, I have felt painfully that the overriding image of Pablo Neruda has been for many a Manichaean image, a statue now so rigid that the eyes of the new generations look at it with that respect mixed with indifference that seems to be the fate of every bronze figure in every public square. To these young people from whatever country of the world, I would like to give them, in the plain speech they would use to greet their friends in the café, an account of a love which itself transcends poetry, a love different in feeling from my love for the poetry of John Keats or of César Vallejo or of Paul Éluard. I would like to speak to them of what happened in these Latin American countries of mine in that first half of a century that for them must seem confused now since the present is a continuation of that past, which everything has devoured and confused.

In the beginning there was woman; Eve preceded Adam in the Buenos Aires of the 1930s. We were very young and poetry came to us under the imperial seal of Symbolism and Modernism, Mallarmé and Rubén Darío, Rimbaud and Rainer Maria Rilke. Poetry was gnosis, revelation, orphic opening, disdain for conventional reality, aristocracy rejecting the stale and tired lyricism of many a South American bard. We were young cougars anxious to sink our teeth down to the very core of a deep and secret life, to reach to the back of our lands, to our own voices. We were also innocent and impassioned traitors shutting ourselves up in the conclaves of the café and in bohemian rented rooms. Then came Eve speaking Spanish from a little pocket-sized book born in Chile, *Veinte poemas de amor y una canción desesperada.* Few knew Pablo Neruda, this poet who so suddenly returned us to what was ours, who pulled us from a vague theory of beloved ladies and European muses and placed us in the arms of a woman immediate and tangible. He showed us that the love of a Latin American poet could be given and written about *hic et nunc,* in the simple words of the day, with the smell of our streets, with the simplicity in which we could discover beauty without having to agree to a grand purple style and divine proportions.

Pablo had known it; he knew it early on. We did not resist that invasion which liberated us, that mighty reconquest. Because of this, when we read *Residencia en la tierra* we were no longer the same: the young cougars had been cast out on their own, on the prowl for a prey so long denied. After Eve we witnessed the coming of the Demiurge resolved to overturn a biblical order that we Latin Americans had never established.

Now we were going to assist in the verbal creation of the continent: fish were going to be called fish in an American voice. Objects and lives were proposed and outlined from an original matrix which we had made for everyone, without the comforting sanction of the Linneos and the Cuviers and the Humboldts and the Darwins who paternally willed us their models and nomenclatures. I remember, I remember it all: Ruben Darío was displaced with dizzying speed in my poetic geography; like night passing on to day he passed across the border to become a great foreign poet like Quevedo or Shelley or Walt Whitman. In our expansive, deserted and savage mental terrain, which we had filled with so many necessary and idle mythologies, *Residencia* swept through Argentina like San Martin so many years before in Chile, to liberate it, like Bolivar spurring his eagles on from the north. Poetry has a military history of its own, one of conquests and battles. The word is legion and loaded and the life of every man sensitive to the word keeps for him in his memory the uncountable wounds gotten in those profound, unspeakable reckonings between yesterday and today, between the artificial and the authentic. It is useless to mutter that the opposite of this doesn't exist. Chile is here today to prove the point to which military history ignores poetry, that it ignores what is in its final instance humanity in its highest exigency, where justice throws down the blindfold which the system puts over its eyes and smiles like a woman watching a child at play.

Neruda did not give us enough time to recover ourselves, to gain that distance intelligence establishes even with what it holds most beloved, so that its reason for being is in an incessant *ne plus ultra*. To accept and to assimilate *Residencia en la tierra* required accordance to a different dimension of language and, after that, an *American* way of seeing that had not been seen until then. (Some of us inspired by stumbling across it in bookstores or hearing about it through friends had already entered with the same amazement into another new phase of the inconceivable metamorphosis of our world: César Vallejo's *Trilce,* which came to Buenos Aires from the north like a trembling, secretive traveller, bringing different keys to unlock the same American consciousness.) But Pablo did not give us enough time to look at it from all sides, to make the first elementary equations necessary to understand that multiplied explosion of poetry. Vast poems which would later form part of the third *Residencia* were heaped tumultuously onto the first great cosmogony to refine it, to specify it, and to bring it each time more into the present and into history. When the Spanish Civil War brought him to write *España en el corazón,* Neruda had taken the final step that transported him from the actor's stage to the

human earth. His political definition, which so many had misunderstood
as ignoble, had surged forth and broke over Latin America. It had the necessity and simplicity of a beloved birthday, of possession in the final surrender, and it is easy to see that the signs of the times have changed since
then. The slow, impassioned enumeration of the fruits of the earth given
by a sad and solitary man has become today the persistent call to recover
those fruits never savored and unjustly lost, the proposition of a poetry
forged at length from word and from action. In Buenos Aires, the capital
of forsaken history, this second and more terrible of Neruda's jolts was
enough to make many masks fall. I was struck to see (it is an ironic testi-
monial) how Neruda's fans suddenly repudiated his poetry while oppor-
tunists exalted to a wind which simply swallowed their voices a work
which was to them palpably unintelligible, except in its most obvious signi-
ficances. There remained those who merited it, whether committed on a
political level or not (I say this expressly, setting it down that I needed even
the Cuban Revolution to wake me up), and for them Neruda's work continued to be a pulse, a great and deep American breath of life where there
were only delinquent *pasatistas* and fidelities to foreign canons that were
growing more and more ridiculous. I know that I owe Pablo Neruda for
access to Vallejo, to Octavio Paz, to Lezama Lima, to Cardenal, poets as
separate as they are united, as individual as they are related. But I repeat,
he did not give us a program; he never made a program for us. Poem after
poem, book after book, his imperious compass performed its revision on
our course, calling to us without imposing itself on us, without the petty
paternalism of a major poet, of a grandfather Hugo in Latin America. He
simply put another book on the table and the pale ghosts fled to their hid-
ing places. When *Canto general* appeared the cycle of creation entered its
last necessary day; later there would follow others, memorable or simple
celebrations, bringing well-earned poems in which he felt moved to recall
his life with his friends, like the intimate *Estravagario* and many moments
in *Memorial de Isla Negra*. Neruda grew old without giving up the smile
of a mischievous boy; he entered through the force of objects into the cycle
of solemnities, through all usable roads. The unnecessary blessing of the
Nobel Prize was the final pat on the head from a system trying to recover
the irrecoverable, the open air, the cat on the roof playing with the moon.

Much has been written about *Canto general* but its deepest sense escapes literary criticism and any reduction aimed only at its poetic expression. This immense work is an achronological monstrosity (Pablo said this
one day, when he looked at me with one of his long looks, like a shark
caught in a trap), and because of this, proof that Latin America is not only

outside of European historical time but has a perfect right and, what is more, the piercing obligation to be so. Like Jose Lezama Lima's *Paradiso*, which exists in a terrain which is not much different when all is said and done, *Canto general* decided to make a *tabula rasa* and begin anew. And even if only a little, it does. Because contemporary European and American poetry never thinks of this, of a province or a territory that is at once within the verbal field of expression *and* within the personal experience of the poet, it is almost obvious that it is an enterprise definitively limited. What I am saying is that contemporary poetry, including socially-motivated poetry like that of an Aragon, or a Nazim Hikmet or a Nicolás Guillén (who are the first to come to mind but by no means the only ones), is giving place only to determined situations and intentions. This is still more noticeable in uncommitted poetry, which in our age and in all ages tends to concentrate on the elegiac, on the erotic, or on a poetry of manners. And into the context of this poetry, even if I do not negate it for its infinite beauty and richness but because it has helped me live my life, came *Canto general* one day. It was a kind of absurd, prodigious Latin American genealogy, that is, a poetic enterprise of the most general branches. It was like a gigantic warehouse full of groceries, or one of those hardware stores that carried everything from tractors to tiny screws. The difference is that Neruda sovereignly refused anything prefabricated where words were concerned: *their* museums, galleries, catalogues, and files would come to us proposing a vicarious understanding of our physical and mental terrain. Neruda left out everything created by culture and included everything created by nature. He was an insatiable eye returning to original chaos, a tongue running along stones one by one in order to know their tastes and textures, an ear in which one by one the first bird calls entered, a smell which grew intoxicated on sand, salt, and on the smoke of factories. Nothing so much had been done by Hesiod in order to embrace the mythological skies and the work of the fields. Lucretius intended nothing else, nor did Dante, the cosmonaut of souls. Like some of the Spanish chroniclers of the conquest, like Humboldt, like the English travellers on the Río de la Plata (but at the very limits of what was tolerable), he refused to describe that which was still to exist. He gave the impression in every verse that before it there had been nothing, that this bird had no name and that this village had not existed. And when I spoke of him of this, he looked at me at length and came back to fill my glass, a sure sign that you were well in agreement, old brother.

Because of things of this nature I believe that the work of Pablo Neruda has been for the Latin Americans of my time something that transcends the usual parameters in which the reader of poetry and the creator of poetry move dialectically. When I think of it, the word *work* has for me an architectonic consistency, a measure of the stone cutter's craft to it, because what it does for many of us is not only give fulfillment on a general level of ontological enrichment, which all great poetry gives, but also on a level at which there is a direct line of contact with the matter, form, space and time of America. Who will be able to come to the Chilean coastline and fall in love with the relentless Pacific without the verses of the "Barcarola" coming to them from the now distant *Residencia en la tierra?* Who will be able to climb to Macchu Picchu without feeling that Pablo came before them with that endless theory of steps and hives? I say it at risk, I say it in pain: how much poetry that I have loved ran through my fingers after this terrible shower of minerals and cells! And I also say it in gratitude: because no poet ever murders another poet, simply the order of another set of manners in a trembling library of sensibility and memory. We have lived and read on loan, although what we borrowed was indeed beautiful. We loved in poetry something like a diplomatic immunity, a favored extraterritoriality, a verbal nepenthe of such stupid tyranny and such insolent exploitation of our public lives. Humbly, without reproaching us for our precious abstractions, Neruda opened up for us the widest of gates to this flood of consciousness which will one day be called in verse liberty. Now we could go on reading Mallarmé and Rilke, placed in their precise orbit, but now we could not deny that we were Latin Americans. I know, the most urgent part of my being knows, that no one goes away the loser in that furious confrontation of the very materials of these two types of poetry.

Because of this, I invite those who much too easily forget to reread *Canto general* so that in the light (and not in the darkness) of what happens in Chile, in Uruguay, in Bolivia—complete for yourself the endless list—they can verify the relentless prophecy and unconquerable hope of one of the most lucid men of our age. It is impossible to encompass this horizon, this rose of the four winds that comes back moistened and vivid and pointing out its many directions. I will refer only to the portrait of that great dictator, of that great tyrant whom Neruda named without wavering in this book, as if he knew what was to come later for his unfortunate people. His denunciation encompassed a future itself where the nightmare was waiting once again. I invite them, not to quote more than one, to reread the poem in which González-Videla is accused of being a traitor to his country, and to substitute his name for that of Pinochet, whom Salvador Allende also named a traitor before falling to an assassin.

I invite them to reread the verses in which Neruda transcribes letters and testimonials of tortured Chileans, taunted and murdered by dictatorship. One would have to be blind and dumb not to feel that these pages of *Canto general* had been written in the last two months, or last night, or at this very moment, written by a dead poet, written for our shame and, perhaps, if we ever deserve it, for our hope.

I did not know Pablo Neruda the man very well, since among my faults is that one of not being close to other writers, egotistically preferring the work to the person. Two incidents have had their effect on me, however: one concerned a pair of dedicated books which brought me to Paris and without which I never would have received whatever I can call my own, and a letter he sent to some journal whose name I do not remember in which he generously tried to suggest a false and absurd polemic between José María Arguedas and me on the subject of "residential" writers and "exiled" writers. When Salvador Allende assumed the presidency in November of 1970, I wanted to be in Santiago, close to my Chilean brothers, to attend something which was for me much more than a ceremony—the first great opening up to socialism in the southern part of the continent. Someone called my hotel and a voice that flowed like a slow river said: "They tell me that you are very tired, come to Isla Negra for a few days. I know that you still don't like to be around people. We will be alone with Matilde and my sister. Jorge Edwards will bring you a car. Matta and Theresa will come for lunch, no one else." I went, naturally, and Pablo gave me a poncho from Temuco as a gift and showed me the house, the sea, the solitary fields. As if he feared tiring me out, he left me alone to wander at length, looking among the empty rooms and to visit at my leisure the cave of Aladino, with its Xanadu of endless marvels. Almost immediately, I understood that rigorous correspondence between poetry and objects, between matter and the word. I thought of Anna de Noailles asking a friend the name of a flower she glimpsed along the walkway and being amazed: "Ah, this is the same one that I've mentioned many times in my poems." I felt that this came from a poet who never named anything without feeling it first, who lived what he named. How much he resented it; how enviously he ironized that day on the figureheads he collected, on the atlas, on the compasses, on the ships in the bottles, the first editions, the stamps and dolls. He did not understand that that house, that all of Neruda's houses were also poems, replicas and corroborations of the nomenclatures of *Residencia* and of *Canto*. They were proof that nothing, no single substance, no flower had ever entered his verses without being looked at and smelled at length, and only then being given and getting the right to live forever in the memory of those who will receive openheartedly that poetry of verbal incarnation, of contact without mediation. Even the death of Pablo Neruda among the trash and uniformed rats—is that not the ultimate poem of struggle? We knew that he was stricken with cancer, that it was a question of time and perhaps he would have died the day he did anyway, although the vengeful troops would not have destroyed and ransacked his house. But fate has it sketched out to the last detail how it would like things to be. Voluntarily or not, now strange to the surroundings or looking at the ruins of his house with those pelican-like eyes which nothing escapes, his death today is his most terrible verse, spit in the eye of the hangman's naked face, like Ché Guevara's death in his time, or like Nguyen Van Troy's, like the deaths of all those who died without surrender. I recall the last time I saw him, in February of 1973, when I came to Isla Negra. It was enough to see the great door closed to know that there are still no guarantees in medical science, as Pablo had said to me, perhaps as a way of saying goodbye. My wife had hoped to tape a talk with him for French radio. We looked at each other without speaking and the tape recorder stayed in the car. Matilde and Pablo's sister took us to the bedroom from which he carried on his dialogue with the sea, with those waves that rose like lids from the great eye of life. Lucid and hopeful (it was election eve and the Unidad Popular had secured its right to govern), he gave us his last book. "Now that I can't go to the demonstrations or talk to the people, I want to be there in these verses which I wrote in three days." The title explained everything, *Incitation to Nixonicide and Praise for the Chilean Revolution,* verses to be shouted on the streetcorners, to be set to music by the popular singers, for the workers and field laborers to read in the town centers and at home. A television at the foot of the bed kept him up to date with all of the proceedings of the election; detective novels, which he enjoyed so much, were a better sedative then the injections which nevertheless were becoming more and more necessary. We spoke of France, of his last birthday in the house at Normandy where friends came from all over so that Pablo might feel a little less the geometric solitude of a famous diplomat. With paper hats and long swigs of wine and music we said goodbye (he knew it and we knew he knew it). We talked of Salvador Allende who still came unannounced to visit him in those days, sending Isla Negra into shock with his helicopter. And that night, although we insisted on going, Pablo made us watch with him a horrendous vampire movie on television, fascinated and distracted at the same time, giving himself over to a present where those phantoms were more real to him than a future he knew was locked. On my first visit, two years before, he embraced me with a promise to see me soon, which we fulfilled in France. Now he looked at us a moment, his hands in ours, and said: "It's better that we not say goodbye, then . . . ," his tired eyes already far away.

So it was; it was not necessary to say goodbye. What I have set down here is my presence next to him and to Chile. I know that one day we will return to Isla Negra, that his people will enter by the door and find in each stone, in the leaf of every tree, in every sea-bird's call, the poetry of this man whom I loved so much living forever.

E. RODRÍGUEZ MONEGAL

A Personal Poetry

A change in the circumstances of the outside world (above all the partial abandonment of the doctrines of socialist realism) and a change in the internal temperature of the poet brought forth a new poetry from Pablo Neruda—less explicitly new and revisionary than the *Odes* at the moment of its appearance, but no less important to a total understanding of the poet. Between 1958 and 1964 Neruda published, among others, five books of verse and one book of prose that expressed exactly the ambivalence of his vision in a form that the *Odes* had not achieved and which permitted, for the most part, access to a personal experience of the highest complexity. These are the years of *Cien sonetos de amor* (1960), and *Cantos ceremoniales* (1961), in which the poet of the free and serpentine poetry of the *Odes* subjected himself voluntarily to the discipline of the sonnet and practiced many times over the high art of verse. But these are also the years of *Estravagario* (1958), perhaps the most personal and whimsical of Neruda's books, his greatest, most intimate revelation; and these are the years of *Plenos poderes* (1962), in which the form and soul of many of the *Odes* coexisted with the openness of *Estravagario*. They are the years of his *Memorias* in prose, those *Lives of the Poet* which were published serially in Rio de Janeiro's *O cruzeiro*, and of *Memorial de Isla Negra*, his partial autobiography in verse.

Whatever their form or content, these five books of verse and one book of prose belong to the same family. They are the autumn leaves of the poet and, like the autumn, somber and glowing, permeated by a mild

From *Neruda: El viajero inmóvil.* © 1977 by Monte Avila Editores, C.A. Original translation by Frank Menchaca.

love, by the heat of memory, and by the shifting winds with their premonitions of snow. The poet counts his steps and his days, figuring the balance of his riches and enumerating his passion for Matilde Urrutia. He listens to the sound of his own breathing with a strange intensity and puts everything into each verse, burying his head in the warm, living matter of today. He dons the toga of the poet or crafts alexandrines or composes grave songs with the solemnity of that invisible doctorate of poetry which no one has as yet granted him. Like Picasso in his greatly prolonged autumnal period, Pablo Neruda invented sequence after sequence, undoing with one hand what the other had done with considerable skill. He rejoiced in outwitting, confusing, and infuriating his critics who were always and inevitably marching many steps behind the poet, who was drunk on the quintessences of his own being.

Of those five books of verse, the most completely realized is without a doubt *Estravagario,* and it is easy to begin to speak of the personal poetry of Pablo Neruda with it. The others, even if not quite as ripe as this one, are also important works which generally have not received the critical consideration they deserve. It is inevitable that before a poet of such a great and overwhelming output, a critic feels outdone. But in this injustice another circumstance has played a part as well: the frivolity and laziness of many critics who have preconceived ideas and whom the poet surprises with each new pirouette or with the sudden presence of a deep and unexpected voice. Thus it is necessary to examine these five books, not only *Estravagario,* with a certain parsimony which would permit the restoration of an important image: that of the poet at the very moment in which he has entered this most fecund autumn.

I have already discussed elsewhere how *Estravagario* burst irrepressibly forth, at a time when Neruda was engaged in the creation of another collection of poems (the *Cien sonetos de amor*), and how the need to create it forced Neruda to postpone precisely this sequence in homage to Matilde Urrutia. Confidence is of primary importance because *Estravagario* demonstrates, down to its very typography, the mark of a very personal work. The first edition, published by Losada, was under the artistic direction of Andres Ramón Vázquez and Silvio Baldessari but the true inspiration for the volume came from the poet himself who, with the help of Matilde Urrutia and Homero Arce Cabrera, selected drawings for it from the *Libro de objetos ilustrados* (San Luis Potosí, Mexico, 1883), those ingenious engravings that more effectively give the tone of this work which is at once popular and personal. Already in the *Tercer libro de las odas,* Neruda had dedicated an ode "To a Book of Stamps," which perhaps was inspired by this old Mexican book. It says:

Libro
liso
como
un
pez
resbaloso,
libro
de mil
escamas,
cada página
corre
como
un corcel
buscando
lejanas cosas, flores
olvidadas!

(Book
smooth
as
a
slippery
fish,
book
of a thousand
scales,
each page
rushes by
like
a charger
in search
of faraway things, forgotten
flowers!)
                    (tr. Frank Menchaca)

   The poet also went searching in the work of the first French illustra-
tors of Jules Verne (P. Ferat, Rieu, A. de N.), those melodramatic engravings that seem to reproduce only one instant of the narrative but, outside
of their context, turn out to be filled with a romantic inner life: Captain
Nemo contemplating the dawn from inside his submarine, the *Nautilus;* a
sailor spying from behind the motionless silhouette of an officer; the unequal fight of other sailors with a huge octopus; another sailor, bearded

like Crusoe or the Count of Monte Cristo telling, almost breathlessly, some extraordinary adventure to his astonished companions. The key to both the popular and more refined aspects of the book lies in these illustrations which, nevertheless, were left out of the *Obras completas*.

Like the old sailor of the French engraving or of Coleridge's poem, Neruda recounts in *Estravagario* an incredible and quotidian experience: the discovery of an autumnal self, a total cartography of his new autumnal skin, an inventory of his slow autumnal blood, of his life and of his contact with autumn. But he also goes on to reveal in his discourse the joys of love in the time of the fall and the sadness of the chilling winds of irreversible time. The hand of death (laying lightly at times, at times crude and vulgar, sinister or insidious) weighs upon many of these verses with a gravity which can also be felt in the twilight poetry of another great American poet, Rubén Darío. More than a few of these poems seem to allude to that poem, "Lo fatal," which concludes so funereally the *Cantos de vida y esperanza*. In one Neruda now says:

> No hay espacio mas ancho que el dolor,
> no hay universo como aquél que sangra.

> (There is no space wider than pain,
> there is no universe like the universe which bleeds.)
> (tr. Frank Menchaca)

In another poem the same note resounds:

> Nuestro corazón es futuro
> y nuestro placer es antiguo.

> (Our heart is in the future
> and our pleasure is ancient.)
> (tr. Frank Menchaca)

Like his immediate precursor, Neruda was and is a great sensual poet, in love with matter, covetous of objects which he collected with the greatest fancy, erotic to the point of delirium. As in Darío, the hand of autumn was worth one peso and its entire stock was expected in return. Unlike the Nicaraguan poet, the Chilean was able now to assume a slower, less anguished tone because he had burnt his candle out with greater parsimony and advanced along the waters of time with the assurance that he had lived his life fully.

It is not Darío but rather another American precursor who anticipates the tone with which *Estravagario* begins: a popular tone, persistent and admirably faithful to the most intimate states of the poet's being. It is in José Hernández and *Martín Fierro* that Neruda goes in search of this wise and blissful tone for many of the popular verses of his new book, even from the first long poem, "Pido silencio" ("I Ask for Silence"), in which so many of these echoes come together:

> Ahora me dejen tranquilo.
> Ahora se acostumbren sin mí.
>
> Yo voy a cerrar los ojos.
>
> Y sólo quiero cinco cosas,
> cinco raíces preferidas.
>
> Una es el amor sin fin.
>
> Lo segundo es ver el otoño.
> No puedo ser sin que las hojas
> vuelven y vuelvan a la tierra.
>
> Lo tercero es el grave invierno,
> la lluvia que amé, la caricia
> del fuego en el frío silvestre.
>
> En cuarto lugar el verano
> redondo como una sandía.
>
> La quinta cosa son tus ojos,
> Matilde mia, bienamada,
> no quiero dormir sin tus ojos,
> no quiero ser sin que me mires:
> yo cambio la primavera
> porque tu me sigas mirando.
>
> Amigos, eso es cuanto quiero.
> Es casi nada y es todo.
>
> (Now they can leave me in peace,
> and grow used to my absence.
>
> I am going to close my eyes.
>
> I only want five things,
> five chosen roots.
>
> One is an endless love.
>
> Two is to see the autumn.

I cannot exist without leaves
flying and falling to earth.

The third is the solemn winter,
the rain I loved, the caress
of fire in the rough cold.

My fourth is summer,
plump as a watermelon.

And fifthly, your eyes,
Matilde, my dear love,
I will not sleep without your eyes,
I will not exist but in your gaze.
I adjust the spring
for you to follow me with your gaze.

That, friends, is all I want.
Next to nothing, close to everything.)

                            (tr. Alastair Reid)

The poem and the book continue in this tone, which is the tone of the
popular song, of verse which is sung with the guitar, with the intimacy of
the intonation of Spanish singing. In referring back to Hernández, Neruda
is releasing a poetry which flows toward the great popular source of the
Spanish language. This accent is perhaps new for the poet, although its intention is very old, as the first book of the *Odas elementales* shows, where
the poet sings to the popular poets and affirms:

Así quiero que canten
mis poemas,
que lleven
tierra y agua,
fertilidad y canto,
a todo el mundo,

(Thus I want them to sing
my poems,
to carry
land and water,
fertility and song,
to all of the world.)

                            (tr. Frank Menchaca)

Many of the devices of popular poetry, in particular the dialogue or interpolation of the listener, appear in the *Odes*. Thus, in the "Oda al camion colorado cargado con toneles" ("Ode to a Red Truck Loaded with Barrels"), the poet sets the tone for this hallucinatory personal experience through the characteristic devices of popular poetry:

> Amigo, no se asuste.

> (My friend, don't be
> afraid.)
> (tr. Frank Menchaca)

He advises near the beginning, and then much later:

> No pasa nada. Espere.

> (Nothing's happened. Wait.)

which he will come back to reiterate, this time transformed to:

> Esperemos, espere.

> (Let's wait, wait.)
> (tr. Frank Menchaca)

Through this medium he goes on giving his emotions in short doses and alerting his imaginary interlocutor. But this technique finds an even broader use in *Estravagario,* where the poet utilizes even in the titles of the poems expressions similar to those coined by popular usage. One is called "Pacaypalla" ("Here, There, Everywhere"), and "Cantasantiago" ("Santiago-song"), is another in which there is an echo of the authors Neruda read around the time of *Residencia en la tierra.* Thus, in this poem to Santiago the last few verses bring together the popular temperament and the pun, which is also an affect of the poet:

> Y no sólo cuento contigo,
> sino que no cuento sintigo.

> (And not only do I count on you,
> but rather I don't count without you.)
> (tr. Alastair Reid)

By means of this technique, Neruda disovers not only the poets of the guitar and the popular couplet, but also some of the most delicate and subtle artifices of the language since Antonio Machado, echoes of whose work appear at times in *Estravagario.* In the poem entitled "No tan alto" ("Not

Quite so Tall"), Neruda asserts in a tone of voice reminiscent of the creator of Juan de Mairena the following:

> Yo soy profesor de la vida,
> vago estudiante de la muerte
> y si lo que sé no les sirve
> no he dicho nada, sino todo.

> (I'm a professor of life,
> a vague student of death
> and if what I know is no use
> I have said nothing and everything.)
>
> (tr. Alastair Reid)

Antonio Machado also discovered in the autumn of his life and his poetry this accent, at once intimate and public, this confessional tone that was also modest enough to permit the heart to open up and continue speaking as if the poet were no one or, more properly, everyone. Neruda had achieved in *Estravagario* what he had not in the *Odes,* although they were deliberately public: the accent of a man speaking for himself because he knows it is the best way of speaking for others. Montaigne had already discovered in his *Essays* the essential impersonality of a certain kind of confessional tone. Through the experience of his own autumnal season, Neruda arrived at the essential experience of all humanity. The baroque and surrealist poet of past confusions (I am thinking, above all, of the obsessive *Residencia* poems) had now discovered a sublime simplicity, the baroque essences of popular song which could be distant and decorous but also openly confessional at the same time.

Although *Estravagario* seems like a book created at the greatest liberty, according only to the whim of the moment, (the name itself suggests the strange vagrancy of the poet)—it is, like all of Neruda's books, a rigorous as well as fantastic work. It is possible to find behind its apparent gratitude and disorder a series of themes which interlace without strictness but rather with an inner coherence. These themes are, above all: life and death, which the poet balances on each side of the scale of his autumnal equilibrium, yielding at times to the second in order to favor the first after all. Another theme is the return of the past, which is increasingly stronger and more vivid, in a manner which is tied to the convictions that to remember is to relive and that what is full of life should never be allowed to die. There is the waking and dreaming of the poet, which are two forms of the same activity, the same creative process (Poet at Work, as the sign on the bedroom door of the surrealist poet used to say). And finally, there is the love which overcomes all obstacles, which Neruda turns to as his only firm conviction in a changing world, and the theme of the worst enemy: himself, Pablo Neruda.

Some of these themes have already been suggested in previous books, but in this one they acquire a particular coloring. The past had already begun to take on a solid and more concrete form in the more autobiographical passages of *Canto general*. But now they assume a kind of autumnal totality which produces verse of intimate pathos, such as in the poem "Regreso a una ciudad" ("Return to a City"), where the poet discovers:

> No encuentro ni la calle ni el techo
> de la loca que me quería.

> (I can't find either the street or the roof
> of the crazy girl who once loved me.)
> (tr. Alastair Reid)

It is a poem in which the allusion is doubtlessly to Josie Bliss, the woman of Neruda's eastern years who provoked "El tango del viudo" ("The Widower's Tango"), and other impassioned poems in *Residencia en la tierra*. The past occupies the poet once more and builds up such an internal pressure in the poet that only the powerful flow of autobiography can alleviate it. Because of this, in the same poem in which he returns to the city, the poet recalls:

> Ahora me doy cuenta que he sido
> no sólo un hombre, sino varios.

> (Now it dawns on me that I have been
> not just one man, but several.)
> (tr. Alastair Reid)

This is the phrase which will footnote the subtitle of his *Memorias* in prose: the *Lives of the Poet*. In the same poem he notices or is made aware that:

> Es peligro caminar
> hacia atrás, porque de repente,
> es una cárcel el pasado.

> (It is dangerous to wander
> backward, for all of a sudden,
> the past turns into a prison.)
>> (tr. Alastair Reid)

The consciousness of having lived many lives and of having been many men comes at the end of a lucky revelation in which the poet discovers what has always been obvious: that the worst enemies are not the antipathetic critics or the unfaithful friends, but himself. In a poem entitled "El miedo" ("Fear"), Neruda comes to the sad conclusion that:

> Tengo miedo de todo el mundo,
> del agua fría, de la muerte,
> soy como todos los mortales,
> inaplazable.

> Por eso en estos cortos días
> no voy a tomarlos en cuenta,
> voy a abrirme y voy a encerrarme
> con mi más pérfido enemigo,
> Pablo Neruda.

> (I am afraid of the whole world,
> afraid of cold water, afraid of death.
> I am as all mortals are,
> unable to be patient.

> And so, in these brief, passing days,
> I shall put them out of my mind.
> I shall open up and imprison myself
> with my most treacherous enemy,
> Pablo Neruda.)
>> (tr. Alastair Reid)

Contemporaneously with this confession, Jorge Luis Borges wrote a short piece (an essay or prose poem) entitled "Borges y yo" ("Borges and Myself") in which he subtly unfolded the difference between the public figure of the poet (Borges) and the private figure (myself). An echo of this same sentiment, of a deep awareness of an inner division, appears also in Neruda's poem, which is less rationalizing but perhaps imparts the same agonic consciousness of horror at the self. In another poem this is even more explicit. It is called "Mucho somos" ("We Are Many"), and begins:

De tantos hombres que soy, que somos,
no puedo encontrar a ninguno:
se me pierden bajo la ropa,
se fueron a otra ciudad.

Cuando todo está preparado
para mostrarme inteligente
un tonto que llevo escondido
se toma la palabra en mi boca.

Otras veces me duermo en medio
de la sociedad distinguida
y cuando busco en mí al valiente
el cobarde que no conozco
corre a tomar con mi esqueleto
mil deliciosas precauciones.

(Of the many men who I am, who we are,
I can't find a single one;
they disappear among my clothes,
they've left for another city.

When everything seems to be set
to show me off as intelligent,
the fool I always keep hidden
takes over all that I say.

At other times, I'm asleep
among distinguished people,
and when I look for my brave self,
a coward unknown to me
rushes to cover my skeleton
with a thousand fine excuses.)

                                    (tr. Alastair Reid)

These poems from *Estravagario* reveal a distinguished manner. They are the visions of a man for whom the complexity of the world has returned as concrete personal experience. In the *Odas elementales* there is always a turn at the end of every poem that converts pain into hope, death into rebirth, desire into returned love. Here Neruda places in full view, without the sugar-coating of any credo, both the bright and dark aspects of life. Because of this, even his own personality is open to question. Because of this, the poems in this book are filled with a tone which is generally bittersweet, but which at times leans quite frankly more towards the bitter, a quality which has been missing from the poet's work since his political conversion. Because of this, he can write a poem like "No me preguntes" ("Don't Ask"), which begins:

> Tengo el corazón pesado
> con tantas cosas que conozco,
> es como si llevara piedras
> desmesuradas en un saco,
> o la lluvia hubiera caído
> sin descansar, en mi memoria.

> (My being is tired
> knowing so many things.
> It's as if I were lugging in a sack
> stones of different sizes,
> or as if rain had been falling
> restlessly in my memory.)
> (tr. Alastair Reid)

It is certain that there is the intimation of hope and that a positive note wishes to sound. The poet addresses his listeners:

> Y si oyen ladrar la tristeza
> cerca de mi casa, es mentira:
> el tiempo claro es el amor,
> el tiempo perdido es el llanto.

> (And if they hear sadness howling
> close to my house, it's a lie.
> Love is clear weather,
> weeping is time wasted.)
> (tr. Alastair Reid)

What prevents the poet from concluding with this stanza is really perhaps that:

> Así pues, de lo que recuerdo
> y de lo que no tengo memoria,
> de lo que sé y de lo que supe,
> de lo que perdí en el camino

entre tantas cosas perdidas,
de los muertos que no me oyeron
y que tal vez quisieron verme,
mejor no me pregunten nada:
toquen aquí, sobre el chaleco,
y verán como me palpita
un saco de piedras oscuras.

(So, of what I remember
and what I don't remember,
of what I know and knew,
of what I lost on the way
among so many things lost,
of the dead who never heard me
and perhaps wanted to see me,
better they ask no questions—
let them put a hand here, on my waistcoat,
and they'll see how I still tremble,
a sack of dark stones.)

(tr. Alastair Reid)

It would be easy to show that this tone is not the only one in the book, that there are still a number of poems that stand out for their dry humor, their coarseness, or a sudden burst of ingenuity, qualities which Neruda rarely makes obvious. It is certain that in *Residencia en la tierra* there are many good examples of this ironic Neruda: "El tango del viudo" ("Widower's Tango"), is perhaps the most notable, although it is not the only one. In *España en el corazón* (*Spain in the Heart*) and in *Canto general* the wrath of the poet tends to assume savagely humorous forms. There are many poems in *Estravagario* in which the the poet laughs at himself and at others, in which he insults the friends who have abandoned him or denounces those who persist in their maliciousness to young lovers and asks them to leave them in peace, rebelling against the tyranny of others. In almost all of the poems the satiric or joking Neruda predominates. But many times the presence of death is lingering on the fringe of the laughter, as in one of the engravings by the Mexican José Guadalupe Posada which decorates the volume. Because of this, humor (although present) is not the definitive tone of *Estravagario*. In two poems the ultimate key to the poet's twilight vision can be found.

One of those, "Olvidado en otoño" ("Forgotten in Autumn"), is based on one of the most annoying of everyday confusions: the poet is on a

streetcorner in Paris, waiting for someone ("for someone or other" he says
with a euphemism that reveals the importance of the absent party); it is
7:30 on an autumn afternoon. Neruda is waiting and waiting. Suddenly,
he feels alone:

> Me quedé solo
> como el caballo solo
> cuando en el pasto no hay noche ni día,
> sino sal del invierno.
>
> Me quedé
> tan sin nadie, tan vacío
> que lloraban la hojas,
> las últimas, y luego
> caían las lágrimas.
>
> Nunca antes
> ni después
> me quedé tan de repente solo.
> Y fue esperando a quién,
> no me recuerdo,
> fue tontamente,
> pasajeramente,
>
> pero aquéllo
> fue la instantánea soledad,
> aquélla
> que se había perdido en el cambio
> y que de pronto, como propia sombra
> desenrolló su infinito estandarte.
>
> Luego me fuí de aquella
> esquina loca
> con los pasos más rápidos que tuve,
> fue como si escapara
> de la noche
> o de una piedra oscura y rodadora.
> No es nada lo que cuento
> pero eso me pasó cuando esperaba
> a no sé quién un dia.
>
> (I was left alone
> like a solitary horse

which knows no night or day in the grass,
only the salt of winter.

I stayed
so alone, so empty
that the leaves were weeping,
the last ones, and later
they fell like tears.

Never before
or after
did I feel so suddenly alone.
It was waiting for someone that did it—
I don't remember,
it was crazily,
fleetingly,
and suddenly just loneliness,
that moment,
the sense of something
lost along the way,
which suddenly like the shadow itself
spread the long flag of its presence.

Later I fled from that
insane corner,
walking as quickly as possible,
as if running away from the night,
from a black and rolling boulder.
What I am telling is nothing,
but it happened to me once while I was waiting
for someone or other.)

(tr. Alastair Reid)

The experience is minimal, even trivial; nevertheless, for the poet it is terrifying. The shell of everyday life is cracked and the poet discovers the void. It is the void left from solitude (which he does not resist, living constantly surrounded, mobbed by friends, witnesses to his life), the void of abandonment, of mournful compassion for oneself. Once again, in the full maturity of his fifty long years, the poet discovers without actually admitting that, in some corner of the world, he is the same solitary child of the rainy south. This emotion had been almost completely repressed since the days of *Residencia en la tierra*, but now it is forcefully reborn, naked and with the serene terror of the irrefutable. Because of this the poet feels as if the shadow of night has overtaken him, and he flees, disconsolate, to the company of men, until the testimony of the eyes of others certify (once and once more) his existence. The poet has met up with nothingness on this undisclosed streetcorner in Paris.

   The last poem in *Estravagario* is called "Testamento de Otoño" ("Autumn Testament"). It is long and somewhat contradictory but it is also secretly filled with the new vision of the poet, this rich, sad, but also hopeful vision of the mature poet. There is a vital affirmation from the very beginning in which the poet introduces himself (with the guitar accompaniment of popular poetry) and defines himself:

> Entraré si cierran la puerta
> y si me reciben me voy,
> no soy de aquellos navegantes
> que se extravían en el hielo:
> yo me acomodo como el viento,
> con las hojas más amarillas,
> con los capítulos caídos
> de los ojos de las estatuas
> y si en alguna parte descanso
> es en la propia nuez del fuego,
> en lo que palpita y crepita
> y luego viaja sin destino.

> (If they close the door, I'll go in;
> if they greet me, I'll be off.
> I'm not one of those sailors
> who flounder about on the ice.
> I'm adaptable as the wind is,
> with the yellowest leaves,
> with the fallen histories
> in the eyes of statues,
> and if I come to rest anywhere,
> it's in the nub of the fire,
> the throbbing crackling part
> that flies off to nowhere.)
>   (tr. Alastair Reid)

   But in the next stanza this ambiguity, this being and non-being of values, fades away and is replaced by the new internal tone of the poet.

On the surface there is an attitude that could be classified as *m'enfichisme*
(the attitude of the popular poet who learns by the Devil but learns more
by old age), but beneath that a deeper and more grave attitude is revealed:
that which recognizes the equally legitimate existence of contraries:

> A lo largo de los renglones
> habrás encontrado tu nombre,
> lo siento muchísimo poco,
> no se trataba de otra cosa
> sino muchísimas más,
> porque eres y no eres
> y esto le pasa a todo el mundo,
> nadie se da cuenta de todo
> y cuando se suman las cifras
> todos éramos falso ricos:
> ahora somos nuevos pobres.

> (Along the margins
> you'll have come across your name;
> I don't apologize,
> it had to do with nothing
> except almost everything,
> for you do and you don't exist—
> that happens to everybody—
> nobody realizes,
> and when they add up the figures,
> we're not rich at all—
> now we're the new poor.)
>   (tr. Alastair Reid)

Later he speaks of his enemies, of his party (to which he left behind
all of his worldly goods in *Canto general*), of those well-meaning people
who accused him of obscurity until they took heart in accusing him of simplicity. He also parcels out his sufferings:

> ¿A quién dejo tanta alegría
> que pululó por mis venas
> y este ser y no ser fecundo
> que me dió la naturaleza?
> He sido un largo río lleno
> de piedras duras que sonaban

con sonidos claros de noche,
con cantos oscuros de día
¿A quién puedo dejarle tanto,
tanto que dejar y tan poco,
una alegría sin objeto,
un caballo solo en el mar,
un telar que tejía viento?

(Has anyone been granted
as much joy as I have
[it flows through my veins]
and this fruitful unfruitful mixture
that is my nature?
I've been a great flowing river
with hard ringing stones,
with clear night-noises,
with dark day-songs.
To whom can I leave so much,
so much and so little,
joy beyond its objects,
a lone horse by the sea,
a loom weaving the wind?)
(tr. Alastair Reid)

Because of this he parcels out his sufferings to those who make him suffer. Because of this he renounces the hatred which occupies so many of his pages after *España en el corazón* and which misguides so many of his political poems. Because of this he turns in ecstasy to his companion Matilde Urrutia of whom he never tires of singing. For her he writes these verses which are so revelatory of his autumnal invalidity:

Matilde Urrutia, aquí te dejo
lo que tuve y lo que no tuve,
lo que soy y lo que no soy.
Mi amor es un niño que llora,
no quiere salir de tus brazos,
yo te lo dejo para siempre:
eres para mí la más bella.

(Matilde Urrutia, I'm leaving you here
all I had, all I didn't have,
all I am, all I am not.

My love is a child crying,
reluctant to leave your arms,
I want to leave it to you for ever—
you are my chosen one.)
                              (tr. Alastair Reid)

In the beloved the poet has found at last the refuge that he lost almost
from birth. He has reached back to feel within himself the sad child of his
early poems of the South, the child in need of maternal affection. When he
sings of his beloved it is as a man who does not tire of enumerating her
erotic attributes. When he feels this way in the most intimate parts of his
being, he is scarcely the young child who cries and seeks the warmth of a
woman's embrace. In one of the most beautiful stanzas of this testament,
Neruda explains this earthy identity which he finds in Matilde Urrutia:

Tu cuerpo y tu rostro llegaron
como yo, de regiones duras,
de ceremonias lluviosas,
de antiguas tierras y martirios,
sigue cantando el Bio-Bio
en nuestra arcilla ensangrentada,
pero tú trajiste del bosque,
todos los secretos perfumes
y esa manera de lucir
un perfil de flecha perdida,
una medalla de guerrero.
Tú fuiste mi vencedora
por el amor y por la tierra,
porque tu boca me traía
antepasados manantiales,
citas en bosques de otra edad,
oscuros tambores mojados:
de pronto oí que me llamaban:
me acerqué al antiguo follaje
y besé mi sangre en tu boca,
corazón mío, mi araucana.

(Your face and your body come from
hard places, as I do,
from rain-washed rituals,
ancient lands and martyrs.

The Bio-Bio still sings
in our bloodstained clay,
but you brought from the forest
every secret scent,
and the way your profile has of shining
like a lost arrow,
an old warrior's medal.
You overcame me
with love and origins,
because your mouth brought back
ancient beginnings,
forest meetings from another time,
dark ancestral drums.
I suddenly heard myself summoned—
it was far away, vague.
I moved close to ancient foliage,
I touched my blood in your mouth,
dear love, my Araucana.)
                                    (tr. Alastair Reid)

This part of the Testament concludes (in a manner reminiscent of Quevedo), with an affirmation of the triumph of love over death:

Alguna vez si ya no somos,
si ya no vamos ni venimos
bajo siete capas de polvo
y los pies secos de la muerte,
estaremos juntos, amor,
estranamente confundidos.

(Sometime when we've stopped being,
stopped coming and going,
under seven blankets of dust,
and the dry feet of death,
we'll be close again, love,
curious and puzzled.)
                                    (tr. Alastair Reid)

Their dust will be the dust of lovers, as the great Spanish poet said, and now Neruda paraphrases and completes his statement:

Nuestras espinas diferentes
nuestros ojos maleducados,

nuestros pies que no se encontraban
y nuestros besos indelebles,
todo estará por fin reunido,
¿pero de que nos servirá
la unidad en un cemeterio?
¡Que no nos separe la vida
y se vaya al diablo la muerte!

(Our different feathers,
our bumbling eyes,
our feet which didn't meet
and our printed kisses,
all will be back together,
but what good will it do us,
the closeness of a grave?
Let life not separate us;
and who cares about death?)
                              (tr. Alastair Reid)

Death, you are dead, another great sensual poet of the Spanish Middle Age said. Neruda does not quote the great Juan Ruiz out of love for him and perhaps not even to demonstrate the rhetorical theme of Planto for a dead lover. He quotes him to actively affirm concrete reality, to deny that he is a being whose life turns full circle and comes to an end, that it is and continues being. This affirmation predominates in the final sections of the poem, a farewell in which the poet takes account of his friends, recognizes his identity in the people, and asserts himself affirming humanity. But even here, even in this note of salutatory optimism, *Estravagario* does not leave out the introduction of some notion of contrariety:

De tantas veces que he nacido
tengo una experiencia salobre
como criaturas del mar
con celestiales atavismos
y con destinación terrestre.
Y así me muero sin saber
a qué mundo voy a volver
o si voy a seguir viviendo.
Mientras se resuelven las cosas
aquí dejé mi testimonio,
mi navegante estravagario,
para que leyéndolo mucho

nadie puede aprender nada
sino el movimiento perpetuo
de un hombre claro y confundido,
de un hombre lluvioso y alegre,
enérgico y otoñabundo.

Y ahora detrás de esta hoja
me voy y no desaparezco:
daré un salto en la transparencia
como un nadador del cielo,
y luego volveré a crecer
hasta ser tan pequeño un día
que el viento me llevará
y no sabré cómo me llamo
y no sére cuando despierte:

entonces cantaré en silencio.

(From having been born so often
I have salty experience
like creatures of the sea
with a passion for stars
and an earthy destination.
And so I move without knowing
to which world I'll be returning
or if I'll go on living.
While things are settling down,
here I've left my testament,
my shifting extravagaria,
so whoever goes on reading it
will never take in anything
except the constant moving
of a clear and bewildered man,
a man rainy and happy,
lively and autumn-minded.

And now I'm going behind
this page, but not disappearing.
I'll dive into clear air
like a swimmer in the sky,
and then get back to growing
till one day I'm so small

that the wind will take me away
and I won't know my own name
and I won't be there when I wake.

Then I will sing in the silence.)
(tr. Alastair Reid)

It would be useful to compare "Testamento de otoño" ("Autumn Testament"), with the successive testaments which the poet inserted in the last section ("Yo soy" ["I am"]) of *Canto general.* Although there is a shared atmosphere of happiness and self-assurance in all three, and although the poet affirms life in the same moment he recounts it in order to confront death with a careful equilibrium, what is missing from the Testaments of 1949 is the ambiguous notion of being and nonbeing, of the simultaneous presentation of contraries which is characteristic of the new vision and wisdom of the poet. Faith continues, the appetite for life does not wane, love goes on enveloping the poet, but autumn has laid its fiery shadows upon the interior landscape. Now the poet is knowing and this internal wisdom has made him richer, more honest. Now the poet can accept his share of darkness and return to the past with a generosity lacking in the epoch of *Canto general.* Now the poet has accepted the world as it is. He has accepted himself and he has accepted being "a clear and bewildered man," "a man rainy and happy, / lively and autumn-minded." This acceptance is the line which marks his maturity.

In "Autumn Testament" there is a line which might serve as the motto of this new awareness:

Toda claridad es oscura.

(All clarity is dark.)
(tr. Frank Menchaca)

This is according to the poet who yesterday did nothing less than raise the name of Simplicity in rebellion against all obscurity. The line is not accidental. In another book which the poet was writing at the same time, in which he also celebrated Matilde Urrutia (*Cien sonetos de amor, One Hundred Love Sonnets,* 57), he comes to assert proudly:

Y cuando me envolvió la claridad
nací de nuevo, dueño de mi propia tiniebla.

(And when clarity enwrapped me
I was born anew, master of my own darkness.)
(tr. Frank Menchaca)

And in *Plenos poderes* (Fully Empowered), he will say only a few years later:

A plena luz camino por la sombra.

(In full light I walk in shadow.)
(tr. Frank Menchaca)

The poet has lived through a deep internal change. When he discarded in anger the anguished obscurities of *Residencia en la tierra* for the somewhat artificial light of *España en el corazón, Tercera residencia, Canto general, Las uvas y el viento* until *Odas elementales,* Neruda made a choice that cut him off from a good part of himself, that altered him and reduced him, that obliged him to live (and to write) trying to escape from the darkest roots of his own song. Now, at the height of autumn, he has been born again, master of his own darkness. This conquest, or reconquest, of a new dimension of voice prepares him to encounter a poetry that is richer and more his own, poetry of shadow and light, poetry accepting of contrariety.

GORDON BROTHERSTON

Neruda's Canto general *and the* Great Song of America

Neruda's great American work, *Canto general,* was first published in Mexico in 1950, though he began it a decade before and added to it afterwards. His main stimulus to a major poem of this kind was given him in the late 1940s when the Chilean Communist Party (which he joined in 1945) commissioned him to compose a new history of that country. Soon afterwards his violent conflict, as a senator, with the national president González Videla, resulted in a long pilgrimage which took him as far as the Urals. Unable to finish the poem as it had been planned he made of it something yet more ambitious; and this, with all its imperfections, amounts to the grandest profession of American faith by a Spanish-speaking citizen of that continent.

Of the fifteen sections of the poem (each a canto in itself) the first five fit most obviously into a historical and ideological design. We move from the earliest America, as yet unnamed continentally (1), which he himself would know through the remains of the Inca city Machu Picchu (2), to the chronicle of Conquest (3) and of Liberation (4), and to the betrayal of that Liberation (5). Neruda's view here both coincides with and differs sharply from that of his predecessors. As for them, the first America was paradise; "a green uterus" of rivers, plants, animals, and of men who had barely learned to speak or name themselves, let alone work their environment. These he addresses as "pastoral brothers," now quite preterite, over and done with. The Zapotec flowers are simply scented shade, and the singing of the Guaraní is in the past tense. Faced with this massive absence

From *Latin American Poetry: Origins and Presence.* © 1975 by Cambridge University Press.

he determines to find a centre for both it and himself, in the most genital part of the land, paradoxically seeking out an umbilical link with virgin America. Through the "terrible tangle of the lost forests" from which Chocano never reemerged, he ascends to Machu Picchu, the mysterious abandoned city in the Andes, first discovered by the modern world as late as 1911. Machu Picchu becomes the mother of those who built her and of those like him who would now be reborn as their heirs. He approaches this "mother of stone" asking to be accompanied by American love ("sube conmigo, amor americano"), a phrase which, curiously enough could derive as well from the Inca's speech in Olmedo's Ode as from Whitman.

In *Canto general* the Conquistadors again violate, rape, spoil, outrage, torture and all but destroy original America. But as before, and "despite wrath" at their behaviour, Neruda credits them with an advance in humanity that is seen to be just as "necessary" as it was by Bello: an unavoidable if rude awakening. The final poem in canto 3, brief and allusive as it is, registers that, despite the daggers, light came to Indian America with the Conquest, virginal "Asia" surrendering to the more "advanced" Europeans:

> Asia entregó su virginal aroma.
> La inteligencia con un hilo helado
> fue detrás de la sangre hilando el día.
> El papel repartió la miel desnuda
> guardada en las tinieblas.

(Asia surrendered her virginal aroma. Intelligence with a frozen thread came after the blood threading the day. Paper spread out the naked honey kept in darkness.)

By the fourth part of the work, however, Neruda's divergence from literary precedent, already manifest, quite eclipses his consistency with it. For the liberators of his America are by no means identical with the heroes of Independence. In fact the very concept of Independence as it had been understood hitherto disappears entirely in his verse, along with the complex and unresolved problems it had entailed. With Neruda liberation is something much older and much more recent, stretching from Cuauhtemoc's valiant resistance to Cortés in 1520 to the founding of the Chilean Communist Party by Recabarren, and Prestes' rebellion in Brazil in this century. Between these events stand figures as diverse as Las Casas, the Araucanian Lautaro (who displays an odd similarity with Hiawatha), Tupac Amaru, Lincoln, Martí, Zapata, Sandino, as well as some of the champions of Latin American Independence in the nineteenth century. Neruda's treatment of these last brings home his disagreement with standard histories and intimates the coherence he would wish for his own. Instead of military prowess and sundry lists of creole generals, and instead of the patriarchal, part-Hispanic part-Indian, tradition espoused as an alternative by Darío and Chocano, we are given mass virtue: the persistent and sometimes unconscious struggle for an America of the people. Like Whitman (who he claimed taught him to be American) he would turn to his advantage the very difficulty of subjecting Americans to paternal authority, vindicating them in their myriad being. In this view even the Spanish epic poet Ercilla, in the most confident days of conquest, is shown to be impotent before his "material":

> Deja, deja tu huella
> de águila rubia, destroza
> tu mejilla contra el maíz salvaje,
> todo será en la tierra devorado.

(Leave your blond eagle trace, destroy your cheek against the wild maize, everything will be devoured in the land.)

The first "hero" of Independence that he sings is Bernardo O'Higgins, who, foreign to pomp and nobility, is presented first of all as a "son of love," one who carries in him the "popular" strength of illegitimacy and abandonment. So deeply does Neruda immerse himself in the people, thus understood, that the consciously aristocratic leanings of a figure like Darío seem not so much vicious as amusing (at his ease in the house of President Balmaceda, Darío is fleetingly noticed as "a young Minotaur with his head wrapped in river mist"). At the same popular level Neruda establishes a bond from the first between European invader and Indian victim in human want: both know the prime reality of hunger and exploitation. Fame and honour were the spur of few of America's discoverers:

> El hambre antigua de Europa, hambre como la cola
> de un planeta mortal, poblaba el buque,
> el hambre estaba allí, desmantelada,
> errabunda hacha fría, madrastra
> de los pueblos, el hambre echa los dados
> en la navegación, sopla las velas:
> "Más allá, que te como, más allá
> que regresas
> a la madre, al hermano, al Juez y al Cura,

a los inquisidores, al infierno, a la peste.
Más allá, más allá, lejos de piojo,
del látigo feudal, del calabozo,
de las galeras llenas de excremento."

(The old hunger of Europe, hunger like the tail of a mortal
planet, peopled the ship, hunger was there, decrepit, vagrant
axe of cold, step-mother of peoples, hunger throws the dice on
board, puffs the sails: 'On, on, or I eat you, on, on, or you'll
return to your mother, your brother, the Judge, the Priest, the
Inquisitors, hell, the plague. On, on, far from the lice, the feudal
lash, the dungeon, and the shit-filled galleys.)

In many points of detail Neruda can be seen echoing artists before him
with similar politics, Mayakovsky for example. His picture of the lonely
mechanical Cortes is transcribed from the Mexican muralists (Diego Rivera and David Siquieros in fact illustrated the first edition of *Canto general*). And into his saga of liberation he intercalates popular songs, from
the Mexican Revolution, or the *cueca* from Chile, in the way Nicolás Guillén did in his "West Indies Ltd." But the larger vision is his, or at least
first expressed by him.

Whatever difficulties Neruda may have had in making his vision coherent, in attributing to his various liberators a common cause and alle-
giance, were in large measure obviated in the fifth canto, "La arena
traicionada (The Sand Betrayed)." There a common enemy, at least, is
sharply defined, an opponent less ambiguous than the Conquistadors
whose arrival was residually necessary, as we have seen. After initial and
uncertain notes on such "tyrants" as Dr. Francia of Paraguay, and the Ar-
gentinian Rosas (now, incidentally, abhorred far less by Latin American
Marxists), Neruda issues into angry denunciation of the havoc wrought in
America specifically by the capitalists of Europe and above all, the U.S.
The traitors are those who connived with these interests, middle-men who
sell their lands and people for private gain, protected diplomatically and if
need be militarily by power that is foreign to the extent that it wants only
to exploit. Whatever Neruda's simplifications of the situation are, and they
are often gross, and however much the politics of the Cold War determine
the detail he emphasizes or ignores, this canto greatly strengthens his "general" argument and first intimates the depth of his personal interest in it.
With invective of lacerating intensity he reviews the behaviour of such figures as the Cuban Machado, the Guatemalan Estrada (Chocano's patron),
the Venezuelan Gómez, and the Chilean González Videla, his persecutor.

Using the strongest weapons of the satirist, he then addresses poems to the source of the evil, entities such as Standard Oil, the Anaconda Copper Mining Company, and the United Fruit Company:

> Cuando sonó la trompeta, estuvo
> todo preparado en la tierra,
> y Jehová repartió el mundo
> a Coca-Cola Inc., Anaconda,
> Ford Motors, y otras entidades:
> la Compañía Frutera Inc.
> se reservó lo más jugoso,
> la costa central de mi tierra,
> la dulce cintura de América.
> Bautizó de nuevo sus tierras
> como "Repúblicas Bananas,"
> y sobre los muertos dormidos,
> sobre los héroes inquietos
> que conquistaron la grandeza,
> la libertad y las banderas,
> estableció la ópera bufa:
> enajenó los albedrios,
> regaló coronas de César,
> desenvainó la envidia, atrajo
> la dictadura de las moscas,

(When the trumpet sounded everything was ready on earth, and Jehovah handed out the world to Coca-Cola Inc., Anaconda, Ford Motors, and other entities: the United Fruit Company reserved for itself the juiciest bit, the middle coast of my land, the sweet waist of America. It rechristened its lands "Banana Republics," and on top of the sleeping dead, the unstill heroes who won greatness, freedom and banners, it set up a comic opera: it alienated choice, bestowed Caesarean crowns, unsheathed envy, brought in the dictatorship of flies.)

To close this section he turns again to González Videla, heaping on him insults of exhaustive detestation. He concentrates in this figure the treachery of the continent and suggests that only by squashing this "rat" will his people again recover their destiny.

In this fifth section of *Canto general*, then, Neruda begins to identify the story of the continent with his own, the likeness of the two becoming ever clearer as the poem develops. At first he, Neruda, is virtual, shadowy and anonymous, when he searches for obscure umbilical origin in Macchu Picchu or when he only alludes to the hated father's presence in images of Conquistadors, blond, bearded and surprisingly often named Reyes (the paternal name Neruda disowned). With time the struggle between "orphaned" or bastard Americans, of "disastrous birth," and their treacherous exploiters is increasingly incorporated into his personal history as it is into theirs. He thus prepares for the daring gesture of canto 6: "América, no invoco tu nombre en vano (America, I do not invoke your name in vain)," where he takes on the continent, matching himself with it. By contrast with what has gone before the poems here are remarkably disparate, and lack all obvious "theme." They are personal memories ("Winter in the South, on Horseback"), the description of a particular place like Santos ("On the Coast") or Patagonia, a comment on a time of life ("Youth") or a moral quality ("The Crimes"), or the image of a given hero ("Varadero in Cuba"). Yet in context they generate and are generated by a centre of energy, and feel like short stabs from it. The American soul which Bello held back except as an educator, and which Chocano's schizophrenia prevented him from knowing wholly, is manifest in the way Neruda describes himself in the next to last poem in the canto: "I am, I am surrounded by days, months, waters that only I know, by hooves, fish, months that I establish." In the perhaps not altogether successful last poem he further describes this "I":

> América, no invoco tu nombre en vano.
> Cuando sujeto al corazón la espada,
> cuando aguanto en el alma la gotera,
> cuando por las ventanas
> un nuevo día tuyo me penetra,
> soy y estoy en la luz que me produce,
> vivo en la sombra que me determina,
> duermo y despierto en tu esencial aurora
> dulce como las uvas, y terrible,
> conductor del azúcar y el castigo,
> empapado en esperma de tu especie,
> amamantado en sangre de tu herencia

(America, I do not invoke your name in vain. When I subject the sword to my heart, when I put up with the leak in my soul, when through the windows a new day of yours penetrates me, I am and I exist in the light that produces me, I live in the shade that determines me, in your essential dawn I sleep and awake sweet like grapes, and terrible, a conductor of sugar and punishment, soaked in sperm of your kind, suckled on blood of your inheritance.)

The remaining sections of *Canto general* (7–15), though consistent in themselves, have overall a similar disparateness in appearance. Some deal with himself and his country: the "Canto general de Chile," once the extent of the poem (7), his flight from González Videla ("The Fugitive," 10), a miners' strike in Punitaqui (11), a "New Years Carol for the Country in Darkness" of 1949 (13). The others range from poems to, and ostensibly by, ordinary people ("The Land Is Called John," 8), an appeal to the common people of the U.S. ("Let the Rail-Splitter Awake," 9), letters and odes to other writers ("The Rivers of Song," 12), to the more overtly comprehensive final statements "The Great Ocean" (14) and "I am" (15). This second group of cantos interacts with the first (1–5) through the isthmian invocation of America, to the extent that no part of the poem can work properly in isolation from the rest. When first expressing the time and space of America, in a sequence readily relatable to "objective" history and geography, from pre-Columbian days to the present, and from "the peace of the buffalo to the shipped sands of the final land," Neruda, as we noted, persistently indicated his own interest in them. The "personal" approach to Macchu Picchu, for example, is later echoed in a highly lyrical elegy intercalated into section 3 between "accounts" of what was done by the "cruel pig" Pizarro. The possible truth of such accounts in themselves is further integrated into the poet's own by being referred to a continuous present. Within the "broad" scheme countries and places are arranged at random, in patterns of the conjuring mind; chronology is effortlessly inverted or ignored (Francia precedes Rosas, González Videla surfaces repeatedly at unexpected moments). And events are often announced like news, in the manner of Brecht, flashes of an actual reporter: "They are coming over the Islands," "Now it's Cuba," and so on. Neruda thus enhances his claim to be speaking for the people when by that is understood an ever-present and widely-spread consciousness.

By canto 6 Neruda has achieved a first-person presence, within which the "separate" phenomena of the rest of the poem can be contained and enlivened. As in the classic epic the acts and attitudes of individual characters, the miners of Punitaqui, González Videla, implicate the whole cast, though the "essential dawn" Neruda guards in himself is now no longer drawn out comprehensively into geography and history. In this sense he himself can act as another such "character," the "hero" if there is one.

Like Whitman celebrating himself, he makes of his "I" the designator by turns of the people ("soy pueblo") and of a personal biography. He may deliberately narrow his persona for a moment with phrases like "I am going to tell you a little story," only for us to discover a few lines later that the story (*historia*) has indeed again become history. At the end, almost as a tour de force, in his last will and testament, the most "individual" of acts and disposals of property, is incorporated a larger message, his small death, as he put it, becoming the "huge death" that defines the continent in space and life, also after he has gone.

It would be hard to exaggerate Neruda's achievement as an American poet, and his great work, dividing the century, will surely come to seem one of the major poetic contributions to it in the Spanish language. Yet there are moments in *Canto general* which are inadequate for just that generality of vision, and belie a vestigial uncertainty in the poet's created self which in turn issues from his being, once again, a *Latin* American. With his creed of liberation, betrayal and solidarity he unquestionably overcame the dilemma of "independence" that had thwarted his predecessors. But he was not always equal to the enormous psychic effort it demanded. A clear indication of delimited scale comes in the canto "Let the rail-splitter awake," despite its rousing title. Here he forces entry into the heart of the enemy camp, willing himself a beloved corner near the Colorado River as a foothold. From there he fraternally addresses the U.S. Veteran of the Second World War, who comes back to his simple home, only to find it plagued with unwelcome guests: racists, all-powerful capitalists, inquisitors into "un-American activities." But very soon he is warning North Americans as a whole not to try and spread their empire further (Greece, China, Nicaragua, Puerto Rico, Peru, Cuba), because they will be implacably resisted at every step: "If you touch this wall you will fall burnt like factory coal." In fact the passion of this admonishment contrasts astoundingly with the ensuing suggestion that none of this should happen, that the woodcutter should awake to make life in the U.S. less corrupt and more peaceful ("Let the young white and the young black march singing and smiling against the walls of gold, against the manufacturer of hatred"). And his reveille is further muted by rhetorical modesty on his own part:

> Yo aquí me despido, vuelvo
> a mi casa, en mis sueños,
> vuelvo a la Patagonia en donde
> el viento golpea los establos
> y salpica hielo el Océano.

> Soy nada más que un poeta: os amo a todos,
> ando errante por el mundo que amo:

(I say goodbye here, I go back home, in my dreams, I go back
to Patagonia where the wind lashes the stables and the Ocean
sprinkles ice. I'm nothing more than a poet: I love you all, I go
wandering through the world I love.)

This nomadic disclaimer cannot but alert us to that problem of moral and
geographical identity otherwise resolved or suppressed in the poem. For
earlier he had striven to incorporate the people of the U.S. into his general
song, and to find a fraternal bond with them: "you are what I am, what I
was, what we should protect, the fraternal substratum of purest America,
the simple men of the roads and the streets." Thus he would share his essential dawn with the woodcutters and rail-splitters, Lincoln's heirs. To do
this he worked his way from Colorado River out, drawing constantly on
Whitman's sense of a vast unconscious landscape, and in it the minutiae
of daily life. Yet in a move ultimately reminiscent of Rodó's suppression
of Whitman in *Ariel,* Neruda does not invoke that poet directly at this
point or openly credit the U.S. with keeping his faith alive at home. Indeed
Neruda appeals directly for the voice of his "deep brother," and the weight
of his "buried chest," to sing not the U.S. at all, but the reconstruction of
Soviet Russia after the war, which he views from his high point in the
Urals ("From here I see extensive zones of man, the geography of children
and women, love, factories and songs, schools," and so on). Whitman's
voice is made here not to awaken his sleeping *camerado* at home but to
swell the chorus of defiance from abroad. Neruda thus tacitly relinquishes
his prospecting, from Colorado out, for a pure America from pole to pole,
and settles back into an attitude towards and against the U.S., from somewhere else. When the party line is most firmly drawn, that is the Urals;
when it softens, he subsides rapidly right down to Patagonia, the "extreme
south of America." From one or other place, his popular American voice
being thus delimited, he resorts to the kind of oratory Darío used to con-
ceal an absence or plurality of position.

Yet more radical than this divisiveness between Latin and Saxon
America (which Neruda elsewhere certainly overcame, notably in the urgent unpunctuated flow of "Wind of Lincoln") is that between Latin and
Indian America, which despite everything dogs *Canto general.* A Spanish-
speaking American whose culture in childhood and adolescence was substantially western, Neruda endeavoured to unveil the original America in
Macchu Picchu, in the second canto of the poem. Doing this he showed he

was wholly alert to the dangers of fetishism, of "kissing the stones" for their sake only. He would always wish the city to invoke those who once inhabited it, the dead of a single abyss, the vanished common folk. Denouncing their possible suffering and praising their skill he says furthermore, in the most revealing line in the section, that he would speak for them:

> Yo vengo a hablar por vuestra boca muerta.

This can mean "I come to speak on behalf of your dead mouth," or "through" it. In either case it is clear that he would be the Indians' spokesman, in the absence of live witnesses. He has already asked the River Willkamayu, in vain, "what language do you bring to the ear," and has interrogated the stones themselves for information. Given the presence of over a million Quechua speakers in the Andean area, who are aware of the Inca past, choosing to enter a "dead" city like Machu Picchu must seem no less of a subterfuge than his description, in the first canto, of Guaraní (the main language of Paraguay) as a language of the past. Neruda's evasion of the live Indian part of the American people appears even stranger in view of his own quotation of Tupac Amaru's Quechua as an epigraph to the canto of the Liberators.

Neruda has been widely criticized for indulgence of Indian America, for forgetting the blood-thirsty imperialism that was practised there long before Columbus arrived. It might just as pertinently be remarked that he sells the Indians short, saying that the conquest was needed to shed intellectual light, when in fact the Maya had even reckoned the phases of the moon more accurately than their contemporaries in Europe. But in any case, although Neruda would continuously deny or denigrate his paternal Spanish heritage, it is in the vocabulary and images of just that heritage that he is constrained to interpret the very heart of his indigenous America.

> Pero una permanencia de piedra y de palabra:
> la ciudad como un vaso se levantó en las manos
> de todos, vivos, muertos, callados, sostenidos
> de tanta muerte, un muro, de tanta vida un golpe
> de pétalos de piedra: la rosa permanente, la morada:
> este arrecife andino de colonias glaciales.

(And yet a permanence of stone and language upheld the city raised like a chalice in all those hands: live, dead and stilled aloft with so much death, a wall; so much life, a blow of stone petals: the everlasting rose, our home: this reef on Andes of glacial colonies.)

As Robert Pring-Mill has pointed out, such imagery is "part of the general Catholic heritage of South America," and of an extended frame of reference in the poem. Some of the commonest words in Neruda's language (rose, blood, chalice, stone), far from having their Roman cultural origins and their semantic identity challenged (as they were by Vallejo), effectively silence whatever "popular" voice may have spoken from the Andean survivors of Machu Picchu.

Ultimately this leaves Neruda in the same dubious position as those poets before him who were anxious to avenge their maternal line without knowing much about it: an ignorance which in turn has traditionally indicated deep psychological reasons for thinking of America's cradle as "disastrous." For all his desire that America may awake and grow in a popular spirit of professedly orphaned brothers and comrades, he is still caught up in the anger of sexual shame and continues a radical ambiguity towards the Indian "race." He shares too that compensatory fantasy of an Indian father nobler and more potent than the relentlessly effective European fecundators of the American womb. In the very first poem of his work Neruda reaches out for him: "I looked for you, o father of mine, young warrior of darkness and copper." This imaginary warrior forebear (discussed at length by Jung with reference to North America), closely resembles Darío's Caupolicán (also invoked later by Neruda), Chocano's Toltec bowman, and even recalls the potency of Bello's maize: "haughty chief of the spiked tribe who swells his grain."

At one point, going beyond anything anyone had expressed before him, Neruda takes the consequences of this fantasy, to produce verse of spine-chilling ferocity. This is how he describes how he and other Liberators ate Pedro Valdivia's heart, after drinking his blood:

> Entonces, de la tierra
> hecha de nuestros cuerpos, nació el canto
> de la guerra, del sol, de las cosechas,
> hacia la magnitud de los volcanes.
> Entonces repartimos el corazón sangrante.
> Yo hundí los dientes en aquella corola
> cumpliendo el rito de la tierra:
> "Dame tu frío, extranjero malvado.
> Dame tu valor de gran tigre.
> Dame en tu sangre tu cólera.
> Dame tu muerte para que me siga
> y lleve el espanto a los tuyos.
> Dame la guerra que trajiste.

Dame tu caballo y tus ojos.
Dame la tiniebla torcida.
Dame la madre del maíz.
Dame la lengua del caballo.
Dame la patria sin espinas.
Dame la paz vencedora.
Dame el aire donde respira
el canelo, señor florido."

(Then, from the earth made of our bodies, was born the song
of war, of the sun, of the harvests, up to the size of the volcanoes. Then we shared out the bleeding heart. I sank my teeth in
that corolla fulfilling the rite of the earth: "Give me your cold,
wicked stranger. Give me your great tiger courage. Give me
your wrath in your blood. Give me your death so that it follows
me and takes fear to your people. Give me the war that you
brought. Give me your horse and your eyes. Give me the
twisted darkness. Give me the mother of maize. Give me the
horse's tongue. Give me the fatherland without thorns. Give me
conquering peace. Give me the air where the cinnamon
breathes, flowered lord.")

These lines rush like electricity from the savage to the tender. Flesh consumed, Valdivia, the foreign father, is hated and loved at the same time,
as in many ancient American rites. As a frame of reference for the work
this functions markedly better than the crypto-Christian and ecclesiastical
imagery imposed on Machu Picchu, and arguably as a more primeval or
interestingly surreal version of it. Such expression lies closer both to Neruda's sense of America and to his own propensities as a poet.

Standing as near to the end of *Canto general* as *The Heights of Macchu Picchu* does to the beginning, the "Great Ocean" canto in large measure answers it and expresses most successfully the vision of the whole
poem. The sea may incidentally be Chile's realm, the arena of its own imperial aspiration (Easter Island, the Antarctic). But much more important,
it is the analogue of American genesis and growth. The sexual metaphor
of conquest and necessary awakening, so brutal and unacceptable, so
keenly felt by Neruda, in the historical cantos at the start of the poem, is
here taken to ultimate depths, where violence and impregnation, rape and
shame need not be denied as part of life.

Estrella de oleajes, agua madre,
madre materia, medula invencible,

trémula iglesia levantada en lodo:
la vida en tí palpó piedras nocturnas,
retrocedió cuando llegó a la herida,
avanzó con escudos y diademas,
extendió dentaduras transparentes,
acumuló la guerra en su barriga.
Lo que formó la oscuridad quebrada
por la substancia fría del relámpago,
Océano, en tu vida está viviendo.

(Star of swelling waves, mother water, mother materia, invincible marrow, tremulous church raised on the mud: life in you felt nocturnal stones, drew back when it came to the wound, advanced with shields and diadems, extended transparent rows of teeth, accumulated war in its belly. That which the darkness, broken by the cold substance of lightning, formed, Ocean, in your life is living.)

As in the terrible absorption of Valdivia Neruda does not exult in retribution (certainly not vengeance) but tempers this awesome view into life's intimacy with supreme tenderness, his marvellous quality as a poet. This leaves the way open for one of the finest poems in the book, "La noche marina," which closes the ocean sequence, where Neruda, lover of life "soaked in sperm," opens himself as totally to the sea and its huge potency as Whitman did to his land and its people:

Quiero tener tu frente simultánea,
abrirla en mi interior para nacer
en todas tus orillas, ir ahora
con todos los secretos respirados,
con tus oscuras líneas resguardadas
en mí como la sangre o las banderas,
llevando estas secretas proporciones
al mar de cada día, a los combates
que en cada puerta—amores y amenazas—
viven dormidos.
                    Pero entonces
entraré en la ciudad con tantos ojos
como los tuyos, y sostendré la vestidura
con que me vistaste, y que me toquen
hasta el agua total que no se mide:
pureza y destrucción contra toda la muerte,

> distancia que no puede gastarse, música
> para los que duermen y para los que despiertan.

(I want to have your simultaneous forehead, to open it in my inside to be born on all your shores, to go now with all the breathed secrets, with your dark shielded lines in me like blood or banners, bringing these secret proportions to the sea of every day, to the combats which at every door—loves and threats— live asleep. But then I shall enter the city with as many eyes as yours, and I shall uphold the garment you clothed me with, and may they touch in me right to the total water that is not measured: purity and destruction against all death, distance that cannot be spent, music for those who sleep and for those who wake.)

JAIME ALAZRAKI

Music as Silence in Neruda's Eight Posthumous Books of Poetry

At his death on 23 September 1973, Pablo Neruda left eight unpublished volumes of poetry: *El mar y las campanas* (The Sea and the Bells; Buenos Aires, 1973), *La rosa separada* (Separate Rose; Buenos Aires, 1973), *Jardín de invierno* (Winter Garden; Buenos Aires, 1974), *El corazón amarillo* (Yellow Heart; Buenos Aires, 1974), *2000* (Buenos Aires, 1974), *Libro de las preguntas* (Book of Questions; Buenos Aires, 1974), *Elegía* (Elegy; Buenos Aires, 1974) and *Defectos escogidos* (Chosen Defects; Buenos Aires, 1974). The public poet, who since *España en el corazón* (Spain in the Heart; 1938) had raged and bitterly reproached the old poets for their egocentric and constant flirtation with their own selves, now opens up his poetry to the intimacy of the self, to the silence of solitude, to the magic blow of the wave of mysteries. It is a return, the last return, to home, to the old house of the self. "Se vuelve a yo" ("Return to Oneself") from "The Sea and the Bells" is Neruda's last answer to the Neruda of the *Elementary Odes* (1954–59), who wrote: "No tengo tiempo para mis asuntos" ("I Have No Time for My Business"):

> One returns to the self as to an old house
> with nails and grooves, so it is
> that one tires of oneself,
> as of a worn-out suit full of holes,
> and tries to walk naked to feel the rain,
> man wants to immerse himself in primordial water,
> in elemental wind, but he only manages
> to return to the pit of himself,

From *Books Abroad* 50, no. 1 (Winter 1976). © 1976 by the University of Oklahoma Press.

> to the minute preoccupation
> of whether he existed, of whether he was able to utter,
> or to pay or to owe or to discover,
> as if I were so important
> that I should or should not be accepted
> by the earth with its vegetal name,
> in its theatre of black walls.

In the poem "Perdón si por mis ojos . . ." from "The Sea and the Bells" the major motifs of Neruda's posthumous poetry meet: solitude as an inalienable right, the sea as the embodiment of the poet's secret self, death as a reconquered unity, as a "sunken song (canto sumergido)" which joins the total song of the great ocean. From these motifs a fourth one derives—silence—which, although already present in his later poetry, fully unfolds in his posthumous books. In the poem "El golpe" ("The Blow") from *Las manos del día* (The Hands of the Day) Neruda despairs of language, of that long river of ink and countless voices, and proposes "just one dark blow without words (un solo golpe oscuro sin palabras)." It is therefore a silence which contains all the words, the same silence with which the minute oceanide (a word Neruda recoined to mean sea creatures) and the tiny coleopteros build themselves with materials extracted from their own essence—a silence which rejects names and forms, interpretations and explanations, in order to realize itself in an absence which nonetheless comprises all presences. Here also, as in other instances, Neruda coincides, in a subliminal choice, with some recurring images of the *Upanishads*. In *Svetasvatara Upanishad* a silence of many is mentioned, a silence which is "pure radiance of beauty and pefection" and through which a cosmic consciousness is expressed, a silence whose substance is the peace of all. Another image from the Vedantic text, tantamount to that of silence, represents God's unifying principle as "a white radiance which contains all the colors of creation," reminiscent of the image of the ink stain in "The Blow." But in "Perdón si por mis ojos . . ." Neruda takes a step forward with regard to the meaning of that silence:

> so is my solitude:
> sudden leaps of salt against the walls
> of my secret self, in such a way
> that I am part
> of winter
>
> . . . .
>
> and of a tail-like silence,
> silence of algae, sunken song.

"I am part of a tail-like silence, / silence of algae" refers as much to a consumed life as to the wordless blow which encloses all the words. In "Pedro es el cuando . . ." from the same book, one notices an impatience with words which, like deceiving masks, disguise us and adulterate us: "Everybody walks with prepositions, adverbs, nouns . . . / Where are we going with the precautionary merchandise / wrapped in petty words, / dressed in nets?" Neruda despairs of the so-called "language of communication" which has resulted in clogging communication, a language of alienation with which we understand each other and yet do not understand: knick-knacks, practical commodities, clothing which we put on and take off every day. In contrast to these signals and countersignals, which take us everywhere without taking us anywhere, Neruda suggests: "one must hear what is voiceless, / one must see those things which do not exist"—a language which resolves itself in silence and whose realization is the negation of language.

Octavio Paz has written that "modern poetry is an attempt to do away with all conventional meanings, because poetry itself becomes the ultimate meaning of life and of man; therefore it is at once the destruction and the creation of language, the destruction of words and meanings, the realm of silence, but at the same time, words in search of the Word." An absurd undertaking and yet inevitable: the poet is condemned to words but must transcend them. He seeks to reveal meanings which escape words, and to do that he must resort to words. The poet's paradoxical endeavor consists of using language in order to abolish it, of defining with words meanings which overpower words. Thus poetry becomes a prism with an opposite function, for it attempts to recompose the colors separated into the spectrum in order to restore the fragmented unity of light. The gamut of dispersed colors thus recovers its primal condition: white light comprised of all colors, reestablished unity, fragments restored to their primordial mold. The silence of poetry also reintegrates in one white space the multitude of sounds that form language, crushed splinters of what, according to Paz, was once the Word:

> Everything belonged to everyone
> Everyone was everything
> There was only one immense and irreversible word
> A word like a sun
> One day it broke in minute fragments
> They are the words of the language we speak
> They are the splintered mirrors where the world
> Can see itself shattered.

Neruda does not approach the subject with the same pointedness as does the Mexican poet, but his repeated references to silence aim in a similar direction. The Chilean poet returns here to a segment of modern poetry which sees in silence an exit from the limitations of language, a route of return to "that Word immense like a sun." Mallarmé had already postulated a poetics which seeks in poetry "une musique du silence," and in more contemporary poetry this poetics of silence is reformulated through writers like René Char ("Beauty is born from dialogue, from the rupture of silence and the renewal of this silence"), Pleynet ("silence resembles the word"), Bonnefoy ("Word by my side / What is there to seek but your silence?"), Dupin ("let silence, / slowly unfolding, rule") and, of course, Octavio Paz, in whose poetry silence assumes the stature of a major theme: "How does one say the obelisk of silence," "silence that talks without talking," "Man is inhabited by silence and emptiness." In all of them this nostalgia for silence, far from being an expression of nihilism toward poetry, represents an effort to recover its power, a faith in the alchemy of language, a search for a unity lost in the fragmentation of the word and the world, an attempt at reunion with a totality divided and squandered by a rational race aiming at ordering the world. Science says, "Let's classify and order," to which poetry answers, "Let's unclassify and confound"; science says, "Let's fragment the world into countless concepts," to which poetry replies, "Let's reencounter the world in a silence which unifies all words in its primal unity."

In the poem "Animal of light" from *Jardín de invierno* Neruda expresses a very human fatigue toward a life segmented into countless and bewildering facts, and he reaffirms the necessity, also very human, to reencounter a unified voice which avoids meanings and becomes "the unburied sound of a wave," "the course of a silence" in whose matter the poet recognizes his truth and his destiny:

> I, the man, the mortal, tired
> of eyes, of kisses, of smoke, of roads,
> of books thicker than the earth.
>
> And today, deep in the lost forest,
> he hears the enemy's rumor and flees
> not from the others but from himself,
> from the endless conversation,
> from the choir that sang with us,
> and from the meaning of life.
>
> Whereupon once, whereupon a voice, whereupon a
> syllable or the course of a silence

> or the unburied sound of a wave
> leave me face to face with truth,
> and there is nothing more to decipher,
> and nothing more to talk about: that was all:
>
> the gates of the forest were closed,
> the sun travels through opening foliages,
> the moon rises like white fruit
> and man adjusts himself to his destiny.

Silence is here a route of return to poetry as the oracle of the poet's self, as a sibylline penetration into the mysteries of his being, as a yearning for a primordial unity. In an earlier book, *Aún* (1969), Neruda perceived silence as the invisible receptacle of all explanations that man has resolutely attempted to define. In poem 20 from that book, which anticipates much of the tone of his posthumous poetry, Neruda describes an experience which has all the traits of an illumination. It occurs in the desert, near Antofagasta, where "the air is vertical" and there is nothing: "there are no animals (not even flies) / only the earth . . . without roads / only the inferior plenitude of the planet." In this lunar landscape of dreams and complete solitude, silence assails the poet as a revelation:

> I was there alone, seeking the reason of the earth
> without names and without wings, powerful,
> alone in its magnitude, as if it had
> destroyed one by one all lives
> to establish its silence.

The ultimate meaning of creation thus becomes that great silence in which the poet finds his home and moves into it as into a shelter of peace. That seems to be, too, the sense of the poem "Una estatua en el silencio" ("A Statue in the Silence") from *El corazón amarillo*. Silence is here described in terms of a dwelling in which the poet resides. It is not an uninhabited home or a mere museum of remembrances; it is a world made of the lives of the poet, which now resolves itself into an absorbing silence, into a peopled silence whose population is but the poet himself. The first two stanzas read as follows:

> So much happens amidst the uproar,
> so many bells were heard
> at the time of love or discovery
> or at the time of bestowing honors
> that I distrusted the tumultuous crowds

and quietly came to live
in this zone of silence.

When a plum falls,
when a wave faints,
when golden girls roll over
the voluptuous sands,
or when a succession
of immense birds precedes me,
in my quiet exploration
there is no sound, no howl, no thunder,
nobody whispers or murmurs:
hence I chose to live
in the music of silence.

This poem could be defined as a manifesto of silence, a declaration of motives through which the poet explains his moving to "the zone of silence,"
or perhaps as a necessity to bring to an end the turmoil of outcries and
gestures of the public world in order to go back to that "music of silence"
in which the poet hears himself as a whole and also recognizes himself as
a drop reintegrated with the great ocean. Neruda, who in an interview
with Robert Bly had defined Mallarmé as "a great poet of stuffy rooms,
all full of curtains, no air," finds now in the dusty image of the French
poet his own voice. It makes sense. His posthumous poetry is also a poetry
of enclosed spaces, a poetry distilled in the old house of the self and woven
in a quiet dialogue with silence.

The ultimate meaning of that silence is defined at the end of the poem
"Otoño" ("Fall") from *Jardín de invierno*:

I return to the sea wrapped by skies:
between one wave and another, silence
establishes an ominous suspense:
life dies, the blood quiets down
until the new movement breaks up
and there resounds the voice of the infinite.

Silence is in this poem that point at which a pendulum seems to stop, the
outermost extremity of its arc; an instant of suspended movement between
one wave and another, it is the evening exuding death at dusk. Life, Neruda seems to say, is subject to a similar movement: there are many deaths,
but there is no death; a new movement is born out of that instant of mo-
tionlessness of the pendulum, a new wave grows out of the death of the
other. Life is made up of this ebbing and flowing of deaths and resurrec-

tions. The wave that dies singing on the sand is reborn deep within the sea in a silence of suspended time. Life whittled away by time blooms in other lives, life stripped of its multitude of forms dies, yet life triumphs unyielding in its everlasting and singular movement.

Cusanus, the fifteenth-century humanist who proposed to substitute reason for intuition as the basic way to knowledge, said that "every straight line is the arc of an infinite circle." From an infinite perspective, death is that state of immobility in which the oscillation of the pendulum seems to be suspended, that "dangerous suspense that silence establishes between one wave and another." The sea does not stop in its endless ebb, nor does the pendulum of life pause. Quevedo once wrote: "You are born dying and you die living." Neruda adheres to this conceptist dialectics but derives from it a measurement—the voice of infinity, the eternal self of the sea—which triumphs over the closed circle from within the circle itself; in its infinite recurrences, that circle breaks its wheel and overcomes death:

> I die with each wave each day.
> I die with each day in each wave.
> But the day doesn't die
> never.
> It does not die.
> And the wave?
> It does not die.

The poem ends with the word *gracias,* which ratifies a notion intuitively perceived: like the day and the wave, the poet's life, every life, is subject to the same flux and reflux which transmutes it and redeems it from death. *Gracias* restates with a wintry quietude his faith in the relentless regeneration of life through its deaths both great and small.

Libro de las preguntas (Book of Questions), another posthumous book, is a collection of about four hundred questions on those enigmas of creation for whose secrets the poet has neither explanations nor answers. In terms of form, this poetry renews a modality initiated in *Estravagario* with the poem "Por boca cerrada entran moscas" ("Flies Enter through a Closed Mouth"). In his *Libro de las preguntas* Neruda writes regarding death:

> What does it mean to persist
> in the alley of death?
> . . . .
> When all the bones are gone
> who lives in the final dust?

The entire book is a new effort to show that the secrets of life defy the capabilities of human intelligence, that those marvels and miracles to which we have become accustomed are more powerful than our fragile logic. But at times, as in the two examples cited, the question contains the seed of its answer. Neruda leaves only tacit answers, but in formulating them he opens up vistas for his poetry, windows through which he peeks and peeps to convey later the images of his visions; and often he only answers with new questions: "Will not death finally be / an endless kitchen?" "Will your destruction fuse / in another voice and another light?" "Will your worms form part / of dogs or butterflies?" Life wins also through death, because with its powers life recycles death into its own nourishment. In the vital cycle of nature, the wastes and excretions of death are life-sustaining. Being and not being are equally materials of a great kitchen; life and death mix together and complement each other as essential ingredients of a broth from which we are all fed.

It is in the poem "El egoísta" ("The Egotist"), which opens the collection *Jardín de invierno,* that Neruda offers a more explicit answer to death. The word "winter" appears insistently again and again throughout his posthumous poetry, here supplying the title to the most intense book of the group. Also, in his memoirs, *Confieso que he vivido* (1974), the winter in Isla Negra is described as a season of shadows and solitude. A gloomy and lonely season, winter also becomes a metaphor for the state of the poet's soul. Neruda feels it as a final season, a season of introspection and solitude, a season on whose bare branches a cycle of permutations dies and a circle of days, months and seasons closes. But winter is also the season which defines itself in the life of the poet as a reencounter with a solitude once unwanted but now welcome as a return to home—the old and long unvisited house of the self—and as an immersion into the great silence, where death is perceived as a liberation and as an act of final integration. From the center of his winter garden Neruda proclaims an irrevocable faith in the arrival of a new season, a new spring which converts the residue of the winter into the roots of new resurrections. Like nature, the poet recognizes himself as part of the same regenerative process, in which to die is also to be born, or reborn.

BEN BELITT

Pablo Neruda: A Revaluation

THE LAUGHING NERUDA

Criticism of Neruda both in this country and South America has paid long homage to the fact—a profound, rather than a peripheral one—that whoever touches his work, touches Chile; and that ultimately, whoever touches Chile touches the whole ambience of Spanish letters. With the passing of time, however, it has become clear that appraisal has languished as well as prospered on this account; for while the achievement of Pablo Neruda has gone on crossing boundaries and denying "establishments," comment has remained singularly narrow, inbred, and positional. Too often the effect has been to decant the total essence of a much displaced identity into a "Chilean Indian from Parral," chemically inseparable from the stones, the forests, and the coastal waters of his own country. Both his admirers and his detractors dwell obsessively on particulars of Chilean landscape or Chilean politics which diminish rather than enlarge an intransigent personal vision. Compiling a long index of placenames and public occasions, they have turned a poet's dispensation to the world into a family quarrel or a South American property.

To be sure, any program which includes the *Canto general de Chile, Las piedras de Chile,* and *Memorial de Isla Negra,* and teems with anecdote and personal history, requires a glossary for North American readers. An overlay of continents, jungles, rivers, cities, and oceans seems to cover Neruda's world like a cartographer's isinglass; and much of *La arena traicionada, Crónica de 1948,* and *Las oligarquías* will require the fine print

From *Adam's Dream: A Preface to Translation.* © 1978 by Ben Belitt. Grove Press, 1978.

of topical Hispanists to be wholly intelligible to readers [in 1978]. Nevertheless, it is a fact that the *Canto general de Chile* was ultimately absorbed into a *Canto general,* and as the poet went on to explain: "Amidst all these visions, I wanted to paint a portrait of the struggles and victories of America as part of our very zoology and geology . . . It is a lyric attempt to confront our whole universe." The true range of Pablo Neruda will never become apparent (especially to Swedish Academicians) until one has reckoned with explicit directives furnished us by his titles. His "lyric" mode embraces (1) songs (*Veinte poemas de amor y una canción desesperada,* 1924), (2) chants (*Canto general,* 1950, *Cantos ceremoniales,* 1960), (3) odes (three books of *Odas elementales,* 1954–59), (4) sonnets (*Cien sonetos de amor,* 1959), (5) sonatas (*Sonata crítica,* 1964), and (6) barcaroles (*La barcarola,* 1968). His range is "general," "elemental," "ceremonial," and "memorial," rather than topical; and his "residence," three times over, is "on earth" (*Residencia en la tierra, I, II, III*)—or when it is not on earth, it is airy, fiery, or oceanic.

A bibliography of Pablo Neruda guides us to these key terms as surely as it detains us en route in Punitaqui, Machu Picchu, Spain, Asia, and Isla Negra. It is to these terms, as indices to the further range of Pablo Neruda, that I should like to address myself in an introduction intended, for once, not as a translator's primer for non-Hispanic readers, but as one poet's meditation on another. I shall assume, because his essential gravity pulls the depths and meanings that way, that the poetry of Pablo Neruda is part of everything else I know and sense about work of genius everywhere; that it is not a special *barrio* or ghetto of the contemporary mind known only to the case worker and the Spanish-speaking expert in segregated mentalities; that we have wrangled too wastefully about public commitment and thought too little of the solitude of an interior stance; that his work, given "free and innocent passage," resonates against literatures other than his own, including the English, from which he has translated Blake, Joyce, and Shakespeare, and that this resonance is the true measure of his long traffic with the democracy of letters.

Any revaluation of the achievement of Pablo Neruda must, I think, pause for a long, second look at a volume published after four volumes of "odes" under the fanciful title of *Estravagario* in 1958, and apparently more important to Neruda than to his critics and countrymen. Partisans of Neruda's odic and "residential" manner, fellow travelers for whom the "only" book is *Rail-Splitter, Awake!,* devotees of his *Twenty Love Poems,* and cultists of Macchu Picchu have all tended to set it aside as an interim work, like his youthful *Crepusculario* (1923)—which the oddity of its title may serve to recall. Precisely how to render the neologistic force of the title is a translator's problem which need not detain the reader for long. It is a word of prismatic obliquity, splitting the glancing illuminations of *extraviar:* to get lost, to wander off course, to divagate; *extravagante:* extravagant, eccentric, way out; *vagar:* to loiter or potter; and to English ears, at least, *vagary,* whimsy, caprice. If it is possible to call *Crepusculario* Neruda's *Book of Twilight* it may be permissible to call *Estravagario* his *Book of Vagaries.*

The titular linguistics are important only because an unplaceable word may also help to locate an unplaceable intonation and suggest the humors which invest it like an aura. The "unplaceable" factor is, indeed, something more than an aura: it is both a destination and a predicament. As "destination," its intent is to throw the complacent reader, for whom Neruda is either a monolith or a public convenience, off-course; and as a predicament, it offers a comic bath of "negative capability" in which the poet romps like a water weasel. On the one hand, his "delights are dolphin-like," and "show his back above / The element they liv'd in": on the other, they toil in the "thick rotundity of the world" for the center of a poet's disturbance, groping for transparency. Neruda's avowed penchant for "impurity," however, constantly deflects him into private caprice, a *coquetería* of unanswered solicitations, digressions of the mind's finalities into the absurd, the quizzical, and the imponderable. With good reason, he enlists the "camp" of antiquarian steel engravings from an obsolete *Works of Jules Verne,* and the "pop" of a *Book of Illustrated Objects* resembling a Sears-Roebuck for the Mexican provinces, printed in San Luis Potosí in 1883. Against this iconography of persiflage, savored by a mind that shrugs away all fictions of solution, including the political, Neruda enters his defense of ignorance as an aspect of the world's redeeming impurity.

The epistemology of ignorance is the constantly augmented theme in a work which might otherwise seem a packet of damp squibs, rather than the fuse to a spiritual explosion. It begins vaguely with a cluster of unexamined intuitions: "It is dark in the mothering earth / and dark within me"; "the whole world frightens me—death and cold water"; "I am tired of the hard sea and the mysterious earth," of old hens, bad *aperitifs,* good education, statues, of concessions, of "everything well-made" and "that ages us." Who would have surmised, asks Neruda, that "earth would change her old skin in so many ways?"—with an afterthought out of Wonderland itself: "We go falling down the well of everyone else." His best hunch brings him close to the anguish of his three *Residencias:* "We are crucially alone / I propose to ask questions / let's talk man-to-man . . . No one knows what he's talking about / but all agree it is urgent."

Meanwhile, a sense of self-loss and the withering away of the known renders both question and answer increasingly remote. There is mockery as well as pathos in his clown's grimace: "My heart is so heavy / with the things that I know / it's like dragging / a dead weight of stones in a sack"; or "No matter how many we are or I am / at the moment / I can never meet up with a soul: they lose me under my clothing / they went off to some other city." At times a child's recalcitrance edges the irony of the poet's denial: "I'm not asking anyone anything / but every day I know less": "Why (do I) recognize nobody / and why does nobody recognize me?" The comedy of the amateur's stage fright, pinned down by spotlight and audience, does not escape him: "I don't know what to do with my hands / and I've thought of doing without them / —but how will I put on my ring? / What an awful uncertainty!" Sheepishly, quizzically, he calls out from his treadmill: "I don't come, I don't go / I don't dress, I don't walk about in the nude / I've thrown forks, / spoons and knives into the well. / I smile only at myself / I don't ask indiscreet questions." "Which is which, which is how?"

The true distress of the poet, however, is never far from his vagaries, and is frequently summed up in a cry: "What must I do to sort myself out? / How can I provide for myself?" The hazards of the absurd show their darkened as well as their lighted side: "A shadow moves over the earth / man's spirit is shadow / and therefore it moves." There are admonitions, cautionary asides: "I don't want to mislead myself again / it is dangerous to walk / backward, because all at once / the past is a prison." In stroboscopic changes of dark and light the poet can only assure others grimly: "From time to time, at a certain remove, / one must take one's bath in a grave"; and himself: "I'm going to open and close myself up / with my most treacherous friend, / Pablo Neruda."

The result is a parody of Socratic quest in which Neruda, committed to the "clarification of things," puts his question to priest, physician, gravedigger, and "specialists in cremation," in turn. No one will miss, under his shifting humors, macabre and impudent by turns, the shock of the poet's concussion with Death, like a roadblock barring the way to the motorist turning a curve at top speed: "The minute vanishes, vanishes over one's shoulder," and "suddenly we have only one year to move on / a month, a day, and death touches our calendar." The responses, as I have tried to suggest, are riddlingly diverse, from the child's game of hide-and-seek: "Let's count up to twelve now / Then: everyone—quiet!", to the radiologist's glare: "Everyone sees / the plight of my shocked viscera / in radioterrible pictures," to spiritual panic: "Help! Help! Give us a hand! / Help us to be earthier day after day! / Help us to be / holier spray, / come airier out of the wave!" Since finalities and outcomes are hardly germane to a *Book of Vagaries,* the answer remains sibylline to the end: "When the wind skims / your skull's hollows / it will show you enigmas / whispering the truth / where your ears used to be." His ultimate impersonations are perhaps three: "I am one who lives / in mid-ocean, close to twilight / and further away than these stones"; "I am he who makes dreams; / in my house of feather and stone / with a knife and a clock / I cut clouds and waves / and out of these elements / I contrive my calligraphy."

The significance of this glancing look backward at Neruda's book of vagaries may not yet be apparent to the casual reader. It is, in the literal sense of the word, a pivotal book: it veers away sharply, like that "swimmer of heaven" in his concluding Testament, from the resolute materiality of his odes and "general songs," and "leaps into transparency." Certain only that "those who would give me advice / become crazier with each passing day"—including the "politically astute" who note down all deviations, who "wrinkle, grow gray, and can't stomach their chestnuts"—our hero of comic impurity, like the celebrated squire from La Mancha, retires to take counsel. In full sight of the utopian dream and the "sad countenance" of his master, he parodies his predicament with the country humors of a yokel: "Now I don't know which way to be— / absentminded or respectful; / shall I yield to advice / or tell them outright they're hysterical? / Independence, it's clear, gets me nowhere. / I get lost in the underbrush / I don't know if I'm coming or going. / Shall I take off, or stand firm, / pay for tomcats or tomatoes?" His decision, in the owlish "Parthenogenesis," is stubborn, circular, and mocking: "I'll figure out as best I can / what I ought *not* to do—and then do it . . . If I don't make mistakes / who will believe in my errors? . . . I'll change my whole person / . . . and then when I'm different / and no one can recognize me / I'll keep doing the same things that I did / since I couldn't possibly do otherwise."

Apart from the immediate drolleries of this soliloquy, which in effect returns a rebellious Sancho Panza to the service of a dream, there would be some somber things to say. Philosophically, it poses questions regarding the nature and uses of "advice" as a species of knowledge, about the validity of the "independent" stance as a clue to autonomous reality, about standing firm, moving off, and tactical error as a test of identity, about the changeable, the innate, and the learned. All are recognizably "existential" preoccupations, all are recklessly and joyously engaged in page after page of the *Estravagario.*

In this sense, Neruda at times comes close to the mood of his younger countryman, Nicanor Parra, with whose "anti-poems" the harlequinade of

Estravagario has often been associated by South American critics. Certainly, it would be a mistake to overlook the affinities of the two major talents of Chile who in 1958—the year of the publication of *La Cueca Larga* and *Estravagario*—undertook to scrutinize each other at length in an exchange of *Discursos* concerned with the criteria and intent of poetry in a new decade of the South American idiom. It would be equally misleading to overlook the fact that the "anti-poem" was *always* present in the protean repertory of Pablo Neruda, in poems such as "Walking Around," from the *Residencias,* in the hard-bitten reportage of *Canto general* and the witty emaciations of the *Odas;* and that, indeed, the whole premise of an "impure" poetry invoked by Neruda in 1935 is the true precursor of the "anti-poem" both in Nicanor Parra and South American letters as a whole. The "anti-poem," after all, is an importation and not an invention of Parra's: it predates the *Poemas y anti-poemas* of Parra in the work of Corbière, Apollinaire, Pound, Eliot, Cummings and Brecht, among others, and has been endlessly adumbrated in a genre of "anti-plays," "anti-novels," "anti-worlds," "non-essays," et cetera, which bear witness to the deflationary trend of the modern imagination in the service of the ignoble, the apostate, and the absurd. In purely Hispanic terms, it is written into the whole of *Don Quixote* where, as another avowed enemy of the baroque, Antonio Machado, liked to point out, the "Cervantine fiction" or anti-romance, calls for a "double time" and a "double space," a "twinned series of figures—real and hallucinatory . . . two integral complementary consciousnesses conversing and forging ahead" in a "book of harlequinade creating a spiritual climate which is ours to this day."

It is equally proper to suppose that the poems of *Estravagario* represent, politically, a kind of "revisionism" by a servant of good will, in the aftermath of extraordinary devotion to party lines, dogmas, tactics, and disciplines. In this case, the disengagements of *Estravagario* show both the irreverence and autonomy of Neruda's commitment to an ideology. Consulting the Presidium of his own pulses, testing the "equivocal cut of my song," he discovers he is no man's Establishment ("rector of nothing"), and in the realignment of checks and balances, opens the way to a decade of unprecedented self-scrutiny. It is to this later decade that we now turn.

A HOUSE OF FOURTEEN PLANKS

Despite the prominence given it in the title and the body of the sonnets themselves, the key word of Neruda's *One Hundred Love Sonnets* (*Cien sonetos de amor,* 1959) is not "love" but "clarity" (*claridad*). The almost Parnassian abstraction of the term may jog some startled memories of the "très-chère," "très-belle / Qui remplit mon coeur de clarté" of Baudelaire, with his equally troubled dream of a voyage under "wet suns" and "disheveled skies" to consummations where "tout n'est qu'ordre et beauté." It is significant that, in the protean world of tidal impulses, oceanic disorder, diurnal and seasonal change which shapes the progressions of the Sonnets—Neruda's characteristic insistence upon the impurities of function and the unfolding telluric and human improvisations of a lifetime—it is *claridad* that the poet has come to espouse, literally, in the person of the Beloved.

The more closely one follows the word through the poet's calendar of "morning, afternoon, evening, and night" with its intimations of changing seasons glimpsed through the "salt disaster" of water, the "mash of the light," "all that shudders below / underfoot, underground," "the insubstantial fog," "an untimely autumn," "today, tomorrow, yesterday" that "destroy themselves in passing," the more one comes to feel its spiritual rather than its cerebral force in the poem. Only occasionally does it connect with the world of quantitative and syllogistic order, as when, viewing the Southern Cross through the "night of the human," Neruda invokes its "four zodiacal numbers" in an image of cosmological serenity. Even here, the numbers and elements connect "for a passing minute only"; the "green cross" is straightway vegetalized into parsley, animalized into fish and firefly, carbonized into diamond, absorbed into the chemistry of fermenting wine.

However imperfectly seen, it is the *claridad* of Matilde Urrutia which constitutes the poet's vision of love's permanence and the world's changes. It is Neruda's word for the beautiful—just as *integritas, consonantia, claritas* came to constitute a triad of spiritual properties of the beautiful for St. Thomas—with the special anguish of Neruda's passion for the secular way. On one hand we have the "waves' shock on unconsenting stone," "the seaweed's sodden aroma," "the towering spumes of Isla Negra"; on the other, we have the "dear Orderer" (*Ordenadora*) who "thrust[s] herself into the subterranean world," bringing definition, the "order [that] apportions its dove and its daily bread": recognizably sacramental images of providence and redemption. In between, moves the "flying hand" of the housewife, arranging cups, saucers, casseroles, "walking or running, singing or planting, sewing or cooking or nailing things down / writing, returning": and in the realm of brute nature, the tides, the breakers, the "ocean's tormented pavilions," the "machinations of the wasp / who toils in behalf of a universe of honey," and the poet's "leaky barge adrift / within a double skyline: dream and order."

The latent "religiosity" of crosses, doves, bread, wine, honey, the

"crown of knives," the "scarecrow smiling his bloody smile," "mockers
and backbiters," merits some passing notice, despite Neruda's wry disa-
vowal of any "plaiting and peddling of thorns." If the doves of Sonnet 78
have more in common with the doves painted by Picasso for the Second
Congress of the Defenders of Peace, and if the bread is the bread written
into the traditional slogans of proletarian revolt from the French Com-
mune to the Petrograd uprisings of 1917, the special *claridad* of the Sonnets makes them resonate freshly against universal archetypes which have
attended the strivings of the spirit in all ages. It is no disservice to the hard-
won contemporaneity of Neruda to point out that his mystique of an
"impure poetry" for engaged poets everywhere has Christian as well as existential overtones in its insistence on a "corruptible" state upon which
imaginative transcendence depends. The impure, the fallen, the perishing,
all that "escapes the interstices" when the net of human order has been
knotted by the rational orderer, dominate the watery brooding of Neruda
throughout the whole of the poet's later *oeuvre,* since the *Estravagario.*

The task of the *Cien sonetos de amor* is to retrieve an "immaculate
day" in all the temporal impurity of its hours, phases, seasons, alternations
of feeling and light, fixed in the last, happy *claritas* of love. On the compositional level, the labor begins with a "profanation" of the sonnet form itself, which, despite its careful count of fourteen lines apiece, omits both
the end rhymes and the metrical profile which dynamize the "sonnetifica-
tion" of feeling and argument, and leaves the thought to work its way
through tercets and quatrains as an act of nature. Indeed, it is Neruda's
intent, according to his dedicatory note to the light-and-dark lady of his
sonnets, to turn the sonnet form itself *wooden.* "In proposing such a project for myself," he writes, "I was well aware that, along the edges of each
[sonnet], by deliberate preference and for purpose of elegance, poets in every age have set rhymes to ring out like silver or crystal or cannon shot.
In all humility, I have made these sonnets out of wood, given them the
sound of that opaque and pure substance, and they should be so heard by
your ears. You and I, walking through forests and sand wastes, by lost
lakes and cindery latitudes, gathered those splinters of pure timber, beams
delivered to the inconstancy of the water and weather. Out of the very
smoothest fragments of all I have fashioned, with hatchet, penknife, and
cold steel, these lumberyards of love and raised little houses of fourteen
planks where your eyes, so sung and adored, may live on."

The seasoned reader of Neruda, aware of the poet's long apotheosis
of wood as an image of the strenuous materiality of the world's body, will
know how to make the most of this courtly compliment. The poet of the
Araucanian forests who wrote:

> Whatever it is that I know
> or invoke again,
> among all the things of the world,
> it is wood that abides
> as my playfellow,
> I take through the world
> in my flesh and my clothing
> the smell
> of the sawyer,
> the reek of red boards.

proffers his "lumberyard of love" as confidently as sonneteers of the past have come with their more traditional nosegays and proud disavowals of marble and gilded monuments. The realism of Neruda is not pejorative. It is, however, "impure." His "century of wooden sonnets," while retaining the classical count of Quevedo and Góngora and addressing itself to themes as Petrarchan as the prosody they espouse, keep open-ended, like a paragraph of prose. Read against the tailored profiles of his great predecessors, the shagginess and waywardness of his sonnets are constantly apparent. They contract at will to the minimal beat of

$$\text{Trajo el amor su cola de dolores}$$

or spring open like a sonnet by Gerard Manley Hopkins:

$$\text{No solo por las tierras desiertas donde la piedra salina}$$

from one sonnet to the next. As little "houses of fourteen planks" unfenestrated by end rhyme, they remain resolutely functional and unadorned: they house only large movements of the mind and show the grain and the knot of the poet's intention, rather than the scrimshaw of the prosodist's virtuosity.

On the other hand, it would be a mistake to assume that they comprise a landscape of blockhouses and framed plank, like those pioneering encampments of the poet's childhood which went up in periodic holocausts and were rebuilt by Temucans "who know how to build in a hurry." Viewed against the profile of the wonderfully spindled and granulated *Odes*—or indeed, from any vantage point along the circumference of poetry as such—his "century of sonnets" registers with remarkable elegance as a city of the mind in which passion and meditation come and go with powerful strides toward a noble objective. Indeed, it is with something of surprise that one comes to realize—as an afterthought, rather than a concession to the "rail-splitting" Neruda—that the customary stabilizers and parquetry of sonnet are not regularly present in the unfolding poem. This is due, in part, to the "feminine" genius of latinate discourse as such, with its functional repetition of identical or assonantal slack syllables which makes it almost impossible, at least to Anglo-Saxon ears, for Italian and Spanish not to *seem* to rhyme.

Closer reading reveals, however, the deeply traditional source of both the eloquence and the concord of the *Sonnets*. The density of a quatrain like the following, for example, should be apparent even without the translator's gloss:

> Ay de mí, ay de nosotros, bienamada,
> sólo quisimos sólo amor, amarnos,
> y entre tantos dolores se dispuso
> sólo nosotros dos ser malheridos.

The eloquence is there because the elegance is there, the traditional rhetoric of invocation and lament balancing romantic outcry with Gongoristic refinement, parallel syncopation of key words: *sólo, nosotros, amada, amarnos*. In Sonnet 66, where all is sparely set on the bones of the sonnet, and end rhyme is regular, Neruda proves that he can, at will, produce a sonnet in the classical vein of the Spanish masters, where the combining elements—marked density, parallelism, repetition, and a "Shakespearean" prosody so adroitly fused with the "Italianate" as to create a continuous texture of two end rhymes used six and eight times respectively—all point the way to the sources in Quevedo and Góngora so highly esteemed by the poet.

On the whole, the effect of Neruda's constant *sauvización* of the lines is to exchange the rail-splitter's hatchet for the eloquence of the cabinetmaker and the artisan. The fact that the eloquence is virile, flexible, intimate, need deceive no one, just as his earlier identification with Lincoln as railsplitter (*El Leñador*) and Vallejo as "carpenters, poor carpenters," is inseparable from his compositional integrities as an artist. The *Cien sonetos de amor* are a landmark in the literature of the sonnet that confirms again the catholicity of Neruda's genius at its flood tide, at the same time that it breathes new life into dry sticks. It accomplishes the miracle of transforming that most servile and feudal of forms—the sonnet's long complaint of knightly self-denial and court compliment contrived for the express delectation of a patron—into a husband's book of hours, grievances, privacies, troubled meditations. It removes the inamorata, once coy and cruel by turns, from her medieval tower, into the kitchen, with its recognizably bourgeois panoply of "cups and glasses / cruets of oil and oleaginous golds," sets her, sharp as a snapshot, against a background of "blue salt, with the sun on the breakers," as she emerges, "mother-naked . . . taking her place in the world." It eternizes her in "ovens of clay with Temuco adobe," without the Renaissance boast of indestructibility for "this scribbling on the paper." In its fusion of both the elegant and the immediate, it proves again the eventual sophistication of Neruda's premise of the Impure as a species of "pastoral," in which, as Empson once pointed out, the complex man goes to school to the simple man "to mirror more completely the effective elements of the society he lived in."

THE MOURNING NERUDA

The year 1961–62 is notable, in Neruda's long chronicle of plenty, for the publication of three volumes of verse, each differing from the other in form and subject matter, and all in marked contrast to the special rigors of the Sonnets: *Las piedras de Chile* (*The Stones of Chile*), *Cantos ceremoniales* (*Ceremonial Songs*), and *Plenos poderes* (*Full Powers*). *The Stones of Chile,* which the poet with good reason calls his "flinty book," not only follows the format of a volume by Pierre Seghers celebrating the stones of France, with photographs by Antonio Quintana, but, we are told in a preface, was "twenty years in my mind." During those years, Neruda contemplated the coastland of Chile with its "portentous presences in stone," which he later transformed "into a hoarse and soaking language, a jumble of watery cries and primordial intimations." The result is a "memorial" which organizes Neruda's lifelong fascination with the craggy, the telluric, and the metallurgical into a veritable Stonehenge of exact and monumental fantasy. The dimensions and intensities shift from poem to poem and image to image, from gigantic evocations in the vein of *Macchu Picchu,* to pebbles for the passing delight of a child, to memorial cairns and barrows elegizing the metamorphoses and convulsions of geological time. This is no mere programmatic picture book of curiosities, however, ready-made for the sightseer—no tourist's guide to the stones of Chile as "house," "harp," "hairy ship," "big table," or a bestiary of playful petrifactions including a bull, an ox, a lion, a turtle, and three ducklings. It is a freehand lithography of time and the spirit.

In any other hands, *The Stones of Chile* might well have turned into a marginal rather than a residual book, a mineralized eschatology. What is remarkable is the speed and the certainty with which Neruda, working in sportive and approximate contexts—the profiles which distance and illusion confer on stones—divines a deeper subject twenty years in the making, like antediluvian artifacts in the "corings" of a geologist. The poet's *aficiones* for wood, water, cereals, stars, shells, are already well-known staples of his substantive world, manifestations of his deep purchase on the "impure." His essay on "oceanography," with its spacy trajectory from the Pillars of Hercules to the *krakens* of Copenhagen and the *narwhals* of the North Sea, his conchologist's passion for the artifacts of the sea floor, his delight in plankton and the sea horse (rendered doubly attractive by the Spaniard's whimsical equivalence: *"unicornio marino"*) similarly confirm his passion for the oceanic. *The Stones of Chile* takes a titan's step forward to fix them all in a massive *assemblage* of images, Medusan in its genius for turning to stone all it gazes upon.

The result, curiously enough, is not frozen Heraclitus or stopwatched Bergson, but a set of poems which yield to the imagination at every turn: which breathes, dissolves, nourishes like those visceral deposits secreted by the ambergris whale so often observed by the poet from his Isla Negra window. Nothing is less static or earthbound than the stones of Neruda's Chile: by his "Great Rock Table" the "child that is truth in a dream / and the faith of the earth" waits "for his portion"; in his Harp, nothing moves but "a world's lonely music / congealing and plunging and trying its changes"; his Ship sails placelessly through deaths and distances; and out of his Blind Statue, he "cut[s] through the stone / of my joy toward . . . the effigy shaped like myself," devising "hands, fingers, eyes." Caliban's world of rock and primordial ooze is transformed into Ariel's domain of light, speed, scintillations, island music, ether:

> In the stripped stone
> and the hairs of my head
> airs move
> from the rock and the wave.
> Hour after hour, that changing of skins,
> the salt in the light's marination.

Despite the frequently "hoarse and soaking language," the "jumble of watery cries and primordial intimations," the impact of the volume is neither sodden nor wooden. Its contour remains, as it should, sculptural, mobile, diaphanous: "weddings of time and the amethyst," "marriages of snow and the sea" which mirror "the heart's whole transparency / in / the boulder / the water."

By contrast, the *Ceremonial Songs,* also dated 1961, is a more diverse work than either the book of sonnets or the book of stones. The title at once directs us to a difference of tempo, scale, intonation. In opting for the

"ceremonial," certainly, Neruda is removing himself from the "general"—
a designation he was happy to claim for that heroic compendium embracing fifteen volumes and 568 pages in the original edition published in 1950
(*Canto general*). Since the poet himself does not dwell on the "ceremonial"
factor as such, one is left to deduce its attributes from a scrutiny of the
constituent songs: their content, their form, the whole ambience of the
"ceremonious" inflection. One notes, first of all, that it is a book which
deals in sequences, concatenations, trains of poems, rather than "taciturn
castles" of stone or "little houses of fourteen planks"; it is a book of long
poems—the longest in twenty-two sections and the shortest in four—of a
decidedly meditative and exploratory cast. The subjects fall readily into
four general categories: commemorative pieces devoted to literary and historical personages (Manuela Sáenz, lover of Simón Bolívar; de Lautréamont); seasonal pieces, embracing midsummer and the rainy season;
landscapes (Spain, Cádiz, the cordilleras of Chile, the ocean); and intro-
spective pieces like "Cataclysm" and "Party's End," in which the poet contemplates his world, his person, and his scruples with a characteristic
rotation or circuition of the troubled matters it contemplates.

The range of *Ceremonial Songs,* then, is ambitious: there is no attempt on the poet's part to mitigate the gravity and duration of his induc-
tive labors. On the contrary, it seems to be one of the shaping criteria of
the "ceremonial" that it aggrandizes and solemnizes whatever it touches.
To be "ceremonious," apparently, is to be formal, speculative, unhurried:
to build more and more *time* into the unfolding of the mind's apprehen-
sion of itself. In the realm of content, it is also, clearly, to celebrate and to
elegize. However diversely the subject veers from persons to places, and
from places to the things which embody them, the unity of mood, temper,
tone, throughout the *Ceremonial Songs*—a kind of spiritual seepage—remains inviolable to the end.

At first reading, the persisting factor is felt to be a pervasive melancholy; but successive rereadings fix the melancholy as profoundly elegiac
in origin. Only by adding the elegiac weight of the *Ceremonial Songs* to
the cosmic and erotic melancholy of the sonnets and the book of stones,
can one begin to intimate the distinguishing cachet of the later poetry of
Pablo Neruda. What remains to be noted in the whole vista of the late
Neruda, from its whimsical inklings in *Estravagario* to the processional
densities of *La Barcarola;* is the *de-ideologizing* of his subject, and its nervy
containment in immediate acts of the poet's mind: his increasing reluctance
to terminate existing doubts by rational acts of the will. It is this that imparts to all the hopes, apprehensions, positional assurances of the poet,

their penumbral melancholy. And it becomes the task of "ceremony" to mediate between melancholia and the world, summoning up what is left of the old dispensation and casting out despair by reimagining the real in existential rather than ideological terms.

In short, the "ceremonial" songs serve notice that we have to do with a *mourning* Neruda, a *"poeta enlutado"*: not in the pusillanimous guise which Neruda rejects both for himself and a perishing world ("The stones do not mope!") but the mourning once deemed "becoming" to Elektra, orphaned exemplar of the world's kinship. Certainly it would be a disservice to suggest that the "mourning Neruda," like the "music-practising Socrates," is not sustained and consoled at every turn by political particulars which, in the striker's militant parlance of the 1930s, *organize* in the midst of mourning. Indeed, nothing is more apparent in the spectrum of Neruda's labors as poet and humanist than the energizing genius of both his melancholy and his empirical anguish. On the other hand, the abiding presence of the *poeta enlutado*—to which he testifies everywhere without guile or reservation—is equally apparent as a constant of his imaginative sensibility. If, in 1924, he begins with a ratio of "twenty love poems" to "one desperate song" (*Veinte poemas de amor y una canción desesperada*), the evidence of his work throughout the three *Residencias* makes it clear that the desperate song was actually unending, and determined the "surrealistic" displacements eventually wrought by his prerevolutionary acedia. ("It so happens I'm tired of just being a man.") And if, as Luis Monguió has suggested, the emergent politics of Neruda turns the world's melancholy into a celebration in which *"every* song is a love song," the seminal reciprocities of love and melancholy remain significant.

A sampling of the progressions of the most ingratiating of the pieces will serve to illustrate both the tactics and the dynamics of the "ceremonial": *Fin de fiesta / Party's End*—the terminal book of the poem as a whole. To all intents and purposes, the occasion of this vortical poem in thirteen parts is scenic and seasonal: the "first rains of March," the seacoasts of Isla Negra, and the omnipresent changes of the Ocean. Underneath this amalgam, however, like a tidal force under a breaker, a deeper theme asserts itself: the confrontation of renewable nature with unrenewable man. It manifests itself first in the motif which gives the poem its ironically lackadaisical title: the theme of *"fiesta."* By "fiesta," it appears, Neruda intends the gregarious drive that assembles, celebrates, and eventually disperses all things—not merely the single "reveler," but the corporate being of his "words and mouths," the "roads," by which he materializes and disappears. By section 2, the poet has accomplished a kind of symbiotic fusion of the Season, the Man, and the Festival, into a single aspect of the world's temporality.

The motifs of seasonal rain and the sea return in section 3, "exploding in salt," ebbing, delaying, "leaving only a glare on the sea," and are churned into a "spray" of eschatological wonderment. On the one hand, the "submerged things" of the universe ask: "Where are we going?" and on the other, the algae riding the currents ask: "What am I?" They are answered by "wave after wave after wave," with Heraclitean enigmas: "One rhythm creates and destroys and continues: / truth lies in the bitter mobility."

The word "bitter (amargo)" is a clue to the encompassing melancholy that thereafter seeps into the matrix of the piece and turns all into an elegiac meditation on the efficacy of human exertion—the people, footprints, dead papers, "transportation expenses (gastos de transportes)" of man's efforts to match the unkillable being of the world with acts of the will and imagination. Here the weariness of the poet is such that he asks for a suspension, if not indeed a liquidation, of the inhabited world: inhabited poems, inhabited beaches, inhabited time, where the "habitable" is construed as the "distinguishing mark" of individual initiative: "for a moment let no living creature enter my verse." For the first time since the *Residencias* of his youth, Neruda, looking away from causes, factions, ideological commitments, into the void where the crystal expands, the rocks climb the silence, and the ocean "destroys itself," restates that heresy of all engaged protagonists: "It so happens I'm tired of just being a man." A more haunting issue, apparently, has presented itself with his returning acedia: it is Antony's enigma of the "marring of energy," and the miracle by which "the ocean destroys itself without marring its energy." The quantitative anguish of things is summed up by Neruda in another outcry, which measures the inadequacy of a world in which "our fathers in patches and hand-me-downs . . . entered the warehouses as one entered a terrible temple": the consumer's outcry of *How much?*

Thus, a third of the way into a shifting and many-sided poem, the backlash of baffled intentionality reasserts itself in political and polemical terms. A new insistence on expedient protestation—on "the whithers and wherefores / wherever it pleases me—from the throne to the oil-slick / that bloodies the world," mounting as the "grains of my anger grew greater," turns the purchaser's *How much?* into the prophet's and the revolutionary's *How long?* There follows another turn of the poet's imagination as a new assault of personal choice on the inequalities of the human condition flows into the voids and pockets of his initial melancholy. It is this systole-diastole of his meditative patterns that is the distinctive mark of the "mourning and organizing" Neruda. Indeed, he seems to breathe as naturally as a sponge on the ocean floor of his exacerbated discomfiture. He absorbs doubts, contradictions, passing flotsam in the great baths of richocheting images and uneasy afterthoughts which he inhabits, rocking in the play of altering pressures, volumes, thermal densities, speeds. No one has written more vividly than Neruda of the thermodynamics and psychology of the deep-sea diver (See "Ode to a Diver"); and somewhere, at the critical depths which break or sustain the human violator of the oceanic and the subterranean, Neruda has known how to anchor the rational balances which turn chaos into meditative order.

The result is an elegiac poem not unlike the *Elegien* of Rilke in both the discontinuities of its empirical search for hard answers, its preoccupation with "the dead with the delicate faces," the "preciously dead," and its insistence on "clarity," joy, a strenuous humanism which asks nothing of "angels" in its pursuit of the heart's fears and the spirit's intimations. It differs from Rilke's "ceremonial" amalgam of melancholy, skepticism, and temporal love, of course, in its *visceralization* of thought—its commingling of thought with "the thorn's languages / the bite of the obdurate fish / the chill of the latitudes / the blood on the coral / the night of the whale"— and its pendulum backswing toward "men." The "Engel-nicht—Menschen-nicht (Not men, not angels)" of Rilke's impasse, glimpsed only briefly in Section Four, is promptly exchanged for "the brutal imperative . . . that makes warriors of us, gives us the stance / and inflection of fighters," as Neruda crosses his "bridge of commitment (lo que hicimos)" into the "pride of a lifetime" and its "organized splendor (el esplendor organizado)."

If the accomplishment of Neruda in *Party's End*, however, were merely tactical and ideological, one might well prefer to sweep backward to the derogated Rilke for truer confrontations of the human condition. The triumph of *Party's End*, however, is that its oceanic circuits stay nowhere for long, are not positional. The day sought by Neruda, in the end, is neither paradisiac nor ideological: it is an "expendable day," "a day bringing oranges," rather than a day of reckoning—though some hint of the social dream clings to the afterthought: "the day / that is ours if we are there to retrieve it again." At the close of the poem, the "white spindrift," the "ungratified cup of the sky," the "watery autumn" move in again, and with them, the obdurate mobilities of a poet who remains "just as I was / with my doubts, with my debts, / with my loves / having a whole sea to myself." Apparently, it has been enough to "come back," to touch his "palms to the land," to "have built what I could / out of natural stone, like a native, open-handed," to "have worked with my reason, unreason, my caprices, / my fury and poise." No longer "deracinate (sin mis raices)" as man, as poet, as Chilean, clouded and luminous by turns, Neruda can now

> say: "Here is my place," stripping myself down in the light
> and dropping my hands in the sea,
> until all is transparent again
> there under the earth, and my sleep can be tranquil.

This redistillation of serenity clings to the whole of Neruda's *Plenos poderes* (1962), imparting to each of the thirty-six poems that unmistakable "fullness of power" to which its title bears witness. Weary "neither of being nor of nonbeing," still "puzzling over origins," professing his old "debts to minerality," yet wavering "as between two lost channels under water," the poet "forges keys," "looks for locks," opens "broken doors," pierces "windows out to living." What was plaintive or suspended in the *Ceremonial Songs* brightens in the up-beat of re-examined commitment, for which Neruda's distinguishing word is *"deberes":* obligations, and its ancillary variations in *deber:* ought, should, must, owe. Thus, in the introductory poem entitled "Deberes del poeta" ("The Poet's Obligations"), his concern is less with possibility than with necessity—the imperatives freely imagined and professed by the poet, to which Yeats gave the name of "responsibilities." The options subsumed under the "responsible" are at once explicit and mysterious: "I must hear and preserve without respite / the watery lament of my consciousness," "I must feel the blow of hard water / and gather it back in a cup of eternity," "I must encounter the absent," I must tell, I must leave, journey, protect, become, be, eat, and possess. Elsewhere, the poet alludes to the "responsibility of the minute hand," the accumulation of "persons and chores," "the imperious necessity for vigilance," "lonely sweetnesses and obligations," "mineral obligations," and "obligations intact in the spume." These, the poet explains, are compelled upon him "not by law or caprice, / but by chains: / each new way was a chain"; he calls for "caution: let us guard the order of this ode," but his mood is blithe: "I am happy with the mountainous debts / I took on . . . the rigid demand on myself of wachfulness / the impulse to stay myself, myself alone . . . my life has been / a singing between chance and resiliency."

Side by side with the theme of resiliency ("la dureza, la dura realidad"), goes a theme of *pureza*, purity, as both a measure of the poet's effectiveness and a reward of his happy "obligation." A table of variations would include not only a multitude of passing allusions—pure waves, pure lines, pure towers, pure waters, pure bodies, pure hearts, pure feet, pure salts—and their variants in *claro* (clear lessons, clear capitals, clear vigilance, as well as "clarities" that are smiling, cruel, and erect) but entire poems like "Para lavar a un niño" ("To Wash a Child") and "Oda para planchar" ("In Praise of Ironing"). All, says the poet, must be cleansed, washed, whitened, made clear: as in a Keatsian dream of "pure ablution round earth's human shores," the land's outline is washed by the salt ("sal que lava la línea") and the land's edge washes the world ("La línea lava el mundo"). Not only does Neruda invoke "a time to walk clean" in the name of the newly washed infant, and insist on "ironing out" the whiteness of the sea itself ("hay que planchar el mar de su blancura"); in the end poetry itself is made white: ("la poesía es blanca").

Thus, between *dureza* and *pureza* (resiliency and purity) and *deberes* and *poderes* (obligations and powers) the poet "writes [his] book about what I am (escribo un libro de lo que soy)" with stunning mastery of all the themes which embody a total identity. The "mourning carpenter (enlutado carpintero)" of *Estravagario* and the *Sonnets* is still there, "attending the casket, tearless, / someone who stayed nameless to the end / and called himself metal or wood": he contributes two of the volume's eulogies, one addressed to the dead "C.O.S.C." and the other, to the nine-and-a-half-year old "little astronaut" whose "burning car" touches "Aldabaran, mysterious stone," and "crosses a lifeline." The old preoccupations with the lost and remembered of a poet bemused by the sacramental character of all change are found again in poems like "The Past" ("Pasado"); and the old melancholy ("To Sorrow," "A la tristeza"): "For a minute, for / a short life, / take away my light and leave me / to realize / my misery, my alienation." So, too, are the dead, "the poor dead (al difunto pobre), the people (el pueblo), the nights and the flora of Isla Negra (Alstromoería, la noche de Isla Negra), farewells (adioses), births (los nacimientos), ocean, water, sea, planet, tower, bird"—each lending new force to that fullness of power by virtue of which a master of chiaroscuro "in the full light of day" paradoxically still "walks in the shade."

THE BURNING SARCOPHAGUS

The great watershed of the sixth decade of Pablo Neruda—the work which, at the present writing, soars like the terminal pylon of a bridge spanning four epochs including the *Residencias, Canto general,* and the

Odas—is, of course, the *Black Island Memorial* (*Memorial de Isla Negra*), published in 1964 to solemnize the poet's sixtieth birthday. In effect, it constitutes a fourth gargantuan span over which flows the spiritual traffic of more than half a century, on its way to destinations as hazardous and uncharted as those previously inhabited by a poet who warns us:

> I have never set foot in the countries I lived in,
> every port was a port of return:
> I have no post cards, no keepsakes of hair
> from important cathedrals.

Its trajectory supports the weight, the diversity, and the architectural stresses of everything encountered en route: exile, deracination, embattled ideologies, and the vested enmity of the world. All that the poet has written, imagined, foresuffered in purgatorial changes of forms and allegiances: shapes of the "crepuscular," the erotic, the tentative, the "enthusiastic," halfway houses of wood and stone, and "residences" that metamorphose into bloody bivouacs in Spain, consulates in Rangoon, Ceylon, India, Mexico, France, flights into Russia, China, Mexico, Peru, "voyages and homecomings" to his native cordilleras—all the wanderings of Ishmael and The Prodigal Son, debouch like a great estuary into the pages of *Black Island Memorial,* from whose terminus "Casa La Chascona," a poet's "house of dishevelment," arises like a hand-hewn Acropolis.

One puts the case a little grandly because the poet's conception is almost orientally pyramidal in its vision of a monument built by the living for a residence *not* of this earth, as well as on it. *Black Island Memorial* is a chieftain's or a pharaoh's personal cenotaph, calling to mind the *alcázares* of Andulucía and the Heorots of Anglo-Saxon myth, hung with shields, talismans, shaggy animal pelts and precious stones, whalebone curiosities of the "seafarer" and "far-wanderer," and encircled by the ocean like a moat. How barbarously or how cunningly Neruda has built his vast *Memorial,* what artifacts, prophecies, legends and gods he has carried over his hearthstone, what enigmas still await him in island, mainland, and ocean, remain to be examined.

The critic's first task, confronted with the grandeurs and *longueurs* of this conception, must be a qualitative one: how to align the "memorial" with the "general," the "elemental," and the "ceremonial" as four phases in the orientation of a talent. I should like first of all to suggest that the "memorial" mode is *nonhistorical:* in Coleridge's words, it "emancipates [the poet] from the order of time and space," whereas the general, the elemental, and the ceremonial may be subsumed under it as modes and dimensions of the temporal. The dynamic that gave *Canto general* its unwearying sweep and thrust after three anguished *Residencias,* was history: history as the court chronicler and the anthropologist conceive it, and History as the polemical Marxist conceives it in an escalating dialectic of freedom and bondage. It is the historical mode, in this layman's understanding of the term, that induced Neruda to join his private chronicle with the perfidies and restorations of Chile, and the Creation story with a multinational saga of the death of kings, conquistadors, quislings, duces, and assorted "satraps" in a Century of Perishing Capital. His chronicle is roughly vertical in its sequences: into its rational progressions stream real wars, personal memoir, autobiography, topical villains and saviors, political reportage, global and national disasters, up to the final page, signed, in the poet's own hand, "today, 5 February, in this year / of 1949, in Chile, in 'Godomar / de Chena,' a few months before / the forty-fifth year of my life."

The pentad of Isla Negra, on the other hand, is concerned with memory rather than history. Into its five volumes there tumble a disorganized *recherche* of events, ruminations, obsessive image, words, doubts, allegiances, political mandates and spiritual recoils in an *ordre du coeur* rather than an *ordre raisonné.* Their point of departure and their point of return are essentially the same: *time present,* in which the poet, brooding daily on the change and the permanence of things from a seacoast in Isla Negra, is induced to evoke an answering dialectic from within. The dialectic is not Marxian, but metaphysical, and its polarizing genius is not History but Memory—the same power invoked by St. Augustine as "the belly of the mind" in book 10 of the *Confessions.* The scene, for all its flashbacks into the displacements of a lifetime, is Isla Negra, to whose sea changes, cloudscapes, and seasonal immediacies the poet constantly returns for a "residence on earth" fixed at last by the heart's choice and due process of mortality.

Visitors to Isla Negra have, between jest and earnest, alluded increasingly to the islanded Neruda as Buddha, guru, and lama—a kind of Latin amalgam of Merlin and Prospero. More often than not, the epithets are irreverently, if affectionately, intended: but the "saintly" Neruda, with his unflinching gaze on the "four perturbations of the mind: desire, joy, fear, sorrow" and his Augustinian assault upon Memory, is an exact distillation of the impact of the *Memorial.* Coming into "the plains, caves, and caverns of my memory" from the secular engagements of a lifetime, he says, almost in Augustine's words ("There meet I with myself and recall myself, and when, where, and what I have done, and under what feelings"):

I also would see myself coming
and know in the end how it feels to me
when I come back to the place where I wait for myself
and turn back to my sleep and die laughing.

The laughter of Neruda is a special dimension of the Hispanic—the Cervantine gift of the *quixotic,* in the presence of the Impossible, as it has flowed into the parlance of the world from the uplands of La Mancha. Like both Quixote and Augustine, however, Neruda is called back, out of History to the "reasons and laws innumerable of numbers and dimensions, none of which hath any bodily sense impressed," and to the "deeper recesses" where "all must be drawn together again, that they may be known; that is to say, they must as it were be collected together from their dispersion"; and, indeed, "re-collected." Thus, we have Neruda's:

MEMORY

All must be remembered:
a turning wind, the threads
in the threadbare event must be gathered,
yard after yard of all we inhabited,
the train's long trajectory,
the trappings of sorrow.

Should a rosebush be lost
or the hare's track dissolve in the night,
should the pillars of memory
topple out of my reach,
I must remake the air,
the steam and the soil and the leaves

. . . .

I was always an avid forgetter:
in my two human hands
only the untouchable things of the world
live unscathed,
and the power of comparison
is the sum of their total destruction.

Forgetting, destroying, comparing, the human rememberer, "toiling in the heavy soil" of his being, like Augustine, discovers not sequence and consequence, but the plasm of identity itself, the ego which has been the subject of the poet's wonder in Whitman, in Hopkins, in Neruda, and Aurelius

Augustinus of Tagaste and Carthage. "What is nearer to me than myself?" asks Augustine. "It is I myself who remember, I the mind." Ransacking the world of "things, either through images, as all bodies, or by actual presence," he comes upon the mind's own testament of what it has committed to memory, "that same memory where before [all] lay unknown, scattered, and neglected." Augustine has suggested the exaltation and despair of the chase, with Nerudian avidity: "Over all these do I run, I fly; I dive on this side and on that, as far I can, and there is no end . . . Thus do I remember Carthage." And Eliot in our own century has nodded acerb consent: "To apprehend / The point of intersection of the timeless / With time, is an occupation for a saint."

This I take to be both the task of Neruda's *Memorial,* and a measure of its "sanctity" for which no fashionable mystique need be sought. Again and again, over the record of personal loves, circumstantial and topical particulars, names, dates, habitations, concretions, a persisting query is heard, turning the knowable into a "dangerous world" of wandering lights and haunted misgivings: "Who was I? What? What were we both?" In a poem taking its title directly from Blake's great archetype of spiritual quest, "Little Boy Lost," Neruda suggests the malaise of the saintly identity:

> Nothing answers me now: let it pass.
> *Being* never was once: we went on being
>
> . . . .
> All kept on happening,
> one man impurely persisting,
> son of the purely born son,
> till nothing remained as it was
>
> . . . .
> Sometimes we remember
> the presence that lived with us,
> there is something we want from him—that he remember us,
>   maybe,
> or know, at least we were he and now talk
> with his tongue,
> but there in the wreckage of hours
> he looks at us, acknowledging nothing.

The note is sounded again, plangent and ardent by turns, in "Those Lives":

"That's how I am," I'll say, leaving this
pretext in writing. "This is really my life."
But everyone knows that's not how it happens at all.
Not only the cords in the net, but the air
that escapes the interstices matters:
The rest remains as it was: inapprehensible.

and again:

I live as I can
in my destiny's ruthless lucidity,
between the luminous and the desperate halves,
disowned
by two kingdoms which never were mine.

and again:

Who is that Other I am? He who never
contrived how to smile and died of his perfect deprival?
Who outlasted the festival bells and the gala
carnation, and toppled the lecterns of cold?

Late, it grows late. I go on with it all. I pursue
this or that paradigm, never guessing the answer,
knowing myself, in each of the lives I have lived,
both absent and present, at once the man who I was, and I
    am.

Does the rub of mysterious verity lie there?

The quest for "mysterious verity" is constant throughout these volumes of
palpable and impalpable stock-taking, jarring all that clings to the poet's
ego, from its moorings in the historical past. In the "memorial" world of
Isla Negra, the poet's *verdad* is exactly equivalent to the lover's search for
claridad in the Sonnets—with which it is eventually fused. Keeping "stead-
fastly triangular," seeing all "at first hand," affirming the "power of the
real to augment / and enlarge us," yet "cherish[ing] the equivocal cut of
my song," Neruda writes "on the card of our hunger / an order of bread
and an order of soul for the table." For this purpose, he returns to that
most elusive and obsessive of his themes: the Song of Myself, and its complementary theme of Non-Being—the *Ser-y-no-ser*, the *Nada*, and the
Sueño that link him to the great Hispanic tradition of self-contemplation
in Calderón, in Unamuno, in Machado, in Guillén. It is in his unappeas-

able self-absorption, from *Twenty Love Poems and a Desperate Song,* up to the present—his solipsistic meditation on the "water and rock" of "realism and idealism, both parts of my world"—that his love and his desperation have their source.

A closer look at the first of the five volumes of his *Memorial* may help to illustrate. It begins, as did the concluding section of *Canto general* (flamboyantly entitled *Yo soy: I Am*) twenty years before, with a retrospective account of the childhood and the young manhood of the poet. The title of the present volume, however, focuses upon a habitation rather than a name, on a landscape rather than an ego: Temuco of the alternate droughts and rains, the earthquakes, the timberlands, the holocausts— *Donde nace la lluvia (Where the Rain Begins).* In his singularly appealing essay on "Childhood and Poetry," published in 1954, ten years before his *Memorial,* Neruda has given us a prose recitative for his Song of Temuco: a personal history from the days of his great-great-grandparents who planted their vines in Parral, to the remarriage of his father, "a nondescript farmer, a mediocre laborer, but a first-class railroader," and his removal to Temuco.

It would appear that Neruda has deliberately set out, in *Where the Rain Begins,* to produce a versified "Childhood and Poetry"—a kind of Wordsworthian *Prelude* to a chronicle of wanderings and revolution, over which the "Spirit of the Place" broods to the end, as the Lake Country broods over the musings of Wordsworth. Where the prose chronicler informs us, for example, that "My mother could pick out in the dark, among all the other trains, precisely the train that was bringing my father into the Stationhouse at Temuco or taking him away," the Spirit of the Place remembers: "The brusque father comes back / from his trains: / we could pick out / his train whistle / cutting the rain, a locomotive's / nocturnal lament / in the dark. Later / the door started trembling." The plank houses, alternately soaking and burning, the mother "dead in Parral not long after I was born," the "tutelary angel" of his father's remarriage, Doña Trinidad Candia, the "glacial" cold of the Temucan schoolhouse, the midsummer forays into the Arucanian forests, the "searing" Cautín and the summits of Nielal, the swans of Lake Budi, the green plums, the beetles, the *copihues,* the secret world of Sandokan and Sandokana, and above all, the omnipresent whistle of the night train cutting fatefully through flood, distances, and darkness with the wail of a vanished paternity—all are transcribed from the essayist's pages.

Here, it would appear, History and Memory are well matched. The way is vertical, if circuitous, and the elements are in sequence: Birth, First Journey, The Stepmother (*La Mamadre*), The Father, The First Ocean, The

Southern Earth, Winter School, Sex, Poetry, Timidity, Swan Lake—such, literally, is the order of his book. Precisely when all is in readiness for a triumphal affirmation of consciousness, however, the Spirit of the Place materializes like a wraith to reaffirm the poet's total disbelief in the buoyant historicity of his chronicle. The pivot which triggers his melancholy significantly takes its title from the poem by Blake already referred to: "Little Boy Lost" ("El niño perdido") and the theme of loss—*"lo perdido"*—is thereafter never absent from the long circuit of the *Memorial*. As it happens, the word is one of the most multiple—and therefore least translatable—in the rich overlay of its contexts in Spanish. Beginning somewhat lamely with its nominal denotation—"lost"—it traverses an equivocal spectrum from "vanished," "absent," "lapsed," "destroyed," "forgotten," "fallen," to "dead"—always with a nostalgic look backward. Its blood cousin, the multifaceted word to which it generally points, like a needle to a magnet, is *soledad,* or aloneness, loneliness, isolation, self-engrossment, intactness, alienation. Between, whirls a mob of grieving mutations: *confuso* (confused), *secreto* (secret), *indeciso* (indecisive), *enlutado* (mournful)—the *no-sé-que* (I-don't-know-what) of empirical metaphysics on its way to the limbo of the *No-Ser* (Non-Being).

A sampling of the pages of *Where the Rain Begins* must suffice to suggest both the persistence of the lost (*lo perdido*) and its absorption into the spectrum of the solitary (*soledad*). There are *pasos perdidos* (lost footsteps), *fiebre o alas perdidas* (lost fever or wings), *bodega perdida entre las trenes* (shop lost among trains), *grité perdido* (I cried out, lost), *se perdía mi infancia* (my childhood was lost), *perdí los arboles* (I lost the trees), and the *estudiante triste perdido en el crepúsculo* (sad schoolboy lost in the twilight)—which brings the poet up to the publication of his second volume, *Crepusculario, The Book of Twilight*. In between, glows an *ignis fatuus* of flickering modulations which are the special illumination of the memory asserting its bafflement at the intersection of time with the timeless. Here, too, the contexts are diverse: *se me confundo los ojos y las hojas* (my eyes and the leaves are confused), *la confusa soledad* (the confused solitude), *una luz indecisa* (an indecisive light), *entro indeciso* (I enter undecided), *la enlutada noche* (the mournful night), *yo, enlutado, severo, ausente* (I, mournful, severe, absent), *volví con el secreto* (I returned with the secret), *en el secreto mundo / caminamos / con respeto* (in the secret world / we walk / with respect), *no distingo entre labios y raíces* (I do not distinguish between lips and roots), *no sé, no sé de donde* (I don't know, I don't know whence), *no sabía qué decir, mi boca / no sabía / nombrar* (I did not know what to say, my mouth did not know how to name).

Specification is in order here because the total effect, in *Black Island*

Memorial, flickers from point to point like marsh gas, with no expectation
of an explosive outcome. It is not given to Neruda, as agonist of the Lost,
to shield his eyes in the presence of the mind's transfiguration: neither
blinded nor prostrate, he looks steadily into the impurities of duration—
animal, vegetal, and mineral,

> while a luster is borne underground, antiquity's princeling
> in his natural grave-clothes of sickening mineral,
> until we are tardily there, too late to be there at all:
> being and not being, life takes its being from these.

Only once is he permitted to see "plainly: one evening, / in India" when,
gazing steadily into the flames of a riverside suttee, he sees "something
move out of the burning sarcophagus / —call it smoke or a spirit—" and
remains until all is consumed, leaving only "night and the water, the
dark / and the river, steadfast in that place and that dying." The world's
body and the combustion of the world's body: these are the themes of the
saint's vigil and man's image of the world's loss.

The point finally to be made, in this uneasy reading of an equivocal
legend, is that the *perdido* pursues Neruda throughout the whole compass
of his *Memorial,* as a function, rather than a defection, of memory. One
could, I am sure, make a tidy case for the first four volumes as the poet's
odyssey or hegira through all four elements of the substantive universe—
(1) Water (*Donde nace la lluvia: Where the Rain Begins*), (2) Air (*La luna
en el laberinto: The Moon in the Labyrinth*), (3) Fire (*El cruel fuego: The
Cruel Fire*), and (4) Earth (*El cazador de raíces: The Root-Hunter*). Since
History and Memory weave themselves equally into his great design, it
might be specified for the curious that Water is cognate with the poet's
Temucan childhood, Air, with the erotic and the passional, Fire, with revolutionary upheaval and world war, and Earth with the poet's return to his
sources on the Chilean mainland: a thoroughly Blakean cosmology. Over
this tidy collocation of elements and events, however, as over the burning
suttee, moves the Spirit of the Place, surrounded by all the paraphernalia
of quantitative optimism, brooding on the Lost, like Dürer's Lady of the
Melancholies. If there is any question regarding the persistence of the Lost,
one has only to follow the path of the *perdido* into the fifth and final volume, which Neruda somewhat misleadingly has entitled *Sonata crítica (Critical Sonata)*, as though disengagement and perspective had at last been
achieved. Here the tally is no less obliterating than in Book One: Neruda,
as card player, "plays for the sake of losing (juego / para seguir per-
diendo)"; he is "lost in the night (perdido en la noche)"; "there is no

longer left [him] a place to lose / the key, the truth, or the lie (no hay donde perder / la llave, la verdad, ni la mentira)"; we have "all lost the battle (todos perdimos la batalla)"; "the truth has died (ya se murió la verdad)"; humanity "loses its way (esta humanidad que pierde el rumbo)"; the pure being is "lost between words (el casto ser perdido entre palabras)"; life is "passed or lost (cuanta vida / pasamos o perdimos)"; memory "trembles in the lost shadow (tiembla mi memoria en la sombra perdida)"; the "salt is scattered and lost (una sal esparcida y perdida)"; the wind's sigh remains "lost in the leaves (sigue el susurro del viento perdido en las hojas)"; but, none the less, "I have found my lost roots (encontré mis raíces perdidos)".

It would be both mischievous and myopic to suggest on the basis of such passages that *Black Island Memorial* is the labyrinthine complaint of a defeated and despairing man. On the contrary, Neruda's steadfast confrontation of the Lost, his avid immediacies and open-ended determination to live "between the luminous and the desperate halves," measure the strenuous vitalism of his position. It is the Muse of Memory, as Keats' Hyperion was also to discover in the fallen world of Titans, sifting the passing event for its "Names, deeds, gray legends, dire events, rebellions, / Majesties, sovran voices, agonies, / Creations and destroyings" that "shows the heart's secret to an ancient power" with an intimacy impossible to History. And it is the double vision of the later Neruda, committed equally to Mnemosyne and Clio, that demands an exact accounting from the poet of "what is past, and passing, and to come." Neruda, looking back at his bulking *Memorial,* unfinished to the very end, declares in the *Critical Sonata:* "He who sings both dies and does not die, he who sings goes on living and dying"; he "sings the earthly and heavenly tower from the abyss." It is thus that the *poeta enlutado,* reading the oceans and weathers of Black Island, construing interstices, gaps, collapses, losses, with a passion that dazzles the imagination, holds in his keeping the plenty and certainty of the world. No poet living has braced the whole of his talent on that "point of intersection of the timeless / With time" with a comparable freedom from cant and preconception, or more resolutely approximated the "occupation for a saint."

RENÉ DE COSTA

The Vanguard Experiment: Tentativa del hombre infinito

$\mathbf{M}$ost readers in 1926 reacted, quite naturally, to what *Tentativa* did not have. The book's so-called "formlessness" was then most disturbing; even the pages were unnumbered. Today we can view the same book from a postvanguard perspective and see it for what it actually does contain: fifteen separate compositions of unique and varied strophic patterns. In the love poems Neruda had experimented with a new kind of lyric discourse; in *Tentativa del hombre infinito* he gives this discourse a new form. The result is a highly cohesive work.

If we return to the original text we can see that the series of cantos was arranged according to a definite plan whose unity—dissembled in subsequent printings—was rather prominently stressed in 1926 through a prefatory declaration immediately following the title page: "Poema de Pablo Neruda" ("A Poem by Pablo Neruda"). This announced poematic unity is more than confirmed in the system of textual correlations which artfully bring the cantos together in a singularly coherent whole. The sequential organization is particularly evident: moving from dusk ("a la siga de la noche"—"in pursuit of the night" [canto 3]) to dawn ("a la siga del alba"—"in pursuit of dawn" [canto 13]), the poem is patterned around the theme of the imaginary voyage ("embarcado en ese viaje nocturno"— "embarked on this nocturnal voyage" [canto 13]) as a personal quest for the absolute.

The disciplined organization of each of the separate cantos is visually apparent from the outset. In the first, for example, the perfect symmetry

From *The Poetry of Pablo Neruda.* © 1979 by the President and Fellows of Harvard College. Harvard University Press, 1979.

of the strophic arrangement gives a sense of balance to the disquiet of the
nocturnal scene:

> hogueras pálidas revolviéndose al borde de las noches
> corren humos difuntos polvaredas invisibles
>
> fraguas negras durmiendo detrás de los cerros anochecidos
> la tristeza del hombre tirada entre los brazos del sueño
>
> ciudad desde los cerros en la noche los segadores duermen
> debatida a las últimas hogueras
> pero estás allí pegada a tu horizonte
> como una lancha al muelle lista para zarpar lo creo
> antes del alba
>
> árbol de estertor candelabro de llamas viejas
> distante incendio mi corazón está triste
>
> sólo una estrella inmóvil su fósforo azul
> los movimientos de la noche aturden hacia el cielo

(pallid fires turning about at the edge of the nights dead smoke
invisible dust clouds race on   black forges sleeping behind
darkened hills the sadness of man tossed in the arms of
sleep   city from the hills at night the reapers sleep debated at
the last fires but you are there pegged to your horizon like a
ship at the dock ready to sail I believe at dawn   tree of creaks
candelabra of old flames distant fire my heart is sad   only
one star immobile its blue phosphorescence the movements of
the night agitate toward the sky.)

(canto 1)

Here the suppression of punctuation has the obvious effect of making the
reader more sensitive to other basic modulating devices such as strophic
unity and the syntactic order of the discontinuous discourse. Thus, the imagery may readily be seen to be organized around the single, almost elemental simile of the central strophe comparing the city lights on the
horizon to those of a ship readying to sail at dawn ("ciudad desde los
cerros . . . como una lancha al muelle"). The opening and closing strophes,
devoid of subjective referents, serve as a kind of objective frame to the tris-
tesse expressed in the intermediate couplets which, in turn, envelop the
lyric content at the core of the canto. The lack of punctuation is no mere
vanguardist caprice, but a sophisticated literary device largely responsible
for the poem's run-on quality, its curious sense of suspension amidst seem-

ingly perpetual motion. Some idea of the calculated effectiveness of the artifice can be gleaned from the opening couplets where the rush of the unpunctuated lines is fixed in each strophe by parallel gerundial constructions that attribute a certain atemporal quality to the verbal process and give a kind of substantive permanence to the imagery of flux. A flux, moreover, whose enduring character is controlled throughout the rest of the canto by the consistent use of the present tense in the conjugated verbs, a maneuver which tends even further to freeze the motion, to lock it into perpetuity. The net result rather resembles a movie still, or, perhaps more precisely, a series of stills. Each strophe presents an arrested image of an action.

Extending the analogy with film offers some insight into the process of the canto's movement. At the risk of oversimplification, a "zoom" effect seems to have been achieved in the succession of images from strophe to strophe. Holding the point of view constant while the angle of vision is changed permits the first couplet's mysterious fulgor of fire to come into view sequentially as the flickering of the city lights, a moored ship, a candelabra, stars, and finally a single star, the brightest in the firmament (Sirius, in an earlier version). The vision is completed through a sequence of images whose associative element—light at night—brings together the counterpoised descriptions of the earth and the sky which frame the composition.

The suppression of punctuation is an artistic aid to the extent that it permits a loosening of the discourse, thus making possible in the first canto the special kind of elliptic continuity that results in the composite, cosmic vision of the nocturnal void. In this way Neruda succeeds in presenting a new version of an old theme: the nocturne; poetized not in the traditional fashion of mysterious divagation, but from the vanguard position of marvelous reality, a prelude to the book's principal theme—the "viaje nocturno," the nocturnal voyage.

Tentativa del hombre infinito was an ambitious undertaking for Neruda at the time. Describing an imaginary sleepwalk through space and time, he arranged the book's fifteen separate cantos in an interrelated series making up the classic pattern of a quest. If we look at the second canto we can appreciate how it was made to resonate with the first through a kind of verbal parallelism:

> *ciudad desde los cerros* entre la noche de hojas
> mancha amarilla su rostro abre la sombra
> mientras *tendido sobre el pasto* deletreo
> ahí pasan ardiendo sólo yo vivo

> *tendido sobre el pasto mi corazón está triste*
> la luna azul araña trepa inunda
>
> emisario ibas alegre en la tarde que caía
> el crepúsculo rodaba apagando flores
>
> *tendido sobre el pasto* hecho de tréboles negros
> y tambalea sólo su pasión delirante
>
> recoge una mariposa húmeda como un collar
> anúdame tu cinturón de estrellas esforzadas

(city from the hills in the night of leaves yellow stain your face
opens the shadow while spread out on the grass I am spelling
out there they pass along blazing only I am alive   spread out
on the grass my heart is sad the blue moon scratches creeps in-
undates   emissary you were going along happy in the afternoon that was falling the twilight rolled on putting out
flowers   spread out on the grass made of black clovers and
only its delirious passion totters   grab a butterfly humid as a
necklace fasten me with your cinch of striving stars.)

(canto 2, emphasis mine)

The same syntagmas ("ciudad desde los cerros," "mi corazón está triste")
around which the basic imagery of the book's opening verses had been organized are here strategically repeated for an effect which is both unifying
and episodic; in resonance with the nocturnal metaphor of the first canto,
they serve now to make the solitary figure of the speaker stand out as he
is imagistically linked to the previous description of the night. Syntagmatic
repetition, strophic unity, even the prosaic positioning of the temporal adverb ("mientras," while) all combine to highlight the narrator's role as protagonist in the creative present of the poem: "ciudad desde los cerros . . .
mientras tendido sobre el pasto deletreo . . . mi corazón está triste." The
result is a composite vision of the somnambular lyric poet as narrator-pro-
tagonist alone in the nocturnal void.

The strophic distribution of the second canto is a unique controlling
device no less significant than that of the first: descriptive symmetry cedes
to an accumulative sequence of verbal actions in which the narrative tense
is made to shift from the present to the past and back again to the present
in a staccato delivery of lyric sensations. Through a succession of discrete
strophic visions, verbs of aimless striving ("trepar," "rodar," "tambalear")
accumulate in intensity while a new syntagma of position ("tendido sobre
el pasto") emerges to function as an imagistic anchor for the structured

view of the poet as narrator, participant, and witness of the nocturnal quest. The second canto thus effectively builds upon the first: moving in a similar fashion from the glow of the city lights to the flickering of the stars, the sudden identification of the speaker as protagonist and the subsequent layering of short strophes combine to increase the tempo of the yearning for cosmic communion so urgently voiced—"tendido sobre el pasto"—in the canto's closing verse: "anúdame tu cinturón de estrellas esforzadas."

Neruda's artistic approach to the personal, experiential dimension of the poem is now quite different, although as in the love poetry, his frustrated affair with Albertina is still the source of inspiration. We may recall that in one of the letters of the period, he had written: "Spread out on the grass, in the evenings, I dream of your gray cap, of your eyes that I love, of you. I go out every night at around five, to wander around the deserted streets, to wander through the countryside." The difference between the two books, between the two kinds of discourse in *Tentativa* and the love poetry, is a difference of purpose. The poems of love were entreaties to an absent lover; the cantos purport to be the somnambulistic ramblings of a preconscious state of mind. Hence, the importance of a certain amount of reader confusion and the variety of devices employed to maintain an air of uncertainty and vagueness.

The entire book is a vanguard experiment in different styles and techniques. For example, in the third canto, when the "nocturnal voyage" actually gets under way, the measured strophic divisions of the earlier compositions are abandoned in favor of a single unit of nineteen uninterrupted lines simulating the headlong rush into the vortex of the night. In this manner the poetic voice in the canto of departure achieves a subtle distancing effect, building up to the ecstasy of a participant, before shifting over to the lyric "you," and finally fading out to that of an impersonal observer:

oh matorrales crespos adonde el sueño avanza trenes
oh montón de tierra entusiasta donde de pie sollozo
vértebras de la noche agua tan lejos viento intranquilo rompes
también estrellas crucificadas detrás de la montaña
alza su empuje un ala pasa un vuelo oh noche sin llaves
oh noche mía en mi hora en mi hora furiosa y doliente
eso me levantaba como la ola al alga
acoge mi corazón desventurado
cuando rodeas los animales del sueño
crúzalo con tus vastas correas de silencio
está a tus pies esperando una partida

porque lo pones cara a cara a tí misma noche de hélices
    negras
y que toda fuerza en él sea fecunda
atada al cielo con estrellas de lluvia
procrea tú amárrate a esa proa minerales azules
embarcado en ese viaje nocturno
un hombre de veinte años sujeta una rienda frenética
es que él quería ir a la siga de la noche
entre sus manos ávidas el viento sobresalta

(oh crisp-leaved thickets toward which sleep advances
trains / oh mound of enthusiastic earth where standing up I
sob / vertebrates of night water so distant restless wind you
break / also crucified stars behind the mountain / raise up its
thrust a wing passes a flight oh night without keys / oh night of
mine in my hour in my furious and pained hour / that lifted me
up like algae on the wave / sieze my unfortunate heart / when
you surround the animals of sleep / crisscross it with your vast
straps of silence / it is at your feet awaiting a departure /
because you put it face to face to yourself night of black
propellers / and may all force in it be fecund / tide to the sky
with stars of rain / procreate hitch yourself up to that prow
blue minerals / embarked in this nocturnal voyage / a man of
twenty holds on to a frantic rein / it is that he wanted to go
off in pursuit of the night / between his hands the wind leaps
forth.)

(canto 3, emphasis mine)

Whereas the first person is used to express the physical sensation of being
immersed in the night—"eso me levantaba como la ola al alga (that lifted
me up like algae on the wave)"—the third person is relied upon to achieve
a certain narrative distance, to objectify the cosmic voyage, even prosai-
cally to explain the motivation for embarking—"es que él quería ir a la
siga de la noche (it is that he wanted to go off in pursuit of the night)."

    Tentativa del hombre infinito belongs to the tradition of the modern
voyage poem. While it undoubtedly has its origin in certain earlier efforts
(Rimbaud, "Le Bateau ivre"; Baudelaire, "Le Voyage"), in the context of
the Hispanic avant-garde it turns out to be seminal to the development of
the book-length metaphysical poem (Alberti, *Sobre los ángeles;* Huidobro,
Altazor; Gorostiza, *Muerte sin fin*): a poetic venture based on the illumi-
nating concept of the mythic quest. To this end, the first three cantos fall

into an epic pattern of departure: the scene is set, the call is received, the quest is undertaken. In the next three (4–6), after the imaginary voyage begins, another pattern emerges as the hero is subjected to a series of trials, the rites of passage.

As the adventure continues to unfold, the camera-eye objectivity of the earlier narrative style is replaced with a new loquaciousness communicating a sense of participatory awe and wonder; the protagonist, loosed of terrestrial bonds, experiences the nocturnal phenomena from a changed and changing perspective. Certain imagistic constants drawn from the introductory cantos are used to create an effect of narrative continuity. Not surprisingly, Sirius, the "estrella inmóvil" that closed the hermetic metaphor of the first canto, reappears transmogrified at the opening of the fourth: "estrella retardada entre la noche gruesa (star bogged down in the thick night)." Starry imagery remains central to the other compositions as well. In the sixth canto the vast void of night is figuratively conquered, hyperbolically envisioned as an inverted well: "los ojos caían en ese pozo inverso / hacia donde ascendía la soledad de todo (the eyes fell down into that inverted well toward which the solitude of everything was ascending)." Accordingly, the tone of the narrative voice changes, and the somnambulic poet finally begins to speak out with a pronounced assurance.

At the outset, syntagmatic repetition was used to fix the narrative situation of the imaginary voyage ("tendido sobre el pasto deletreo" [canto 2]); now ellipsis is used for an almost breathless effect, running together imagery of joy and loquacity as the speaker whirls on into the center of the night:

> no sé hacer el canto de los días
> sin querer suelto el canto la alabanza de las noches
> pasó el viento latigándome la espalda alegra saliendo de su
>   huevo
> descienden las estrellas a beber al océano

> (I don't know how to make a daytime canto / without wanting to I let loose the canto the praise of night / the wind passed by whipping my back happy coming out of its egg / the stars descend to drink in the ocean.)

> (canto 6)

Midway through the book, in cantos 7–9, there is a kind of climax, an encounter with the night itself that is poetized in a lyric style not unlike that of *Veinte poemas de amor*. In canto 7 physical union realized through

the sexual act becomes a metaphor for ultimate oneness: "torciendo hacia
ese lado o más allá continúas siendo mía . . . en otra parte lejos existen tú
y yo parecidos nosotros (turning toward that side or farther away you
continue being mine . . . in another place far away you and I exist something like ourselves)." And in the ninth canto the body of woman is directly metaphorized as the vehicle of ecstasy, the "navío blanco (white
ship)" of the imaginary voyage:

> ah para qué alargaron la tierra
> del lado en que te miro y no estás niña mía
> entre sombra y sombra destino de naufragio
> nada tengo oh soledad
> sin embargo eres la luz distante que ilumina las frutas
> y moriremos juntos
> pensar que estás ahí navío blanco listo para partir
> y que tenemos juntas las manos en la proa navío siempre en
>   viaje

> ah why did they stretch out the earth / on the side from which I
> am looking at you and you are not there my little girl / between
> shadow and shadow destiny of shipwreck / I have nothing oh
> solitude / nevertheless you are the distant light that illuminates
> the fruit / and we shall die together / to think that you are there
> white ship ready to depart / and that we have our hands joined
> at the prow ship always in motion.

After the cosmic union is realized the speaker's references to himself
become more explicit. In the latter portion of the poem—less cinematically
descriptive and more impressionistically memory-oriented—movement
between the narrative present and the remembered past is generally com-
pressed in the same strophe, a device that effectively serves to contempo-
rize the flashbacks:

> ésta es mi casa
> aún la perfuman los bosques
> desde donde la acarreaban
> allí tricé mi corazón como el espejo para andar a través de mí
>   mismo
> . . . .
> yo no cuento yo digo en palabras desgraciadas
> aún los andamios dividen el crepúsculo
> y detrás de los vidrios la luz del petróleo
> era para mirar hacia el cielo

this is my house / even now the forests perfume it / from where it was carted in / there I shattered my heart like a mirror in order to walk through myself . . . I don't tell stories I say it outright in words without grace / even now the scaffolding divides the twilight / and behind the windows the petroleum lamp / was for looking up at the sky.

(canto 10)

The clipped assertive narration is characteristic of the later cantos (10–12) and stands in sharp contrast with the lyricism of the central portion of the poem. Hyperbole is now reversed and used to augment the role of the narrator rather than merely to reduce that of the universe. In canto 10's verses the unfinished house of the poet's birth, without walls or roof, is aggrandized; the scaffolding is viewed as superimposed on the sunset, while the artificial light of the house-lamp is seen to illumine the sky. This is the kind of creative liberty with language made possible by the experimental attitude of the avant-garde. But *Tentativa del hombre infinito* is primarily a poematic quest for the absolute and only secondarily an experiment with new writing techniques; Neruda, mindful of his narrative plan, keeps his hero moving on toward a kind of atonement with the past. At one point though, the narrator becomes engaged, *Residencia*-like, in a meditative search for self:

> admitiendo el cielo profundamente mirando el cielo estoy
>   pensando
> con inseguridad sentado en ese borde
> oh cielo tejido con aguas y papeles
> comencé a hablarme en voz baja decidido a no salir
> arrastrado por la respiración de mis raíces
> inmóvil navío ávido de esas leguas azules

(letting the sky in profoundly looking at the sky I am thinking / with insecurity seated on the edge / oh sky woven with water and papers / I began to speak to myself in a low voice decided not to come out / dragged along by the respiration of my roots / immobile ship avid for those blue leagues.)

(canto 11)

In the concluding portion of the book Neruda utilizes with particular effectiveness the avant-garde technique of juxtaposition. The narrator, denied his camera-eye objectivity and stripped of his neoromantic role as anxious participant of the cosmic flux, emerges most concretely toward the end in the assigned role of "hombre infinito (infinite man)." In canto 13, as the nocturnal adventure draws to a close—"el alba se divisa (dawn is visible)"—time and space are stretched out and treated materially in a unique imagistic recital of the hero's return:

> el mes de junio se extendió de repente en el tiempo con
>   seriedad y exactitud
> como un caballo y en el relámpago crucé la orilla
> ay el crujir del aire pacífico era muy grande

> (the month of June suddenly extended itself in time with seriousness and exacitude / like a horse and on a lightning bolt I crossed over the edge / ay the creaking of the peaceful air was very great.)

(canto 14)

The fifteenth canto functions as a kind of epilogue and, through the reuse of certain expressions drawn from the earlier cantos (for example, "mi corazón está cansado"), ties together the narrative plan of the work: "estoy de pie en la luz como el medio día en la tierra / quiero contarlo todo con ternura (I am standing up in the light like midday on the earth / I want to tell it all with tenderness)." Anticipating yet another nightfall, the poem's closure implies a certain cyclical continuity:

> espérame donde voy ah el atardecer
> la comida las barcarolas de océano oh espérame
> adelantándote como un grito atrasándote como una huella oh
>   espérate
> sentado en esa última sombra o todavía después todavía

> (wait for me where I am going ah the evening comes / the dinner the ocean boats oh wait for me / getting ahead of you like a shout getting behind you like a footstep oh wait up / seated on this last shadow or still later / still.)

(canto 15)

At the end, as at the beginning, the gerundial run-on constructions and the accumulative repetition of temporal adverbs combine effectively to lock the poematic quest in a timeless present.

This is a major work. It brought the interior monologue into Neruda's poetry without the Surrealist dependence on automatic writing. Moreover, this book, for its innovative use of language and its highly charged lyric content, constitutes the link between two extraordinary masterpieces: *Veinte poemas de amor* and *Residencia en la tierra*. Yet, for all its perfection, it never gained the readership Neruda wanted it to have. Accepted only by the literary avant-garde when it first appeared, it was quickly passed over and was all but forgotten until quite recently. Over the years Neruda, continuing his campaign of 1926, kept on insisting that critics go back and read this work to find the origins of his disciplined approach to poetry. In 1964, for example, we find him stressing the seminal importance of the *Tentativa* experiment:

> *Tentativa del hombre infinito* is a book that did not achieve what I wanted it to, it was not successful for a variety of reasons in which even day to day circumstances intervened. Nevertheless, even with its smallness and its minimal expression, it assured more than any other work of mine, the path I was to follow. I have always looked upon *Tentativa del hombre infinito* as one of the real nuclei of my poetry, because working on those poems, in those now distant years, I was acquiring a consciousness that I didn't have before, and if my expressions, their clarity or mystery, are anywhere measured, it is in this little book.

Neruda was right of course. And, in the context of his own evolution, it seems clear that around 1925 he began to forsake the refined prosodic system of Hispanic poetry; he then managed to creatively combine the liberties of the literary avant-garde with such elemental and seemingly artless devices as the parallelism of key syntactic units, the modulation of the poetic line, the organizational power of the strophe, and the disciplined use of the quest theme in order to structure the fifteen cantos of his *Tentativa del hombre infinito* in the meaningful trajectory of a voyage through space and time in search of the absolute. To be sure, the quest for ultimate oneness was one of the constants in the later Modernist literature of Spain and Spanish America, and it was essentially from this aesthetic perspective that Neruda himself had earlier dealt with the theme in the final poem ("La canción desesperada") of his *Veinte poemas de amor y una canción desesperada*. However, only after abandoning the hollow shell of rhyme and meter and freeing his expression from the logical concatenation of continuous discourse was Neruda able to attain the unusual inner cohesion and high degree of poetic tension that stylistically link his vanguard experiment of 1926 to the expressive system of the *Residencia* cycle.

MANUEL DURÁN

Pablo Neruda and the
Romantic-Symbolist Tradition

There can be, I think, no doubt about the modernity of Neruda's poetry. It does not need to be underlined that Neruda is one of the most typical poets of our century. Yet, he has his roots in the past. This past is the nineteenth century, specifically the tradition of Coleridge and Victor Hugo, of Shelley and William Blake, of Baudelaire and Rimbaud. This is the central tradition of Western poetry, more important to us if we want to understand Neruda's poetry than the Baroque tradition of Quevedo and the mystical and mythical tradition of the Upanishads, no matter that Neruda was attracted to both Quevedo and the Upanishads.

It is true that the visions of Neruda are not strictly spiritual like Blake's, that Neruda can be called a "cosmic materialist." It is equally true that for Coleridge there was no barrier between poetic imagination and religious revelation. Octavio Paz has observed in his *Children of the Mire* that Shelley's atheism—and the same can be said about the atheism of much contemporary poetry—was a religious attitude, a religious passion. Neruda's poetic materialism is, I think, not different from the materialism of a Shelley or a Rimbaud. In order to define Neruda's poetic roots we must follow an oblique path: tradition helps us to understand Neruda and vice-versa Neruda's poetry will redefine and validate tradition.

Since it is an all too obvious fact—what might be called an open professional secret—that we critics tend to be rather proud, it is, perhaps, a bit risky to suggest that the best way to approach a poet, to approach the essential definition of a poet and of poetry, is to ask another poet for such

From *Actes de VIIIᵉ Congrès de l'Association Internationale de Littérature Comparée*. © 1980 by Manuel Durán. Stuttgart: Bieber, 1980.

a definition. Yet it seems logical and quite normal that it should be a poet who can most rapidly and profoundly penetrate the poetic material of another writer; and it is to a poet, a great poet, that I am going to turn now in order to try to arrive at a quick and precise definition of an important aspect of Pablo Neruda's work. In his latest book (*Y otros poemas,* published in 1974), the Spanish poet Jorge Guillen offers four verses which constitute, in essence, a portrait, a miniature of Pablo Neruda:

> Este sultán soñoliento,
> Si vuela, cae de pie,
> Imagina lo que ve,
> Se convierte en elemento.

Leaving aside the physical or psychological description of the poet, what I am interested in stressing here is the last verse: "se convierte en elemento." This conversion, fusion or diffusion of the "I" into the material elements—imagined or not—which surround it, is, I believe, the essential characteristic which gives unity to Neruda's mature poetry. It is this, above all, that I would like to demonstrate; and, concretely, I would like to show that if we compare a poem from Neruda's first maturity, i.e. from *Residencia en la tierra,* with another mature poem, this time from *Odas elementales,* i.e. from what can be called his second and final maturity, we will see a clear relationship, an identity. It is the type of identity found in a single tapestry, seen in one case from the front, and in another case from the reverse side. In both poetical works, we are dealing with an extreme psychological aperture—with clear stylistic consequences—towards the world of sensations, the world which surrounds the poet; simultaneously, a partial abdication of the unifying conscience occurs, a diminishing of the judge's conscience, of the poet's role as arbiter or tutelar god of the external treasure.

Neruda writes the poems collected in *Residencia en la tierra* as the result of profound crises and disorienting personal experiences, it is true. But he also writes them as the heir of a tradition of crisis in Western poetry. From the German romantics and Blake to Eliot, Joyce, Kafka and the surrealists, the poet's "I" passes through multiple avatars which tend to diminish its value, to crumble it, to crush it between an external world which has lost its symbolic and transcendent value, and a conception of personality which is more and more atomized and chaotic. Blake and Novalis were still visionaries full of hope; poetry, they believed, could be converted into action, it could be the new religion of the modern world. During the course of the nineteenth century, this vision dims or becomes corrupted.

As Octavio Paz has written, "al extirpar la nocion de divinidad el racionalismo reduce al hombre. Nos libera de Dios, pero nos encierra en un sistema aún más férreo. La imaginación humillada se venga y del cadáver de Dios brotan fetiches atroces; en Rusia y en otros paises, la divinizacion del jefe, el culto a la letra de las escrituras, la deificación del partido; entre nosotros, la idolatria del yo mismo. Ser uno mismo es condenarse a la mutilación, pues el hombre es apetito perpetuo de ser otro. La idolatría del yo conduce a la idolatría de la propiedad; el verdadero Dios de la sociedad cristiana occidental se llama dominación sobre los otros. Concibe al mundo y los hombres como mis propiedades, mis cosas. El árido mundo actual, el infierno circular, es el espejo del hombre cercenado de su facultad poetizante." Neruda, the American poet, for many, perhaps the most typically American poet of the last few decades, also responds to this long European tradition.

In identifying this European tradition, which Neruda, in his own way, continues, I want to limit myself to two names: Rimbaud and Mallarmé. Of the two, Rimbaud is the most vulnerable and the most open ("par délicatesse / j'ai perdu ma vie" he writes); Mallarmé is more consequential, logical, complete. For both, God has disappeared, and man is a "small god" who takes His place; immediately the universe vacillates; chaotic, it invades the poet. Rimbaud's work is the product of an invasion by an unordered universe which the poet's "I" cannot and does not want to resist: illuminations, delirium, senseless explosions: "je devins un opéra fabuleux"; Rimbaud's poetry simultaneously reveals an affinity for the world of raw material, of unworked, natural material, material which has not been humanized nor industrialized. This is, of course, the same world which we find in the Neruda of the *Odas elementales:*

> Si j'ai du goût ce n'est guère
> Que pour la terre et les pierres.
> Je déjeune toujours d'air,
> De roc, de charbons, de fer.

For Mallarmé, the relationship poet-language-world has deteriorated: the world, as an image, has evaporated; language has become transparent, "aboli bibelot d'inanité sonore," and behind that transparency, appears probability, the "perhaps" which reveals a universe which is, probably, empty, which in any case is an uninhabitable world, void of human meaning. The disappearance of the image of the world signifies that true reality is not to be found outside, but rather within, in the head and in the heart of the poet. Yet what modern psychology, beginning with and even predating Freud, demonstrates is the complexity of the human psyche, and its lack of unity; and what Breton and the surrealists—and also Joyce—affirm is a faith in the creative potential of language, viewing it as superior and in certain ways independent, imposing itself on any individual mind, as eminent as that mind might be. Various critics [like Octavio Paz] have seen that the "movimiento general de la literatura contemporánea, de Joyce y Cummings a las experiencias de Queneau y a las combinaciones de la electrónica, tiende a restablecer la soberanía del lenguaje sobre el autor." In 1934 Neruda arrives in Madrid. It is a decisive moment for his own work and for the fate of Hispanic poetry as a whole. The official revered model of poetry in that moment is so-called "pure poetry." No one has ever been able to define this wave with great precision, and yet from San Juan to Juan Ramón Jiménez, this poetic river had run, sometimes subterraneously, through the waters of the history of Hispanic literature. Neruda puts forth another model which opposes this one. His model is derived both from his own experience and from the disintegration of the symbolist tradition; it is an "impure poetry." Propelled by Neruda—and not only by Neruda, but also by Lorca, Larrea, Miguel Hernández, Emilio Prados, to name just a few who enter into the battle—the new model rejects the narrow aristocratic ideals of the "pure poets." Juan Ramón Jiménez, the supreme idol of these years, chooses to enter the fight through an intermediary, and he unleashes the rages of a lesser poet, but a tough and brilliant polemicist, Juan José Domenchina. Domenchina fiercely attacks the tendencies of the young rebels, and wages his battle from a position of great influence, from the pages of *El Sol,* the period's leading newspaper, where he serves as literary critic. The struggle is ferocious, and the outcome remains in doubt for some time. Juan Ramón Jiménez's modernist aesthetic, deriving in some aspects from symbolism and related in a certain sense to Valéry's poetry, confronts what I have called the nihilistic wave of symbolism: a lack of confidence in the "I" and in the external world, combined with a growing belief in the liberation of language as a creative agent. Naturally, in this regard, the new wave coincides with the surrealist movement, which is an inevitable and—almost—logical way continues its fundamental concepts. And, nonetheless, the dangerous, almost accursed word "surrealism" is rarely mentioned. As Juan Cano Ballesta, one of the most astute observers of the Spanish literary situation of this period, points out, "llamativo es el caso de *Caballo Verde para la poesía* (octubre de 1935) [a magazine, we might add, which was inspired and founded by Neruda] en cuyos manifiestos no se invoca nunca el surrealismo, a pesar de su proximidad con él y su orientación hacia las esferas instintivas y oníricas ... También resulta curioso que Miguel Hernández escriba un ensayo sobre la *Residencia en la tierra* de Neruda sin hacer la más leve alusión a la escuela de Breton: No es nada extraño, ya que el mismo Neruda hablaba años más tarde del surrealismo como de 'un pequeño clan perverso, una pequeña secta de destructores de la cultura, del sentimiento, del sexo y de la acción.' Tales palabras resultan llamativas en un poeta que se inspiró poderosamente en las técnicas surrealistas."

During his residence in Spain, and prior to the civil war, Neruda politicizes his poetry, and does so in an extremely rapid and dramatic fashion. We should not forget, however, the examples of Emilio Prados and Luis Cernuda who chronologically predate Neruda in politicizing what earlier had been, for them, their own version of "pure poetry." Rafael Alberti is another early example of conversion to "impure poetry," to social poetry, to poetry stained by the mire and blood of social struggle. "Poésie engagée"—socially committed poetry—will be the goal, the watchword, of all those seeking to put an end to the aristocratic and elitist poetry proclaimed by Juan Ramón Jiménez and defended by Domenchina from the pages of *El Sol*. Beginning in 1933, the magazine *Octubre* becomes the expressive forum for the spokesmen of "poésie engagée": Rafael Alberti, Arturo Serrano Plaja, Pla y Beltrán, César M. Arconada, Luis Cernuda, Antonio Machado are counted among its contributors. As J. Lechner has observed, *Octubre* "contribuyó sin duda a polarizar la conciencia del público lector y a preparar el ambiente de solidaridad que reinaría a partir de los primeros momentos de la guerra civil entre los artistas e intelectuales disconformes." Juan Cano Bellesta points out: "La batalla contra la poesía pura aún no estaba ganada. Paul Valéry y Juan Ramón Jiménez, árbitros supremos del buen gusto, aún están en su pedestal, reciben honores y son homenajeados. En la primavera de 1933, Paul Valéry hace una visita a Madrid. ¡Gran acontecimiento para la poesía! Juan Ramón Jiménez, que no asiste a la recepción, le envia un manojo de rosas. *Hoja literaria* publica una página del poeta francés. 'A propósito del "Cementerio Marino," en que se resalta la importancia dada a la forma, la palabra, agotando sus posibles combinaciones embellecedoras y alejándose lo más posible de la prosa. Pero cada día abundan más los ataques irrespetuosos de la juventud iconoclasta. Juan José Demenchina se enfrenta con esa pléyade juvenil de 'imberbes epigonos' que 'fingen ignorar el pábulo con que se nutren' y se entregan 'con voluptuosidad de roedor' a la 'ratería poética.' "

We all know that Neruda's support, his presence, his poetry, his manifestos in the magazine *Caballo Verde para la Poesía* were of decisive importance in this battle against "pure poetry." What I am interested in stressing now is that the literary climate in Spain in those years had already begun to change very rapidly; that Neruda was understood precisely because there were many poets who were already proceeding along the same lines. One example can suffice: Neruda publishes his most important manifesto, on the front page of the October, 1935 edition of *Caballo Verde*. In it, he affirms the necessity of broadening poetic material, of opening poetry to new sensations. Neruda defends "una poesía impura como un traje, como un cuerpo, con manchas de nutrición y actitudes vergonzosas, con arrugas, observaciones, sueños, vigilias, profecías, declaraciones de amor y de odio, bestias, sacudidas, idilios, creencias políticas, negaciones, dudas, afirmaciones, impuestos." An entire body of chaotic material is thus incorporated into the poetic business of the moment. Luis Rosales gives witness to the impact of Neruda's words: "aquellos que lo vivimos no lo podemos olvidar. El manifiesto de Neruda tuvo un acierto extraordinario, nos confirmó en nuestras creencias a los que entonces éramos jóvenes y nos abrió perspectivas insospechadas." And Juan Ramón Jiménez, "desde el Olimpo de su retiro" (the description is Juan Cano Ballesta's), "fulmina sus rayos contra los revoltosos": "Siempre tuve a Pablo Neruda ... por un gran poeta, un gran mal poeta, un poeta de la desorganización; el poeta dotado que no acaba de comprender ni emplear sus dotes naturales ... Tiene Neruda mina explotada y por explotar; tiene rara intuición, busca extraña, hallazgo fatal, lo nativo del poeta; no tiene acento propio ni crítica llena. Posee un depósito de cuanto ha ido encontrando por su mundo, algo así como un vertedero, estercolero a estos, donde hubiera ido a parar entre el sobrante, el desperdicio, el detrito, tal piedra, cual flor, un metal en buen estado aún y todavía bellos. Encuentra la rosa, el diamante, el oro, pero no la palabra representativa y transmutadora." But Neruda was not alone; some months before his incisive and controversial manifesto, the poet León Felipe proclaimed a rather similar aesthetic attitude, when in the foreword to his *Antologia,* published in Madrid in 1935, he described his own conception of poetic material: "Y todo lo que hay en el mundo es mío, y valedero para entrar en un poema, para alimentar una fogata, todo, hasta lo literario, como arda y queme. Y no vale menos un proverbio rodado que una imagen virginal, un versículo de la Revelación que el último 'slang' de las alcantarillas. Todo buen combustible es material poético excelente."

What all of this shows us is that the "impure poets" (Among the Spaniards Alberti and León Felipe, the latter undoubtedly inspired by the example of Walt Whitman; and Neruda, a reader of the symbolists and especially of those we have called "left-wing" symbolists, Rimbaud and Mallarmé, and of Huidobro and César Vallejo, as well) had to defend theoretically the type of poetry that they were, in practice, developing. Two of Neruda's poems from these years give a very precise idea of the new attitude, an attitude which deals, above all, with making oneself porous, open, vulnerable; with accepting the material which surrounds the poet; the poet is no longer seen as a proud and aesthetic "I," controlling his language and his materials; rather, the poet is invaded, his senses, tense, exasperated, passively accept what come to them. We see this in a poem which, significantly, is entitled "Arte poética."

> como si llegaran ladrones o fantasma,
> y en una cáscara de extensión fija y profunda,
> como un camarero humillado, como una campana un poco
>   ronca,
> como un espejo viejo, como un olor de casa sola
> en la que los huéspedes entran de noche perdidamente ebrios,
> y hay un olor de ropa tirada al suelo, y una ausencia de flores,
> —posiblemente de otro modo aun menos melancólico—
> pero, la verdad, de pronto, el viento que azota mi pecho,
> las noches de substancia infinita caídas en mi dormitorio,
> el ruido de un día que arde con sacrificio,
> me piden lo profético que hay en mí, con melancolía,
> y un golpe de objetos que llama sin ser respondidos
> hay, y un movimiento sin tregua, y un nombre confuso.

"Impure poetry," then, is poetry in which the vigilant and aesthetic "I" has been relinquished and transformed into a passive receiver of everything it sees ("I am a camera," Christopher Isherwood will write); and what it sees is a type of sinister invasion, as if thieves or phantoms stealthfully approached. The poet is "una cáscara de extensión fija y profunda" which the external world will fill with its echoes, confused echoes which the poet, in turn, will reproduce "como una campana un poco ronca" and which will leave him occupied, engrossed, in the service of everything which solicits his attention, "como un camarero humillado," reflecting imperfectly, "como un espejo viejo" what he sees, invaded like a house which receives "huéspedes . . . perdidamente ebrios."

I have reproduced only one half, the second half of Neruda's poem; in it we can distinguish two parts, the first, which runs from "como si llegaran ladrones" to "de otro modo aun menos melancólico" (and in passing we can observe in the repetition of "melancólico" and later, "melancólicamente," the surviving echoes of later modernism, sentimental modernism of the type written by Amado Nervo); and the second and final section of the poem, from "aun menos melancólico" to the final words, "y un nombre confuso." This second section signals a change in rhythm; everything moves more quickly, everything is more dynamic, everything demands that the poet be more porous, more open, that he listen more and that he absorb more rapidly the growing chaos; "pero la verdad, de pronto, el viento que azota mi pecho" are the words which initiate this change; there is more, there is much more material in the external world, it is essential to abolish even further the "I" which filters and judges and orders this chaotic external world: there are "noches de substancia infinita," there is a "día que arde con sacrificio"—that is, Time, the infinite, and not only concrete objects, invade the poet—and, in effect, the last two verses indicate that the assault of the external material is so brutal, so inundating, that it is no longer possible to assimilate it, to register it, to respond: "y un golpe de objetos que llaman sin ser respondidos / hay." The poem ends in a growing chaos: "y un movimiento sin tregua, y un nombre confuso." It is the perception of a visionary who does not believe in transcendency; it is a vision which is in contrast to Blake's (whose work Neruda knew and translated), but which is very close to Rimbaud and his illuminations.

In "Walking Around," another fundamental poem, this dissolution of the critical and aesthetic "I" is perhaps even more apparent:

> Sucede que me canso de ser hombre,
> Sucede que entro en las sastrerías y en los cines
> marchito, impenetrable, como un cisne de fieltro
> navegando en un agua de origen y ceniza.

(We can note the subversion of the modernist symbol, the swan, which here is converted into an antipoetic object, a type of hat which navigates in a sea of ash). In his own way, which is, of course, different from González Martinez's, Neruda has "twisted the swan's neck." Neruda wanders without direction, "walking around," and the images, in this chaotic accumulation—as in the unconnected catalogue to which Leo Spitzer has referred in a memorable essay—start mounting, negatively, invading.

> Hay pájaros de color de azufre y horribles intestinos
> colgando de las puertas de las casas que odio,
> hay dentaduras olvidadas en una cafetera,
> hay espejos
> que debieran haber llorado de vergüenza y aspento,
> hay paraguas en todas partes, y venenos, y ombligos,

It is clear that we are dealing, above all, with an urban landscape: the poet wanders through "calles espantosas como grietas" (Blake had already launched his curses against the "dark Satanic mills" of modern industry and urban civilization). The "pájaros de color de azufre" are not part of Nature; rather, they are a subversion of Nature by industry, by the chemical and mechanical world. The hanging intestines bring to mind a vision of the city as butcher-shop. The set of teeth in a coffee pot is the absurd surrealist detail, which, like the revolver with white hairs, is in accord with both Lautréamont's well-known definition and the French surrealists in general. The mirrors are, perhaps, an image of man, of the poet who reflects the chaotic world into which he has been born, and who continues observing this world, in its entirety:

> Yo paseo con calma, con ojos, con zapatos,
> con furia, con olvido,
> paso, cruzo oficinas y tiendas de ortopedia,
> y patios donde hay ropas colgadas de un alambre:
> calzoncillos, toallas y camisas que lloran
> lentas lágrimas sucias.

The instability has been transmitted to the witness, who passes from calm to fury and then to forgetfulness: the chaos has become internal. Tired "de ser hombre," of organizing with his intelligence and his "buen gusto" what his senses transmit to him, the walk has carried Neruda to a point where the external sadness and chaos reflect the observer's inner sadness and chaos, both culminating in a blurry mirror of dirty tears. (We should point out here that despite the will to open himself to chaos, there is still, in these final verses, a remnant of traditional poetic language, in its most rudimentary, its most primitive and ancient form: the use of alliteration: "un alambre: / calzoncillos, toallas, y camisas que lloran / lentas lágrimas sucias.")

As a final note or colophon to these brief remarks, I think it is necessary to point out the existence of "another" Neruda, who is, nonetheless, "the same" Neruda, the double of the pessimistic and solitary Neruda ("pessimistic" and "solitary" due to personal circumstances, but also, essentially, due to a lack of faith in any form of transcendence). It is the Neruda of the *Odas elementales,* whose newly acquired faith is certainly not of a traditionally religious or transcendental nature. Rather, it is a faith based on confidence in the future of man and of history as seen through a Marxist prism, and based also on a profound identification with Nature. (It should be remembered that Neruda's most atrociously negative poems in *Residencias* always refer to the city, and that the great majority of the *Odas elementales,* in contrast, sing of natural, predominantly vegetal products.) One should also keep in mind that abdication of the critical and aesthetic "I" in the Neruda of *Residencias,*—as effective and dramatic as it is—is never total. It is sufficient to remember that in the first poem we looked at, everything ends with a crescendo, comparable to the finale of many of Beethoven's symphonies, while in the second poem, the alliteration, consciously or not, reminds us of the reiterations and variations found in Mozart and other great Baroque composers. Boilueau's famous verse is clearly appropriate here: "ce beau desordre est un effec de l'art."

I think that to truly appreciate the personal shades of the optimistic Neruda, the Neruda of the *Odas elementales,* it would be necessary to compare one of the poems from this period with, for example, one of Jorge Guillen's "materialist" poems, such as "Naturaleza viva," which appears in the first *Cántico.* Or perhaps with some of the poems written by the great French poet Francis Ponge, the author of *Le grand recueil,* who, given the date of his birth and literary publications, develops his work in a form parallel to that of Neruda.

The optimistic Neruda of the *Odas elementales* continues exposing his "I," passively, to the atmosphere which surrounds him. The great difference is to be found in the fact that the ruins and the chaos—and the loneliness—of the big city, have been substituted by a great vivifying wave of sensations created by the world of Nature. Thus, for example, in "Oda al olor de la leña":

> Como una mano
> de la casa oscura
> salió el aroma
> intenso
> de la leña guardada.
> Visible era el aroma
> como
> si el árbol
> estuviera vivo.
> Como si todavía palpitara.
> . . . allí estaba experándome
> el olor
> de la rosa más profunda,
> el cortado corazón de la tierra,
> algo
> que me invadió como una ola
> desprendida
> del tiempo

> y se perdió en mí mismo
> cuando yo abrí la puerta
> de la noche.

The typography—which is an integral part of Neruda's poems—has also changed; before, the lines were an irregular and chaotic mass, like ruins and rubble; now, sinuous and vertical, they remind us of volutes of smoke, of thin celery stalks, of the branches of a lemon tree. What has not changed—and what I have tried to underscore—in these remarks today— is the aperture and the submission of the "I," of the poetic consciousness, enveloped by and submerged in the sensations which surround the poet like an immense, unending wave.

JOHN FELSTINER

Translating Alturas de Macchu Picchu

FROM VOICE TO VOICE

Perhaps the real "original" behind any translation occurs not in the written poem, but in the poet's voice speaking the verse aloud. Roger Caillois was lucky to be there that day in 1945, for as "litany followed upon invective and grief upon anger," he was hearing in Neruda's voice the formal and the emotional components of *Alturas de Macchu Picchu*. In more specific ways, a translator may also pick up vocal tones, intensities, rhythms, and pauses that will reveal how the poet heard a word, a phrase, a line, a passage. To get from the poet's voice into another language and into a translator's own voice is the business of translation. It depends on a moment-by-moment shuttle between voices, for what translating comes down to is listening—listening now to what the poet's voice said, now to one's own voice as it finds what to say.

In order to go between but not get between the author and the reader, a translator constantly makes local choices in diction and phrasing that tune the new version as it goes. With *Alturas de Macchu Picchu* in particular, the choices matter because this poem marked "a new stage in my style and a new direction in my concerns," as Neruda said. But newness emerges from what came before. Into Neruda's long poem may have fed anything from his life up until August 1945—childhood, love, travel, politics, previous writings. A knowledge of these things should feed into the translator's work as well, if only to bring about some lexical echo, or shift

From *Translating Neruda: The Way to Macchu Picchu*. © 1980 by the Board of Trustees of the Leland Stanford Junior University. Stanford University Press, 1980.

191

in tone, or emphatic rhythm that shows what the newness actually consists of. This [essay] recounts in detail the process of making an English version of *Alturas de Macchu Picchu*—that is, of creating yet another stage, another direction for the poem itself.

To make a new version is to reimagine the original poem, and in this process the translator develops particular affinities with the author: a shared historical or philosophical perspective, a parallel emotional impetus, a kindred linguistic task. Occasionally one great poet translates another and brilliantly proves the affinity. Rilke translated Valéry's "Cimetière marin" into German with "an equivalence I scarcely thought could be achieved," he said; "my resources so corresponded with his great, glorious poems that I have never translated with such sureness and insight." Or in the ultimate case, Samuel Beckett makes faithful but firsthand versions of Beckett's French—they are just what he would say in English. When the translator is other than a great poet, those emotional and linguistic affinities are put to the test: each choice, each rendering attempts to realize in English what the author has said—that is, both to comprehend and to make actual. This is the heart of the process, this twofold incitement. Sometimes it strains the language of translation, whose words must keep to an original and yet set their own pace too. But often enough a happy chance will render the original fully and at the same time let the English verse do what it wants to.

The translator becomes obsessively alert to words, as certain of them spring into relief from the page or from the poet's recorded voice. Perhaps an ambiguous term in *Alturas de Macchu Picchu* occurred in earlier poems or prose in such a way as to clarify its present usage. In translating as prolific a writer as Neruda, one builds up a kind of concordance from work to work. A number of weighted words turn up more than once in *Alturas de Macchu Picchu*: "manantial (spring, source)," "hundir (to sink, plunge)," "entregar (to give up, hand over)," and others become familiar tokens that keep their meaning. One can hear something slightly different in each context, but maybe those shadings signify less than the pattern and the resonance that emerge in translating the word identically as often as possible. There can be no hard-and-fast rules for deciding between the demands of the original and those of the translation. So I write from within the Spanish and without, feeling for the pulse and pressure of Neruda's verse but also keeping a distance at which my new version becomes just that—a new version of the story now discernible in both poems. What follows, then, is a close account of the translator's basic activity, the to-and-fro movement between Spanish and English.

CANTOS 1, 2: "THE EXHAUSTED HUMAN SPRING"

Opening the first half of the poem, the stage before his life brought him to Machu Picchu, Neruda draws us right into that life, saying where he has been and when, how he has acted, and what he has missed so far. But with all that, his syntax and imagery still unfold somewhat obscurely:

> Del aire al aire, como una red vacía,
> iba yo entre las calles y la atmósfera, llegando y despidiendo,
> en el advenimiento del otoño la moneda extendida
> de las hojas, y entre la primavera y las espigas,
> lo que el más grande amor, como dentro de un guante
> que cae, nos entrega como una larga luna.

Even a close, practically word-for-word rendering requires a dozen decisions (some of them made while thinking out these paragraphs) that affect the sense and movement of the passage:

> From the air to the air, like an empty net,
> I went on through streets and thin air, arriving and leaving
> behind,
> at autumn's advent, the coin handed out
> in the leaves, and between spring and ripe grain,
> the fullness that love, as in a glove's
> fall, gives over to us like a long-drawn moon.

Other translations begin "From air to air." Though it is often possible to drop the definite article when translating Neruda, here I think his opening movement belongs to "the air" we all live in. That movement also needs a protracted rhythm. He is dragging the air, as it were, searching his surroundings for something, coming to the fruits of summer and autumn but then leaving them behind.

The syntax of these lines has troubled readers and translators, since "llegando y despidiendo" could make an independent unit, "arriving and saying goodbye." But "despedir" may have a stronger transitive meaning here, "dismiss" or "renounce." Perhaps "leaving behind" splits the difference between saying good-bye and renouncing. To settle then on "la moneda (the coin)" as the object of "despedir," a comma between "otoño" and "la moneda" would help: "leaving behind, / at autumn's advent, the coin." No editions have a comma there, but Neruda does pause markedly in two phonograph recordings (the third is noncommittal). So despite the pun, I think we see him leaving behind or forsaking the season's

generosity, what the leaves and what love have to give. Not to relate him
to them would ignore the emptiness of his net, the very need that set him
writing his poem. In *Veinte poemas de amor* (1924) Neruda had said, "I
cast my sad nets in your oceanic eyes." That yearning for fulfillment, baffled for so many years, becomes the initial memory in *Alturas de Macchu
Picchu*—a memory of failing to connect with nature and humankind.

Some of the translator's choices in these lines have a more local significance. Neruda's "moneda extendida," the "extended" coin, calls not
only for a visual image but also for a figurative sense, as in coin "handed
out." And when love "nos entrega" (literally, "delivers to us"), which in
the first of the *Veinte poemas de amor* suggests passive surrendering, Neruda's verb here can carry as well an active sense of giving. The phrase
"give over" blends both ideas and also modulates away from the trivial
rhyme of "glove" with "love." Within this same figure, the preposition
"dentro (within)" poses a more crucial question. If the fullness of love
comes "dentro de un guante que cae," literally "within a glove that falls,"
does it somehow come within the glove itself or—a more compelling
thought—within a moment, "as in a glove's fall"? Neruda locates this experience, like the swelling calabashes of "Galope muerto" twenty years before, in high summer, "between spring and ripe grain." This is the kind of
love we are offered but seldom grasp. It can concentrate and reveal itself
in a moment, yet extend "como una larga luna (like a long-drawn
moon)"—"larga" implying duration rather than distance, as in "ese sonido
ya tan largo (that sound so drawn out now)," from "Galope muerto." In
that poem Neruda perceived a kind of consummation that could seem a
moment's doing yet stretch on endlessly. Both nature and passion gave him
instances of it. Then *Alturas de Macchu Picchu* subjected that consummation to the demands of history.

After Neruda's "empty net" drifts through the streets, reaching then
leaving behind seasons of ripeness, a sudden parenthesis interposes four
images of forceful passion:

> (Días de fulgor vivo en la intemperie
> de los cuerpos: aceros convertidos
> al silencio del ácido:
> noches deshilachadas hasta la última harina:
> estambres agredidos de la patria nupcial.)

These images, with each phrase bearing four marked stresses, need the
directest possible conveyance into English:

(Days of live brilliance in the storm
of bodies: steels transmuted
into silent acid:
nights raveled out to the final flour:
battered stamens of the nuptial land.)

The figures surge up into Neruda's narrative from a deeper stratum than the lines around them. They all imagine a passion that is now only latently possible—is too brilliant, too consuming to take form yet as a clause or sentence. The last line, "estambres agredidos de la patria nupcial (battered stamens of the nuptial land)," poses problems in translation. For one thing, "fatherland" or even "homeland" at the end would dissipate the rhythm too much—why is it that English has nothing but compound words for this idea? And "estambres" can mean either "stamens" or "threads," which are both germane to the poem. Italian and French have cognates that retain both meanings, but the English word "stamen" has lost the root sense of "thread," and a choice must be made. Whereas "threads" would pick up "raveled" from the previous line, "stamens" does better by bringing out a regenerative potential in the "nuptial" land. But then why such violence in "agredidos (assaulted, injured)"? The previous figures embody a memory and a hope of sexual passion; in "battered stamens of the nuptial land" Neruda may momentarily be envisioning the damaged lives at Macchu Picchu and their difficult rebirth.

Following the parenthesis occurs a change of tense that can easily get lost in translation. Before, Neruda had said "iba yo," "I was going" or "I went on" rather than "I went" through streets and air. Now he moves from the imperfect into a full sentence with preterite forms, "hundí, descendí, regresé (I plunged . . . dropped down . . . went back)." The change marks a departure: from a drifting to a willed descent. Canto 1, then, not only sets in motion the imagery of fruitless wandering but also imagines a decisive journey that will not actually occur until canto 6—an ascent that requires descending because the site is buried, sunken out of consciousness. Having spoken of a "patria nupcial," Neruda in this opening canto enters "a world like a buried tower (un mundo como una torre enterrada)." Both "patria" and "torre" will come back later as epithets for Machu Picchu, and the "human spring" Neruda seeks in this canto is echoed when he calls the city "High reef of the human dawn" (6). In his beginning, Neruda's words prefigure his end.

Canto 1 also sets the poem's coordinates in time and space. Through the unfulfilling streets and seasons Neruda moves horizontally, but after imagining "days of live brilliance" he drops vertically like a buried tower, a sinking spiral, a sword, a plunging hand (the same verb, "hundir," can yield both sinking and plunging in this sentence). "Hundí la mano turbulenta y dulce / en lo más genital de lo terrestre (I plunged my turbulent and gentle hand / into the genital quick of the earth)." It seems a semantic windfall that the best rendering of "dulce (gentle)," softens the sound of "turbulent" and then chimes etymologically with "genital." As for "lo más genital" (literally "the most genital"), "the genital quick" tunes up Neruda's Spanish slightly—I hope he would approve the change. Every quest is sexual, it seems, and so Neruda thinks of penetrating to some progenitive source beneath earth and ocean, even more purposefully here than in "Entrance into Wood." Because the source has been spent or forgotten, his descent along the vertical axis must also take him back in time, "back . . . to the jasmine / of the exhausted human spring." In the Caedmon recording, Neruda misreads "jazmín (jasmine)" as "jardín," as if it were the "garden" of the exhausted human spring, and that odd slip corroborates his return to some lost Eden. The "primavera humana," being a natural as well as a historical source, may justify in translation the pun on "spring" as a fountain. Or perhaps that word needs capitalizing, so that other meanings of "spring" do not obscure Neruda's search for a season of renewal and rebirth.

His search has the elements of a mythic or ritual procedure, a spellbound underworld and undersea descent. To mark that quality throughout the canto's final lines, I give them more rhythmic shape than English free verse usually has, establishing an iambic pentameter base and varying it with anapests and dactyls:

> and deeper yet, in geologic gold,
> like a sword sheathed in meteors
> I plunged my turbulent and gentle hand
> into the genital quick of the earth.
>
> I bent my head into the deepest waves,
> dropped down through sulfurous calm
> and went back, as if blind, to the jasmine
> of the exhausted human spring.

Neruda himself recited much of the poem in an incantatory tone and rhythm, as if conscious that only a heightened utterance would carry him on this journey.

Having gone back to the "human spring," he begins canto 2, "Si la flor a la flor"—echoing the poem's opening, "Del aire al aire"—and then goes on to show why the human spring is exhausted. The trouble lies in our dissonance with nature:

> Si la flor a la flor entrega el alto germen
> y la roca mantiene su flor diseminada
> en su golpeado traje de diamante y arena,
> el hombre arruga el pétalo de la luz que recoge
> en los determinados manantiales marinos
> y taladra el metal palpitante en sus manos.

> While flower to flower gives up the high seed
> and rock keeps its flower sown
> in a beaten coat of diamond and sand,
> man crumples the petal of light he picks
> in the deep-set springs of the sea
> and drills the pulsing metal in his hands.

The equation between natural and human existence, which is lyric poetry's main source of metaphor, carries an inescapable logic: instead of crumpling the flower, "man (el hombre)" should conform to the example of nature's regenerative process. Neruda's clauses by their very placement reveal the crux of his method. Flowers give, but man crumples: what's broken is the metaphoric connection sought so avidly in Neruda's love poems. That is, human life should be embodying and enacting metaphors from nature.

In translating "la flor entrega (flower gives up)," it is worth echoing canto 1, where love "nos entrega (gives over to us)": our own generousness and nature's ought to coincide. By the same token Neruda's next line is crucial: "y la roca mantiene su flor diseminada." Across the word "flor" a tensile arc gives shape to the line, connecting two verbs whose meanings might be opposed: "mantener (maintain)" and "diseminar (disseminate)." What holds them together is the idea that giving does not entail loss, that in spending passion and energy one need not lose substance or identity. Neruda's political exertions from 1936 to 1945 taught him this, and now on the way to Macchu Picchu he can put it in a single line.

That word "mantiene" marks Neruda's first use of the root "tener (to hold)," which will occur in critical ways throughout the poem. Whether as "maintain," "sustain," "contain," or "detain," the root implies a dynamic form—some kind of matter or energy held in, yet holding its own. In translation, short Germanic verbs seem better than the Latinate words for holding this line's tensile shape: "and rock keeps its flower sown." "Sown" also lends a stronger sound and rhythm to the whole passage than "disseminated," and "keeps" has the sense of at once containing and prolonging. The rock that "keeps its flower sown" can give us intimations of Macchu Picchu, a stone structure that may have kept life stirring within it.

Since this first half of *Alturas de Macchu Picchu* essentially recapitulates the experience of Neruda's twenties, images of denatured life from his earlier poems keep turning up. The "clothing hung from a wire" in "Walking Around" can be seen here in "clothes and smoke" and "hostile trappings of the wire." The "amapola (poppy)," a frequent symbol for passion in his love poems, appears now in a striking figure from canto 2, where Neruda asks:

> quién guarda sin puñal (como las encarnadas
> amapolas) su sangre?
>
> (Who, [like the crimson poppy] keeps
> no dagger to guard his blood?)

In the earlier love poems it was usually enough to say something like "the color of poppies sits on your brow." Here, human and physical nature remain disjunct. Societal anxiety closes parentheses around the poppy, nature's example of passionate openness. More specifically, the word "guard" implies that we would lose less through openness than through constraint; that we might thrive within organic forms of existence rather than rigid forms of control.

In canto 2, nature provides the touchstone for sexual and social acts though not yet for political existence. The passage beginning "How many times in the city's winter streets" drifts with no verb through four long lines of loveless human scenes until "me quise detener (I wanted to stop)." "Detener (stop, pause, arrest)," a common verb, was one Neruda often used revealingly. "Galope muerto" finds him "deteniéndose"—"in what's immobile, holding still, to perceive"—and in "Sonata y destrucciones" he is "detenido," a journeyer "held" between shadows and wings. His prose also uses the word at important moments: in Spain "my poetry paused" amidst the anguish, and then "roots and blood began to rise through it"; and going home in 1943, he says, "Me detuve," "In Peru I stopped and climbed to the ruins of Machu Picchu." Here in canto 2 the verb "detener" interrupts a frustrating horizontal movement, what Eliot's *Four Quartets* calls "the waste sad time / stretching before and after," and creates, in Eliot's words, a "point of intersection of the timeless / with time":

me quise detener a buscar la eterna veta insondable
que antes toqué en la piedra o en el relámpago que el beso
     desprendía.

(I wanted to stop and seek the timeless fathomless vein
I touched in a stone once or in the lightning a kiss released.)

Eliot's word "timeless" (for "eterna") helps in translation, since both poets
conceived of profound and heightened experience along a vertical axis, out
of time. And because Spanish has another word for human veins ("vena"),
my translation relies on "fathomless" to locate this mineral "veta" underground or perhaps undersea. In wanting to stop in mid-career and to descend, the poet recalls some early joy and anticipates in "a stone" some
future one.

Right after Neruda recalls the stone and "the lightning a kiss released," an extended vision arises, showing what that vital touch was and
what it might be like again. This vision arises between parentheses, as if
caught and held against the stream of daily experience:

(Lo que en el cereal como una historia amarilla
de pequeños pechos preñados va repitiendo un número
que sin cesar es ternura en las capas germinales,
y que, idéntica siempre, se desgrana en marfil
y lo que en el agua es patria transparente, campana
desde la nieve aislada hasta las olas sangrientas.)

These lines, as the translator comes to realize, develop no main clause: beginning "lo que (that which)," they form a kind of instantaneous subliminal flash depicting what the poet stopped to seek:

(Whatever in grain like a yellow history
of small swelling breasts keeps repeating its number
ceaselessly tender in the germinal shells,
and identical always, what strips to ivory,
and what is clear native land welling up, a bell
from remotest snows to the blood-sown waves.)

Moving through progressive verb forms, a present tense, and the verb "is,"
this passage never resolves into a main verb but remains in suspension. Life
given over to time and change ("history," "repeating," "ceaselessly," "germinal") is not exhausted, but through that very change keeps its form
("grain," "breast," "number," "shell").

The key phrase is the strangest, "idéntica siempre," and needs close rather than interpretive translation. Tarn says that the grains shell "always the same way," but I think Neruda means they are "identical always": no matter how much generation the germ of life goes through, it keeps its essential identity, it remains one and the same. Like the parenthesis in canto 1, which closes with "battered stamens of the nuptial land," this parenthesis closes with a presage of the mountain site: "y lo que en el agua es patria transparente, campana / desde la nieve aislada hasta las olas sangrientas." No English verse could equal the way Neruda's *ah*-sounds move through "agua" to the "patria transparente," then into the roundedness of "campana," and finally resonate throughout the landscape of the last line. I have played with the sense a little to get rhyming vowel sounds—"clear native land welling up, a bell / from remotest snows to the blood-sown waves"—though that mixture may be somewhat rich.

The parenthesis closes and Neruda's narrative voice now returns, in the past tense again, saying he could not "touch," he could only "grasp" hollow faces or masks. In this alienation, he imagines finding some responsive touch in a place that will be either "running" or "firm":

> No tuve sitio donde descansar la mano
> y que, corriente como agua de manantial encadenado,
> o firme como grumo de antracita o cristal,
> hubiera devuelto el calor o el frío de mi mano extendida.
>
> (I had no place to rest my hand,
> none running like linked springwater
> or firm as a chunk of anthracite or crystal
> to give back the warmth or cold of my outstretched hand.)

The translation can, like the original, enrich its language by association: "my outstretched hand" reaches back to "the coin handed out in the leaves" in canto 1, as well as forward to moments when Neruda's hand will touch the city's stones and reach for the men who dwelt there. A place "running like linked springwater" will be found in canto 9's epithet for the city, "wellspring of stone (manantial de piedra)," and my word "linked," instead of the literal "chained" for "encadenado," will again be heard when Neruda says to the Indian workers in canto 12, "Tell me everything, chain by chain, link by link." I choose "linked" in canto 2 because the word suggests controlling yet releasing a life-giving source: it anticipates the Incas' ingeniously stepped conduits and irrigation runnels at Macchu Picchu, which link the levels of the city, harmonizing hard natural fact with human need. One more phrase in this passage, "No tuve sitio," also looks ahead through the poem as if through the years. Here Neruda says, "I had no place" to rest, and the need for one is so sharp that it carries through to canto 6, where he will announce simply: "éste es el sitio (this is the place)."

CANTOS 3, 4, 5: "WHAT COULD NOT BE REBORN"

Because this poem prepared a new stage in his work, it "came out too impregnated with myself," Neruda said. "The beginning is a series of auto-biographical recollections. I also wanted to touch for the last time there upon the theme of death." He said this after being exiled as a Communist between 1948 and 1952, during which time he was welcomed throughout the Soviet orbit and in China, saw *Canto general* translated into twenty-five languages, and felt persuaded that poetry's task was to hearten the common struggle. These conditions made him sensitive to the poem's subjective, dispirited vein. Yet it is hard to imagine *Alturas de Macchu Picchu* without Neruda's presence, particularly the constantly inquiring force of his voice.

"What was man?," Neruda cries at the close of canto 2, and the next canto opens with another figure from nature:

> Lives like maize were threshed in the bottomless
> granary of wasted deeds
>
> . . . .
>
> and not one death but many deaths came each man's way.

What troubles Neruda most about this way of living, which feels like a "lamp snuffed out in suburban mud, a petty fat-winged death," is that such dwindling and death have no communal matrix, no shared vision, no common *logos* to redeem them. "Alone," he says in canto 4, "I roamed round dying of my own death." Even the workers whom he evokes fairly strongly, "the drover, the son of seaports, the dark captain of the plow," remain isolated as "cada ser" or "cada uno" or "cada hombre": "each being," "each one," "each man." One can question whether Neruda's vision really is shared commonly. In translating, it is hard to see "hijo" ("son" or "child"), "uno," and "hombre" as generic rather than gender-linked: this canto does not suggest that for women, as for drovers and sailors and farmers, "their dismal weariness each day was like / a black cup they drank down trembling."

Canto 4 opens with "La poderosa muerte." Whether a "powerful," "mighty," "irresistible," or "overmastering" death, as translators have heard it, it is in any case the "one death," which canto 3 opposed to the "many deaths" that isolated men die day after day. By complex figures of speech—death was like salt in the waves, like sinking and height—Neruda connects this "poderosa muerte" to other ideas in the poem. It is not simply that his writing runs to figures of speech, but that in those figures he evolves the deeper-than-narrative structure of his poem, particularly through words the translator has noticed and will come upon again:

> La poderosa muerte me invitó muchas veces:
> era como la sal invisible en las olas,
> y lo que su invisible sabor diseminaba
> era como mitades de hundimientos y altura.
>
> (The mightiest death invited me many times:
> like invisible salt in the waves it was,
> and what its invisible savor disseminated
> was half like sinking and half like height.)

The literal sense of "diseminaba" seems called for (and enriches the sound) in this instance. Along with its corrosiveness, salt has enhancing and preserving qualities, and these fit Neruda's idea of a death that sustains the potential for rebirth. In canto 12, for instance, he will say to the buried American, "Give me your hand out of the deep / region seeded by all your grief"—your "dolor diseminado." The analogy in canto 4 imagines death "como mitades de hundimientos y altura"—literally, "like halves of sinkings and height." The available verse translations miss Neruda's drift, I think. [Ben] Belitt's "height, or the ruin of height, a plenitude halved" eludes my understanding, and [Nathaniel] Tarn's "fragments of wrecks and heights" skirts the exact sense of "mitades (halves)," the idea that death is a whole made up equally of what sinking and height connote. The image of sinking need not have negative force, as Belitt and Tarn imply; for Neruda it leads to the deep pole, the basis, the root. The words "hundir" and "altura" take various forms both early and late in the poem, suggesting that an encounter with Machu Picchu involves the full scale of what we can experience: from the unconscious to the spirit, from sexual earthiness to transcendent ecstasy, from past to future, from death to renewal.

Even when a profuse and vaguely symbolic imagery in *Alturas de Macchu Picchu* makes translating uncertain, it is well to trust rather than paraphrase Neruda, for a logic usually underlies what he says. In the poem's opening image he had stopped wandering through the streets to sink into earth and sea. Now in "suburban mud" or "cluttered streets" (3) he looks for the dimension that people lack, crying out to it "ancho mar, oh muerte! (broad sea, oh death!)" (4). Then a little later he says: "quise nadar en las más anchas vidas, / en las más sueltas desembocaduras." The choice of rendering "anchas" again as "broad"—"I wanted to swim in the broadest lives, / in the openest river mouths"—indicates that life can have great breadth, like that of death.

Neruda is seeking a consummation in the "openest river mouths" and the undifferentiated primal element from which life emerged and to which it returns. A source for this idea can be found in some impressions he sent from Ceylon to a Chilean newspaper in 1929, during the period these early cantos represent. He was talking about the effect of Hindu belief on life in the Orient:

> Origin and duration are antagonistic states: original being is still immersed in spontaneousness, in the creative and destructive element, while day-to-day lives go on abandoned, deprived of beginning or end. With no loss of itself, and losing itself, being goes back to its creative origin, "like a drop of seawater to the sea," says the *Katha Upanishad*.

In 1929, trying to find some meaning in his own day-to-day life, Neruda saw this potential immersion in the primal sea of being as "a source of impossible and fatal obscurities." But what he called "duration" or daily life had by 1945 come to be in need of "its creative origin." Having seen so many abandoned, deprived lives around him, and seeking to recover an American genesis, Neruda at Machu Picchu felt impelled to plunge his hand or sink like a drop through earth and sea to the human spring.

The poet's "turbulent and gentle hand," from canto 1, now in canto 4 has found men denying him as if he made a Christ-like demand on them: they shut themselves off "so I would not touch / with my streaming hands their wound of emptiness (para que no tocaran / mis manos manantiales su inexistencia herida)." There seems no good way to specify in translation the recurrent image of "manantial (source, spring)," as here in "manos manantiales," though Tarn's "divining fingers" hits on an ingenious solution. As "streaming hands" they could easily be Walt Whitman's hands touching his fellow creatures or dressing the wounded, and in fact another passage, from canto 5, also begins much like Whitman:

I lifted the iodine bandages, plunged my hands
into meager griefs that were killing off death,
and all I found in the wound was a cold gust
that passed through loose gaps in the soul.

It begins like Whitman, at least, but ends more like Eliot, whose vision of urban and suburban spiritlessness in *Four Quartets*—"men and bits of paper, whirled by the cold wind / . . . Wind in and out of unwholesome lungs"—is strikingly akin to Neruda's.

Eliot would never play the healing or suffering servant of humanity as Whitman and Neruda do, and they in turn could hardly live with Eliot's austere deprecation of sensuality. Yet Neruda's and Eliot's ideas share similar forms, if they differ in substance and tone. Eliot's sense of a "darkness to purify the soul," where "the darkness shall be the light" (which in fact derives from the Spanish mystic San Juan de la Cruz), resembles Neruda's vision of death as a "gallop of nighttime clarity" (4), except that Neruda's paradox seems homemade, instinctive. And in canto 5 Neruda's formula for the empty human shuffle around him—"Era lo que no pudo renacer (It was what could not be reborn)"—might well be translated by Eliot's fine discrimination of what keeps humankind from spiritual rebirth: "that which is only living / Can only die." What distinguishes Neruda from Eliot, at least in *Alturas de Macchu Picchu,* is that finally he aims at a secular rebirth and makes himself the agent of it.

CANTOS 6, 7: "LIVING, DEAD, SILENCED, SUSTAINED"

"Entonces"—in Neruda's recordings the word is weighted, slow, sonorous:

Entonces en la escala de la tierra he subido
entre la atroz maraña de las selvas perdidas
hasta ti, Macchu Picchu.

Our word "then" sounds too thin and brief for such a crucial moment. "Then, then" (depending on how it's spoken) might get a dramatic emphasis at this point, but once one begins such compensating for an adequate English rendering, the door opens too wide.

Then on the ladder of the earth I climbed
through the lost jungle's tortured thicket
up to you, Machu Picchu.

This is the watershed of the poem, as of Neruda's entire poetry, and it makes a beautifully timed cadence. For "hasta ti, Macchu Picchu," I am tempted to say "up to thee, Machu Picchu," to preserve the Spanish form used with one's intimates or when praying to God. Even without that archaism in English, we can hear Neruda speaking to Machu Picchu in the directly personal way he spoke a canto earlier to death: "Solemn death, it was not you," "No eras tú, muerte grave." He may feel equally close to both and may also in some way mean to identify the two.

Another small semantic event in canto 6's opening lines has larger implications that might go unnoticed or remain vague without the specific focus that occurs in translation. Neruda climbs "en la escala de la tierra (on the ladder of the earth)," and immediately invokes Machu Picchu as "Alta ciudad de piedras escalares"—"High city of laddered stones," as a Spanish ear might hear the phrase, though "stepped" or "scaled" describes the actual construction more closely. By echoing "escala" in "escalares," Neruda makes the cut stone and the earth congruent with each other. A human construction conforms superbly to raw, ineluctable nature: this is what gives Machu Picchu its mythic aura. The physical site and the city do exhibit this conformity in the way the steep, rocky slopes give rise to flights of stone steps and mortarless walls as smooth as the day they were fitted. Unlike the urban scene in "Walking Around," with its "hideous intestines hanging from the doors of houses I hate," Neruda finds stone buildings that fuse the primordial presence of the Andes with the aspirations of an indigenous people.

That fusion of nature and history explains another image from the beginning of canto 6. "En ti," Neruda says to the site,

> En ti, como dos líneas paralelas,
> la cuna del relámpago y del hombre
> se mecían en un viento de espinas.

> (In you like two lines parallel,
> the cradles of lightning and man
> rocked in a wind of thorns.)

Tarn interestingly chooses the figurative sense of *línea* and has two "lineages" issuing in one "cradle both of man and light." His choice of "light" for Neruda's "relámpago (lightning flash)" tends to assimilate this image to a biblical genesis. "Lightning," on the other hand, not only recalls Neruda's glimpse of ecstasy in canto 2, "the lightning a kiss released," but finds a dazzling, threatening energy at the cradle of a cosmos more secular than biblical. Neruda's cradles identify Machu Picchu as a remote source of both natural and human phenomena, of "lightning and man." In the scheme of *Canto general* (1950), Neruda used *Alturas de Macchu Picchu* as the second of fifteen books, thus placing it far back in the epic's chronology. It follows directly upon the poems about untouched minerals, wild plants, solitary birds, and invisible Arauco, and it comes before the third book, *The Conquistadors*. In effect, then, Machu Picchu occurs between a Creation and the first human cataclysm. It stands suspended, untouched (as was indeed the case) by the incursions of history.

The poet in canto 6 continues invoking this place with honorific yet pointed epithets:

> Mother of stone, spume of condors.
> High reef of the human dawn.
> Spade lost in the primal sand.

Catalogs of attributes are a vital convention in medieval oral poetry: addressed to a god, a ruler, a sacred place, they establish the qualities or powers that a people value. Here Neruda, whose emphatic, alliterated lines sound rather like Anglo-Saxon verse, reinforces Machu Picchu's twofold aspect as a human construction and a fact of nature by calling to the "Mother of stone" alongside the "spume of condors." His second epithet does much the same: "High reef of the human dawn"—a natural metaphor for a primal history. But if he sees the city as a reef, long-lasting and visible, he also imagines it as a spade lost in the sand: Machu Picchu appears emergent and yet buried. In Neruda's next line the verb tenses embody a similar double vision: "Ésta fué la morada, éste es el sitio (This was the dwelling, this is the place)." "Sitio" could of course be translated as "site," but that risks giving it a merely archaeological significance. The past tense balanced against the present and the matching half-lines divide Machu Picchu's genius equally between the city that people formerly dwelt in and the natural site a poet now announces.

Neruda's assurance that past and present time can fuse through the poet's agency takes even more concrete form later in canto 6, in a particular sequence of tenses:

> Miro las vestiduras y las manos,
> el vestigio del agua en la oquedad sonora,
> la pared suavizada por el tacto de un rostro
> que miró con mis ojos las lámparas terrestres,
> que aceitó con mis manos las desaparecidas
> maderas.

As it happens, the first-person, present-tense "miro (I look at)" takes only a change in accent to become, three lines later, the third-person past, "miró (looked at)." English cannot quite match that economy:

> I look at clothes and hands,
> the trace of water in an echoing tub,
> the wall brushed smooth by the touch of a face
> that looked with my eyes at the lights of earth,
> that oiled with my hands the vanished
> beams.

Using one English verb for "miro" and "miró" helps in recognizing Neruda's presence as both a pilgrim now and a native then. Tarn varies the verb, saying "I gaze" and then "a face that witnessed," because "gaze" has a strength that is needed here and "witness" has suggestive overtones. Neruda's kind of witness can also gain from simplicity and immediacy. His double residence at Machu Picchu, in the present and the past, can bear every possible emphasis in translation, for it matters vitally to him. (In his urgency Neruda even says that the face not only looked, it also "oiled.") He recited these lines passionately, putting unusual stress on "mis ojos" and "mis manos": "that looked with *my* eyes," "that oiled with *my* hands."

This emphasis also clarifies Neruda's surprising use of "porque (because)" in the very next line. Why does he look at the trace of water, the vanished beams, the wall brushed by "a face / that looked with my eyes"?

> porque todo, ropaje, piel, vasijas,
> palabras, vino, panes,
> se fué, cayó a la tierra.

> (because everything, clothing, skin, jars,
> words, wine, bread,
> is gone, fallen to earth.)

Having for years let my translation of "porque todo . . . se fué" remain as "for everything . . . is gone," I now see it fails to intensify the logic of Neruda's statement. Precisely "because" every rudiment of that previous life is now gone, he says "my" eyes long ago looked and "my" hands worked. We may not want to assent to that illusion, but it fosters a crucial idea. Unless renewed in the person of the poet, these beams, jars, and wine remain utterly lost to us now. To redeem the past, to translate it over the centuries into his own eyes and hands, requires an act of imagination—not, as ultimately for Eliot, an act of religious faith. Neruda does allow a hint of resurrection (or transubstantiation) by including "palabras, vino, panes (words, wine, bread)," among the things we may have lost. Tarn calls the "panes" "loaves," giving a more specific Christian coloring to Neruda's redemptive mission.

To translate "panes" as "loaves," the way Tarn does, and in the next canto "vaso" ("glass" or "vessel") as "chalice," accentuates an already difficult question. Neruda has been faulted for making use of his Spanish Catholic heritage while at the same time lamenting the Conquest, and no doubt that is a real split in him as in many Latin Americans. In *Alturas de Macchu Picchu*, I think he deliberately highlights neither Christian nor indigenous imagery because he is addressing a general audience, both Latin and American. It is also held against him that he speaks for pre-Columbian peoples while ignoring present-day Indians—another tendency in countries such as Peru and Mexico. He calls up slaves from the Inca past without a word for modern Quechua speakers, but here again I believe he does so to be heard by modern workers in general, for whose plight he finds a deep basis at Machu Picchu.

Eliot's *Four Quartets* (1943), published a few years before Neruda's poem, also doubles back to a neglected site and summons forgotten ancestors. In "East Coker," he revisits the village his forebears emigrated from, and we see the dancing of sixteenth-century rustic feet "long since under earth / Nourishing the corn." This scene shares with the return to Machu Picchu an assumption that, in Eliot's words, "We are born with the dead"; that we need the past just as the past needs us. Eliot's third quartet, "The Dry Salvages," evokes scenes from his childhood but—tellingly enough—does not try specifically to recover any American place or time from oblivion. The final poem, "Little Gidding," locates in England a site essentially like Machu Picchu: a seventeenth-century Anglican chapel and refuge from civil war, later destroyed by Cromwell's Puritans. Eliot shows the way there, telling us "to kneel / Where prayer has been valid. . . . / And what the dead had no speech for, when living, / They can tell you, being dead." Although Neruda says as much of the dead at Machu Picchu, the effect of their message differs radically. Eliot leads us—or rather, he leads the English in wartime—to reconcile past with present strife and suffering in a formal pattern, and thus to approach a purified condition founded on Christ's. Neruda, though he also imagines transfiguring past and present agonies, would do so by questioning, by refusing to accept the hunger and toil of South American Indians. And where Eliot wants the poets in his tradition, such as Dante, to infuse his own language, Neruda would speak for the voices utterly lost.

The communication Neruda feels he has opened at Machu Picchu lets him, in canto 7, directly and collectively address those who died there as "vosotros" (in this case, "os"). A translation cannot pick up that sound, which Latin Americans associate mainly with the way they are spoken to in church or at political rallies, but I would borrow Tarn's excellent solution, "You dead":

> Muertos de un solo abismo, sombras de una hondonada
>
> . . . .
>
> desde los capiteles escarlata,
> desde los acueductos escalares
> os desplomasteis como en un otoño
> en una sola muerte.

> (You dead of a single abyss, shadows of one ravine
>
> . . . .
>
> from the red-topped columns,
> from the laddered aqueducts
> you plummeted as in autumn
> to one sole death.)

It would help to hear the plural pronoun and verb ("os desplomasteis"), for Neruda now believes that these dead in "a single abyss" died the consuming and unifying death barred to the isolated individual today.

They "plummeted," Neruda says, calling to mind the city's sheer architectural lines. This powerful vertical movement again signals a revelatory event. At first the poet dropped as if blind through the deepest waves, and then on reaching Machu Picchu he said: "Here the broad grains of maize rose up / and fell again like red hail" (6). Now the inhabitants themselves take part in this archetypal movement. Neruda speaks in this canto of an "árbol poderoso," a "mighty tree" cut down, and throughout *Canto general* an "árbol" stands for a race of people (often Araucanians) arisen from the earth. Here the tree "sostuvo una mano que cayó de repente / desde la altura hasta el final del tiempo": it "held up a hand that fell suddenly / down from the height to the end of time." Neruda's image implies that the people as an organic entity sustained this individual hand. Then the hand "fell," and in translation that common word allows not so much an allusion to Adam's fall as an association of Neruda's story with the most elemental and familiar events: leaves fall, rain falls, towers fall, Rome falls. Tarn sees instead "a hand that suddenly pitched / from the heights to the depths of time." Although "pitched" has more force than "fell," it does not pick up the lament from canto 6, where "everything . . . is gone, fallen to earth"; nor does it anticipate a later moment in canto 7, where Neruda will say to the dead: "cuanto fuisteis cayó (whatever you were fell away)." Tarn's "depths of time" makes sense, but in fact Neruda

used a more surprising image: the hand fell from the height to "el final del
tiempo (the end of time)." If ordinarily we imagine time stretching horizontally to its end, *Alturas de Macchu Picchu* reaches down to that end
along a vertical axis.

In ritual response to the fall of an entire community, the next lines
begin: "Pero una permanencia (Yet a permanence . . . rose up in the
hands / of all)." These lines contain essential statements within ambiguous
syntax, so that translating them requires more decisions than usual about
what the lines really mean:

> Pero una permanencia de piedra y de palabra,
> la ciudad como un vaso, se levantó en las manos
> de todos, vivos, muertos, callados, sostenidos,
> de tanta muerte, un muro, de tanta vida un golpe
> de pétalos de piedra.

I have restored three commas from the poem's first appearance in a Venezuelan magazine (1946), putting them after "palabra (word)," where
"Obras completas" has a colon, and after "vaso (bowl)" and "sostenidos
(sustained)," where there is no punctuation. The pauses in Neruda's recordings of the poem support these changes, and his meaning gains as
well:

> Yet a permanence of stone and word,
> the city like a bowl, rose up in the hands
> of all, living, dead, silenced, sustained,
> a wall out of so much death, out of so much life a shock
> of stone petals.

Those commas after "word" and "bowl" bring the permanence of stone
and word right into apposition with the city. After all, the whole poem
depends on such a possibility. The city's physical buildings have persisted,
yet the permanence the poet claims for them depends on the word as well
as the stone. Neruda's genius in alliterating "permanencia" with both "piedra" and "palabra" gets washed away in translation, but even without it
a new idea comes clearly into view. This "palabra" belongs not only to the
poet but to Machu Picchu's inhabitants, whose "words, wine, bread" have
fallen to earth. His advent and response, his words, now form part of the
city's permanence.

Neruda introduces this idea momentarily and passes on to "la ciudad
como un vaso (the city like a bowl)." Taken strictly, "vaso" denotes

"glass" or "vessel," but a more formal "vessel (vasija)" occurs in the next passage, and "glass" seems inappropriate to the place and the occasion. Other translators use "cup" or "goblet," and Tarn elects "chalice," which sounds Eucharistic. Like "vaso," "bowl" implies a cavity that might contain much life and death, and the word also resonates with "stone" and "rose" on either side of it. Neruda's image suggests both that the people's hands held the city up and that in turn the city holds on to its people— "vivos, muertos, callados, sostenidos (living, dead, silenced, sustained)." A comma after "sostenidos" balances this sequence so that those in the true city, the one Neruda's poem re-creates, are living though dead, silenced yet sustained. (Semantically I would prefer "held fast," but "sustained" does more for the verse.) After "sostenidos," the next phrases articulate so loosely that they are practically impossible to render with any confidence: "de tanta muerte, un muro, de tanta vida un golpe / de pétalos de piedra." The preposition "de" covers many relationships; here it is probably "out of" or "from": "a wall out of so much death, out of so much life a shock / of stone petals." Perhaps Neruda means that with so much labor and death in it the city has become a wall, sealed off yet buttressed against further loss; and that latent with so much life, it has the energy to shock or to flower. But finally the line is anyone's guess.

Throughout the last verse paragraph of canto 7, hints of ambivalence and irony continue to tug at Neruda's language, making the city more than simply a vanished glory. Its "dead of a single abyss" he now sees as man "all tangled in his hole," over which the unpeopled city remains an "exactitud enarbolada," an "unpraised exactitude." If the root "árbol (tree)" could survive translation, it would recall the growth and wholeness of an indigenous people, but against that sense Neruda's word "exactitude" begins to suggest the exactions of life under Inca rule and the human cost of perfecting that city. Two lines later Neruda's epithet for the city has an even darker coloring: "la más alta vasija que contuvo el silencio (the highest vessel that held silence in)." Whereas the verb "sostener," however translated, carries a sense of supporting, prolonging, or holding on, by "contener" Neruda means something more constraining—not the vessel's openness but its enclosure. And another crucial word in this line can come through whole, for once, into English: "silencio." But the silence that the city held in remains profoundly ambiguous: is it a kind of purified suffering or a mute defeat? Canto 7 then closes with an entire line that presents absolutely no problem in translation, a line whose simplicity offers the clearest kind of insight into what Machu Picchu means: "una vida de piedra después de tantas vidas (a life of stone after so many lives)."

CANTOS 8, 9: "THE DEAD REALM LIVES ON STILL"

If tragic affirmation could sum up Neruda's quest, the poem might have ended there, with "a life of stone after so many lives." But he had still to come at Machu Picchu in different ways: a prolonged interrogation in Canto 8, a sequence made purely of epithets in 9, a radical revision of city's human story in 10 through 12. These cantos do what only a long poem like Neruda's or Eliot's can do: they take varying perspectives on a subject, they move from narrative to lyric and other forms, they take on new voices and tones of speech. As a long poem, *Alturas de Macchu Picchu* develops the reach of an epic without losing the intensity of lyric verse. And by personifying the city, evoking its people, and persisting in his own voice and person, Neruda also creates an unusual dramatic form that finally governs our experience of the poem.

In canto 8 a new mood, the imperative, along with a series of insistent questions, begins to draw us into a tighter relation with Machu Picchu. The same verb with which Neruda first says "I climbed (he subido)" through the lost jungle, he now uses in a new way: "Sube conmigo, amor americano. / Besa conmigo las piedras secretas (Climb up with me, American love. / Kiss the secret stones with me)." The "love" Neruda addresses is not a consort but a kind of pilgrim, who like himself once probed the unloving world alone and now has a strange community to encounter. Perhaps Neruda is also summoning the reader—ourselves—into intimate touch with Machu Picchu. Yet the poet in his own person continues to provide our only perspective. In this canto he confronts the river, the Urubamba winding down through its gorge two thousand feet below the peaks that flank the city: "La plata torrencial del Urubamba / hace volar el polen a su copa amarilla (The torrential silver of the Urubamba / sends pollen flying to its yellow cup)." Like the grain's "yellow history" in canto 2, this image would seem to indicate a life-giving source, but it is hard to tell, since Neruda also describes the river as "crystal and cold, a buffeted air / dividing the clash of emeralds." Other ornate figures follow as the poet says to his companion, "Love, love, . . . study the blind child of the snow," and then begins a long interrogation of the river's "arterial waters" and "rapid swords" and "tormented flashings."

Besides using heavily figurative language, Neruda also composed this canto wholly in the classic Spanish eleven-syllable meter. To carry over that formalness, I keep mainly to four-stress lines in translation, but not to the extent of padding them. With this canto, the poem's longest by far, I find myself awkwardly situated as a translator. It seems bloated, its metaphors merely jostling each other. Yet one engages to make as vital and convincing a version as possible—which is, after all, the only thing to do, short of impermissible cutting or "tuning up."

My sense, then, is that in canto 8 Neruda pulled out the stops on his verse without yet having a distinct dramatic purpose. Why is it that "the empty vine goes flying"? Why does "the blind child of the snow" have "rapid swords"? Neruda's metaphors typically take one of three forms, with which the translator becomes quite familiar, especially in this canto. He will speak of the river's "war-worn stamens," where neither term, "war-worn" or "stamens," suggests the tenor of the metaphor; or he will combine adjective and noun so that one term analogizes while the other specifies the river, as in "arterial waters" or "cascading hands"; or he will create metaphors with a genitive link, such as "the bitter greeting of the dew." All these examples show Neruda instinctively linking natural with human life, and in that sense they have some point. But often his metaphors come to hand too readily, in translation as well. They are surprising but not surprisingly true, and at such times Neruda virtually parodies himself. In this canto a spate of images makes the reader, like the would-be translator, careless of what they signify and whether they add up. Such is not the case in canto 2, whose extended analogy between flowers, rocks, and people develops their critical relationship; or in canto 9, whose sheer accumulation of epithets demonstrates in itself the poet's hold on the city.

Canto 8 does serve to begin Neruda's questioning of Macchu Picchu, though his vague "American love" has little purpose as a companion—the speaker himself ends up asking all the questions. He calls on the Incas' sacred river, changing from "Urubamba" to a more ancient Quechua name as if to trigger deeper truths about the city's original condition:

> Oh Wilkamayu of resonant threads,
> when you shatter your bands of thunder
> into white spume, like wounded snow,
> when your steep gale
> sings and slashes arousing the sky,
> what language do you bring to the ear
> barely uprooted from your Andean foam?

It is a dire view of the sacred river. Possibly I have injected more violence into Neruda's question than he intended: my word "shatter (rompes)" could be "break," and "slashes (castiga)" could be "punishes." Yet he does seem to have displaced the breakdown of a city and a people onto the everlasting river below them. His question also suggests that the river in some way acts to translate that breakdown to the listener: "qué idioma traes a la oreja (what language do you bring to the ear)."

Then Neruda makes it clear that Machu Picchu's ruin involved the essence of a people, their voice. The river manifests a breakdown in the power of speech, of self-expression:

> What do your tormented flashings say?
> Your secret insurgent lightning—did it
> once travel thronging with words?
> Who goes on crushing frozen syllables,
> black languages, banners of gold,
> bottomless mouths, throttled shouts
> in your slender arterial waters?

The Incas had neither written language nor picture writing like that of Central America, which makes the fall of their civilization even more drastic and irrevocable. Whatever songs, whatever oral tradition they had, lapsed utterly. It is a painful thought for a poet.

The canto's final imperative says: "Ven a mi propio ser, al alba mía / hasta las soledades coronadas (Come to my very being, to my own dawn, / up to the crowning solitude)." (In the first line I have adopted Tarn's good rendering.) Apparently Neruda situates his own dawn on the heights of Machu Picchu—a fairly ambitious conceit. His next line, however, objectifies that thought with lapidary compactness: "El reino muerto vive todavía." English can compact it further—"The dead realm still lives"—but that aborts the rhythm and fails to set life against death as directly as "muerto" and "vive" do, or to prolong a keen sound the way "vive" feeds into "todavía." Saying "The realm that died is still alive" slips into singsong, and Tarn's "The fallen kingdom survives us all this while" imports something new. Perhaps to suggest Neruda's rhythm and cleave to his idea a simple sentence will do: "The dead realm still lives on." But that lightens the accent on "lives," whereas Neruda's strongest accent falls on "vive": "El reino muerto vive todavía." I will leave it at this: "The dead realm lives on still," and let Neruda's vigor remain in Spanish, where anyway the reader has probably absorbed it by now. Yet given Neruda's earlier questioning, the canto cannot close there, on an affirmative note. His final image, which I think refers to a stone altar for sun worship at Machu Picchu, reminds us that this dead realm still lives in a threatened time: "And across the Sundial like a black ship / the ravening shadow of the condor cruises."

In contrast to this canto's ornate questioning, canto 9 shores up the ruined city with a series of terse, impersonal metaphors. It makes a unique text for translation: forty-three lines, again in strict hendecasyllables, with no stanza break, each line stopped at the end and containing one or more often two epithets addressed to Machu Picchu. The canto opens:

> Águila sideral, viña de bruma.
> Bastión perdido, cimitarra ciega.
> Cinturón estrellado, pan solemne.
> Escala torrencial, párpado inmenso.
> Túnica triangular, polen de piedra.

As pure invention, Neruda's phrases call for literal English renderings; that is, anything idiomatic or interpretive would belie them. They call as well for the balanced stresses—two in each half-line—of ritual invocation:

> Sidereal eagle, vineyard of mist.
> Bulwark lost, blind scimitar.
> Starred belt, sacred bread.
> Torrential ladder, giant eyelid.
> Triangled tunic, pollen of stone.

Because many of these words have occurred before in contexts closer to narrative—eagle, mist, lost, blind, bread, torrential, ladder, pollen, stone— their reappearance here in set formulas shows Neruda gathering fragments that were dispersed, so as to sustain and maybe even reconstruct the city with his words. The half-lines abut each other, and one measured verse is set upon the next like fitted stones. In fact, near the beginning, seven successive lines close with something made "de piedra": "pollen of stone . . . bread of stone . . . rose of stone . . . well-spring of stone . . . light of stone . . . vapor of stone . . . book of stone." In opening the whole *Canto general*, Neruda dedicates himself to "my land without name, without America," and here in canto 9 he makes the poet's primary activity that of naming.

"Manantial de piedra," and the English "wellspring of stone," call the unmoving stone city a vital, fluent source, and "Madrépora del tiempo sumergido (Coral of sunken time)," sees it growing durably though invisibly. Two other images in this canto imply something essential about Machu Picchu. "Vendaval sostenido en la vertiente (Gale sustained on the slope)," describes a force, both violent and elemental, that would naturally have spent itself but for something holding it up, some vital collective spirit as in the earlier uses of "sostener." The epithet that follows, "Inmóvil catarata de turquesa," suspends "'cataract" between "immobile" and "turquoise": as "immobile" keeps it from perishing, the forceful fall of water takes on the formal beauty and stillness of a precious stone, giving a dynamic form to the ruined city.

Not every epithet here makes so condensed or original an insight. "Torre sombrera, discusión de nieve," sounds impressive as "Shading tower, dispute of snow," but hasn't very much meaning. "Cúpula del silencio, patria pura," could be "cupola" or "vault" or "Dome of silence, purebred homeland," but "patria" does not gain much in that combination. "Bastión perdido, cimitarra ciega," enlists the somewhat suggestive adjectives "lost" and "blind," but what is gained by "bastion" and "scimitar," notions alien to the Inca city? A few of Neruda's paired epithets could even be scrambled mischievously in translation without much damage: "Serpiente andina, frente de amaranto," could come out "Serpent of amaranth, Andean brow," and go unnoticed; "Serpiente mineral, rosa de piedra", might as well be "Serpent of stone, mineral rose." This interchangeability demonstrates the random process by which Neruda sometimes finds his metaphors. A hostile critic of his, the Spanish poet Juan Larrea, makes this point and goes so far as to "continue the game" of canto 9 by composing an even longer syllabic sequence but with images more endemic to Inca civilization. Larrea calls Neruda's canto a dadaist grab bag, which is only partly so, and says that it parodies the litany to the Blessed Virgin, which may in a sense be true. Neruda does exploit the cumulative and attributive qualities of litany; he may also be playing on a Catholic rhythm to tantalize and shock the reader into regarding Machu Picchu sacredly. More seriously, Larrea faults him for a lack of interest in Machu Picchu itself. Why aren't such terms as "quipu (the Incas' knotted-cord system of communication)," "amauta (a sage)," "quena (an Andean flute)," "chicha (fermented maize)," "coca," and others present in the canto? One reason may have been that Neruda, as he once said, felt "Chilean, Peruvian, American," in Machu Picchu: he had the Araucanian past along with all of Latin America's past and present in mind when he wrote.

Apart from this complaint, Larrea does have a point. The ruined city acted strongly as a catalyst for Neruda's poetic development, and particularly in later cantos where the theme of hunger emerges, he projects his ideas onto Machu Picchu rather than trying to do justice to the place itself. Whether this invalidates the poem's redemptive treatment of American place and time, as Larrea also claims, is another question. Canto 9's closing lines provide both strong and weak examples of that treatment:

> Volcán de manos, catarata oscura.
> Ola de plata, dirección del tiempo.

"Volcano of hands" puts an eruptive force (familiar in Mexico and Chile if not in Peru) into human hands, which might emblematize a workers' revolution, but "dark cataract" is vague and reiterative. "Ola de plata (Silver wave)" also seems an empty gesture, but not "dirección del tiempo," which a motto from *Four Quartets* might serve to gloss if not actually to translate: "In my end is my beginning." Three ways of envisioning time coverage in Neruda's epithet: "dirección," meaning "guidance," "route," or "aim, address," places the city in the beginning, along the way, and at the end of American history. Probably the truest choice for "dirección del tiempo" is the literal one, "direction of time," which fits all three meanings, but Tarn's "destination of time" is more compelling.

CANTOS 10, 11: "LET ME GRIND STONE STAMENS"

These cantos gather to a climax everything that *Alturas de Macchu Picchu* has ventured so far: the poet's personal stake, his dismay at a sick, isolated human condition, the contrast between this moribund existence and a communal amplitude of life and death, the inspiration of a towering site whose people worked and then fell silent. After interrogating the river's "bottomless mouths" in canto 8 and then reciting an impersonal litany to the city in 9, Neruda himself now totally pervades the last quarter of the poem. His voice and presence animate every passage, indeed every line, which means that his reader is more than usually governed by the poet's disposition. It also means that the translator's attempt to find in English an authentic idiom and tone, a voice that feels right, becomes an oddly subjective experience—one of possessing and being possessed, which may be just what the poem requires.

Canto 10 begins outright with a question: "Piedra en la piedra, el hombre, dónde estuvo? (Stone upon stone, and man, where was he?)." The speaker makes a more direct demand than in canto 8, and where the epithets of canto 9 touched mainly on Machu Picchu's natural or man-made aspects ("vineyard of mist. / Bulwark lost"), this canto concerns the people themselves. In the first line "el hombre" is strung syntactically between "la piedra" and a question, "where was he?" Suddenly it occurs to Neruda that the city's inhabitants may not have "plummeted as in autumn to one sole death" (7): perhaps they ground their lives away in 1445 no less tediously than people do in 1945. To a translator, that thought occurs in rendering the imagery from canto 10 in such a way as to recall the poem's earlier images of human attrition: "Were you too then the broken bit / of half-spent humankind," Neruda asks in 10, recalling "a bit of petty death"

(5); "your empty mouth" in 10 recalls "his empty skin" (5). And the wasted "days of unraveled light" that Neruda now attributes to Machu Picchu recall ironically the passionate "nights raveled out" that he had hoped for in canto 1. These verbal recurrences along with many others bring about the twofold vision of *Alturas de Macchu Picchu,* which is the poem's reason for being. Neruda, having known contemporary misery such as he found in northern Chile's bleak mining region, focuses both on the society around him and on the misery of Machu Picchu's forgotten inhabitants: one vision responds to the other. It is a difficult but desirable historical perspective—one which compels him to question the magnificent city.

That Neruda's tone and the very shape of his verse have changed in canto 10 immediately affects the job of translation. Most noticeably, the sixteen sentences that make up the canto are without exception questions and imperatives. Ranging from one to eleven lines long, they either ask or demand to know something the city has not revealed:

> Hunger, coral of humankind,
> hunger, hidden plant, root of the woodcutter,
> hunger, did your reef-edge climb
> to these high and ruinous towers?

The shock of this question in Spanish is its message to the ear and the eye that nothing keeps "hambre (hunger)" from "hombre (man)" but one small vowel:

> Hambre, coral del hombre,
> hambre, planta secreta, raíz de los leñadores,
> hambre, subió tu raya de arrecife
> hasta estas altas torres desprendidas?

In this triple invocation of "hunger," Neruda seems to be calling an oracle out of the city, an unwilling or clandestine oracle. To ask if hunger "climbed" to the city he uses "subir," the same verb he used when he himself climbed "through the lost jungle" (6) and when he bid his "amor americano" "climb up with me" (8). By that measure, hunger retains as active a presence, as dramatic a role, at Machu Picchu as the poet does. What's more, by calling hunger both a "root" and a "reef," he makes it organic to the site and also gives it another lexical hold on Machu Picchu, the "high reef of the human dawn" (6).

Neruda has moved pass the spectacle of "stone upon stone" to the lives beneath them. At this moment, one of the poem's most intense, he presses his interrogation into an imperative mood that would commit him bodily to the human fact at Machu Picchu:

> Yo te interrogo, sal de los caminos,
> muéstrame la cuchara, déjame, arquitectura,
> roer con un palito estambres de piedra,
> subir todos los escalones del aire hasta el vacío,
> rascar la entraña hasta tocar el hombre.
>
> (I question you, salt of the roads,
> show me the trowel; architecture, let me
> grind stone stamens with a stick,
> climb every step of air up to the void,
> scrape in the womb till I touch man.)

Something about our word "architecture," probably its flat accenting and dim vowel sounds, makes it much less potent than "arquitectura" to stand as the poet's interlocutor, so I shift its position a little to help my "I" confront the city's monumental form. In almost any other context, grinding "stone stamens with a stick" would create an inexcusable alliteration, but here that very insistence reinforces Neruda's need to work his way into the makings of the city. Now it is not the "alturas" of Machu Picchu he reaches but "la entraña." Although the word means "entrail" or "inmost recess," I would risk translating "rascar la entraña hasta tocar el hombre" as "scrape in the womb till I touch man," because Neruda has penetrated to the origin, the "mother of stone" whose sons lie buried in her. (I also have the best precedent for hearing "entraña" as "womb": Neruda himself translated a phrase from Blake—"the virgin ... shall awaken her womb"—with the word "entraña.") With this quasi-filial yet sexually invasive entrance into Machu Picchu, he can now "touch man" where before he could not "touch with my streaming hands" (4) those who denied him. What's more, in asking to grind the stones he comes to delve in the womb: that is, by committing his own handwork to the ruined city, he discovers its human basis.

Further questions—were rags, tears, and blood the human lot?—lead to canto 10's strongest imperative: "Devuélveme el esclavo que enterraste!" Anything but the directest possible version—"Give me back the slave you buried!"—would vitiate the anger audible in Neruda's voice when he reads this line. Larrea, assuming Inca governance to have been provident, disallows the assumption of misery and exploitation behind "esclavo." Even if he is right, for Neruda it matters more to create a continuum between then and now, a deep-seated incentive behind the present struggle for social justice. Though his Mexican and Peruvian friends, such as Diego Rivera and Uriel García, found inspiration in a specifically Indian heritage, Neruda could make more human contact and moral cause with the poor as such, with the worker. It matters most to him that the worker at Machu Picchu was undeniably anonymous and is now forgotten. "Tell me how he slept," Neruda asks, and "if every course of stone / weighed down his sleep, and if he fell underneath."

Then he turns and speaks to another face of Machu Picchu: "Antigua América, novia sumergida (Ancient America, sunken bride)." It is not a mother now, or a slave, but some potential innocence that Neruda imagines was exposed to the "empty height of the gods," the "bloodstained body of the new grain." These forces—perhaps they signify Inca religion and forced labor—provoke the canto's final question to a "buried America":

> América enterrada, guardaste en lo más bajo,
> en el amargo intestino, como un águila, el hambre?

> (buried America, did you keep in the deepest part
> of your bitter gut, like an eagle, hunger?)

Again the tolling word is "hambre," but unlike the previous lines, which began "Hambre, coral del hombre," these prolong the question until its last word is inevitable. In Spanish the ear does not notice an unstressed syllable at the end, as in "hambre," because virtually every line has one. In English the ear does mind it. I could end emphatically on "your bitter gut," but would rather let Neruda's accusation reach its true close with a slightly troubling sound and rhythm: "like an eagle, hunger."

No more questions are needed. Now an imperative based on Neruda's key preposition, "a través (through, across)," finally completes the gesture begun in canto 1 when he plunged his hand into the earth. Canto 11 opens:

> A través del confuso esplendor,
> a través de la noche de piedra, déjame hundir la mano
> y deja que en mí palpite, como un ave mil años prisionera,
> el viejo corazón del olvidado!

> (Through the dazing splendor,
> through the night of stone, let me plunge my hand
> and let there beat in me, like a bird a thousand years
>   imprisoned,
> the old forgotten human heart!)

To make the kind of rolling rhythm that Whitman's poems often start with, this passage could have gone: "Down through the dazing splendor, / down through the night of stone let me plunge my hand." I still regret not letting it go that way, but "a través" alone does not quite justify "down," even if the verb "hundir (plunge)" might. (Now and then, in an account such as this, one can have one's cake and eat it too, by being discreet in translation and then reckless in commentary.) In canto 1, Neruda had moved instinctually down to the genital quick. Now, having found hunger in America's "deepest part" (10), he descends into history with the same gesture of plunging his hand—and with ambiguous suggestions of the Aztec ritual in which an Indian's heart was cut out alive. The human heart Neruda seeks is "a thousand years imprisoned," or might I have said "arrested"? Though that word takes "prisionera" too literally and makes an unwanted pun on cardiac arrest, it would suggest the working of history in *Alturas de Macchu Picchu,* where an original American life, arrested for centuries as if frozen in stone, needs the poet to release it.

Neruda's passage, another four-line imperative, moves toward the verb "caer (fall)." In "Galope muerto," "Agua sexual," and throughout most of *Residencia en la tierra,* the word had signaled a kind of dripping away, a decadence or death that the poet had somehow to counter. Only in "Entrada a la madera" could he "fall . . . / to a forgotten room in ruins" and still come up with new life. Earlier in *Alturas de Macchu Picchu,* Neruda says twice that everything that used to support the city's life is fallen. Now "caer" occurs to him as he makes a vital descent from the splendid structure down into human nature:

> Déjame olvidar hoy esta dicha, que es más ancha que el mar,
> porque el hombre es más ancho que el mar y que sus islas,
> y hay que caer en él como en un pozo para salir del fondo
> con un ramo de agua secreta y de verdades sumergidas.
>
> (Let me forget today this joy that is broader than the sea,
> because man is broader than sea and islands
> and we must fall in him as in a well to rise from the bottom
> with a branch of secret water and sunken truths.)

The verb "caer" comes almost to signify plunging rather than lapsing, as if by some mythic, pre-Christian descent and return, Neruda would redeem the life that fell away at Machu Picchu. Still, this passage poses a puzzling choice. The third-person construction, "hay que caer en él como en un pozo," means "it is necessary to," "one must fall in him as in a well," but that sounds too impersonal at such a juncture. The question is whether

Neruda wants to instruct or to include the reader: "you must" or "we must"? It would thicken the poem's dramatic plot to have him turn here and say "you must," addressing us directly for the first time. But I think he means to involve himself (and the reader no less) by saying that "we" must fall into humankind to rise with sunken truths. These "verdades sumergidas" are sunken in the sense of being forgotten, out of reach, but also latent—we remember the inchoate energy that "Galope muerto" locates in a "sumergida lentitud" or "sunken slowness," and the germinal core of things to which Neruda falls in "Entrada a la madera." We risk falling in order to discover these truths.

A startlingly kindred idea to Neruda's exists in North American poetry—not in Eliot, for whom descent usually meant purgation, but in William Carlos Williams. A brief, little-noticed chapter from *In the American Grain* (1925), entitled "Descent," honors Sam Houston for leaving civilization to spend many years among the Cherokee Indians. "It is imperative that we *sink*," says Williams, giving us a perfect English equivalent for Neruda's "hay que caer." Both poets decried any system that either repressed or transcended human sensuality and suffering. Both sank a taproot into the common clay where they lived.

Something must be keeping Neruda from reaching mankind's sunken truths if it takes so many imperatives to get him released: "let me grind stone stamens . . . let me plunge my hand . . . let there beat in me . . . let me forget." It is in fact the sublimity of Machu Picchu, which gave his poem its title and which here he calls "this joy" and "dazing splendor," that now keeps him from the city's human basis. Canto 11 goes on:

> Déjame olvidar, ancha piedra, la proporción poderosa,
> la trascendente medida, las piedras del panal,
> y de la escuadra déjame hoy resbalar
> la mano sobre la hipotenusa de áspera sangre y cilicio.

> (Let me forget, broad stone, the sovereign symmetry,
> transcendent measure, honeycombed stones,
> and from the square edge let me this day slide
> my hand down the hypotenuse of haircloth and bitter blood.)

He has been fascinated, gratified, exalted, but is now not to be confined by the architectonics of Machu Picchu, its harmonious geometry of rectangles, squares, trapezoids, triangles, polygons, diagonals, perpendiculars, slopes, and curves. If Neruda did not turn on the city this way, demanding to forget the unforgettable stature of it, *Alturas de Macchu Picchu* would remain a powerful but conventional meditation. As it is, he hits on an astonishing image that ties the great structure to its invisible human cost: "and from the square edge let me this day slide / my hand down the hypotenuse of haircloth and bitter blood." Since we share a common geometry with Neruda, his image loses nothing in translation. "Hypotenuse"! What a word for this poem—something that connects the stone's square sides, opposes their perfect angle, and remains unseen by onlookers until the poet traces it with his hand.

The compassion generated in this image leads Neruda back to the bodies of men and women asleep or dead at Machu Picchu. He names three of them: Juan Cortapiedras, Juan Comefrío, Juan Piesdescalzos. Some translators retain "Juan," but since Neruda has given the Indians a common Spanish name, an English one seems called for. "John" sounds too formal. For an everyday worker's name, maybe "Jack" will do. Jack Stonebreaker, Jack Coldbiter, Jack Barefoot. These nuances matter because the act of naming must bring Neruda face to face with his predecessors. He ends the canto by calling them up, reclaiming (only male, it seems) Indians from the bitter gut: "rise to be born with me, brother."

CANTO 12: "AS IF I WERE ANCHORED HERE WITH YOU"

Eliot puts it this way: "We are born with the dead: / See, they return, and bring us with them." Neruda brings them with himself, so that his far and near visions coalesce. When the poet says "rise to be born with me, brother," he is not only summoning the past into the present but urging the present into the future. "Sube a nacer conmigo, hermano": that simple imperative addressed to Indian workers also opens the final canto, and bristles with chances and disappointments for the translator. "Subir" has meant "climb" in this poem: the poet climbed to Machu Picchu, and so did hunger. Now Neruda is asking a dead man to climb up to him, but I hear something more solemn, probably not "climb" but "rise to be born with me, brother." Tarn avoids the revolutionary jargon of "rise" and "brother" by having Neruda say, "Arise to birth with me, my brother," but possibly it should not be avoided. And though it weakens "nacer" to have to translate it as "to be born," changing Neruda's verb into the noun "birth" partly frustrates his call for a momentous act, an act in which the poet is also "to be born." English lacks an active verb for the process of coming to birth, but Neruda had "nacer" and used it throughout his poetry. Perhaps the death of his own mother when he was born and the distressful birth of his only child made him cherish the word, since he attached it to plants, birds, waves, nations, poems, all the things he valued most.

The verb "nacer," carrying a personal weight as well as a political metaphor, brings Neruda to the critical moment of his American genesis—a moment in which personal and political motives are united. "Rise to be born with me (Sube a nacer conmigo)": in renewing himself, the poet would bring others to a kind of rebirth. This double process belongs to the poem's broadly sexual configuration, in which Neruda blends the impulses of a son and a lover. Through the early cantos he has been probing a love-less quotidian world for some passionate response to his "streaming hands" (4), some consummation, some "patria nupcial" (1). Then he climbs to the site through "lost jungles (selvas perdidas)" (6)—they are words he often used for the ambience of his childhood—and reaches the "mother of stone." She is now to be delivered of his brothers, as he scrapes the womb and plunges his hand toward forgotten man. "Look at me from the bottom of earth," Neruda says to him in canto 12, "Mírame desde el fondo de la tierra," and the translator (in a state of ideal alertness) will recall having dealt with that phrase somewhere before. In the opening lyric of *Veinte poemas de amor* (1924), Neruda had told his woman that he digs in her "and makes a son leap from under earth," from "el fondo de la tierra"—the same phrase as in *Alturas de Macchu Picchu*. I translate it differently because in 1924 the lover as husbandman is speaking, in 1945 the visionary pilgrim, but over the years Neruda's impulse remained much the same. As he grounded himself in all of American place and time, the sexual impulse had more to work on. Here in canto 12 it makes him reach into the recesses of Machu Picchu for a passionate connection with his fellow beings.

"Dame la mano desde la profunda / zona de tu dolor diseminado (Give me your hand out of the deep / region seeded by all your grief)." For the demands of this canto, Neruda adopts the eleven-syllable line again, which can be matched by four-stress (and often eight-syllable) English lines. And by this time, a semantic depth can be felt behind the poem's words. Hands of modern man that drilled the pulsing metal; the poet's hands plunging into earth, lifting bandages, looking for love or rest, oiling the vanished beams; the Indians' "spidery hands" that suddenly fell but hold up the city like a bowl—all these hands join in the simplest of utterances, "Dame la mano (Give me your hand)." In canto 12 Neruda imagined Machu Picchu's dead united in "the deepest" ravine. Now in that depth he can see not only their unity but their "dolor diseminado," and the memory of a rock that generously "keeps its flower sown (diseminada)," in canto 2, offsets this later suggestion of Christian suffering in "dolor."

"Give me your hand": Neruda reaches for his "hermano," but then breaks that movement with startling honesty:

> No volverás del fondo de las rocas.
> No volverás del tiempo subterraneo.
> No volverá tu voz endurecida.
> No volverán tus ojos taladrados.

English can only barely approximate those primary negative stresses, much less the multiple assonance in Neruda's lines:

> You won't come back from bottom rock.
> You won't come back from time under ground.
> No coming back with your hardened voice.
> No coming back with your drilled-out eyes.

The repeated pulse of "You won't come back" and the idiomatic abruptness of "No coming back" can help enforce the blank fact of this loss. To redeem the loss, Neruda asks various laborers at Machu Picchu to look at him "from the bottom of earth, / plowman, weaver, voiceless shepherd." He still speaks to them as "tu," as individuals, but then at the end of a long appeal he shifts to the second-person plural: "traed a la copa de esta nueva vida / vuestros viejos dolores enterrados (bring all your age-old buried / griefs to the cup of this new life)." In widening his voice to address them all, Neruda effects a stirring change. All of them fell, died a like death, are equally forgotten, and now can be called back collectively. From here until the end of the poem, a sequence of sixteen such imperatives summons the dead as well as their painful labor: "Show me your blood and your furrow," the old lamps and flints, the stumbling, the whips. Once, even though he has said there is "No coming back with your hardened voice," the poet prompts them to speech:

> decidme: aquí fui castigado
> porque la joya no brilló o la tierra
> no entregó a tiempo la piedra o el grano.

The verb "entregar (give up, hand over)" rings deeper now, thanks to earlier uses when Neruda was reaching out to his fellow creatures for love. Now he has found what he was after all those years:

> say to me: here I was punished
> when a gem didn't shine or the earth
> give forth its stone or grain on time.

He wants to bear it all in mind, including "la madera en que os crucificaron (the wood they crucified you on)."

Neruda's voice takes on a terrific plangency in reading this section aloud. We hear why in a line the poem has been heading for all along: "Yo vengo a hablar por vuestra boca muerta (I come to speak through your dead mouth)." Since "por" can signify either "through" or "for" their dead mouths, he may mean to speak both on their behalf and in place of them, though that would preclude his taking on their pain directly. What is not ambiguous is Neruda's phrase "vuestra boca muerta." Since "vuestra," the possessive of "vosotros," modifies "boca," a singular noun, the dead all have one mouth (thanks to a grammatical twist unavailable in English). Neruda convokes them as a unified community, relying now on the essential medium of speech as the poem's final period begins:

> A través de la tierra juntad todos
> los silenciosos labios derramados
> y desde el fondo habladme toda esta larga noche
> como si yo estuviera con vosotros anclado.

> (All through the earth join all
> the silent wasted lips
> and speak from the depths to me all this long night
> as if I were anchored here with you.)

"All through," which combines the senses of "a través" as both "through" and "across," helps a new idea emerge at this point: the idea that communicating down through the earth with humanity's past puts him in touch across present time as well, with "all / the silent wasted lips." Neruda's twofold presence at Machu Picchu, in pre-Columbian and mid-twentieth-century time, gives him this privilege and lets him speak "as if I were anchored here with you": the subjective "as if I were" says he is and he isn't there, he shares their plight and at the same time his voice translates it into present terms.

"Through me many long dumb voices," Neruda might have been saying. Possibly it seems strange that a line from *Song of Myself* should provide the kind of free translation for *Alturas de Macchu Picchu* that Eliot's *Four Quartets* sometimes provides, since between Eliot and Whitman so little affinity exists. Neruda needed a way of moving through time and place, evoking the past so that at certain points it might come up into the present with a rising, regenerative force: this is the way Eliot moves in *Four Quartets*. Within such a pattern, though, the quality of Neruda's voice and feeling recalls Whitman's: the plasmic human sympathy, the welcoming of materiality and sensousness, the awareness of common lives and labor, the openness toward the human prospect, the poet's volunteering himself as a redeemer.

"Contadme todo, cadena a cadena, / eslabón a eslabón, y paso a paso": "tell me everything, chain by chain, / link by link, and step by step." By this point a full set of related terms has developed within the poem: tell, say, speak, sing, language, word, syllable, lips, mouth, voice, shout, silent, silenced. So much is vested in the act of speech that a reader must ask what connection speech has with other actions and passions. The question, on which theories of language and literature turn, touches *Alturas de Macchu Picchu* in two ways. First, because Neruda moves indistinguishably between actual and symbolic narrative, each kind of narrative shares its virtue with the other: his climb to the ruins goes beyond mere credible fact, while plunging his hand to the earth's quick keeps a physical credibility about it. Second, speech enables the poet to forge a collectivity. Neruda prized the oral, communal nature of poetry and recognized the voiceless anonymity of the poor: in *Alturas de Macchu Picchu* he calls attention to the need for voice-to-voice contact between himself and the city's inhabitants. Perhaps even more critically, he is aware of being a poet, not a worker, and of dealing with workers who are not poets. By establishing speech as an authentic medium between him and them, he can turn his words—"let me grind stone stamens"—into a virtual action, just as the voiceless workers can "tell me everything."

The lines beginning "contadme todo (tell me everything)," go on immediately to say "afilad los cuchillos (file the knives)," as if both kinds of activity, telling and filing, came from the same sphere and followed the same laws. Neruda not only speaks "as if" he were at Machu Picchu, he identifies what can be told with what can be done:

> afilad los cuchillos que guardasteis,
> ponedlos en mi pecho y en mi mano,
> como un río de rayos amarillos,
> como un río de tigres enterrados.

> (File the knives you kept by you,
> drive them into my chest and my hand
> like a river of riving yellow light,
> like a river where buried jaguars lie.)

A passage like this never ceases to need translating, partly because it makes so terrifying a gesture. The knife an Indian would have kept for handwork and for protection against animals or other people—is it to be used on an advocate, the poet exposing himself to whatever energy remains at Machu Picchu? In the United States we have little precedent for this kind and degree of a poet's commitment, except for Whitman's "I am the man, I suffer'd, I was there." So it challenges our resources to make a viable translation.

Take the four lines beginning "afilad los cuchillos (file the knives)." The music in them, the mesh of sound in rhythm, comes from Neruda's brilliant *e*-sounds, two per line, moving through patterns of alliteration and assonance. In English a corresponding music can emerge from bright *i*-sounds—"file the knives you kept by you, / drive them into my chest and my hand"—thanks to the (etymologically unrelated) "file" for "afilad," instead of the more usual "sharpen." For "ponedlos en mi pecho y en mi mano," the fairly bland "ponedlos" literally means "place them," but if Neruda wants to be given knives to defend the helpless dead, why "en mi pecho," in his chest? Does "pecho" here carry its figurative sense of "courage"? Since the preposition "en" can mean either "in" or "into" his chest, Neruda's line is ambiguous. Rather than leave it that way, I make the decision—a risky one, considering how much depends on it—that he wants to suffer the knives, not use them. Clearly Neruda desires to take onto himself the pain of those he is addressing—he has even asked to see the wood they were crucified on. So there is virtual truth in the imperative as I translate it. I hope I am not too influenced by the fact that "drive" resonates with "knives."

What effect has the double simile that follows this image of knives? Neruda's line, "como un río de rayos amarillos," forms such a tense arc of sound that it virtually eclipses the meaning of the words, let alone any equivalent translation of them. What occurs to me is an etymological deepening of "river" into "riving"—"like a river of riving yellow bolts" or "riving yellow light"—since "rayo" means "lightning bolt" or "ray of light." In the second simile, "como un río de tigres enterrados," "tigers" would prolong the bright sound, but "tigres" in South America refers to jaguars. I have felt for years that my literal translation—"like a river of buried jaguars"—needed lengthening into pentameter like the line above it, and needed intensifying as well. Now I see a change that will do it: "like a river where buried jaguars lie." The *i*-sound gets prolonged in "lie," and that word sustains—as the whole poem sustains—an energy not merely buried but latent, recoverable.

When the poet's secular voice asks an ancient people to give their pain to him, saying "file the knives you kept by you, / drive them into my chest and my hand," these wounds (if they really are a kind of stigmata) must

seem strangely familar to any reader of the New Testament. Then two similes extend and sharply modify this image, recasting it in a native milieu:
the pain Neruda takes on will be "like a river of riving yellow bolts, / like
a river where buried jaguars lie." The Urubamba River sends up sound and
mist around Machu Picchu; from the city you see it two thousand feet
below like a yellow ribbon gleaming and twisting. In this image, the river
lends the raw force of nature to the poet's agony. So does the underworld
presence of jaguars, perhaps the most powerful cult god of the Central Andes. For the North American and even the Latin American reader, then,
these two similes carry Neruda's Christ-like assumption of responsibility
beyond familiar ground. They also resist the tendency that any translation
has, by virtue of its being in one's native tongue, to assimilate what is
strange.

Five appeals to the silent lips bring Neruda's poem to a close. The first
two,

> Dadme el silencio, el agua, la esperanza.
> Dadme la lucha, el hierro, los volcanes,

do not demand much energy to translate, which could indicate a hollow-
ness in them—it depends on your mood:

> Give me silence, water, hope.
> Give me struggle, iron, volcanoes.

The next two are astir with possibilities:

> Apegadme los cuerpos como imanes.
> Acudid a mis venas y a mi boca.

Now and then a lucky or last-ditch thought turns up a likely word. For
"apegad," not "attach" or "cling" but "fasten" seems right to me: its
sound attracts it to "magnets (imanes)" and then to "hasten (acudid)" in
the next line:

> Fasten your bodies to me like magnets.
> Hasten to my veins and to my mouth.

These lines embody the kind of adhesive fellow-feeling that Neruda found
in Walt Whitman, and they do more than that. Having taken the forgotten
workers' knives in his chest and hand, Neruda now wants their flesh and
blood transfused into him. Lives that were stifled in the mother of stone
can rise to be born through him—through his veins, because some lamb's
blood he swallowed as a child and some children's blood he saw flowing

in Madrid's streets have brought him to a consangunity with those who
worked and died at Machu Picchu; and through his mouth, because this
genesis begins with a voice, Pablo Neruda's voice. "Yo vengo a hablar por
vuestra boca muerta," he had said, "I come to speak through your dead
mouth." Now the current of speech shifts the other way at last. Neruda
asks his American predecessors, much as the translator asks the poet, to

> speak through my words and my blood,

and this final appeal the poem itself has by now fulfilled:

> Hablad por mis palabras y mi sangre.

AFTERMATHS OF TRANSLATION

Pablo Neruda died on September 23, 1973, twelve days after the military coup in Chile. There was occasion to recite his poetry in translation,
to bring North Americans closer to Chile in whatever way possible. At one
point, I discovered a strange side effect of translating at its most earnest:
the experience of being possessed, the illusion that the lines you've translated are speaking through you and for you. I had memorized passages
from my version of *Alturas de Macchu Picchu* without intending to. There
is, I found, a great difference between writing down translations on the
page and speaking the lines to expectant faces:

> I bent my head into the deepest waves,
> dropped down through sulfurous calm
> and went back.

One naturally feels an empathy with first-person narrative and lyric
speech. As a translator I have felt something more: a strange sense of having authored the lines I am speaking. Maybe this illusion is necessary to
generate in English an idiomatic, lifegiving voice.

From the illusion of authorship an even stranger illusion or self-
deception follows, as a kind of occupational hazard. After steeping myself
in Neruda's Spanish, I set it aside and focus for days on my English version
to make it as authentic as possible. Eventually in turning back to the Spanish, I may by this time have forgotten its exact wording and configuration.
I am astonished to find that somehow it now sounds like an uncannily
good translation of my own poem, with perhaps a few odd spots: "descendí como gota"—that's very good, for "dropped down," but perhaps
"lo más genital" seems a little disappointing, after "genital quick." This

illusion does not last long, but in a deeper sense it does last, and for the engaged reader as well as for the translator. It means that we are liable for what the words have to say.

One last cautionary tale on the hazards of translating Neruda also stems from September 1973. On September 17, a poem was circulated by international wire services in which Neruda was heard to denounce violently Nixon and Pinochet, among others, as "hyenas ravening / our history . . . satraps bribed a thousand times over / and sellouts, driven / by the wolves of Wall Street, / machines starving for pain." I couldn't see how Neruda, extremely ill at the time, could have produced such a concerted outburst. But after hesitating for fear of endangering his position, I was persuaded to translate the poem. It was published immediately on the Op-Ed page of the *New York Times,* carried in many other periodicals, and used as a poster. Then I learned that "The Satraps," as it was called, was actually written by Neruda twenty-five years earlier, about Central American dictatorships backed by the United States. It seems that a Jewish literary magazine in Buenos Aires had adjusted the dictators' names to apply to 1973.

I am chagrined at not having recognized the poem, but feel a good deal more satisfied that I and others were deceived—that Neruda's anger had its impact at another moment of Latin American history. Thousands were being killed in Chile, as that poem says, "with no other law but torture / and the lashing hunger of the people." On looking up the original poem I found that one line had been garbled over the wires. It was not "máquinas hambrientas de dolores," but "dólares"—not machines starving for pain, but for dollars. But the mistranslation had its own truth and I let it stand.

ROBIN WARNER

The Politics of Pablo Neruda's
España en el corazón

In the two decades that have elapsed since Archibald MacLeish complained that "literary legislators no longer argue the question whether poetry *can* make sense of the public experience. They argue the reasons why it can't," critics, in general, have become noticeably more tolerant of politically motivated verse, especially that of the Left. Provided the causes it champions can be regarded as broadly humanistic rather than narrowly sectarian, such verse is not disqualified from critical consideration as serious poetry. Such a criterion begs the important question of the extent to which poetry written in the context of a particular historical situation may be attuned to specific political issues. The question has considerable relevance for present-day readers of Neruda's *España en el corazón,* composed during the Spanish Civil War. The political ideals to which the collection gives expression—freedom, patriotic duty, the dignity of man—are neither narrow nor dated; but the point is not that Neruda sought to demonstrate the rightness of such exemplarily liberal causes, but rather that his support for them served to further the interests of a particular faction among the forces opposed to Franco.

It would serve little purpose here to offer any comment on the respective merits of the conflicting political tendencies within the non-insurrectionary zone, but a summary of the main areas of dissension may be helpful. On one side were ranged those who sought to present and conduct the war as the defence of a legitimate democratic government against military treason aided by international fascism; on the other were those who

From *Hispanic Studies in Honour of Frank Pierce,* edited by John England. © 1980 by Robin Warner. Sheffield University Print Unit, 1980.

viewed the conflict as a process of consolidating the achievements of a popular revolution. The "legitimist" camp not only comprised Republicans and moderate Socialists, but also enjoyed the influential support of the Communists, whose Popular Front policy entailed an alliance with bourgeois-democratic parties not merely against the common enemy, fascism, but also against the "extremist" left. By virtue of its control of censorship and covert manipulation of organizations such as the Alianza de Intelectuales Antifascistas, as well as by its prestige in the eyes of the younger generation of writers and intellectuals, the Communist Party was able to create a certain ideological consensus which Neruda, to judge by the viewpoint expressed in *España en el corazón*, seems to have shared. The Communists campaigned vigorously for recognition of and obedience to centralized civil and military authority, and stressed the priority, over any thoroughgoing assault on social inequalities, of ensuring the survival of the Republican regime; thus they consistently attacked the power of workers' defence committees, collectives and other manifestations of the popular movement which damaged middle-class interests. At the same time the Party was engaged in rallying popular support, boosting combative morale and attracting recruits to its ranks. Thus the strong emotional appeal entailed by such a programme also served to facilitate another important function of Communist propaganda: that of glossing over the contradictions inherent in the policies—in some respects, counter-revolutionary—for which it sought to gain support.

España en el corazón embodies a number of ideological formulas which coincide with the Communist point of view. The most salient of these are: persistent reminders of the need to subordinate personal feelings and aspirations to the war-effort; exemplifications of the invincible strength which stems from national unity, transcending differences of class; advocation of liberal-humanistic principles; a strong appeal to the emotions, together with a stress on the value of visceral (rather than intellectual) commitment to the struggle.

The most obvious indication of the importance attached to the war-effort in *España en el corazón* lies in the number of poems which take the armed forces and their achievements as a theme. Over one third of the collection (aptly subtitled "Himno a las glorias del pueblo en guerra") is devoted to some aspect of the armed struggle, if not to the People's Army in general, to such subsidiary topics as the defence of Madrid, the battle of El Jarama, the International Brigades or the anti-tank units. Other poems, such as "Canto a las madres de los milicianos muertos," clearly illustrate another important facet of Neruda's treatment of the war theme: the essential contribution of the populace as a whole to the pursuit of military victory. Civilians and soldiers are shown to share equally—the militiamen with their lives, the mothers with their grief—the heavy burden of sacrifice for a greater cause. It is instructive to note at this point that the eight-point manifesto issued by the Communist Party in the first months of the war lays repeated emphasis on the need for non-combatants as much as soldiers to submit to discipline, make sacrifices and accept without demur the dispositions of a system of higher authority. It is significant that Neruda's "Oda solar al Ejército del Pueblo" not only makes clear the link between civilians and the military by stressing the fact that ordinary workers and craftsmen have been called from their peacetime trades to serve as soldiers, but also manages to suggest an analogy between the socially beneficial cooperation of different industries and the hierarchical command-structure of the People's Army:

> Fotógrafos, mineros, ferroviarios, hermanos
> del carbón y la piedra, parientes del martillo,
> bosque, fiesta de alegres disparos, adelante,
> guerrilleros, mayores, sargentos, comisarios políticos,
> aviadores del pueblo, combatientes nocturnos,
> combatientes marinos, adelante.

While the war-effort is presented as an enterprise which should absorb all energies and override any hesitations, Neruda also tends to echo the Communist definition of the struggle as a popular national war of independence. It is the traditional ideal of freedom which must be defended at all costs. He assures the *antitanquistas* that:

> La Libertad os recogió en las minas,
> y pidió paz para vuestros arados:
> la Libertad se levantó llorando
> por los caminos, gritó en los corredores
> de las casas.

Madrid is similarly described as "la ciudad española en que la libertad acorralada / pudo caer y morir mordida por las bestias." The unifying principle of the Republican Zone is more frequently presented as "patria" or by the formula "España" than as "el pueblo," although the distinction between these concepts is, in any case, blurred. The enemy forces are characterized as traitors, foreigners or self-interested cosmopolitans and references to "moros" and to Africa are common. The International Brigades, on the other hand, are seen to be composed of men who, although they

have come from abroad ("de lejos y lejos"), have been forced out of their
own homelands and have thus honourably transferred their patriotic alle-
giance. The idea of national unity in defence of the Republic is also supported by Neruda's tendency to describe resistance to the Nationalists in
terms of the fusion of heterogenous elements into a monolithic force. To
take only one example, the inhabitants of Madrid, in suppressing the military rebellion of July 1936, are shown to have acted in an irresistibly concerted fashion:

> reuniendo y llamando con una voz de océano,
> con un rostro cambiado para siempre
> por la luz de la sangre, como una vengadora
> montaña, como una silbante
> estrella de cuchillos.

The polity threatened by the military insurrection, at least in the form it
had taken before the war, is presented as one which made possible a state
of peace and prosperity wherein all men co-operated harmoniously to realize the productive potential of Nature. Such a picture certainly emerges
from Neruda's evocation of Madrid in the immediate pre-war years, before
the onset of war-time shortages:

> Todo
> eran grandes voces, sal de mercaderías,
> aglomeraciones de pan palpitante,
> mercados de mi barrio de Argüelles con su estatua
> como un tintero pálido entre las merluzas:
> el aceite llegaba a las cucharas,
> un profundo latido
> de pies y manos llenaba las calles,
> metros, litros, esencia
> aguda de la vida.

Even when they are torn away from their fruitful toil by the demands of
the war, the soldiers of the Republic, it is suggested, do not lose their relationship with the productive forces of Nature. The heroes of El Jarama are
"formidable y trigal"; the immortal spirits of militiamen fallen in battle
"sonríen desde la tierra / levantando los puños sobre el trigo"; *antitanquistas* lie in wait "sembrados / en los campos, oscuros como siembra." The
enemy forces, on the other hand, are associated with all that is inimical to
the earth's natural abundance and its potential for human fulfilment. Neruda constantly characterizes them as vile excrement, as weeds and stones,

as wild and destructive scavengers. They are unnatural in the sense that they have no place in the natural, creative order of things:

> Chacales que el chacal rechazaría,
> piedras que el cardo seco mordería escupiendo,
> víboras que las víboras odiaran.

Neruda's vision of a new social order, where men live and work at peace with each other and with their environment can be seen as one aspect of the way *España en el corazón* emphasizes the value of "lo humano." Such an emphasis in turn reflects a widespread trend of thought in left-wing intellectual circles during the thirties. Even before the Civil War, Neruda had announced his adherence to this tendency in the poem which first states his resolve to situate his art within a wider social context, "Reunión bajo las nuevas banderas":

> un día
> palpitante de sueños
> humanos, un salvaje
> cereal ha llegado
> a mi devoradora noche
> para que junte mis pasos de lobo
> a los pasos del hombre.

The "new humanism" (the title of a manifesto presented by the editorial board of *Hora de España* on the occasion of the Second International Writers' Congress) certainly comprised elements of Marxist thought, but also had the useful war-time function of reconciling conflictive viewpoints under the banner of a none-too-specific if fervently proclaimed ideal. Thus we find, for example, that the heroism which is extolled in *España en el corazón* is most frequently of the type which derives from the courage and fortitude of ordinary men and women, of "tú que vives, Juan, / hoy, tú que miras, Pedro," who make up the "humana orilla" which turns back the tide of fascist aggression. The numerous descriptions of human suffering reach a climax in "Canto sobre unas ruinas," a poem which transcends the context of the Civil War to express a more comprehensively tragic view of the human condition:

> no hay raíces
> para el hombre: todo descansa apenas
> sobre un temblor de lluvia.

If the Republic is seen as the champion of human values, the enemy, on the other hand, is systematically characterized as abominable. The Nationalists and their allies are frequently described in terms of what is physically repugnant—excremental and pestilential matter of various kinds. Again, they are often given traditionally inhuman attributes—they are referred to as monsters, beasts or savages. Occasionally more conceptual methods are employed to establish that the enemy represents the antithesis of human values. In "Bombardeo," for example, Neruda uses reiterated interrogatives to suggest a callousness which surpasses ordinary human comprehension:

> Quién?, por caminos, quién,
> quién, quién? en sombra, en sangre, quién?
> en destello, quién, quién?

The enemy is often depersonalised by such terms as "sotanas" or "uniformes," or, with an even stronger imputation of inward emptiness, by descriptions such as "sacos" or "los enmascacarados." He is so lacking in human feeling that avenging bullets cannot reach his heart, but only "el sitio del corazón." Perhaps the most striking example of this concept of the abominable is to be found in the curse pronounced on Franco—the fervent hope that he should be barred from the common mortal fate and condemned to be haunted eternally by the human suffering he has caused:

> Maldito, que sólo lo humano
> te persiga, que dentro del absoluto fuego de las cosas,
> no te consumas, que no te pierdas
> en la escala del tiempo.

The humanistic preoccupation of *España en el corazón* is also expressed, in a simplified form, through an emphasis on the primacy of basic human feelings, with an implied devaluation of purely intellectual considerations. The title itself refers to a visceral attachment to Spain on the part of the Chilean poet. As he confesses in "Explico algunas cosas," his feelings are so strong that they override not only his inclination to lyrical poetry but also the claim of his native country on his inspirational loyalty:

> Preguntaréis por qué su poesía
> no nos habla del sueño, de las hojas,
> de los grandes volcanes de su país natal?

The point which Neruda makes in this poem is that the magnitude of events in Spain has impelled him to take his poetry out of the realm of private experience (the peaceful and happy "casa de las flores") and into the public world. To those who would question the wisdom of such a change his answer is a reiterated challenge:

> Venid a ver la sangre por las calles.
> venid a ver
> la sangre por las calles,
> venid a ver la sangre
> por las calles!

There is no scope for rational debate; to cavil would be to deny basic human feelings of shock, grief and anger at the slaughter of innocent children.

The exalted tone of much of *España en el corazón*, the rituals of celebration or mourning, the solemn curses, the abundance of rhetorical questions and emotive repetitions, certainly reflect the importance attached to sentiment. So, less obviously, do the frequent instances of plain statement. The facts, Neruda seems to say, speak for themselves; no poetic adornment could enhance their emotional impact. A good example of this technique is provided by "Tierras ofendidas," where the flow of impassioned but somewhat abstract rhetoric is interrupted by a starkly horrifying reference to the panic-stricken flight from Málaga: "las enloquecidas madres / azotaban la piedra con sus recién nacidos."

Emotion is nothing, of course, if not personal, and it is true that to transfer public issues to the sphere of subjective reaction is to depoliticize them in an important sense (a tendency by no means necessarily inimical to the policies Neruda supports). But we should realize that when, for instance, he states that he witnessed the arrival of the International Brigades "con estos ojos que tengo, con este corazón que mira," he is speaking not simply for himself but on behalf of his fellow citizens who share his feelings of gratitude and admiration. An assumed identity of viewpoint underlies *España en el corazón;* the poet is fully aware of his civic, commemorative function. The matching of public duty and personal feeling is forcefully conveyed in "Paisaje después de una batalla":

> agárrenlo mis párpados hasta nombrar y herir,
> guarde mi sangre este sabor de sombra
> para que no haya olvido.

Or again, in "Batalla del río Jarama," Neruda adds, with considerable verve, a traditional disclaimer of his individual merit:

> Jarama, para hablar de tus regiones
> de esplendor y dominio, no es mi boca
> suficiente, y es pálida mi mano.

The function of certain stylistic features of *España en el corazón* can be fully appreciated only if the ideological framework of the collection is kept in mind. Many of them are associated with a desire to avoid hermeticism and communicate with a wide audience, "no con unos iniciados en los secretos del oficio, sino con las multitudes." The use of traditional (and thus widely acceptable) prosodic features such as regular stanzas, metres and, occasionally, rhyme, is in keeping with such an aim. So too, presumably, is the prevalence of traditional types of metonymy conspicuously absent in Neruda's pre-war verse: "sotanas (the Clergy)," "uniformes (the Military)," "espada (armed aggression)," "Madrid (the populace of Madrid)" and the personification of "Patria," "Libertad" and "Tradición." A tendency to employ conventional epithets ("áspera lucha," for example) might also be classed as part of the poetry's leaning toward wide appeal and intelligibility, although it is true that the conventionality often seems to derive from the clichés of propaganda in phrases such as "solemne patria," "voluntad insigne" or "noble tierra." The use of plain statement, already mentioned as an emotive device, can also be regarded as part of the tendency to expressive clarity; it acquires further significance, however, if we consider its relationship to the recurrent theme of individual self-effacement. By using simple and even prosaic language the poet can suggest that his personal pretensions as an artificer of words must be subordinated to his public duty. Just as Neruda praises the soldiers of the People's Army for abandoning the tools of their trades for a rifle ("Los gremios en el frente"), so he sets a personal example, as a poet, to other "oficios," by renouncing his more refined skills and attuning his expression to the needs of a nation at war. When we read in "Explico algunas cosas" that "por las calles la sangre de los niños / corría simplemente, como sangre de niños," we share not only the poet's horror at what is happening in Madrid (the first city to suffer large-scale aerial bombardment), but also his sense of the inappropriateness of any attempt to devise imaginative correlatives for what he feels. Perhaps the most extreme example of this tendency is provided by "Como era España," where Neruda's complex response to the Spanish situation is conveyed not by a poem in the conventional sense, but by an extensive collage of place-names.

Another frequently used device which has interesting implications is the linking of antithetical qualities, especially when this takes the form of a soft-hard formula. To give only a few examples: bereaved mothers are exhorted to join together their tears "hasta hacerlas metales"; Spain is "proletaria de pétalos y balas"; the hope inspired by the International Brigades is like "un inmenso río con palomas de acero"; the heroic spirit of resistance in Madrid is a "deslizamiento de dulzura dura." Since blood can symbolize both strong passions and suffering or loss of life, its use in such a context is particularly apt. Thus, in "Explico algunas cosas" the shedding of innocent blood is transformed into a motif of unity and resolve to be revenged:

> Frente a vosotros he visto la sangre
> de España levantarse
> para ahogaros en una sola ola
> de orgullo y de cuchillos.

Similarly, it is the "eléctrica sangre" of Madrid which keeps the city's enemies at bay. As we have noted, the ideological content of *España en el corazón* tends to be presented through a series of clearly delineated antitheses, but it would appear that the use of this type of formula corresponds to more complex intentions than the basic propagandistic aim of discrediting the enemy forces and rallying support for the Popular Front. "Soft" elements are associated with human frailty, suffering and compassionate feelings, whereas "hard" ones have to do with solidarity and implacable resolve. The yoking of the two notions exemplifies the transformation of subjective feeling, through rigorous discipline, into effective combative morale, and so lends yet further support to Neruda's persistent call for the subordination of individual points of view to the demands of the war-effort. The appeal for submission to discipline and authority, moreover, is made through an exacerbation of emotional fervour rather than by admonitions against its dangers.

The present study, restricted as it is to features of *España en el corazón* which help us to identify Neruda's precise political orientation, can offer no general conclusions as to the work's poetic value. One important question is posed, however. If we accept that Neruda attempts to attract support not simply for broad principles, but for pragmatic policies as well, then we must concede that *España en el corazón* contains propaganda of the sort often held to preclude successful poetry. One ventures to suggest that the relationship between political ideology and the processes of poetic thought is too complex to permit such easy assumptions.

ENRICO MARIO SANTÍ

Vision and Time

I awake; but between me and nature remains a veil, a subtle
tissue; a mosquito net. Behind it, things have taken their place
in the world: brides receive their flowers, debtors their bills.
Where am I?

Thus begins "Diurno de Singapore," one of a dozen newspaper articles
that Neruda sent back to Chile while en route to the Far East in 1927.
Behind the "mosquito net," a veil separating poet and world, subject and
object, all things assume their place and elude his grasp. The final question
lends itself to two discrete interpretations. A literal reading, provided further in the same paragraph, simply locates the poet in space: "I'm in Singapore." But another, rhetorical option would instead leave the relation
between subject and veil unclear. Where is he, in fact, in relation to that
"subtle tissue"? What position can the poet assume, where can he stand,
in a world whose order somehow excludes him?

The above passage and its attendant questions may serve as a spring-
board for our discussion of *Residencia en la tierra*, the three-book cycle on
which Neruda's reputation as a visionary poet rests. It is in these books
that we can identify what I here call the visionary mode, the interplay of
subject and object as the basis of poetic perception. All prophetic poetry,
I have argued, is visionary in the sense of an imaginative statement predi-
cated on the mimesis of revelation. But to speak of a visionary mode in
particular implies recognition of a privileged perception in the speaker and

From *Pablo Neruda: The Poetics of Prophecy*. © 1982 by Cornell University Press.

its role in the poem's rhetorical structure. In visionary poetry the revelation of an object's truth stems from the perception of an alienated subject. In the above passage, for example, the speaker's visual range, isolated by the mosquito net, allows him to perceive two significant scenes that are related by the punctuation as sequential events. The sudden invasion of daylight accounts for the specifically visual experience, while the veil is but the symbol of the visionary process: the re*vela*tion or un*veil*ing of the object through the *re*veiling of language.

The term "visionary mode" is at once a restrictive and a comprehensive name for modernist poetics, a conception of the poet as an alienated subject who conveys images claimed to be truthful and significant. Such artistic truth, as Frank Kermode notes [in *Romantic Image*], "is unrelated to, and more exalted than, that of positivist science or any observation depending upon the discursive reason." The representation of this truth determines, in turn, a distinct rhetorical effect insofar as the mode depends on the dramatic presence of a passive prophetic speaker or persona. This passive speaker, more an agent than an instrument, is concerned with insightful perception and with knowledge that transforms obscure feelings into clear ideas. Thus the visionary mode identifies what throughout literary history has been variously described as "spots of time" (Wordsworth), "moments privilégiés" (Proust), "epiphanies" (Joyce), or even the Russian formalists' notion of art as defamiliarization—in short, the modernist concept of art as the fresh rearrangement of reality. Each of these formulas has a distinct structure of its own, of course, and my intention in lumping them together is to emphasize their common tenet: that visionary truth is inextricably linked to the artist's estrangement. That meaning was perhaps summarized best by Rimbaud, who in a memorable phrase claimed he was a seer because he was an *other*. "Car *je* est un autre (For *I* is an other)," he wrote to Paul Demeny in a phrase whose grammatical violence concealed a whole theory of poetic vision. The subject's self-distancing—that is, his own internal discontinuity or *dédoublement*—alienates the object in such a way that it prompts its rearrangement in inordinate, perhaps superior, ways unseen by normal eyes.

The assumption that *Residencia en la tierra* is ultimately guided by a visionary poetics has with varying degrees of explicitness governed critical readings since Amado Alonso's groundbreaking study. A visionary syntax or poetic logic can in fact be isolated in the three-book cycle. Each of these books can be read as a stage in the poet's reasoned probe into the subject-object dichotomy that underlies the visionary experience. Time, both as existential concern and aesthetic principle, plays a crucial role in this experience as it urges the self's preservation within an aesthetic project. That is, writing provides a haven for the poetic self against the passage of time, but as it does so it turns that self into a lifeless idol. The three books of *Residencia en la tierra* show the dramatic evolution of a prophetic speaker; by focusing on this dramatic change, we can outline the logic of conversion with which the *Residencia* cycle is brought to a close.

II

A "residence on earth" can be that only for someone not of this earth, someone who is alien or at least alienated. The poet is a guest, a newly arrived visitor, and his "residence" becomes the occasion for either fresh discovery or reacquaintance. From the very title, then, the book insists on the subject's distance from the object and the object's reconstitution in a new light.

Although the earliest poems of *Residencia* date from as far back as 1925, when Neruda was still living in Chile, it was not until he took up residence in Burma, two years later, that he began to give shape to the first book, which covers the years up to 1931. Neruda's alienation can be explained by the bleak circumstances in which he found himself at the time. His meager salary as honorary consul in Rangoon was hardly enough to survive on, and his physical isolation, removed as he was from a familiar geography and climate, was only made worse by his linguistic estrangement. English was the lingua franca of diplomacy in the Far East then (as it still is today) and he was living among people who never had heard Spanish, let alone spoke or understood it. There is even a pathetic letter from this period in which Neruda begged the Spanish poet Rafael Alberti to rush him a dictionary because he feared he was forgetting his native tongue. Indeed, one can hardly slight the linguistic import of Neruda's alienation, since in many ways *Residencia en la tierra* is just that—an estranged poet's refuge within the resources of his own language, a kind of poetic "last stand" within the one residence he knew best.

Yet for all the importance of the language barrier, we must not overlook the broader alienating context of Neruda's personal clash with the East. It is a commonplace that Neruda, unlike other writers who have lived for a time in Asia and adapted to it with much more ease (such as Octavio Paz), was never willing or able to understand Eastern modes of life and thought. "Distance and a deep silence," he wrote years later, "separated me from the world, and I could not bring myself to enter wholeheartedly the alien world around me." Often, however, this acknowledgment is ac-

companied by a view of the poetry as the result of an intellectual imperme-
ability, as irrational exercises, that is, whose ostensible hermeticism
excludes the possibility of representation. To support this view critics invoke the influence of an incipient surrealism, which was fairly strong in
Chile at the time that Neruda wrote the first poems, and Neruda's own
rejection of *Residencia en la tierra* after his involvement in the Spanish
Civil War and his political conversion. Of the two, Neruda's rejection has
provided much critical mileage. For in denouncing poetic abstruseness as
a symptom of social inauthenticity, Neruda seemd to underscore the moral
underside of hermeticism, in addition to explaining, if only from the vantage point of a personal crisis, the reasons for his conversion. To my
knowledge, the influence that Neruda's self-disparagement may have had
on the criticism of *Residencia en la tierra* has never been broached. Nor
for that matter has it ever been questioned that an inability to adopt an
Eastern mode of thought necessarily determines an irrational style. It could
be shown, I think, that there has existed a subtle but pervasive complicity
between Neruda's political prejudices and the arguments often used to approach this early poetry. The issue is not, obviously, that Neruda's opin-
ions should be discarded, but that they should be judged as defensive
gestures that form part of a broader rhetorical strategy.

These distinctions need to be made clear, and the issue of alienation
itself viewed dialectically, if we are to avoid making unwarranted assumptions. For neither a careful reading of the poems nor the extant documents
of this period support the argument for irrationality that has gone unchal-
lenged for so long. On the contrary, both poems and documents point up
a nondiscursive though orderly probe of the poet's alienation and the
knowledge it affords. It is the knowledge that Neruda displays, for example, in another of his articles in *La Nación,* in which he remarks that
"these places only require constant knowledge and attention" and that "in
India human beings form no part of the landscape and there is no discontinuity between oneself and Nature as in the Contemporary West." Neruda
concludes by noting that "everything here seems to be in ruins and tearing
itself apart, but in truth strong elemental and living links join these appear-
ances with almost secret and almost undying connections." We may therefore view Neruda's goal in these poems as an attempt to understand those
"secret and undying connections" not despite but because of his view that
they constitute a dilemma for the Western observer who has internalized
an epistemology based on irony and distance. It should be clear that by
irony I mean not only the linguistic tension stemming from a disparity between intention and expression. I mean, principally, the phenomenology

of Romantic irony, which prescribes the estrangement of the self and the consciousness of an absolute subjectivity as the means to knowledge. It is that knowledge, in fact, that appears at every turn in Neruda's correspondence with Héctor Eandi and José Santos González Vera, writer friends who at the time lived in Buenos Aires and Santiago de Chile: "I believe myself incapable of any communication"; "I've surrounded myself with a certain secret atmosphere." The most pathetic of such remarks appears in a letter he wrote to Eandi in 1930: "At the time I can feel nothing I can perceive, everything seems not empty of meaning but abounding in it. I do feel that all things have already found meaning by themselves, that I form no part of them and that I have nothing to penetrate them with."

The title *Residencia en la tierra* thus provides a governing metaphor for an ironic distance between subject and object which, beginning with "Galope muerto," its first poem, elaborates what I should like to call a "scene of writing"—a textual theater where the self dramatizes its relationship with the writing process. The title of this first poem provides an important link to the book's title, as if the redundancy of the phrase "residencia en la tierra" contained an ironic paradox from which "Galope muerto," the following title phrase, stems. Implicit in the latter, which constitutes an oxymoron or antithetical metaphor, is a translation of the English "dead gallop," a horse's wild run. The Spanish "galope muerto," however, does not convey this figurative meaning; it signifies the antithetical sense of a dead or silent sound. The starting point of the poem, and therefore of the book, is this paradoxical, impossible experience, which originates in the irony of the two titles. Thus juxtaposed, they yield a contextual argument: (1) the subject's ironic distance causes (2) the paradox of a silent sound. This paradox is a vision.

I of course extend the definition of vision to encompass an aural mode. Privileged perception includes sound as well as sight, clairaudience as well as clairvoyance. This first poem can, in fact, be read as the narration of the passage from clairaudience to clairvoyance, hearing to sight, or "audition" to vision, as it recasts the experience of unheard sound, as it were, into intelligible imagery. What seems crucial, in any case, is that this particular communication depends on the title's double rhetorical deviation as both oxymoron and translation, a deviation that signals a retreat from referential meaning and a plunge into a purely linguistic realm. The title pointedly tells us, in other words, that the experience about to be told will prepare the ground for a visionary space that is made up solely of language—the only space in which visions can properly occur.

My explication of the first two titles may seem unduly labored but it is designed to convey that what in the past has been taken to be a baffling "hermeticism" is nothing more than a rich linguistic density that becomes clear if words are simply read in context. "Galope muerto" refers to nothing more than what is says: a dead, impossible sound. It is an aural rather than a visual revelation, the first of a series of poems in *Residencia* on the theme of the poet's gifted sense of hearing. Thus in the passage from the title to the first line the reader must supply the copula that the experience assumes: "Galope muerto *es*"

> Como cenizas, como mares poblándose,
> en la sumergida lentitud, en lo informe,
> o como se oyen desde lo alto de los caminos
> cruzar las campanadas en cruz,
> teniendo ese sonido ya aparte del metal,
> confuso, pesando, haciéndose polvo
> en el mismo molino de las formas demasiado lejos,
> o recordadas o no vistas,
> y el perfume de las ciruelas que rodando a tierra
> se pudren en el tiempo, infinitamente verdes.

(Like ashes, like seas populating / in the submerged slowness, in the unformed, / or as one hears from high atop the roads / the church bells crossing, / having that sound already apart from the metal, / confused, weighty, turning into dust / in the same windmill of forms too far away / or remembered or not seen, / and the perfume of plums, which, rolling down to earth, / rot in time, infinitely green.)

Both the anxious tone and the obsessive simile clauses dramatize a desire to transpose indefinite sound into visual terms. Yet the choppy quality of these similes implies as well the sound's resistance to discursive form. Other sounds—the echo of ringing bells, for example—appear as possible substitutes, along with the images of faintly remembered or unseen shapes. The series culminates in the image of rotting green plums, which, like the title image, constitutes an oxymoron. The first stanza, then, arranges a sequence of image options in an order of viability that culminates, fittingly, in a visual version of the aural paradox described in the title.

After this initial success, the aural experience continues, and so does the poem. Far from being an isolated event, the muted sound appears everywhere, surrounding the speaker as in a state of siege:

> Aquello todo tan rápido, tan viviente,
> inmóvil sin embargo, como la polea loca en sí misma,

esas ruedas de los motores, en fin.
Existiendo como las puntadas secas en las costuras del árbol,
callado, por alrededor, de tal modo,
mezclando todos los limbos sus colas.
Es que de dónde, por dónde, en qué orilla?
El rodeo constante, incierto, tan mudo,
como las lilas alrededor del convento
o la llegada de la muerte a la lengua del buey
que cae a tumbos, guardabajo, y cuyos cuernos quieren sonar.

(All that so fast, so living, / immobile, however, like the pulley
crazily turning on itself, / those engine wheels, that is. / Existing
like the dried stitches in the seams of the tree, / silent, around,
just so, / all the limbs mixing their tails. / It's just from where
to where, on what shore? / The constant round, uncertain, so
mute, / like the lilacs surrounding the convent / or the arrival of
death at the tongue of the ox, / who drops his guard, and
whose horns want to sound.)

The surrounding objects, described with similar oxymorons (they are
both "rápido" and "inmóvil"), appear spread out in a circular pattern.
The first stanza suggests a circle in the image of "molino de las formas,"
which makes no sense until we encounter other circular images: "polea,"
"rodeo constante," "lilas alrededor del convento." These are images of circular or cyclical activity, an endless life-death process to which the
speaker, who assumes a central position, bears witness. Along with a common circular pattern these objects share a strange silence, an uncanny stillness that is enough to arrest the speaker's momentum and persuade him
to pose the experience in far more cautious terms. The encompassing indefinite pronouns, for example, turn out to be "callado," the siege of reality becomes "tan mudo," and as death overcomes the tongue of the falling
ox its horns become a pair of muffled trumpets. The speaker discovers,
that is, a voice buried under surrounding matter. His mission now, as in
the first stanza, is to translate that "dead gallop" into yet another intelligible description, which the three questions pinpointing the origin of the experience are designed to prepare.

> Por eso, en lo inmóvil, deteniéndose, percibir,
> entonces, como aleteo inmenso, encima,
> como abejas muertas o números,
> ay, lo que mi corazón pálido no puede abarcar,
> en multitudes, en lágrimas saliendo apenas

y esfuerzos humanos, tormentas,
acciones negras descubiertas de repente
como hielos, desorden vasto,
oceánico, para mí que entro cantando,
como con una espada entre indefensos.

(For this reason, in the stillness, stopping, to perceive, / then, like wing beats immense, above, / like dead bees or numbers, / oh, what my pale heart cannot bear, / in multitudes, in tears hardly flowing / and human efforts, storms, black actions suddenly discovered / like ice, vast disorder, / oceanic, for me who enter singing, / as with a sword among the defenseless.)

Despite his anxiety—reflected by this point in a virtually telegraphic syntax that confutes grammatical coherence—the speaker resolves to confront the disordered human frailty that he alone perceives in sudden pangs of vision. Like the one-eyed king in the country of the blind, he is a singer amid mute objects, a competent translator of their silence, and consequently an armed prophet whose voice is a sword. But these credentials by themselves cannot account for the nature of the original sound, whose origin he seeks now in explicit terms:

Ahora bien, de qué está hecho ese surgir de palomas
que hay entre la noche y el tiempo, como una barranca
         húmeda?
Ese sonido ya tan largo
que cae listando de piedras los caminos,
más bien, cuando sólo una hora
crece de improviso, extendiéndose sin tregua.

(Well now, of what is that upsurge of pigeons made, / existing between night and time like a damp ravine? / That sound already so long / that it stripes the roads with stones as it falls, / rather, when only one hour / grows suddenly, extending without end.)

The question—which, as John Felstiner notes, is one of only two complete sentences in the poem—restates the mystery. Both "ese surgir de palomas" and "ese sonido ya tan largo," equated as they are by the same demonstrative pronoun, refer to the "dead gallop" whose effect on the speaker is a feeling of boundless temporality. The last stanza, finally, hints at the answer:

Adentro del anillo del verano
una vez los grandes zapallos escuchan,
estirando sus plantas conmovedoras,
de eso, de lo que solicitándose mucho,
de lo lleno, oscuros de pesadas gotas.

(Inside the ring of summer / once the great calabash trees
listen / stretching their moving plants, / of that, of what asking
much, / of the full, obscure with heavy drops.)

The origin remains inside the "anillo del verano," a comprehensive
circle that encloses all the circular objects in a single structure. Within it,
"los grandes zapallos" listen to one another as if engaged in a cosmic conversation whose subject is perhaps the very answer to the riddle that
prompts the poem. The latter image, typical of the early Neruda, echoes
the passage in Baudelaire's "Correspondances" in which the "forest of
symbols" casts an amused glance at the unsuspecting speaker. The final
genitive clauses attempt to answer the question that was posed in the previous stanza. And yet, suspended until now, that answer is no clearer than
the question itself. In the end, that is, we have learned no more than we
knew at the beginning, with the possible exception, perhaps, that we know
that the mysterious sound has accosted the speaker to the point of imped-
ing his articulation of the quest. The origin of the haunting experience, and
thus the reason for the poem, remain beyond the speaker's reach, behind
reality's encircling veil.

"Galope muerto" is the most apposite introduction to the visionary
poetics of *Residencia en la tierra,* a fact that perhaps explains its leading
position in the book. The poem deals with the discovery of the visionary
vocation, and its echo of Baudelaire's famous text is appropriate, as Neruda seems to be responding with a postsymbolist poetics of his own. The
two poems share a view of the poet as a reader or decoder of signs, but
they propose radically different readings. For Baudelaire, reality enjoys a
religious stability afforded by Nature's "temple," an aesthetic monad or
ultimate symbol in which the poet places his faith as the means to ensure
the accuracy of his reading of the world's "gloomy and deep unity." In
Neruda's postmodern text, on the other hand, reality is no less gloomy or
deep, but it hardly affords the unity or stability that Baudelaire enjoys: the
"temple" has turned into "ashes." Baudelaire trusts that his poem will fuse
word and thing by means of the proper symbol—a confidence whose formal correlative is the traditional sonnet of his argument. Neruda dramatizes a radical linguistic distrust by showing the gap that exists between

word and thing—there being no longer an aesthetic unity that can support
this language—and by making the search for a visual analogy the very subject of his poem. The poem's truncated, disjointed structure is the formal
counterpart of the failure of that search. "Galope muerto" may, in fact, be
the extreme version of the theme that Michel Foucault identifies at the root
of classical representation—the anguish of the poet who "beneath the language of signs and beneath the interplay of their precisely delineated distinctions . . . strains his ears to catch that 'other language,' the language
without words or discourse, of resemblance." The modern poet thus fulfills
what Foucault calls [in *The Order of Things*] an "allegorical role" in at-
tempting to read that "other language," "another deeper discourse, which
recalls the time when words glittered in the universal resemblance of
things."

That "Galope muerto" achieves its effect by dramatizing the visionary's anxiety is evident enough. But it would be wrong, I think, further to
attribute the poem's disjointed form, as Alfredo Lozada suggests, to an intuitive source. Rather than attempt to describe the empirical conditions of
the writing subject, it seems safer to notice that the lack of a culminating
vision signals a self-reflection that calls attention to the visionary process
itself. Because of its disjointed form, as if it were the nervous stenography
of a visionary session, the poem can yield only a trace of the manner in
which it came about. The subject sees, in this sense, not only the object
but also himself in the act of seeing and recording. He is a witness to his
own witnessing, as it were, and the poem becomes a visionary cinema in
which he plays the dual role of spectator and actor, audience and protagonist.

Self-reflection is what Amado Alonso called "auto-exégesis," self-
exegesis or commentary, to explain those frequent moments in *Residencia
en la tierra* when the poetry turns to explaining itself. As a critical tool
the term is too limiting, as we shall see, but for the moment it serves to
remind us that in *Residencia en la tierra* self-commentary varies in degree
from poem to poem. In "Galope muerto," for example, the self-reflexive
gesture is never dramatized overtly but remains implicit in the poem's disjointedness. This use of self-reflexive form dates back to *Tentativa del
hombre infinito* (1925), Neruda's first long poem, in which the visionary
speaker at times intrudes into the narrative to describe himself as a seer
and to tell of his efforts to produce the text. As we read the poem we are
left with the impression of automatic writing flowing directly from the unconscious without any guidance from the creative faculties. And yet its argument, as Jaime Alazraki and others have shown, is hardly capricious

insofar as it structures a "visionary voyage," Neruda's contribution to a well-known poetic tradition. "Galope muerto," then, belongs to this earlier experimental stage, in which self-exegesis is a by-product of formal disjointedness.

"Arte poética" is perhaps the best illustration of this self-reflexive poetics, as its title suggests. And the further fact that it occupies a central position within the first book, the seventeenth of thirty-three poems, should convince us of its importance. For these reasons it seems best to discuss it now, profit from its centrality, and backtrack later. It begins by locating the speaker in an imaginary space:

> Entre sombra y espacio, entre guarniciones y doncellas,
> dotado de corazón singular y sueños funestos
> precipitadamente pálido, marchito en la frente
> y con luto de viudo furioso por cada día de vida

> (Between shadow nd space, between garrisons and damsels, /
> gifted with a singular heart and dismal dreams / precipitously
> pallid, with withered forehead / and with a furious widower's
> mourning each day of life)

While the first set of images denotes opposite states of perception— "sombra y espacio," confusion and clarity—the second set assigns the speaker the role of a hero breaking down garrisons to rescue damsels in distress. This self-adulation is complemented by the claim to "gifts," the traits of the Romantic artist and particularly those of the *poète maudit*— a unique heart, a peculiar paleness, and a daily death-in-life. The portrait is stock Romantic, to be sure, and it recalls one text in particular, Gérard de Nerval's "El desdichado" ("le ténébreux, le veuf, l'inconsolé [the gloomy, the widower, the disconsolate]"), to which the fourth line seems to allude. Nor should the irony of the self-portrait escape us. It reworks conventional Romantic traits in order to heighten the speaker's diffidence yet preserve tonal coherence. The alliteration in "*preci*pitadamente *pál*-ido," for example, exaggerates the speaker's paleness enough to turn the portrait into a caricature. Following these lines are two instances of seeing and hearing which, together with the ensuing simile clauses, recall the desperate series in "Galope muerto." This time, however, the additional number heightens the desperate tone as the speaker gropes for the correct analogy. The last of them reveals

> un olor de casa sola
> en la que los huéspedes entran de noche perdidamente ebrios,

> y hay un olor de ropa tirada al suelo, y
> una ausencia de flores,
> —posiblemente de otro modo aún menos melancólico—

(a smell of solitary house / which guests enter at night hope-
lessly drunk, / and there's a smell of clothes thrown on the
floor, and / an absence of flowers, / —perhaps in another still
less melancholy way—)

The "solitary house" is but the "residence on earth" appearing here in spatial splendor, though it seems to be no more than an anonymous guest-
house that lodges the speaker's drunken friends, or perhaps the wraiths of
vision. Its grotesque symbol is a bundle of dirty clothes, whose odor has
displaced that of the Mallarméan bouquet, which, fittingly, is absent from
the scene. By thus spatializing the subject's alienation, the last simile marks
a climactic juncture that is quickly filled by a self-reflexive statement. In
this statement, a dramatic aside, the speaker views the preceding anguish
in ironic retrospect and lumps the first half of the poem into a single unit,
a kind of free-verse sonnet (fourteen lines), as if reflecting upon it in an
aftermath of vision. In addition to the fact that it appears at a crucial juncture, the importance of this ironic statement lies in its use of such a
charged adjective as "melancólico," about which I shall say more later. For
the moment we should note that it carries most of the weight of the irony
and that it refers less to the speaker's weakness than to his perception of
the formal inadequacy of his writing. The poem so far is too sad, he seems
to say, too literary, perhaps, to capture my meaning. It is this ironic statement that underscores and thus uncovers all of the preceding Romantic
themes. And in characterizing the poem as "melancólico," it denounces the
literary conventionality of the description, which thus blocks the speaker's
desire for authenticity, and pleads for a more immediate rendering of the
same experience.

But to attempt a different and less desperate beginning leads ultimately to the same state of things. While the fifteenth line discredits melancholy expression, the ensuing argument returns to it:

> pero, la verdad, de pronto, el viento que azota mi pecho,
> las noches de sustancia infinita caídas en mi dormitorio,
> el ruido de un día que arde con sacrificio
> me piden lo profético que hay en mí, con melancolía,
> y un golpe de objetos que llaman sin ser respondidos
> hay, y un movimiento sin tregua, y un nombre confuso.

(but, the truth, suddenly, the wind that beats upon my breast, / the nights of infinite substance fallen in my bedroom, / the noise of a day that burns with sacrifice / ask me, with melancholy, for all the prophecy there is in me, / and there's a thump of objects that call without answer, / and a ceaseless movement, and a confused name.)

The "truth" that now takes hold is the prophetic power of the same Romantic language denounced earlier. It reappears along with an entirely different imagery: an inspiring wind, nights of revelation, voices promising days of self-sacrifice. The new imagery counters the previous somber sequence, so that both series represent the opposite cognitive poles ("sombra y espacio") to which the first line had alluded. It would appear, then, that such a shift has made the speaker advance from melancholy sickness to prophetic health. And yet the speaker still insists on linking "truth" with melancholy. The abiding question of these lines has thus been the apparent contradiction that confutes the preceding ironic reversal and the attendant shift of images. Emir Rodríguez Monegal's reading, for example, refuted Alonso's earlier interpretation, which had offered the view that melancholy permeates the entire poem, including the end. Monegal countered that both the image shift and the explicit claim to prophecy preclude a melancholy ending. But even a sensitive debate such as this leaves unexplained the seemingly contradictory association of melancholy and prophecy.

To understand the precise sense of this association we need to shift our attention to the long history of melancholy as a literary concept. Melancholy was "black bile," one of the four humors that regulated the body's emotional system, according to ancient medicine. The melancholic personality belonged to the sad and contemplative person whose excess of black bile was thought to induce fits of depression and, in extreme cases, madness. Once melancholy was identified as the source of emotional disturbances, it became part of the mythology of poetic inspiration. Natural philosophers, among them Aristotle, explained poetic frenzy as a melancholic seizure and thus made melancholy known as the painful reward that poet-prophets heroically endured. What in "Arte poética" seems to be a contradiction, then, can be easily explained as a function of this intellectual convention. In fact, once understood in its philological density, the reference to melancholy explains not only the recurring interplay of dark and light imagery throughout Neruda's poetry, but the mythology that underlies the entire visionary mode, its conventions and its structure of vision as estrangement.

Instead of discrediting the role of melancholy, the shift of images affirms it by attributing it to a prophetic function. The last two lines revert to the initial sequence of unheeded objects, secret movements, and confused language. The pun in which the verb "hay" coincides with the interjection "ay!" prepares us for the less obvious one at the end, in which "un *nombre* confuso (a confused name)" sounds the same as "un *hombre* confuso (a confused man)." Whereas the first pun echoes the earlier one in the fifth line, where the interjection plays against the verb, the second pun points out, as did the rhetorical divergences of "Galope muerto," that both the subject and his literary product are purely linguistic entities. And the appearance of both puns in the last line further implies that the reversal to the initial somber state depends on this purely linguistic realm in which man and word, verb and interjection, are kept separate and distinct. The cyclical movement makes the poem end where it began, thus indicating that the previous image shift had been a temporary though still necessary stage of illumination within a consistently somber and confused cycle.

"Arte poética" clarifies the uses of irony and prophecy. Irony and reflexiveness, accordingly, become one and the same. The strategic location of the single most ironic line in the poem suggests that prophetic truth or poetic knowledge stems from a previous self-consciousness, which has arisen from the ruins of visionary exhaustion. As such, irony would seem to be a kind of "pause that refreshes," a fictional mediation whereby the alienated speaker holds in check the power of negativity and is thus able to posit a future reconciliation of spirit and world. Yet far from signaling a reparation, the ironic moment marks a temporal disjunction that exposes the speaker's facticity. That is, the speaker recognizes his inauthenticity; but just as two wrongs can never make a right, knowledge of one's inauthenticity cannot neutralize bad faith. Irony, like allegory, enacts what Paul de Man has called a "rhetoric of temporality," an authentic experience of time "which seen from the point of view of the self engaged in the world, is a negative one." Caught between a consciousness of infinity and temporal facticity, the visionary poet recognizes his own limits and allows that knowledge to subvert the empirical claims of prophecy—that "truth" which suddenly takes hold after the ironic break. Such a subversion of prophetic "truth" allows the speaker to invoke a self-conscious fictionality as the grounds for vision. This explains both the poem's circular structure, which dramatizes an endless process leading to no synthesis, and the speaker's identification, here as well as in "Galope muerto," with the written text, an identification that exposes the poem's fictionality and suspends a union between self and world.

Even the keenest commentators on *Residencia en la tierra* have been reluctant to recognize its ironic content, as if pointing to it would somehow denigrate Neruda's achievement. In his remarks about "self-exegesis," for example, Amado Alonso was sensitive enough to notice this ironic strain, but he invariably explained it away, using Crocean categories, as an anomaly owing to a disjunction of intuition and feeling. A rhetorical model not only seems to go further in explicating these moments, but it helps to identify Neruda's affinity with such Romantic ironists as Baudelaire, Novalis, and Heine. For what Romantic irony identifies is precisely that dissonant gesture evident in the authorial disruptions of whatever realistic illusions the text may create.

The other issue that "Arte poética" clarifies is prophecy. The poem shows the coincidence of a Romantic imagery with the speaker's claim to prophetic identity. Thus by providing a secular, or at least nonbiblical, context, it views prophecy as vision: not a speaking *before* or prediction, but a speaking *forth* or revelation, a mission with more of a rhetorical than an exclusively religious sense. This crucial insight coincides with a strategy of characterization that exploits the dramatic potential of such a title. That is, the speaker's identification of himself as a prophet renders his dramatic presence more immediate than the plainer label "mystic" or "visionary" could do. Such a deliberately dramatic gesture cannot help seeming forced, an authorial disruption groping for a suitable label. For prophecy is, finally, the fiction that identifies the visionary act. Once the visionary subject acknowledges his own facticity and discloses the degree to which his status depends on fiction, all visions are exposed as similar constructs that depend on a system of literary conventions.

III

"The poet should not just do exercises," Neruda wrote to Héctor Eandi in November 1929. "There's a mandate for him—to penetrate life and make it prophetic. The poet ought to be a superstition, a mythic being." The statement recalls the arguments of both "Galope muerto" and "Arte poética," although, as we have seen, the poems themselves go beyond Neruda's plea for the creation of impressive visionary speakers. Nor was Neruda's rejection of poetry as "exercise" as total or as innocent as it may seem. One could perhaps infer from the date of the letter that his injunction was a veiled reference to the Spanish poets of the Generation of 1927—García Lorca, Jorge Guillén, and Rafael Alberti, among others— who adhered vaguely to a notion of art as sport, or perhaps to Ortega y

Gasset's description of the avant-garde poet, in *The Dehumanization of Art* (1925), an an intellectual athlete. One might venture further that Neruda's adverse reaction stemmed from his brief stopover in Madrid in 1927, while en route to the Far East, when he was probably slighted by the ruling poetic intelligentsia. And yet Neruda's contact with these poets was not so extensive during this first visit to Spain, nor were these men so devoted to the abstract imagism that Neruda was then rejecting, as to bear out the argument. Neruda devotes a mere three lines of his memoirs to his four-day visit to the Spanish capital, hardly an indication that he attached great importance to that first trip. Furthermore, and contrary to popular distortions of literary history, Ortega and such poets as García Lorca and Guillén were committed instead to a *rehumanization* of art which would profit from the innovations of the European avant-garde without losing sight of human values and expression. Their affinity to Neruda would be attested to years later when Ortega published three poems from *Residencia en la tierra* in *Revista de Occidente* and the Spanish poet defended Neruda against the charges of plagiarism that were raised in 1934 by his fellow Chilean Vicente Huidobro.

It was in fact to Huidobro, along with the earlier ultraist movement, and not to his more immediate Spanish counterparts, that Neruda seems to have referred in his warning to Eandi. Ultraism had been the Hispanic equivalent and synthesis of the various imagist schools that had sprung up all over Europe in the century's first two decades. Typical of the avant-garde, it conceived of the artist as an intellectual athlete, and of poetry especially as the most cerebral of games. Huidobro, a Chilean poet who in pre–World War I Paris had contributed to Pierre Reverdy's *Nord-Sud* review, soon became the "ambassador" of the French avant-garde in Hispanic circles, and it was largely through his agency, as well as through his claim to having fathered a new poetic school that he called Creationism, that ultraism acquired its fame and resonance. "Any serious artistic school," Huidobro had written in 1925, "must begin with a period of search in which intelligence directs the artist's efforts." Analysis, logical structure, and lucid thought patterns were Huidobro's ingredients for the modern poem. His poetry, like that of the ultraists, readily mixed them to create surprising visual effects through metaphor—what the English at the time called Imagism. Later in the same letter to Eandi, Neruda pointedly alludes to Huidobro by complaining that "people have lost all temperament and devote themselves to intellectual exercise, with pleasure, as if it were a sport," adding further that "even so, all of them seem rather mediocre players." And the allusion seems more pointed still when he charges that "for some time poets' intelligence has cut all human links to what they say; cordiality and friendship toward the poetic message have fled the world."

In referring to poetic "exercise," then, Neruda rejects one cerebral poetry, associated with Huidobro, for another, which he calls prophetic and whose function is "to penetrate life." This is the poetry he claims to have written in *Residencia en la tierra*. What seems suspect about such a dichotomy, however, is its deliberate ease—Neruda's claim that his own poetry penetrates life and his implication that Huidobro's slights it. For Neruda's poetry was less immediate than his letter to Eandi implies, and Huidobro's was less cold and calculating than Huidobro himself claimed. Both, in fact, are versions of the same modernist poetics. Like Neruda, Huidobro sought to write a poetry that captured the unusual traits of objects and thereby altered and refreshed the reader's perception. Like Huidobro, Neruda wrote (at least in *Residencia en la tierra*) a difficult, often baffling poetry, which attests to his skill as a craftsman. Their opposition stems not from conflicting purposes, as Neruda seems to have believed, but from divergent simulations of the poetic experience. While Huidobro's revelations proceed swiftly, in almost mathematical fashion, seeming to result from an intense but orderly cerebral juggling, Neruda's prophetic utterances simulate all the anguish associated with the visionary experience. Neruda's neo-Romanticism, it seems, attempts to correct Huidobro's militant avant-gardism, but his own corrective gesture cannot help leading to a misreading of his precursor, as if mirroring the distortions to which the avant-garde itself subjected Romantic art. For contrary to the claims often made by modernist writers, "the cult of novelty and even of the strange," as Renato Poggioli notes, "was an exquisitely romantic phenomenon even before it became typically avant garde." "Instead of being reciprocal opposites," Romanticism and the avant-garde "came to appear as relatives, reacting to the humanistic and classical opposition in similar ways." And so the poet may not have to do exercises, as Neruda claims, but the reader of *Residencia en la tierra* does, as much as or more in fact than when reading Huidobro's cerebral lyrics. In their textual strategies, at least, Neruda and Huidobro appear to be relatives, though they would have been the first to deny any kinship.

Neruda's antagonism toward Huidobro lasted throughout his life and at times even reached the violence of a true "anxiety of influence" (to use Harold Bloom's term), as when he obliquely disparaged Huidobro's well-known dictum that "the poet is a little god" in his Nobel Prize speech. My concern with Neruda's statements in his correspondence, however, is aimed less at documenting this adverse relationship, interesting as it is, than at pointing up the differential role that prophecy assumed at the time he wrote the poems of *Residencia en la tierra*. Invoking prophecy seems to have helped him to clear a creative space of his own and to distinguish his poetics from an ostensibly frivolous one, such as he judged Huidobro's to be. It is this differential role, I think, that explains the explicit references to prophecy in at least two other poems of *Residencia*. One of them, "Colección nocturna," dramatizes the appearance of prophecy in the form of an angel spreading an ominous "alimento profético (prophetic nourishment)." The reference occurs in the prelude to a dream vision that describes a catalogue of incongruous images in a familiar tone. Following a parade of motley figures and objects (the "colección nocturna" or night collection), the speaker announces the coming of day and admits that the entire vision has been a waking dream that creates the illusion of a bridge between subject and object: "un poco de cada oficio, un resto humillado trabaja su parte en nuestro interior (a little of each job, a humiliated leftover does its work inside of us)." "Communicaciones desmentidas," the second of five prose poems included in the first book, also invokes prophecy in its opening line: "Aquellos días extraviaron mi sentido profético (Those days misled my prophetic sense)." This time, however, the reference forms part of the speaker's struggle to preserve an identity that is dramatized, as in "Arte poética," as a Romantic self-caricature. The poet's faculties are once again stamped upon by melancholy, besieged by circular objects that render him an armed prophet: "aguardo el tiempo militarmente, y con el florete de la aventura manchado de sangre olvidada (I await time in a military style, and with the adventure's foil stained with forgotten blood)." Both of these poems advance prophecy as the principle underlining the visionary mode. Yet neither one approaches the power of such poems as "Galope muerto" and "Arte poética," both of which exploit a deft characterization and the unfolding of a visionary epistemology. In the case of "Arte poética," this epistemology proposes an analogy between the object's cyclical patterns and the structure of visionary discourse. As an order-preserving structure, the cycle constitutes the pattern inherent both in the object and in perception, in reality and in the discourse that identifies it.

It is this sense of vision as an activity that preserves order against temporal dispersion that Neruda repeatedly underscores in his letters to Eandi and José Santos González Vera. Despite the unreliable vagueness of this correspondence, which at times betrays the self-deprecation of a fledgling poet, there are moments of genuine insight in these letters, as when Neruda describes the poems as having "the same movement, the same pressure . . . developed in the same region of my head, like the same type of insistent waves." Scarcely a month had elapsed when the same description, cast in a similar redundant style, reappears: "I've completed almost an entire book of poems: *Residencia en la tierra,* and you will see how I'm able to isolate my expression, making it waver constantly among dangers, and what solid uniform substance I use to make the same force appear insistently." And the same terms appear again a year later, in yet another letter to Eandi, which calls the book "a heap of very monotonous verse" and "something very uniform, one single thing begun over and over, as if eternally and unsuccessfully rehearsed." What strikes one immediately about these statements is the recurrence of such key adjectives as "same," "uniform," "single," and "insistent," all of which convey the idea of singular unity or substance. They are all meant, obviously, as descriptions of the tonal uniformity that links the various parts of the book and provides it with an overall coherence. They describe, that is, an external integrative principle, a cycle, which functions at the broadest level of the book as a unit. Yet the same terms imply as well an internal cyclic principle that concerns the representation, within individual poems, of objective circular structures. Both external and internal cyclic principles coexist in these statements and both could be said to structure the form of *Residencia en la tierra.*

What concerns me now is the way these two cyclic principles actually work to form what I earlier called the book's poetic logic or visionary syntax. I shall begin this inquiry with a reading of "Unidad (Unity)," the fifth poem in the book. The presence of an external cyclic sense depends, as we shall see, on the arrangement of the poems, but in the case of "Unidad" it plays a crucial role because of the poem's own internal cyclic sense. The title itself alludes to the achievement of ultimate cyclicality:

> Hay algo denso, unido, sentado en el fondo,
> repitiendo su número, su señal idéntica.
> Cómo se nota que las piedras han tocado el tiempo,
> en su fina materia hay olor a edad,
> y el agua que trae el mar, de sal y sueño.

(There is something dense, united, seated in the back / repeating its number, its identical sign. / How one notices that the stones have touched time, / in its delicate matter there's a smell of age, / and the water that the sea brings, of salt and dream.)

The first two lines, we should note, echo Neruda's statements in his letters. Repetition and sameness become the signs of a cyclical presence that the next three lines translate as an unrelenting temporal process. Noticing this sign—what the poem puts metaphorically as "olor a edad"—becomes the poet's duty, as it is to register the surrounding circular pattern:

> Me rodea una misma cosa, un solo movimiento:
> el peso del mineral, la luz de la piel,
> se pegan al sonido de la palabra noche:
> la tinta del trigo, del marfil, del llanto,
> las cosas de cuero, de madera, de lana,
> envejecidas, desteñidas, uniformes,
> se unen en torno a mí como paredes.

(One same thing surrounds me, a single moment: / the weight of the mineral, the light of skin, / adhere to the sound of the word night; / the ink of wheat, of ivory, of weeping, / the things made of leather, of wood, of wool, / grown old, faded, uniform, / gather around me like walls.)

The tone is decidedly less desperate and the catalogue itself less deranged than in "Galope muerto." The stanza aligns symmetrical triads of genitive clauses and adjectives, and it is this order that the last line identifies as an immuring fortress. Finally, the third and last stanza summarizes the form of the object as well as the subject's position in relation to it:

> Trabajo sordamente, girando sobre mí mismo,
> como el cuervo sobre la muerte, el cuervo de luto.
> Pienso, aislado en lo extremo de las etaciones,
> central, rodeado de geografía silenciosa:
> una temperatura parcial cae del cielo,
> un extremo imperio de confusas unidades
> se reúne rodeándome.

(I work deafly [engrossed], gyrating upon myself, / like the crow over death, the mourning crow. / I think, isolated in the extreme of seasons, / central, surrounded by silent geography: / a partial temperature falls from the sky, / an extreme empire of confused items / reunites surrounding me.)

The punning adverb of visionary work ("sordamente") implies both stealth and silence, which join to qualify the subject's own wheellike structure as homologous to the object's. This new description echoes the turning pulley of "Galope muerto," but its pointed difference signals the speaker's self-assertion as a result of his growing linguistic self-consciousness. Despite its bewilderment, the siege affords a clarity of vision whose climax the colon at the end of the fourth line discreetly anticipates. It is nothing less than a descent from heaven, though who or what descends we are not told. The compendious image of "confusas unidades" itself approaches the status of an oxymoron and conveys the cognitive tension we have encountered before. The image principally dramatizes the speaker's ability to discern a pattern where there appears to be none and to extract meaning from a set of otherwise unrelated objects. The last line all but reasserts, with a fitting measure of redundance, a circular order that consists of siege and repetition and that recalls the "anillo del verano (ring of summer)" of "Galope muerto."

The paradox of a chaotic symmetry that we find in "Unidad" stems, as we might surmise, from the disquieting method of the visionary mode. As Rimbaud's disordering of the senses was "reasoned," so Neruda's is caused by a tension between cognitive opposites of chaos and system. That such Rimbaldian illumination could result only from a previous leap in the dark we learned in "Arte poética," where melancholy marked the prelude to poetic knowledge. The poem illustrates such a method by harmonizing the motley nature of the object with an impassive orderliness, and it goes one step further in relating this tenuous harmony or "unity" to a cyclic pattern common to both subject and object. The final homology intimates, then, a bridging of the gap that separates the two and a way out of irony and alienation.

One would certainly by tempted, from the vantage point afforded by our earlier reading of "Arte poética," to dismiss such unity as a delusion. But such a dismissal would assume a reading order opposite from the one that the book prescribes. That is, to prejudge "Unidad," the fifth poem, in terms of the lessons reaped from "Arte poética," the seventeenth, would be to reverse a dialectical pattern that the reading order suggests. If we now turn back to those first few poems, up to and including "Unidad," we can continue to trace that same sense and unfold an overall pattern.

We may, in fact, think of "Galope muerto" and "Unidad" as the first stages of two sequential sallies, two inquiries into the subject-object dichotomy. The experience of "Galope muerto" marks the origin of the first inquiry, which includes the argument of the next three poems: "Alianza (Sonata)," "Caballo de los sueños," and "Débil del alba." Earlier we learned that this first stage ended by circumscribing the objective limits of visionary experience within a circle—an "anillo del verano." Acknowledging that impasse, "Alianza (Sonata)," the poem that follows "Galope muerto," takes up the same inquiry and refashions it by conceiving the subject-object relationship as intersubjective. The point of contact is the punning title, which, besides heralding an alliance between two people, transforms the earlier "ring of summer" into an explicitly matrimonial symbol (in Spanish "alianza" also means wedding ring). Yet instead of describing a joyous marriage, the poem begins by admitting the union of failed vision and pervasive emptiness:

> De miradas polvorientas caídas al suelo
> o de hojas sin sonido sepultándose.
> De metales sin luz, con el vacío,
> con la ausencia del día muerto de golpe.
> En lo alto de las manos el deslumbrar de mariposas,
> el arrancar de mariposas cuya luz no tiene término.

(Of dusty looks fallen on the floor / or of soundless leaves burying themselves. / Of lusterless metals, with emptiness, / with the absence of day suddenly dead. / At the height of hands the dazzling of butterflies, / the taking off of butterflies whose light has no end.)

The initial genitive clauses appear to be incomplete only if we fail to infer their grammatical coherence from the title. Thus the "alianza" is *of* failed vision ("miradas polvorientas," "hojas sin sonido") *with* emptiness and absense ("con el vacío, con la ausencia"). The dazzling kaleidoscope of butterflies, looming beyond the speaker's grasp, outlines a visionary horizon and the promise of a brighter union. In the second stanza it is the other person, identified with a familiar second-person pronoun and a female adjective, who appears as the source of that cherished light. The further association of this other person with twilight shows it to be an effulgent though forbiddingly remote landscape. Both a participle and its description as an "objeto de abejas (object of bees)" further expose her passivity, but the third stanza qualifies that passivity as a function of her quiet strength. In contrast to the speaker, who fears the coming of day as preying temporality, she is able to gather those same days in her own "voz de luz (voice of light)," thereby becoming the object on which the speaker hopes to lay the foundation of visionary structure: "Oh, dueña del amor, en tu descanso fundé mi sueño, mi actitud callada (Oh, mistress of love, in thy tranquillity I founded my dream, my quiet posture)." The fourth stanza goes on to underscore their dreamlike relationship, for despite her aid in defining both spatial and temporal dimensions, the subject can feel her presence only "en mi sueño." Finally, in the fifth stanza, the speaker describes the culmination of their alliance as the physical merger of their tears, which, defying the law of gravity, ascend as they are shed by both subjects and meet in the speaker's mind. They "grow" there until they become a turbulent ocean that causes their destruction simply because, we infer, the speaker awakes.

Thus the second approach to the object ends in failure. In the end the speaker awakes and rejects his experience—a third stage must begin. But the rejection, as we soon discover, will be far from total. The next title, "Caballo de los sueños" ("Dream Horse"), suggests that the speaker retains the agency of dreams, first introduced in "Alianza," in the quest for unity. Moreover, it becomes evident at this point that the speaker's fall into an explicit dream state, by providing discreet signs of chronological succession, dramatizes a temporal process that increases in importance as we continue reading. Like the first two, this third title will become a sign of the external cyclic sense. Not only does this title signal the recurrence of a dream vision, but it shows the metaphorical source of the earlier "dead gallop." The sequence therefore suggests a dialectical progression toward an increasingly concrete vision (from "galope" to "caballo") despite, or perhaps because of, the greater frequency of dreams.

While in "Alianza (Sonata)" the speaker creates, however fleetingly, the fiction of another desiring subject, now he begins by admitting his sense of isolation and the contingency of bureaucratic drudgery:

> Innecesario, viéndome en los espejos,
> con un gusto a semanas, a biógrafos, a papeles,
> arranco de mi corazón al capitán del infierno,
> establezco cláusulas indefinidamente tristes.
>
> Vago de un punto a otro, absorbo ilusiones,
> converso con los sastres en sus nidos:
> ellos, menudo, con voz fatal y fría,
> cantan y hacen huir los maleficios.

(Unnecessary, seeing myself in mirrors, / with a taste of weeks, biographers, papers, / I tear from my heart the captain of hell, / I establish indefinitely sad clauses. / I wander from one point to the next, I absorb illusions, / I talk to tailorbirds in their nests: / they often, with a cold and fatal voice, / sing and make curses flee.)

Like a degraded Narcissus, the speaker has only himself to desire, peering into faded mirrors in order to nourish the illusion of a union. He thus turns to writing the sad, self-exorcising poems whose power reflects the voice of nature, which he had heard in the course of his quest. The present poem will therefore attempt to sustain the illusion of a continuum beyond the fleeting experience of reflection. As in mirrors and on film screens, in dreams the subject becomes its own object and therefore creates the illusion that irony has been suspended. The poem's first two stanzas constitute the moment of extreme irony that precedes the dream vision. Once asleep, the speaker journeys to "un extenso país en el cielo (an extensive country in the sky)," seeking to recapture the same sense of infinity that he had felt at the end of "Galope muerto." By the end of the fifth stanza he has reached that goal (as the exclamation points suggest), in the form of an effulgent day—the same visionary horizon intimated earlier in "Alianza (Sonata)." The speaker soars victoriously over churches and army barracks astride the day's "rojo caballo (red horse)," a scene that bears an uncanny resemblance to the surrealist landscapes of the early Marc Chagall. The piled-up references to the horse's gallop in so short a space ("*galopo* los cuarteles desiertos de soldados [I gallop the soldiers' deserted barracks]," "su cuerpo de campana *galopa* y golpea [its bell body gallops and strikes]") call attention to the source of the original sound of "Galope muerto," a discovery that marks the high point of the dream. The latter phrase especially, with its resounding alliteration, renders a total image of the dream horse, while in the last stanza the speaker once again awakes to the contingent world to which his desire binds him. And yet a change has clearly taken place. At first he could desire only his own image, but now he can escape that solipsism and openly vent his wish for illumination beyond his numbered days: "Yo necesito un relámpago de fulgor persistente, / un deudo festival que asuma mis herencias (I need a lightning of persistent splendor, / a festive relative to receive my inheritance)."

So far, then, we have covered three poems that constitute the first three stages of a sequence: first, the initial vision and its impasse ("Galope muerto"); second, a recasting of the subject-object structure as an intersubjective experience that also ends in failure ("Alianza [Sonata]"); third, a plunge into an explicit dream vision that identifies the source of the original vision ("Caballo de los sueños"). "Débil del alba" ("Weakling of Dawn"), the fourth and last stage, which fittingly takes place at dawn as the speaker awakes, describes the aftermath:

El día de los desventurados, el día pálido se asoma
con un desgarrador olor frío, con sus fuerzas en gris,

sin cascabeles, goteando el alba por todas partes:
es un naufragio en el vacío, con un alrededor de llanto.

Porque se fue de tantos sitios la sombra húmeda, callada
de tantas cavilaciones en vano, de tantos parajes terrestres
en donde debió ocupar hasta el designio de las raíces,
de tanta forma aguda que se defendía.

(The day of the luckless, the pale day peers out / with a tearing
cold smell, with its forces in gray, / without neck bells, dropping dawn everywhere: / it's a shipwreck in the void, with a
surrounding of tears. / Because the moist, silent shadow left
from so many places / from so many cavilings in vain, from so
many earthly sites / in which it must have occupied even the design of roots, / from so many a sharp form that defended itself.)

The day cannot help belonging to the luckless, among whom the
speaker numbers himself. His loss of the preceding dream appears to be
written all over the gloomy morning. The description of dawn cites familiar characteristics (paleness, cold, grayness), but includes the more unusual
"sin cascabeles," which suggests the subject's nostalgia for the "dream
horse." In the glaring absence of the dream horse, dawn sprays its dew
over the landscape, as if crying over his loss. And yet, however gloomy,
the day is nevertheless present, as opposed to the "sombra húmeda, callada," which eludes the form he would like to provide it:

Yo lloro en el medio de lo invadido, entre lo confuso,
entre el sabor creciente, poniendo el oído
en la pura circulación, en el aumento,
cediendo sin rumbo el paso a lo que arriba,
a lo que surge vestido de cadenas y claveles,
yo sueño, sobrellevando mis vestigios mortales.

Nada hay de precipitado, ni de alegre, ni de forma orgullosa,
todo aparece haciéndose con evidente pobreza,
la luz de la tierra sale de sus párpados
no como la campanada, sino más bien como las lagrimas:

el tejido del día, su lienzo débil,
sirve para una venda de enfermos, sirve para hacer señas
en una despedida, detrás de la ausencia:
es el color que sólo quiere remplazar,
cubrir, tragar, vencer, hacer distancias.

(I cry in the midst of the invaded, amid the confused, / amid the
growing flavor, placing my ear / in pure circulation, in the
increase, / yielding without direction the way to what
arrives, / to what sprouts dressed up in chains and
carnations, / I dream, carrying my mortal remains. / There is
nothing precipitous, or joyful, or of proud form, / everything
appears making itself with evident poverty, / the light of earth
comes out of its eyelids / not like the bell stroke but rather like
tears: / the cloth of day, its weak canvas, / is good for a patient's bandage, is good for waving / good-bye, behind
absence: / it's the color that only wishes to replace, / to cover,
to swallow, to vanquish, to make distances.)

In the midst of it all stands the speaker, who, like dawn, is crying and
sharpening his ear to the sounds only he can hear, which, together with
the memory of past dreams, help him withstand the onslaught of time. Absorbed in poverty, the world now literally pales in contrast to the earlier
dream. No "proud form" makes its entrance, and even the dawn's weak
light seems to betray its source by slowly peering out of the earth's "eyelids," refracted by the dawn's haze, instead of breaking through the powerful bell stroke, as it once did in "Galope muerto." The day's weakness, like
surgical gauze, resides in its ontological lack—it covers, replaces, or hides
the wounded world, besides isolating and excluding the subject:

Estoy solo entre materias desvencijadas,
la lluvia cae sobre mí, y se me parece,
se me parece con su desvarío, solitaria en el mundo muerto,
rechazada al caer, y sin forma obstinada.

(I am alone among rickety matter, / the rain falls over me and
resembles me, / resembles me in its derangement, alone in the
dead world, / rejected on falling, and without any obstinate
form.)

Once again, the poem ends with an admission of failure, yet proposing at
the same time a negative resemblance, the missing link between subject and
object: derangement, isolation, and formlessness.

After tracing this particular sequence we can place in context such a
poem as "Unidad" and view its stress on cyclicality as the dialectical result
of the texts that immediately precede it. We realize that the emphasis on
repetition and sameness—in short, on "unity," as if in reversion to the initial stage of siege of "Galope muerto"—is a reaction to the elusiveness of

form that we find dramatized in "Débil del alba." Both "Galope muerto" and "Unidad" represent, then, two pauses after scattered movements, regroupings of forces following plundering raids, as it were, during which the speaker takes stock of those structures that guide visionary perception. Indeed, the striking similarity between "Galope muerto" and "Unidad," as well as the position that each poem assumes within the reading order, should persuade us of their analogous roles in the interplay between the two cyclic principles. Within such an interplay internal vision sustains external sequence by providing recurrent pauses during which the speaker is able to regain his sense of direction, an alternation of spasmodic search and withdrawal not unlike the dialectic of melancholy and irony described in "Arte poética."

More important, however, is the temporal process that is implied by such an external cycle. Much has been written about the presence of time as a theme in *Residencia en la tierra,* but the way time actually works in the text has never been explored. The above sequence, I have argued, is built on a dramatic plot or fictional chronology in which the subject attempts several approaches to the object. The unfolding of an intersubjective alliance, its replacement by an explicit dream state, a cruel awakening at dawn are all sequential scenes from a drama of the visionary mind. Within this drama, the poet articulates his displacement through time, which thus becomes a structural principle as well as a major theme. And just as time appears inscribed in the book's title (both in the reference to a "residence" and in the use of dates), so temporal progression conditions the entire poetic experience. Time determines the subject's desire to fuse with the object and thereby attain immediate presence. The poem represents the process whereby the speaker's consciousness is gradually transformed from dullness to ecstasy to meditative calm. But the fusion to which consciousness aspires never takes place, and the realization of that experience, which would signal the achievement of total poetic knowledge, is postponed in each case. What generates each text, then, is a fruitless search, a deferment of presence in time and space as determined by memory. That is, experience in the poems is never immediate, but only remembered, seen in retrospect, and thus subject to the distortions of recollection. And as in any composite collection—a tradition begun, perhaps, by Petrarch—the poems appear to be arranged *as if* they were in chronological order, a sequence of disjointed scenes from which the reader can only infer a "psychology" and a writing project.

Bearing in mind such a temporal progression, we can conceive of *Residencia en la tierra* as a poetic diary, a kind of *journal intime,* or what

Rodríguez Monegal calls the record of a "season in hell." Neruda's text, like Rimbaud's, is structured according to the subject's experience of time, its writing emerging from, as well as fulfilling, an internal discontinuity that the journal format is meant to repair by unfolding "a kind of ontological respiration, an inward and outward of being, itself punctuated and helping to shape the discontinuous life being lived." It is this journal structure that explains, I think, why the poetry of *Residencia en la tierra* is so intent on registering common objects and events (what critics proverbially note as the most definitive trait of Neruda's poetics), as if wishing to fill the vacuum of aimless temporal succession with the dross and regularity of daily experience. Yet writing fills that vacuum not with things, as critics have mistakenly argued, but only with words, the written representation of those things. Instead of allowing the subject to integrate with the object—or, in temporal terms, to attain the experience of infinity—the poem partially temporalizes that object and that goal and removes both from immediate consumption. Writing becomes, instead, an agent of desire: Tantalus' water and fruit. It is the counterpoint of expressive commitment and ironic demystification that causes the dissonance we encounter at every step between the speaker's desire for presence, on the one hand, and his experience of difference—historical or linguistic time—on the other.

IV

To attempt to trace here the entire plot that is reflected by the entries in this poetic diary would be foolhardy, but it seems clear that we can at least draw two provisional conclusions. The first is that, taken as a whole, the poetry of *Residencia* bears a less negative message than the reading of isolated poems has traditionally suggested. What we see, instead, is that the journal structure lends a textured coherence or continuity that rescues the self from time. But precisely because writing is put at the service of the self, it runs the risk of becoming an idolatrous monument in whose sanctuary the self can evade the perils of an authentic temporal destiny, including death. We shall see that this is in fact the outcome of the self in *Residencia en la tierra*.

For the moment, however, we must heed the second conclusion, which addresses the more pragmatic issue of reading these poems. Once we realize that a temporal drama binds them together, seemingly obscure references are seen in a new light. The first line of "Sonata y destrucciones," for example ("Después de mucho, después de vagas leguas [After a lot, after vague leagues]"), refers to the collective reading experience. If we bear in mind the comprehensive dramatic situation, beyond the poem's own, we can better understand the further description of visionary experience ("Amo lo tenaz que sobrevive en mis ojos [I love the tenacity that survives in my eyes]"), as well as the familiar terms of poetic hearing ("Oigo en mi corazón mis pasos de jinete [In my heart I hear my horseman steps]"). Like "Unidad," the poem describes the same visionary method ("Hay entre ciencias de llanto un altar confuso [Among sciences of weeping there's a confused altar]") as a tension between harmony and disharmony. And the concluding stanza describes yet another familiar experience:

> Acecho, pues, lo inanimado y lo doliente,
> y el testimonio extraño que sostengo,
> con eficiencia cruel y escrito en cenizas,
> es la forma de olvido que prefiero,
> el nombre que doy a la tierra, el valor de mis sueños,
> la cantidad interminable que divido
> con mis ojos de invierno, durante cada día de este mundo.

(Thus, I stalk the inanimate and the mourning, / and the strange testimony I bear, / with cruel efficiency and written in ashes, / is the form of oblivion I prefer, / the name I give to the earth, the value of my dreams, / the endless amount that I divide / with my winter eyes during each day of this world.)

The poet's "testimonio extraño" is given with an "eficiencia cruel," another name for the paradoxical unbridled discipline, so to speak, of visionary experience. The disclosure is both self-referential and self-destructive, as writing is here destined for its own oblivion, thereby neutralizing the possibility of effective witnessing.

This is not to say, obviously, that the poems merely repeat the same points or that they differ only in the arrangement of a few common motifs. We have seen, on the contrary, that there is actual dialectical progress within such a cyclical sequence, even if that progress consists mainly of a negative knowledge about the object. What we discover is the unfolding of an all-encompassing dramatic situation that grounds representation, a scene or theater of writing to which the poems refer in order to legitimize visionary discourse. It is this scene of writing that underlies not only the relationship between subject and object but that of the subject with the experience of vision. Such a setting allows, in other words, for an introspection that unveils patterns of selfhood that are as structured as those in the object. Each poem contains, of course, a glimpse of the visionary subject that allows the reader to infer an overall "psychology," and even such poems as "Arte poética" and "Unidad" go so far as to suggest an internal cyclical pattern. Other texts are even more explicit and focus entirely on the subject, as does "Sistema sombrío" ("Somber System"), for example, which in the reading order immediately follows "Arte poética" and with it shares the center of the book:

> De cada uno de estos días negros como viejos hierros,
> y abiertos por el sol como grandes bueyes rojos,
> y apenas sostenidos pos el aire y por los sueños,
> y desaparecidos irremediablemente y pronto,
> nada ha sustituido mis perturbados orígenes,
> y las desiguales medidas que circulan en mi corazón
> allí se fraguan de día y de noche, solitariamente,
> y abarcan desordenadas y tristes cantidades.

(Of each of these days, black like old irons / and opened up by the sun like great red oxen / and hardly sustained by air and dreams / and inevitably and suddenly gone, / nothing has replaced my confused origins, / and the unequal cadences that circulate in my heart / are forged there by day and night, solitarily, / and embrace disordered and sad measures.)

The title image, itself close to an oxymoron, conveys the proverbial tension that echoes in the image of "días negros." The retrospective scope of the first line is deliberately concise. It assumes the reader's familiarity with such temporal experience as well as with the days' "blackness," which derives from the melancholy imagery of "Arte poética." The series of parallel conjunctive clauses in the first four lines forms a logical sequence whose rhythm conveys that very temporal progression, and together with the retrospective glance it reinforces the impression that the text belongs to a poetic diary. Both the opening and metamorphosis of those same days foster visionary illuminations, but they can hardly be sustained (let alone prolonged or enjoyed) because of the passage of time. Temporal sequence is thus unable to penetrate into the deep realm of the self. Like the cognitive tension that fosters vision, the subject's structure fuses opposite poles of chaos and order: "desiguales medidas" embrace "desordenadas y tristes cantidades," images that suggest the finely tuned parts of a clock that keeps time only because its ticking is not synchronous. These images suggest a deep structure, an underlying order of equal cadences, which feed on paradox and antithesis. This structure makes up the visionary subject. The cyclical structure, fittingly, forms part of a "circula-tory" system (the heart's systole / dyastole) that works against surface in-stability:

> Así, pues, como un vigía tornado insensible y ciego,
> incrédulo y condenado a un doloroso acecho,
> frente a la pared en que cada día tiempo se une,
> mis rostros diferentes se arriman y encadenan
> como grandes flores pálidas y pesadas
> tenazmente substituidas y difuntas.

(Thus, then, like a watchman turned unfeeling and blind, / incredulous and condemned to a painful lurking / in front of the wall in which each one of time's days is joined, / my different faces huddle and link themselves / like great pale heavy flowers / tenaciously replaced and dead.)

The last stanza proceeds logically in a cause-and-effect sequence despite the first line's ending with the apparently absurd self-designation of "blind watchman," a reference to the Romantic figure of the blind poet-prophet. As in "Sonata y destrucciones," the vigil is an active lurking, though unlike it. Earlier the seer had witnessed "lo inanimado y lo doliente (the inani-mate and the mourning)"; now he can see only himself. What we have is a visionary cinema on a screen made up of the total recall of temporal ex-perience and a film showing a succession of masks and a parade of former postures. As a watchman, the subject keeps a constant vigil on himself, in an infinite regression: the watchman watches himself in the act of watching a watchman, ad infinitum. The implication is that of a match of temporal succession at the surface with a succession of masks at the core, a synchro-nization of dailiness and depth identity on behalf of visionary freshness. The image of the chain, first suggested in the earlier "viejos hierros," is the emblem for both this summary identity and the scene of writing, the jour-nal or book of memory that links daily succession.

"Sistema sombrío" aims at a holistic picture of visionary identity by describing a closure, self-contained and self-sustaining, whose formal counterpart is its sonnet form (14 lines). In endowing vision with a "sys-tem" of its own, the poem suggests the extent to which visionary discourse has progressed and its articulation improved. So by the time we reach the end of the first book we are able to realize both the extent of that progress and the impasse to which it has led. Indeed, "Significa sombras" ("It Means Shadows"), the last poem, could be read as an oblique response to "Sis-

tema sombrío," as suggested by the same initials, and as a summary, outlined in the series of rhetorical questions in the first two stanzas, of the
issues probed throughout the first book:

> Qué esperanza considerar, qué presagio puro,
> qué definitivo beso enterrar en el corazón,
> someter en los orígenes del desamparo y la inteligencia,
> suave y seguro sobre las aguas eternamente turbadas?

> Qué vitales, rápidas alas de un nuevo ángel de sueños
> instalar en mis hombros dormidos para seguridad perpetua,
> de tal manera que el camino entre las estrellas de la muerte
> sea un violento vuelo comenzado desde hace muchos días y
>   meses y siglos?

(What hope to consider, what pure presage, / what definitive
kiss to bury in the heart, / submit in the origins of despair
and intelligence, / soft and sure over eternally disturbed
waters? / What vital, rapid wings of a new angel of
dreams / install on my dormant shoulders for the sake of perpetual security, / in such a way that the road between the stars
of death / may be a violent flight begun many days and months
and centuries ago.)

The catalogue reads like a review of the entire book: while "esperanza" and "presagio" recall the experience of "Galope muerto," the "defini-
tivo beso" echoes the erotic fiction in "Alianza (Sonata)"; "orígenes" and
"aguas eternamentes turbadas" outline, in turn, interior and surface levels
analogous to those in "Sistema sombrío," and they virtually quote from
the corresponding passage. Similarly, the "ángel de sueños" recalls the one
in "Colección nocturna," and the "violento vuelo" suggests the same
dreamlike soaring of "Caballo de los sueños." Lacking an answer of their
own, the rhetorical questions carry a tone of retrospective contempt toward all these inquiries. The summary gestures make clear, from the strategic standpoint of the end, that the quest for poetic presence has been a
function of the subject's temporal predicament. The "violento vuelo," for
example, is but a flight out of time, just as the subject's "orígenes" stand
against surface instability. Faced with that uncertainty, the speaker attempts in the third stanza both to rationalize past inquiries and to predict
their outcome:

> Tal vez la debilidad natural de los seres recelosos y
>   ansiosos

busca de súbito permanencia en el tiempo y límites en la
    tierra,
tal vez las fatigas y las edades acumuladas
    implacablemente
se extiendan como la ola lunar de un océano recién creado
sobre litorales y tierras angustiosamente desiertas.

(Maybe the natural weakness of zealous and anxious
beings / suddenly searches for permanence in time and limits on
earth, / maybe the fatigues and the implacably piled-up
ages / will extend like the lunar wave of a newly created
ocean / over shores and lands deserted in anguish.)

The split into past and future times through present and past subjunctive verbs is subtly concealed by the sentence's parallel structure, as if suggesting an undifferentiated continuum. Whereas during past and present
the subject sought comfort from spatial and temporal limits, in the future
he will continue to wish for a union between subject and object that would
fuse his reserves of temporal anxiety to the equally barren objective reality.
That wish translates into several forceful resolutions, the first of which betrays a resignation to the effects of time:

Ay, que lo que soy siga existiendo y cesando de existir,
y que mi obediencia se ordene con tales condiciones de hierro
que el temblor de las muertes y de los nacimientos no
    conmueva
el profundo sitio que quiero reservar para mí eternamente.

Sea, pues, lo que soy, en alguna parte y en todo tiempo,
establecido y asegurado y ardiente testigo,
cuidadosamente destruyéndose y preservándose
    incesantemente,
evidentemente empeñado en su deber original.

(Oh, may whatever I am keep on existing and ceasing to
exist, / and may my obedience arrange itself with such iron
conditions / that the tremor of deaths and births should not
move / the deep place that I wish to reserve for myself
eternally. / May whatever I am, then, be someplace and in all
time, / established and assured and ardent witness, / carefully
destroying and incessantly preserving itself, / clearly set on its
original duty.)

The existential doing and undoing disintegrates and in turn reconstitutes the subject according to the cyclical laws that were established in "Sistema sombrío." The "condiciones de hierro," for example, recall the "viejos hierros" of that poem, as does the "profundo sitio" that wrestles against temporal disruption. A note of relieved self-contentment thus sounds through the two references to "lo que soy," as though the speaker had now reconciled himself to the impossibility of total self-definition. He continues to hope for permanence, as we see in the subtle contrast between "alguna parte" and "todo tiempo," but that hope appears mediated by the constraints of visionary identity. The security of visionary witnessing is countered by the risks of a death-in-life cycle that makes the identity possible. The penultimate line, with its chiastic construction, inverting verbs and adverbs, conveys the complexity of that cycle and again links it to the notion of vision as témporal duty. Vision thus becomes "original" in the dual sense of being both new and faithful to origins, the same origins alluded to earlier as an echo of "Sistema sombrío."

At the end of the first book of *Residencia,* then, the reader is left awaiting an answer because there is none to give, except, of course, the one provided by the last poem. The nebulous affirmation that "it means shadows" does not point to the absence of meaning but rather to the fact that whatever knowledge there is remains shrouded within a mystery that poetic vision has failed to penetrate. The poem describes an impasse, a point beyond which no one can see and where the dialectic of poetry is forced to recoil upon itself. If vision and irony are the two motifs that make up the poetics of *Residencia en la tierra,* then the first book ends by allowing irony to displace vision and returning to the conditions that had produced the scene of writing. The speaker has traced a circuitous journey, since at the end of "Significa sombras" he is no better off than at the beginning of "Galope muerto," the knowledge of having an "original duty" being no clearer than the acknowledgment of a privileged sound. In fact, if we weave together the titles of the first and last poems so as to form a single sentence, we unravel the entire thread of the first book: "Galope muerto significa sombras"—"Dead gallop means shadows." The mystery of vision leads the speaker to inquire into his own nature, but this introspection reaches an impasse as soon as he discovers the negative implications of temporal contingency.

FLORENCE L. YUDIN

The Dialectical Failure in Neruda's "Las furias y las penas"

"Todas las mujeres son la furia"
—MIGUEL DE UNAMUNO, *El otro*

Pablo Neruda's *Third Residence* (1935–45) marks a sharp break from the *Second* (1931–35), heralding radical content and diction. At the same time, this volume in the trilogy also speaks with the desperate, angry voices which dominate parts 1 and 2. Within this context of transition, "Las furias y las penas" is a model text: it combines resemblance in tone and imagery to *Residencias* 1 and 2 with Neruda's new social perspective. Thematically, "Las furias y las penas" bridges earlier and later works by means of its hellish vision of individual violence motivated by social decay. What Neruda had previously expressed in terms of personal alienation, he projects from the nadir of collective bankruptcy and the imminence of gratuitous holocaust. Viewed as a whole, *Tercera residencia* illustrates a fluid coherence of innovation with retrospective, creativity with continuity, that would characterize Neruda's entire development.

In 1939, after the Spanish Civil War had propelled Neruda into the arena of commitment, the poet himself drew attention to his new course, singling out the human and artistic values which impelled a pivotal transition: his conversion from poet as outsider to people's rhapsode. His words introduce section 2 of *Tercera residencia,* entitled "Las furias y las penas":

From *Hispania* 68, no. 1 (March 1985). © 1985 by the American Association of Teachers of Spanish and Portuguese, Inc.

(En 1934 fue escrito este poema. Cuántas cosas han sobreve-
nido desde entonces! España, donde lo escribí, es una cintura
de ruinas. Ay! si con sólo una gota de poesía o de amor pudié-
ramos aplacar la ira del mundo, pero eso sólo lo pueden la lucha y el corazón resuelto.
El mundo ha cambiado y mi poesía ha cambiado.)

The historical rupture to which he refers was accompanied by a literary revelation: Neruda's discovery of Spanish Baroque poetry, whose
champion he saw in Quevedo. René de Costa, one of Neruda's most
thoughtful critics, has summarized pointedly the effects on Neruda of this
"revaluation":

> "Not uncharacteristically, he would eventually detail the cir-
> cumstances of the changes in his work; and in a radio speech
> of 1939 ("Quevedo adentro"), he publicly acknowledged not
> only his admiration for the great Spanish poet, but also the ca-
> talytic effect the belated discovery had on his personal outlook,
> moving him from an attitude of anguished despair to a kind of
> social optimism. What most fascinated Neruda—besides
> Quevedo's condemnation of corruption, his civic spirit, and his
> intense passion for love and life—was his notion of "la agricul-
> tura de la muerte.' "

Thus, two consciousness-raising events—Neruda's experience of the Spanish Civil War, his maturing affinity with the poetry of Quevedo—con-
verged to produce major distinctive features in his poetic vision. "The new
posture assumed is that of a radical nonconformist. *Tercera residencia*
must, therefore, be considered in this light, from the dual perspective of art
and society, poetry and politics."
Despite its importance as a major transitional work, the third of the
Residence volumes, is, according to de Costa, "the least studied and most
maligned." Whatever the muddled pretexts for neglect, the biases are crystal clear: Neruda's controversial treatment of society, politics and sex. To
put this differently, the contents, rather than their poetic expression, have
been the real motive for rejection or silence. By default, Neruda's originality in *Tercera residencia* remains to be illuminated. I hope to invite fresh
thinking with an analysis of "Las furias y las penas," the longest poem in
this volume and perhaps the one with the most extreme point of view.
As the epigraph to "Las furias y las penas," Neruda quotes one verse
from Quevedo's sonnet, "A todas partes que me vuelvo, veo." The line,

"Hay en mi corazón furias y penas," opens the first tercet, in which the "I" blames passion's tyranny for his suffering and guilt. Since Neruda's debt is not limited to the verse cited, it is necessary to quote the sonnet in its entirety:

> A todas partes que me vuelvo, veo
> Las amenazas de la llama ardiente,
> Y en cualquiera lugar tengo presente
> Tormento esquivo y burlador deseo.
>
> La vida es mi prisión, y no lo creo,
> Y al son del hierro, que perpetuamente
> Pesado arrastro y humedezco ausente,
> Dentro en mí propio pruebo a ser Orfeo.
>
> Hay en mi corazón furias y penas:
> En él es el Amor fuego y Tirano;
> Y yo padezco en mí la culpa mia.
>
> ¡Oh dueño sin piedad, que tal ordenas!
> Pues del castigo de enemiga mano
> No es precio ni rescate l'armonia.

What does Neruda do with his model? How large is his debt to Quevedo? Both questions are secondary to my purpose in this explication but they are basic to an understanding of Neruda's explosive originality.

"Las furias y las penas" is divided into twenty-four stanzas, varying in length from one to twenty-seven verses. Its proportions and chaotic expression contrast sharply with Quevedo's formalism. More importantly, while both poems share a related theme—male protest of love's psychic torment—Quevedo's complaint is traditional and cerebral, while Neruda's is unconventional and emotionally savage. Of necessity, Quevedo and Neruda selected from the literary tradition of the Furies those characteristics that suited their individual expressive modes—Baroque/Surrealism, respectively. If we examine the mythological sources, it is clear that Neruda preserves but attenuates key Roman contexts, whereas Quevedo omits the more negative and psychically damaging powers that were attributed to the Eumenides.

Paralleling this contrast in topical focus, Quevedo's poem is also more circumscribed in its human and social implications. While the Baroque victim of passion's contradictions and guilt ascribes his dilemma to the human condition ("La vida es mi prisión"), he does not, in contrast with Neruda's spokesman, denounce society as the model and mirror image of his own sexual violence. Whereas Quevedo's complaint ends on a note of personal defeat ("No es precio ni rescate l'armonía"), Neruda's begins with the assumption that society's moral disintegration conditions man's perversion and embodies his perpetual annihilation ("interminablemente exterminados").

Neruda's context is one of circular crime and punishment: *poenas* in the form of psychic torment, with concomitant rage, resulting in an even more violent action which, in turn, increases the despair. This vicious circularity derives from the need for and repetition of sex: "El impulso erótico [es] . . . ciego, tiránico y devorador," as Amado Alonso was the first to observe. Like their ancient counterparts, Neruda's Furies are implacable. For the modern victim, they personify dehumanization and nihilism: an irrational rejection of the self and others. This is, I believe, the central metaphor of Neruda's sulphuric expression. With the quotation, "Hay en mi corazón furias y penas," Neruda confesses his indebtedness to Quevedo; throughout his poem, he elaborates on his own experience with Quevedo's inner torments—*fuego, Tirano,* and *culpa mía*—, intensifying Quevedo's implied human dilemma; then, Neruda makes of his model the pivot around which to construct a poem whose meaning and structure express devastating failure.

Why the nihilism? For what does Neruda need metaphors of violent sexuality? Mainly, I think, to work out what was at the time of composition (1934), a truncated dialectic. From the subterranean point of view, sustained in *Residencias* 1, 2, personal blackout is the answer to institutionalized dissolution. Perceiving no escape hatch, no way to reach and join a community of unbrutalized others, Neruda's protagonist reacts like a raging somnambulist in an infernal habitat. Drunken technology celebrates the reign of order, but fails to anticipate the obscene product of its renewal. From this extreme, volatile perspective "Las furias y las penas" takes its twisted momentum. The base image of society in the advanced stages of dissociation gives rise to the depiction of individuals as crazed primates.

Society's sickness is mirrored through Neruda's impotent dialectic. Even a surface reading of the text reveals that the wild contradictions go nowhere: like irrational fears, there is no letting go of the demons, no time or space for experiential adjustment, no resolution of antitheses; therefore, no dialectical base. In terms of his evolving *Arte poética,* it seems fair to say that Neruda had not yet reconciled personal contradictions with his social project ("deberes de poeta / tareas humanas"). By keeping in mind the brilliant synthesis of life with society he would soon achieve in *Canto general* (1950), we can gauge both the psychic and artistic distance he needed to travel before reaching a livable dialectic.

The opening lines of "Las furias y las penas" express sharply the dominant theme and convey the tone of the poem:

> En el fondo del pecho estamos juntos,
> en el cañaveral del pecho recorremos
> un verano de tigres,
> al acecho de un metro de piel fría,
> al acecho de un ramo de inaccesible cutis,
> con la boca olfateando sudor y venas verdes
> nos encontramos en la húmeda sombra que deja caer besos.

It is unclear in the first seven lines who is the grammatical subject: is it "I" against myself—my Furies—or is it "I" / "You"? This ambiguity appears in other sections of the poem, sometimes marking "ella" / "enemiga," at other times projecting a divided self. With no holds barred, Neruda exposes the animal instincts of mutually destructive partners: enemies joined in the hunt for sexual gratification. In his brief, but incisive judgment of Neruda's imagistic originality (stanza 1), Amado Alonso asserts: " 'Las furias y las penas' toca directamente en la llaga, al encararse sin rodeos ni derivaciones con el impulso erótico mismo."

It is useful to put into perspective the radical diction and naked referents in the poet's expression. Neruda pulled back the trappings of centuries of love poetry to unmask the beast; namely, his version of alienated sex. What remains of human relationship is a mere shadow: both partners abuse each other, in apparent disregard of their common humanity. Thus, whomever he meant to be the subject is antagonist and mirror image: "nos encontramos en la húmeda sombra que deja caer / besos." *Húmedo,* as a natural characteristic, usually carries positive connotations in Neruda's lexicon, as when he refers to the Chilean forest (*Memorias*), or in the context of reconnecting with natural sources ("Entrada a la madera," *Segunda residencia,* 4). But in "Las furias y las penas" even origins are negatively charged because the sex act is both re-birth and death.

Stanza 2 lashes out against the female antagonist, while it also establishes the fierce symbiosis between the lovers:

> Tú mi enemiga de tanto sueño roto de la misma manera
> que erizadas plantas de vidrio, lo mismo que campanas
> deshechas de manera amenazante, tanto como disparos
> de hiedra negra en medio del perfume.

The progression of comparisons suggests unleashed fury, trampling whatever lies in its path, be it animate or inanimate. Mounting aggressivity and
gigantism choke the environs. And like the symbolic inversion of *húmedo,*
campanas announces a frightful menace, rather than the vitality which the
term generally conveys in Neruda's poetry. As if to signal the imminent
onslaught, each imagistic pair in stanza 2 contains a striking antithesis between human and dehumanized reality. Within the gathering war clouds,
surrealistic threats materialize:

> enemiga de grandes caderas que mi pelo han tocado
> con un ronco rocío, con una lengua de agua,
> no obstante el mudo frio de los dientes y el odio de los ojos,
> y la batalla de agonizantes bestias que cuidan el olvido.

Alienated sex is like a re-enactment of one's elemental fears. Neruda suggests this paradigm in icily physical terms; alternatively, each can match
the other's threshold of violence:

> en algún sitio del verano estamos juntos
> acechando con labios que la sed ha invadido.
> . . . .
> tengo también tus ojos de sangrienta luciérnaga
> capaces de impregnar y atravesar rodillas
> y gargantas rodeadas de seda general.
>
> (stanza 2)

Whether such fusion of instinct and conscious ferocity are metaphors of a
primal nature, they clearly reflect mutual hatred and the need to wound.
What the speaker envisions as his own rapacious drive, he projects on the
other, and magnifies the potential violence. As with the repeated criminal
offenses of a single individual, there seems to be the knowledge that once
you have crossed the threshold of violence, it is easy to do again and again.
We recognize this inward and outward looking at cruelty as a radical trend
in certain contemporary arts: "To involve oneself with violence can indeed
compel one into thought about oneself and man and society, sometimes
very painful and disconcerting thought."

Having conceded brutalization as the erotic mode, the victim /
victimizer depicts his female counterpart as a prehistoric amphibian, stalk-
ing the earth, and targeting her prey with polymorphous instinct:

> pero ahí están tus ojos oliendo a cacería,
> a rayo verde que agujerea pechos,
> tus dientes que abren manzanas de las que cae sangre,
> tus piernas que se adhieren al sol dando gemidos,
> y tus tetas de nácar y tus pies de amapola,
> como embudos llenos de dientes que buscan sombra,
> como rosas hechas de látigo y perfume, y aun,
> aun más, aun más,
> aun detrás de los párpados, aun detrás del cielo,
> aun detrás de los trajes y los viajes, en las calles donde
>   la gente orina,
> adivinas los cuerpos.

Both the chaotic description and repeated qualifier ("aun más") suggest the inability of the speaker to define or adequately express the wildly irrational nature of his enemy. His is a dual failure, rooted in the dissolution of identity, bound to the sterility of mutual hatred ("tengo también tus ojos de sangrienta luciérnaga"). With the ghastly words, "adivinas los cuerpos," we view primitive behavior through the lens of surrealism. The chain of verbs that follows plots the course of animalism: "acechas," "rompes," "caes haciendo crepitar," "adivinas los cuerpos." This is not sexual hunger but biological rapacity: a human being driven by anti-human instinct:

> Como un insecto herido de mandatos,
> adivinas el centro de la sangre y vigilas
> los músculos que postergan la aurora, asaltas sacudidas,
> relámpagos, cabezas,
> y tocas largamente las piernas que te guían.
>
>   (stanza 3)
>
> Oh, conducida herida de flechas especiales!
>
>   (stanza 4)

Implicit in these lines is the depiction of woman as pitiless Fury, stronger than life's force, sexually perverse, and bent on death. Yet out of such a totally negative context, Neruda's expressive art produces the beautifully alliterative verse which is the fourth stanza.

The ambiguity of identity, which we examined in the opening lines of this poem, intensifies to such a degree that it is now the male antagonist who points the way to vicious sex: "Mi odio es una sola mano que te indica / el callado camino." Like his mythical counterparts, enraged by the all-powerful Furies, the modern victim rails against himself, only to become the accomplice in a sickening spiral of prostitution:

> con sobresalto: llegas
> y ruedas por el suelo manejada y mordida,
> y el viejo olor del semen como una enredadera
> de cenicienta harina se desliza a tu boca.
>
> (stanza 7)

From the anguish which gives first voice to this poem, a floodtide of alienating phenomena engulfs the antagonists. Their intercourse is a cholerically futile defense against despair. Their habitat is correspondingly inhospitable, a nightmarish admixture of Eros and the grotesque:

> Ay leves locas copas y pestañas,
> aire que inunda un entreabierto río
> como una sol-paloma de colérico cauce,
> como atributo de agua sublevada,
> ay substancias, sabores, párpados de ala viva
> con un temblor, con una ciega flor temible.

In this modern Armageddon, everything converges at the apex of hell: "y duras olas que suben la piel hacia la muerte."

Hell is the vision of the radically alienated; its torments made more savage through inescapable repetition. Amado Alonso understood poignantly the underlying desperation in Neruda's erotic nightmare:

> En ninguna parte baja como aquí nuestro poeta a lo puramente instintivo y animal, y por eso en ninguna parte se declara tan bien como aquí ["Las furias y las penas"] el papel que lo erótico desempeña en el angustiado mundo poético de Pablo Neruda. En medio de la universal desintegración y de la angustia, ceder al vértigo de lo erótico, entregarse al paroxismo fugaz (por eso una y otra vez buscado) de las fuerzas elementales de nuestra vida, es un desesperado intento de huida y de romper la radical soledad.

With stanza 10, the poet draws sharp referential lines around his epigraph, "Hay en mi corazón furias y penas." Lodged in his chest, like a metallic crusher, hatred pounds away:

> Entonces es que estoy verdaderamente, verdaderamente lejos
> y un río de agua ardiendo pasa en lo oscuro.
> Ay cuántas veces eres la que el odio no nombra,

y de qué modo hundido en las tinieblas,
y bajo qué lluvias de estiércol machacado
su estatua en mi corazón devora el trébol.

Perhaps because it harks backward to *Residencias* 1, 2 and pushes forward Neruda's social project, "Las furias y las penas" embodies the dilemma of an irrational dialectic and elaborates an unbearable prospect. If I am correct in taking "el odio" as the antecedent of "su estatua," the speaker is at dead center: exiled, devoid of feeling, self-destroying. Rejection of self and hatred of the devouring other preclude humanity. In the zones of radical negativity which Neruda explores, sex is not renewal; rather, like a ricocheting missile, its destructive energy returns to knock down hunted and hunter. Hatred and despair, rejection and submission, oscillate to the rhythm of nihilism.

The "Furies and Punishments" of failed humanity feed on themselves in Neruda's subterranean vision. With no viable outlet, these irrational outbursts fixate on woman as whore. She is reduced to a single, emasculating function, wearing the scarlet brand of ire and perversity:

> El odio es un martillo que golpea tu traje
> y tu frente escarlata,
> y los días del corazón caen en tus orejas
> como vagos búhos de sangre eliminada,
> y los collares que gota a gota se formaron con lágrimas
> rodean tu garganta quemándote la voz como con hielo.
>
> (stanza 11)

The speaker calls upon the Furies to impose punishment befitting sub-human criminality:

> Es para que nunca, nunca
> hables, es para que nunca, nunca
> salga una golondrina del nido de la lengua
> y para que las ortigas destruyan tu garganta
> y un viento de buque áspero te habite.
>
> (stanza 12)

Isn't this threat the ultimate revenge a poet might conceive? Not to have speech, not to sing, to have one's voice pierced, this is the rhapsode's most bitter attack on his primal enemy.

Given the foregoing contexts of dehumanization, we can expect no fellowship, no reaching out to overcome numbness. In only three instances does the speaker name people other than his "enemiga"; and all appear or are remembered with phantom-like shapes. For the narrator, other men are anonymous forms, like himself, cyphers in a prostitute's bodycount:

> En dónde te desvistes?
> En un ferrocarril, junto a un peruano rojo
> o con un segador, entre terrones, a la violenta
> luz del trigo?
> O corres con ciertos abogados de mirada terrible
> largamente desnuda, a la orilla del agua de la noche?
>
> (stanza 13)

Impelled by insatiable appetite, man's enemy perceives neither individuality nor sensual reality. What she touches is shrunken to the bottom line of brutal indulgence:

> Miras: no ves la luna ni el jacinto
> ni la oscuridad goteada de humedades,
> ni el tren de cieno, ni el marfil partido:
> ves cinturas delgadas como oxígeno,
> pechos que aguardan acumulando peso
> e idéntica al zafiro de lunar avaricia
> palpitas desde el dulce ombligo hasta las rosas.
>
> (stanza 14)

Stripped of any femininity, the erotic enemy pulses through lives, like a laser, grimly implacable.

Stanza 15 makes a transition in which the poem moves away from the particular (you / I) towards a generalization about life's emptiness. Through imagery that links abortive nature with human sterility, the narrator strikes a universally desolate chord: succession, whether in nature, individuals or time, atomizes:

> Por qué sí? Por qué no? Los días descubiertos
> aportan roja arena sin cesar destrozada
> a las hélices puras que inauguran el día,
> y pasa un mes con corteza de tortuga,
> pasa un estéril día,
> pasa un buey, un difunto,
> una mujer llamada Rosalía,
> y no queda en la boca sino un sabor de pelo
> y de dorada lengua que con sed se alimenta.
> Nada sino esa pulpa de los seres,
> nada sino esa copa de raíces.

If a sense of being already dead but still dreaming pervades "Las furias y las penas," here it spreads like a dense fog, under whose cover the illusion of reality terminates.

Disintegration, therefore the impossibility of continuity, formulates one of the poem's key metaphors. Alone, the "I" is spectator and actor in the drama of end-game: "Yo persigo como en un túnel roto, en otro extremo / carne y besos que debo olvidar injustamente." He has wallowed on humanity's sordid bed, "cien veces ocupada por miserables parejas," retelling the story of incessant failure, of nowhere man and woman: "tú y yo / hemos estado juntos derribando cuerpos, / construyendo una casa que no dura ni muere." The deadness of love making is augmented by the inability to connect with other human beings, to bridge solitudes dialectically. Thus, efforts to find a way out of the black, to reverse stasis, end in pulverization:

> tú y yo hemos corrido juntos un mismo río
> con encadenadas bocas llenas de sal y sangre,
> tú y yo hemos hecho temblar otra vez las luces verdes
> y hemos solicitado de nuevo las grandes cenizas.
>
> (stanza 16)

If there are no personal or temporal linkages, each action is a onceness, governed by chance, flat and ultimately absurd. Such is the common thread woven into the last eight stanzas of "Las furias y las penas." But unlike the majority of preceding sections, the final block of verses is characterized by more objective diction and certain rational statements:

> Recuerdo sólo un día
> que tal vez nunca me fue destinado,
> era un día incesante,
> sin orígenes. Jueves.
> Yo era un hombre transportado al acaso
> con una mujer hallada vagamente.
>
> (stanza 17)

As if wiped clean of memory, the speaker has only unmarked time—static continuity—and the fleeting recall of orgasm on which to make his moorings. The terrible alienation of sexual antagonists rebounds grimly in the next sequence:

> nos desnudamos
> como para morir o nadar o envejecer
> y nos metimos uno dentro del otro.
>
> (stanza 17)

The sex act has no apparent climax, only a pathetic finality or an inconclusive dropping off. In this erotic hell, the partners are both loveless and incompatible, briefly joined in a doomed attempt at salvaging a shadow of identity:

> ella rodeándome como un agujero,
> yo quebrantándola como quien
> golpea una campana,
> pues ella era el sonido que me hería
> y la cúpula dura decidida a temblar.

They are irreconcilably separate, each one debasing the other as the agent of his / her unbearable frustration and total failure.

The mixed sequence of tenses in stanza 18 suggests that Neruda meant its verbal structure as a kind of summing up: "Era una sorda ciencia"; "he rodado a las grandes coronas genitales." The circularity, from where the speaker has been to where he is, defines both the content and literary form of "Las furias y las penas." The poet explicitly draws attention to this alliance:

> Este es un cuento de puertos adonde
> llega uno, al azar, y sube a las colinas,
> suceden tantas cosas.

The main idea contained here telescopes the philosophical outlook of the entire poem. What makes up life's narrative ("cuento") are single, unconnected events, governed by chance, and meaningless ("suceden"). Man is out of control, like someone hallucinating one-night stands in sordid places. This statement and the one that follows provide the clearest outline of the thrust and power in "Las furias y las penas."

Stanza 20 correlates the speaker's anguish with his sense of betrayal. We witness the last spark before terminal disillusionment:

> Enemiga, enemiga,
> es posible que el amor haya caído al polvo
> y no haya sino carne y huesos velozmente adorados
> mientras el fuego se consume
> y los caballos vestidos de rojo galopan al infierno?

From the point of view which informs the violence and hopelessness of the poem, Neruda needed radical diction and esthetic nonconformity to carry his expression from wasteland to printed page. Therefore, I believe that it is faithful to the text to understand "Las furias y las penas" as an art of love, in diametric opposition to Ovid's *Ars Amandi*.

Echoing leitmotivs, stanza 21 states in a low key the pain of illusions smashed. Both the kind and quality of desired realities have been banished and will remain locked out of the speaker's future:

> Yo quiero para mí la avena y el relámpago
> a fondo de epidermis,
> y el devorante pétalo desarrollado en furia,
> y el corazón labial del cerezo de junio,
> y el reposo de lentas barrigas que arden sin dirección,
> pero me falta un suelo de cal con lágrimas
> y una ventana donde esperar espumas.

The longed-for intensities, such as the experience of true passion, will be denied. He is hemmed in, totally isolated and without a spark of hope.

In contrast with the plea for repose, stanzas 22 and 23 mandate an ineluctible, berserk future: "corre," "corre," "corre," "golpea," "derriba." With the final image, this devastating wave of frenzy crests in frozen sexual assault:

> y entra en medio del sol y la ira de un día de puñales
> a echarte como paloma de luto y nieve sobre un cuerpo.

In words more dreadful than Quevedo's most piercing *desengaño*, Neruda encloses his "Furias y penas" in the grip of death against life:

> Es una sola hora larga como una vena,
> y entre el ácido y la paciencia del tiempo arrugado
> transcurrimos,
> apartando las sílabas del miedo y la ternura,
> interminablemente exterminados.
>
> (stanza 24)

Thus, hunter and hunted come together in fatal stasis, and the tragedy of their defeat will be played out endlessly in the theater of the absurd. Like the best of Neruda's poetic codas, these lines are remarkable in their fusion of terrible import with beautiful cadence.

The poetic coherence of "Las furias y las penas" derives from its underlying dialectical fault. Like natural rifts, Neruda's is a metaphor of catastrophe. His male / female antagonism feeds on its own bitter divorce; blocked by psychic and moral bankruptcy, the possibility of union, through sexual or social action, could not find entry in his esthetic of dehumanization.

Consequently, "Las furias y las penas" denies man's freedom, debasing the human condition to the denominator of regression:

> y nos quedamos solos y cobardes
> ante la vida que negamos.

Not until he sees a way clear of the blackout, will Pablo Neruda affirm livable synthesis:

> Y juntos
> somos completos como un solo río,
> como una sola arena.

The organic untiy of Neruda's work shows a pattern of evolution plus revolution. In such a dynamics, even the occasional extreme perspective offers adequate textuality. Despite its failed dialectic, "Las furias y las penas" sustains a haunting beauty in meaning and tone. Thus, this major transitional poem bears the unmistakable signature of Neruda's originality and achievement.

ALFRED J. MacADAM

Neruda's España en el corazón: *Genre and Historical Moment*

The visionary, the satirist, and the prophet come together in *España en el corazón,* subtitled *Himno a las glorias del pueblo en la guerra.* Neruda's use of the word "hymn" here points out just what he hopes to accomplish and, paradoxically, just what his poem cannot achieve. It is impossible to separate the hymn from divine worship, from a community's relationship to God. Thus, in elevating the "people" to the condition of deity, Neruda evokes in this title the hymn's "radical of presentation" in order to conjure up Frye's "participation mystique." The poet's "I" becomes a communal "I," just as the generic designation "hymn" constitutes an attempt to overcome or transcend individuality. The poet-prophet is one with his people: They speak through him; he is their voice. But because there is no divinity present in the poem except at the level of rhetoric, we must assume Neruda is really writing an ode and not a hymn, that Neruda's voice remains his own. Paul Fry has elucidated the peculiar relationship between hymn and ode:

> Only the hymn speaks from knowledge, while the ode always hopes for knowledge. . . . Perhaps there is no such thing as a hymn of participation; if so, then the difference between hymn and ode is simply the difference between common prayer and personal prayer. By imitating hymnody, however, an ode reveals *its* conception of a hymn as a being-present to a transcendent, originary voice. The aim of the ode is to recover and usurp the voice to which hymns defer: not merely to participate in the presence of voice but to *be* the voice.

From *Textual Confrontations.* © 1987 by the University of Chicago. University of Chicago Press, 1987.

Fry's remarks apropos of Shelley's "Hymn to Intellectual Beauty" enable us to see just what is at stake in Neruda's "hymn": "In the opening lines [Shelley] pretends that his incomparably esoteric numen is an object of common prayer by singing apparently in behalf of a congregation. . . . Hereafter the poem lapses into the first-person singular and the language of private experience, by no means with the purpose of declaring, with collective intimacy, 'A mighty fortress is my God.' Shelley's hymn is an ode." We may assume, with Fry, irony on Shelley's part and, in Neruda's case, a sincere desire for community. The result for both poets is, nevertheless, an ode.

Neruda invokes the hymn modality in order to sing a song of praise to the Spanish people and to encourage them in a time of trouble. But there is much more than exhortation in *España en el corazón,* precisely because it is not a hymn. It contains a fragment of autobiography (as do Claudel's odes), a great deal of invective against the Nationalists, commemorations of battles, a lyrical evocation of Madrid in 1937, an encomium of the International Brigade, and a final, prophetic paean to the People's Army. Auden's elegy [*Spain*] deals with the individual's need to make decisions in order to maintain his identity and integrity: a stoic, Lucanesque attitude toward death. Neruda's ode exhorts those on the "good" side to fight on, to victory or death. As Fry says, "The ode differs from elegy . . . chiefly in coming upon death while meaning to talk about birth; whereas in the typical movement of an elegy it is the other way around." Auden's melancholy voice preaches a lesson about living, while Neruda's impassioned hymn directs its audience into the jaws of death.

It is absolutely essential we keep in mind the ideas of persona and "radical of presentation": The poet Neruda is not Neruda the man, just as Walt the titanic singer of America is not Walt Whitman, and *España en el corazón* only makes sense if we understand that the poet aspires to speak for a collectivity. His autobiographical interpolation both destroys his prophetic role in an absolute sense and, paradoxically, affirms it. This brief lapse into individuality would have been appropriate in a measured, elegiac self-analysis in Auden's style, a way of documenting how a conversion took place, but Neruda, through his persona, tells instead why a poet of self-expression, of anguished and gigantic ego—one who even here uses his most idiosyncratic metaphors—had to abandon himself and become a socially committed, post-Romantic poet.

The "old man" (in the religious sense) is not dead, just swept aside by circumstance. Neruda, then, is fusing two rhetorics he had previously kept separate, the rhetoric of poetry and the rhetoric of ideology. The occasion of the Civil War is, to be sure, the crucible in which they fuse, but the process had begun earlier, specifically in Neruda's translation of William Blake's *Visions of the Daughters of Albion* and "The Mental Traveller," which he published in the Spanish magazine *Cruz y raya* in 1934.

Neruda's criteria in selecting Blake texts for a Spanish audience are entirely personal. "The Mental Traveller" and *The Visions of the Daughters of Albion* document moments in the cyclical, recurring failure of mankind to achieve what in Blake's terms "Humanity Divine Incomprehensible" attains at the end of *Jerusalem* IV. In that text the Four Faces of Humanity converse:

> And they conversed together in Visionary forms dramatic which bright
> Redounded from their Tongues in thunderous majesty, in Visions
> In new Expanses, creating exemplars of Memory and of Intellect,
> Creating Space, creating Time, according to the wonders Divine
> Of Human Imagination throughout all the Three Regions immense
> Of Childhood, Manhood & Old Age.

This is the moment when the Imagination reaches autonomy, the "Spectre" of doubt banished, when the poet is not "pure and disposed to rise to the stars," but capable of creating the cosmos through his own visionary powers. "To me this world is all one continued vision of Fancy or Imagination" says Blake in a letter to Reverend Trusler, a statement that makes him equal to Rimbaud in postulating a visionary self that would transcend egoism.

"The Mental Traveller" describes the abject human condition: sexual differentiation, instinctive breeding, inability to rise above contingency. The narrator of the poem is a superhuman observer who describes the newborn child as the fruit of contradiction ("born in joy / begotten in dire woe"), and how, if he is male, he is given to an old woman who "nails him down upon a rock, / catches his shrieks in cups of gold." As the boy matures, the woman grows younger: He turns into an aged wanderer, she into a maiden. He pursues her madly until he becomes, once again, an infant. At the end, he is "the frowning Babe," in a grotesque nativity scene. Harold Bloom comments:

> Where the first half of the poem described the mutual betrayals
> between man and nature, the second is concerned with man's
> failure to transmute nature into art, but again the guilt is dou-
> ble. The Poor Man, as he has become, finds a Maiden again, in
> an earlier phase than that of the one who rejected him for an
> earlier vision of himself. But he has learned nothing from his
> defeats, and this embrace costs him the remnants of his imagi-
> native vision.

> *(The Visionary Company)*

The only way this ever-worsening process of repetition can be stopped is
through an explosion of the imagination.

The Visions of the Daughters of Albion also deals with the individual's failure to embrace his own imagination and, like "The Mental Traveller," also concentrates on human sexuality. Here the protagonist is
female, Oothoon, raped by Bromion, a lustful thunder deity, as she is on
her way to her intended mate Theotormon, an anguished ocean god.
Bromion, like Amnon in the story of Absalom, rejects Oothoon as a harlot,
but when she turns to Theotormon for consolation she finds only tormented indecision: He can neither love nor despise her. Oothoon is sexually alive in a world where sexuality is repressed. The end of the poem,
a kind of *Huit Clos,* describes Oothoon lamenting while "Theotormon
sits / Upon the margin'd ocean conversing with shadows dire." The
Daughters of Albion, the female chorus of the text, redouble Oothoon's
lamentations, thereby showing that all women share her doom.

The erotic element in Neruda's poetry (1934 is the year of his highly
erotic "Las furias y las penas" [furies and sufferings]) finds an echo in the
defense of sexuality in the *Visions,* just as Blake's criticism of a society
based on repression and the blind acceptance of dogma would also have
appealed to him. But even more important to him is the central theme of
both "The Mental Traveller" and the *Visions*: the need to transcend social
restraints (including orthodox religion) and individuality in order to become visionary. To be a Visionary is to see all (the motto of the *Visions* is
"The Eye sees more than the Heart knows") and not to need the comforting rules of society to survive. We cannot know if Neruda ever thought
himself a visionary, but we can imagine that in trying to be one he would
take on, most poignantly in 1937, the role of *vox populi,* the prophetic
voice of the people. Neruda's denunciation of things as they are parallels
Blake's, and both evoke a world that might be. In 1937, however, Neruda
concentrates on denouncing what is happening during the Spanish Republic's hour of need.

España en el corazón divides into twenty-four parts, the divisions indicated by a word or phrase in the margin, similar to the marginal tags in "The Rime of the Ancient Mariner." Probably copied from biblical annotation, this technique reappears in Neruda's *Canto general,* but he does not use it in his books of lyric poetry, either before or after *España en el corazón,* no doubt because the *persona* of all those books is a single individual.

The first division of the poem is entitled "Invocación," but who or what the poet seeks to invoke is ambiguous. In the ode, the poet does not follow the model of the epic poet's invocation of the muse to sing through him, in effect to be his memory, although Neruda does to some extent assume the posture of the epic poet here the better to remind the reader of the "arms and the people" aspect of his poem. Nor is Neruda's invocation precisely like the hymn-writer's calling upon God because God, after all, is already present.

His invocation is really an apostrophe. In that device the poet speaks to a place, a person (usually absent), or a *genius loci,* and those mute agencies speak through the poet or allow the poet to blend with them. If we examine Neruda's first poetic sentence, we see it lacks a predicate verb: The two verbs present are an infinitive and part of a modifying clause. This is an extreme example of ellipsis—something important is missing. We see a will or a desire, "la voluntad de un canto / con explosiones, el deseo / de un canto inmenso (the desire for a song / with explosions, the desire / for an immense song)," but the "I" who wills or desires carefully excludes reference to himself. The "radical of presentation" is one in which no mention of the singer is necessary, in which the singer is before us, in profound communication with us. He invokes the energy of imagination—inevitably and fatally his own imagination—to provide him with a song, a verbal metaphor for a substance: "un metal que recoja / guerra y desnuda sangre (a metal that includes / war and naked blood)." This metal would be a kind of war trumpet, but its blast would include love ("la rosa pura y partida [the pure and split rose])" and cosmology ("el origen / de cielo y aire y tierra [the origin / of sky and air and earth])." In the images of the rose and the song about origins, we see two traditions: the amatory (sacred and profane, the rose is "split") and the prophetic. The poet seeks to convoke the traditional powers of the poet in order to reveal the meaning of what is happening in Spain. To do this he uses the traditional poetic devices, images, and the full panoply of tropes. Thus invocation becomes apostrophe: The absent power invoked has always been present in the poet; he will make it visible through his text.

The next division is a genuine apostrophe. Neruda addresses his subject: Spain, the motherland ("Madre natal"). His address is a simple question: "¿Quién? por caminos, quién, / quién, quién? en sombra, en sangre, quién? / en destello, quién, / quién? (Who?, along roads, who, / who, who? in shadow, in blood, who? / in distillation, who / who?)." The poet asks Spain to identify her enemies, those who have turned her into "machacada piedra, combatida ternura, de trigo, cuero y animal ardiendo (smashed stone, fought tenderness, of wheat, hide and burning animal)." Neruda calls civil war matricide, a horror suggested in the confrontation between Julius Caesar and the personification of Rome in the *Pharsalia*. The difference is that, in Lucan, Rome speaks while here Neruda speaks for Spain. Suddenly the questioning is interrupted by violent action, the division entitled "Bombardeo" ("Bombardment").

Neruda's rhetorical intention in this section is to approximate the reality of war insofar as words can represent that turmoil. He combines asyndeton and polysyndeton: "Cae / ceniza, cae / hierro / y piedra y muerte y llanto y llamas (Falls / ash, falls / iron / and stone and death and wailing and flames)," a mixture of concrete substances and abstractions that reaffirms the apocalyptic tone set at the beginning in the invocation-apostrophe. Lists are one of Neruda's favorite devices, especially in *Residencia en la tierra (Residence on Earth)*, and their appearance here indicates that even when Neruda becomes a prophetic poet he does not abandon his earlier hermetic style. He simply subordinates that style to a new intention: Here the topsy-turvy world does not reflect an anguished ego but a situation in which the forces of repression are metaphors for a demonic anti-order. They recreate on an ideological or moral plane the unnamed sources of anguish in Neruda's earlier expressionistic poetry.

The third phase of *España en el corazón*, "Maldición" ("Curse"), is a ritual cursing of the enemy which evokes the magic of satiric vituperation. Ironically, it links Neruda with a poet fighting on the fascist side in the Spanish Civil War, Roy Campbell. In *Flowering Rifle* (1939), which Robert C. Elliott analyzes in *The Power of Satire* as a model of magical invective, Campbell compares his verses to a lasso for catching enemies: "If only once I'd whirled the whistling line / To get them hog-tied with iambic twine." Neruda's curses, especially in his attacks on Generals Sanjurjo, Mola, and Franco, are, like his attempts to recreate war in language, linguistic raids on reality: Here he wants to weave a spell around the enemy generals. This shamanistic desire to use poetry as magic reappears in Neruda's promise that Spain will rise from her own ashes: "Patria surcada, / juro que en tus cenizas / nacerás como flor de agua perpetua, / juro que de tu boca de sed saldrán al aire / los pétalos del pan, la derramada / espiga inaugurada. (Furrowed father land, / I swear that in your ashes / you will be born like a flower of perpetual water, / I swear that from your mouth of thirst will issue into air / the petals of bread, the poured out / inaugurated seed)." There is no inconsistency here because Neruda's interpretation of the ode allows him to mix anything with a call to arms.

The reader is not, therefore, surprised to find an autobiographical section in the text in which Neruda talks about his poetic conversion. "Explico algunas cosas (I shall explain a few things)" is comparable to those passages in Virgil or Spenser where the poet notes his passages from pastoral to epic poetry. Neruda goes further, virtually parodying the style of his own earlier books, especially *Residencia en la tierra*:

> Preguntaréis: ¿Y dónde están las lilas?
> Y la metafísica cubierta de amapolas?
> Y la lluvia que a menudo golpeaba
> Sus palabras llenándolas
> De agujeros y pájaros?
> Os voy a contar todo lo que me pasa.

> (You might ask: Where are the lilies?
> And the poppy-covered metaphysics?
> And the rain that often beat
> On his words filling them
> With holes and birds?
> I'm going to tell you everything that's going on with me.)

Neruda is deliberately conversational and prosaic here in order to point out the sharp division between the present and the past—a past of personal experience and poetic past with its own system of images. He goes on to describe his life in prewar Madrid, his friends Federico García Lorca and Rafael Alberti, the pastoral quality of his flower-covered house and neighborhood despite their urban setting. Then he chronicles the disasters of war, the fire that consumes the idealized past. All that remains is his voice, damning the enemy and urging the reader to come and see the blood flowing in the streets—another device to incorporate the reader into the action.

Neruda dedicates the rest of the poem to listing catastrophes and Republican heroism. Despite his attempts to maintain the hope that a new day will dawn for Spain, his poem becomes increasingly melancholy, almost elegiac. The genre clearly begins to work its effect on the poet at this point. The poet aspires to be the voice of the people, longs to embody its collective spirit, desires both to incite action and to be action, but the very weight of its own rhetorical baggage pulls it back to earth. In the section entitled "Canto sobre unas ruinas" ("Song on Some Ruins"), Neruda turns to the Spanish Baroque for poetic guidance, particularly, as Alain Sicard and others have pointed out, to Rodrigo Caro's "Canción a las ruinas de Itálica" ("Song to the ruins of Italica"). Neruda begins this section in the demonstrative style of all poems on ruins:

> Esto que fue creado y dominado,
> esto que fue humedecido, usado, visto
> yace—pobre pañuelo—entre las olas
> de tierra y negro azufre.

> (This that was created and dominated,
> this that was moistened, used, seen
> lies—poor handkerchief—among the waves
> of earth and black sulphur.)

Neruda talks about Spain as a geographical and moral reality, much in the way Auden describes the entire Iberian peninsula in *Spain* as a "fragment nipped" from Africa. However, where Auden makes the peninsula into a no-man's-land of existential decision, Neruda links it to the tradition of poems that meditate on ruins as metaphors for the ephemeral nature of life. Rodrigo Caro's "canción" begins:

> Estos, Fabio, ay dolor, que ves ahora
> campos de soledad, mustio collado,
> fueron un tiempo Itálica famosa.

> (These, Fabius, oh grief, you see now,
> fields of solitude, parched hill,
> were once famous Italica.)

The two passages complement each other to such an extent that the reader is left wondering whether Neruda is using Rodrigo Caro as a touchstone or as a subject of parody. Is he evoking the great Hispanic tradition of *desengaño,* with its metaphysical invitation to the reader to think about his own "ruin" and his ultimate destiny, or is he mocking that tradition by urging the reader to save Spain from destruction? Despite the oratory of exhortation, the mood here is that of despair.

The rest of *España en el corazón* is an attempt to snatch hope from the ashes of this despair. The final division of the poem, "Oda solar al Ejército del Pueblo" ("Solar Ode to the People's Army"), aside from explicitly linking the entire text to the ode tradition, is an exhortation to the Republican army. But even as he pushes that army forward in space ("adelante, España, / adelante, campanas populares / adelante, regiones de manzana, / adelante, estandartes cereales, mayúsculos del fuego [forward, Spain, / forward, bells of the people, / forward, apple regions, / forward, cereal standards, capital letters of fire]) in a desire to push it foward in time, to the time of victory, the poem seems to confess its inherent despair.

Neruda tells the army that all the implements the people use would like to march with them ("cada instrumento, cada rueda roja, / cada mango de sierra o penacho de arado, / cada extracción del suelo, cada temblor de sangre / quiere seguir tus pasos, Ejército del Pueblo [every instrument, every red wheel, / every saw handle, every plow handle, / everything taken from the soil, every pulse of blood / wants to follow your steps, People's Army]") to that ever-more abstract victory. In conclusion, he tells the army:

> tu luz organizada llega a los pobres hombres
> olvidados, tu definida estrella
> clava sus roncos rayos en la muerte
> y establece los nuevos ojos de la esperanza.

> (your organized light reaches poor, forgotten
> men, your defined star
> sinks its hoarse points in death
> and fixes the new eyes of hope.)

Neruda's ode ends with the word "hope," certainly a tentative notion for a poem that sets out to move an army and a people on to victory. Surely what we see is the ode itself collapsing under the burden of its own tropes, of the individual poet reappearing as the collective voice he sought to embody dissolves, leaving him, as before, alone.

FRANK MENCHACA

"A Language Full of Wars and Songs"

$\mathbf{M}$y first encounter with the poetry of Pablo Neruda came at the age of fourteen at a B. Dalton bookstore in the Walt Whitman Mall in suburban Long Island. I was attracted first by the possibility that *Twenty Love Poems and a Song of Despair* (*Veinte poemas de amor y una canción desesperada*), might have been written by a Spanish poet. (The fact that Neruda was not Spanish but Latin American occurred to me only later because, being a more or less average North American, I made no distinction between the two.)

Adolescence has a way of definitively making one feel like a foreigner, no matter how hard one struggles to hide the feeling of overwhelming strangeness to oneself, one's friends, one's family. I am a first generation American. My father was a Basque and my mother, of Spanish ethnic origin, was born in New York City. I chose to regard myself as more European than American rather than associate myself with what I then believed to be a boorish and ignorant American culture: the canned music and multiplex movie theaters of the very mall in which I was standing. I preferred to think of myself as an inheritor of the dust and blood of the *corrida* that came to me via the images of Hollywood, and of the dark, death-obsessed Spanish soul as described by the flamenco floor show. I thought of myself, in short, as a foreigner and I sought to replace the distance that the age of thirteen or fourteen had dumped in my lap with another kind of distance— the luxurious distance that comes from believing one can neither understand nor belong to one's own culture, from maintaining the tourist's mild bemusement with the novel at home while preserving an ironic detachment.

Naturally, I was predisposed to liking the poetry. Besides being written in the language of preference, I thought the title, *Twenty Love Poems and a Song of Despair,* appropriate. It suggested poetry of a love tainted with tragedy and, at the age of fourteen, any kind of encounter with another human being, most of all an erotic kind, must be thought of as inevitably disastrous. Disaster eliminates the possibility of intimacy and the very possibility of intimacy was, of course, paralyzing. To be introduced to anything about another individual, even superficially, was to be introduced to something about oneself and, once again, being a foreigner had its advantages here.

II

Great poetry, no matter where it comes from, has a way of surviving the stupidity of predispositions and taking the reader completely by surprise. Rilke's "Archaic Torso of Apollo" is about this: how the poem destroys the reader's preconceptions in order to redefine completely his or her relation to it. Like many of the poets writing today in the United States, this poet is in the museum. But there the similarity ends. He posits the poem, the torso itself, as an artifact, as the fragmentary object of the reader's eye. Yet in fourteen lines, the span of one sonnet, the torso begins to change, coming everywhere alive, its eyes ripening like fruit, a lamp hoisted in its chest until the entire scene is turned inside out. Where so many of today's poets would have stopped at deft descriptions of the old masters or at imitations of the American Scene painters (in search of the false sublime), Rilke goes on to transform the museum piece, the poem, into the seer, and the reader into the artifact. The stone bursts like a star until "there is no place / that does not see you." The reader, once observed by the poem, becomes the statue, fixed in time and space, a single dot beneath an enormous evening sky. Its admonition is clear: "Du musst dein Leben ändern (You must change your life)." If the work of art knows anything it is what Lamarck knew—survival through change. It is the poem that becomes organic, mutable. The reader is left to squirm against the dust of his or her own expectations, falling quietly down from the library shelves and from somnolent reading rooms, falling like salt: a drying, burning, curative jacket, harder and worse than stone.

> In recompense, I will feel a glance arising from the work and directed on me: this glance is not the reflection of my interrogation. It is a foreign consciousness, radically other. . . . The work interrogates me.
>
> (Jean Starobinski)

III

E. R. Monegal's and Enrico Mario Santí's chronology in *Pablo Neruda* ends in 1974 with this:

> En Madrid, y sin autorización de sus herederos, se publican *Cartas de amor de Pablo Neruda,* que recoge la correspondencia del poeta con Albertina Rosa Azocar, una de las dos musas de los *Veinte poemas.*

> (In Madrid, without the authorization of his estate, *The Love Letters of Pablo Neruda* are published, which collect the poet's correspondence with Albertina Rosa Azocar, one of the two muses of the *Twenty Poems.*)
>
> (tr. Frank Menchaca)

Can the muse of biography be the muse of poetry?

The cycle as a whole refers less to an actual woman and more to a female figure. "Quién eres tú, quién eres? (Who are you?)" Neruda asks in poem 17 and the question does not seem rhetorical in the least. It has the tone of urgency, even of desperation.

Who is he speaking to then? Wherever she appears (if indeed "she" is even a woman at all), the beloved to whom Neruda sings is at best a shadowy figure, present in the poems by absence.

Therefore the *Twenty Love Poems* are fetishes, more lyrical than most, but fetishes nevertheless. The *disjecta membra* of the poet at the tail end of adolescence. While the sun beat down on the blinds, shut up in his rooms in the university town (Santiago), he imagined, in all the exquisite detail adolescence lavishes upon its fantasies, this woman and these poems followed.

Obviously their subject, the object of Neruda's anxieties and desires, meant a good deal more to him than an afternoon fancy (though there is undeniably an element of the purely masturbatory to these poems).

> Pienso, camino largamente, mi vida antes de ti.
> Mi vida antes de nadie, mi áspera vida.

> (I think, I explore great tracts of my life before you.
> My life before anyone, my sad life.)
>
> (poem 17, tr. W. S. Merwin)

Woman is the territory upon which the poet begins the painful cartography of his existence. She is not only the way into life, a tunnel through to himself, she is what lies on the other side, landscape, *tierra,* earth, all of life itself.

So Neruda's is a kind of sugar-coated machismo. Another man using a woman in the old platonic pursuit of the whole. This is Neruda's hand groping after all. Maybe it is made a bit mild by the romantic glove, but it is still on the prowl for some so-called completion.

> En ti los ríos canta y mi alma en ellos huye
> como tú lo desees y hacia donde tú quieras.

> (In you the rivers sing and my soul flees in them
> as you desire, and you send it where you will.)
>   (poem 3, tr. W. S. Merwin)

If Neruda has cast himself in the role of the Second Cortez to the beloved's New World, his conquest is equivocal at best. If the woman is Malinche or pre-Columbian Paradise, she is also a good translator and has not at all fallen for him as a white god or because of his horse. She has, at times, captured his soul and made it small, made it buoyant, shot it like a pinball, an artificial and intrusive little thing, through her arterial system of rivers.

But if the poet alternately surveys the beloved as a conquered land and is conquered by her currents, the question persists: "Quíen eres tú quíen, eres?"

Although he found it idle to reply to the questions of his readers, Neruda neverthless furnished a delightfully backhanded and evasive answer to precisely this question in his *Memorias,* as E. R. Monegal points out in *El viajero inmóvil.* Neruda invented two women to fill the shoes of his two supposed muses for the *Twenty Poems:* Marisol and Marisombra. As Monegal explains, Marisol is the dark country girl from Temuco with the stars in her eyes and the wild and woody scent of the forest. Marisombra is, of course, the city slicker, the student, the beauty with the grey beret sitting at the cafe table. This is all wonderfully evasive and Neruda goes as far as to indicate which poems pertain to which woman. But Monegal is on to Neruda here, despite his understatement that this "presents the critic with a curious problem." While Neruda has said explicitly that the beret belongs to the urbane Marisombra he has also inadvertently placed it upon the head of Marisol, confusing the two and proving, perhaps with a smile, that his answer need not be taken seriously and that, perhaps, he should not have been asked in the first place.

IV

He has been spoken of as the martyred laureate of Latin America: his houses were ransacked at his death, his funeral was attended by the state police. Those who have wanted to dismiss the senator from Chile as a communist verse-propagandist have used his poems to Stalin and Sandino considerably to their advantage. Still others have viewed him as a sort of guru of the earth, displacing him to the North American midwest where he is allowed to recite his elementary odes to the objects of "nature," thank you, but as soon as something man-made enters into the poem (remember "Sobre una poesía sin pureza"?) he is asked to keep quiet, please.

When Neruda's readers have gone in search of his "real" self in the poetry and hailed its discovery, they have missed what one of the poems in *Estravagario* so beautifully points out: "Muchos somos" ("We Are Many").

> De tantos hombre que soy, que somos,
> no puedo encontrar a ninguno:
> se me pierden bajo la ropa,
> se fueron a otra ciudad.
>
> Cuando todo está preparado
> para mostrarme inteligente
> el tonto que llevo escondido
> se toma la palabra en mi boca.
>
> Otras veces me duermo en medio
> de la sociedad distinguida
> y cuando busco en mí al valiente,
> un cobarde que no conozco
> corre a tomar con mi esqueleto
> mil deliciosas precauciones.
>
> Cuando arde una casa estimada
> en vez del bombero que llamo,
> se precipita el incendiario
> y ése soy yo. No tengo arreglo.
> Qué debo hacer para escogerme?
> Cómo puedo rehabilitarme?
>
> Todos los libros que leo
> celebran héroes refulgentes
> siempre seguros de sí mismos:
> me muero de envidia por ellos,
> y en los films de vientos y balas
> me quedo envidiando al jinete,
> me quedo admirando al caballo.

Pero cuando pido al intrépido
me sale el viejo perezoso,
y así yo no sé quién soy,
no sé cuántos soy o seremos.
Me gustaría tocar un timbre
y sacar el mí verdadero
proque si yo me necesito
no debo desaparecerme.

Mientras escribo estoy ausente
y cuando vuelvo ya he partido:
voy a ver si las otras gentes
le pasa lo que a mí me pasa,
si son tantos como soy yo,
si se parecen a sí mismos
y cuando lo haya averiguado
voy a aprender tan bien las cosas
que para explicar mis problemas
les hablaré de geografía.

(Of the many men who I am, who we are,
I can't find a single one;
They disappear among my clothes,
they've left for another city.

When everything seems to be set
to show me off as intelligent,
the fool I always keep hidden
takes over all I say.

At other times, I'm asleep
among distinguished people,
and when I look for my brave self,
a coward unknown to me
rushes to cover my skeleton
with a thousand fine excuses.

When a decent house catches fire,
instead of the fireman I summon,
an arsonist bursts on the scene,
and that's me. What can I do?
What can I do to distinguish myself?
How can I pull myself together ?

All the books I read
are full of dazzling heroes,
always sure of themselves.
I die with envy of them;
and in films full of wind and bullets,
I goggle at the cowboys,
I even admire the horses.

But when I call for a hero,
out comes my lazy old self;
so I never know who I am,
nor how many I am or will be.
I'd love to be able to touch a bell
and summon the real me,
because if I really need myself,
I musn't disappear.

While I am writing, I'm far away;
and when I come back, I've gone.
I would like to know if others
go through the same things that I do,
have as many selves as I have,
and see themselves similarly;
and when I've exhausted this problem,
I'm going to study so hard
that when I explain myself,
I'll be talking geography.)

                                   (tr. Alistair Reid)

V

Borges and Neruda are rarely spoken of in the same sentence, except when it delineates their differences. Their mutual desire for avoidance carried over into life: when one came to town the other left. Where they meet is at the great American source from which the poetry of each has flowed—Walt Whitman. Doubtless this attests to Whitman's enormous strength. He can sustain any kind of reading, even two which are, in the end, diametrically opposed. It also points to Borges's and Neruda's impressive will and strength as readers and interpreters. But what they share and what they learn from Whitman is that "I" is not only Another but "I" is Others.

The multiplicity of the poetic self takes place in Borges through an exchange between father and son, maker and thing made, writer and reader. The seminal text is "Borges y yo" ("Borges and Myself"). Here Borges parodies (even a little poignantly) the idea that the progenitor, the master of fictions, is ultimately another subject of fictions, be they his own, his inheritor's, or God's. Thus the writer is his own books. Not only the personality but the very substance and being of Shakespeare is spent out to become Hamlet, Lear, Juliet. Whitman is the great poet of the self who would embrace the world and simultaneously look down to encounter the zero his arms were making while trying to do so. "Lo gigantesco puede ser una forma de lo invisíble (The gigantic can be seen as another form of invisibility)," says Borges in "El otro Whitman." What he takes away from Whitman is this: the notion that the very moment one tries to encompass the world in the creative process, one becomes the many parts of that world. One multiplies instantly and exponentially until, ironically and even tragically, one is less real, the creator of nothing.

> you who were Existence
> Yourself forgot to live.
> (Emily Dickinson)

A wildly insightful and informed reader (despite his own self-effacing advertisements for himself), Neruda also must have understood that the self which claims to be everywhere freely available in Whitman's poetry is nowhere to be found. Its parts could never be summed so as to be seen as a whole. It was all around and everyone, a great democracy, without ever really being visible.

In the introduction to *Odas elementales*, "El hombre invisible" ("The Invisible Man"), he writes:

> yo quiero
> que todos vivan
> en mi vida
> y canten en mí canto,
> yo no tengo importancia,
> no tengo tiempo
> para mis asuntos,
> debo anotar lo que pasa,
> y no olvidar a nadie.
>
> (I want
> everyone to live
> in my lfe

and sing in my song,
I am not important,
I have no time
for my own affairs,
I must take note of everything that happens
and not leave anyone out.)

(tr. Frank Menchaca)

It is the Invisible Man's way of becoming the Infinite Man. Not only the lives of this world—the fishermen with their muscular torsos screwed back, heaving the nets, the booksellers, the bricklayers—but objects also take their place upon the empty geographic space of the poet. Like a magnet made of air taking the shape of the continent he attracts, almost sexually, everyone and everything.

VI

It is an erotic life of property, as Lewis Hyde calls it, that Neruda alluded to as far back as 1935 in "Sobre una poesía sin pureza" ("Some Thoughts on Impure Poetry"):

Es muy conveniente, en ciertas horas del día o de la noche, observar profundamente los objetos en descanso: Las ruedas que han recorrido largas, polvorientas distancias, soportando grandes cargas vegetales o minerales, los sacos de las carbonerías, los barriles, las cestas, los mangos y asas de los instrumentos de carpintero. De ellos se desprende el contacto del hombre y de la tierra como lección para el torturado poeta lírico. Las superficies usadas, el gasto que las manos han infligido a las cosas, la atmósfera a menudo tragica y siempre patética de estos objetos, infunde una especie de atraccion no despreciable hacia la realidad del mundo.

(It is worth one's while, at certain hours of the day or night, to scrutinize useful objects in repose: wheels that have rolled across long, dusty distances with their enormous loads of crop or ore, charcoal sacks, barrels, baskets, the hafts and handles of carpenters' tools. The contact these objects have had with man and earth may serve as a valuable lesson to a tortured lyric poet. Worn surfaces, the wear inflicted by human hands, the sometimes tragic, always pathetic, emanations from these objects give reality a magnetism that should not be scorned.)

(tr. Margaret Sayers Peden)

There is an exchange, a negotiation between objects and humans. The dissimilar arrangement of their atoms and molecules does not preclude them from a shared life, a common energy.

In the painting "La philosophie dans le boudoir" by René Magritte, female breasts of flesh and blood grow from a white dress, hanging on its hanger on a rack. A pair of high-heeled shoes end in two sets of human toes. In a sense, these images, like Neruda's images of emanating objects, are those of the fetishist.

Both kinds of imagery engage a paradox. In the case of the painting, these objects radiate a life of energy all their own precisely because they are removed from their living and erotic matrix: the body. The white dress and the pair of shoes, worn by the woman, would at the very least lose some of their power for the observer and most probably cease to have any special attraction at all. Fetishism, it seems, depends wholly upon the particularity of an object's context.

(It is classified as a neurosis and one thinks of it in terms of illness. Yet the moment in Magritte's painting when the dress and the shoes begin to pulse with life is also a visionary moment. Things somehow respond to the aimless love and anxiety of the observer by exchanging their lives as things for an instant of another life, one which will squeeze into them the qualities which radiate love's and anxiety's object. Then the observer sees. Things release their energy. Then the observer dreams. Things readjust to their places on shelves and in closets, fitting themselves back into their jackets of dust.

Neruda's own peculiar form of fetishism also moves one as a vision of the extensional world, in all its vibrancy and beauty, based upon an overwhelming solitude. In the *Odas elementales,* his celebration of the physical world, he is reduced to the giant invisible man. In the *Veinte poemas,* it is precisely because the beloved is so far away, that the poet must make love to what is near. It is her absence that inhabits the world and causes the mirror and the towel to weep, and the pearl necklace to throb.)

Similarly, the objects and lives that hold so much allure for the poet somehow evaporate him once he embraces them. The sexual solidity of matter, its delicious tangibility, vaporizes the vessel that touches it. This notion forms part of one of Neruda's most difficult and paradoxical poetic stances.

Thirty-six years after "Sobre una poesía sin pureza," in his Nobel Lecture, this notion still obsesses him. But here he posits his poems as something more than the products of a transaction between the poet and the world and its ten thousand things. They are objects with a life all their own:

> Cada uno de mis poemas pretendió ser un instrumento útil de trabajo: cada uno de mis cantos aspiró a servir en el espacio como signo de reunión donde se cruzaron los caminos, como fragmento de piedra o de madera en que alguien, otros, los que vendrán, pudieran depositar los nuevos signos.

> (Each and every one of my verses has chosen to take its place as a tangible object, each and every one of my poems has claimed to be a useful working instrument, each and every one of my songs has endeavored to serve as a sign in space for a meeting between paths which cross one another, or as a piece of stone or wood on which someone, some others, those who will follow after, will be able to carve new signs.)

(tr. Frank Menchaca)

He began with an intense, inward appreciation of objects in poetry. Now he places his poems in the world as objects. A convenient and reductive way of describing this development is as the development of an art of fetishism into an art of carpentry. Yet the movement that it describes, from inner to outer, is, I think accurate. Neruda's progression from *Residencia* to *Canto general* follows this pattern.

VII

Alluding, perhaps, to the Whitmanian image of the tally, he described his poems late in his career as the point at the center of X, as the circle in which contradictory forms and energies deposit their signs and write their names.

The chaotic enumeration, as Leo Spitzer has called it, of the *Residencia* poems foreshadows this. Here the self is the locus which amasses the heterogeneous objects that will constitute it in one all-encompassing poetic cycle. The individual strains to become the single manifestation of the entire democratic nation, in Whitman's terms. Yet as the lines of the great catalog, the declaration of interdependent independence, pile one on top of the other, the self somehow becomes less real. As Spitzer points out, the creative process Neruda has taken from a Whitmanian poetic tradition now consists of "actividades desintegradas (disintegrating activities)." The end result is opposite from the original intention. Writing of the entire

world leaves the poet nowhere where, to use the title of one of the most
famous *Residencia* poems, he is simply "Walking Around":

> Hay pájaros de color de azufre y horibles intestinos
> colgando de las puertas de las casas que odio,
> hay dentaduras olivdadas en una cafetera,
> hay espejos
> que debeiran haber llorado de verguenza y espanto,
> hay paraguas en todas partes, y venenos, y obligos.
>
> Yo paseo con calma, con ojos, con zapatos,
> con furia, con olvido,
> paso, cruzo oficinas y tiendas de ortopedia,
> y patios donde hay ropas colgadas de un alambre:
> calzoncillos, toallas y camisas que lloran
> lentas lágrimas sucias.

> (There are birds the color of sulphur, and horrible intestines
> hanging from the doors of the houses which I hate,
> there are forgotten sets of teeth in a coffee-pot,
> there are mirrors
> which should have wept with shame and horror,
> there are umbrellas all over the place, and poisons, and navels.
>
> I stride along with calm, with eyes, with shoes,
> with fury, with forgetfulness,
> I pass, I cross offices and stores full of orthopedic appliances,
> and courtyards hung with clothes on wires,
> underpants, towels and shirts which weep
> slow dirty tears.)

(tr. W. S. Merwin)

The dramatic effects of the Spanish Civil War and Neruda's subsequent conversion to communism changed this elemental response to Whitman, making him a different kind of poet, but no less a poet of the self.
For Neruda, the poetic self had somehow to embrace the entire world
without passing into an oblivion of scattered objects and faces which,
however brilliantly arranged, exhaust and deplete the poet. This was the
problem he had to solve in moving from the hermetic, self-enclosed and
covertly Whitmanian poetry of *Residencia*. For those poems were almost
like extraordinary postcards from an oblivion of the self, faced with a
whirlwind of things, people, and places and backed by a language which
transmitted the chaos and clangor of the self under construction through

these things. The Blake of *The Four Zoas* comes to mind when one reads these accounts of the forging of an imagination, of the violent conception, division, and creation of the self. (Neruda, in fact, knew Blake and went on to translate *The Visions of the Daughters of Albion*.) In a sense, they are Whitmanian poems of the self taken totally to the extreme.

"It's poetry with no way out," proclaimed Neruda himself, in an interview with Rita Guibert. However bold and brilliant they are, the *Residencia* poems represented danger. They had absorbed the world so totally that they blocked the passage through which a world-absorbing poetic self might be born. Their drama is the drama of this struggle for space, for emergence, for resolution of the deep self-contradiction upon which they also depended for their creation. Their sense of doom at the outcome of that struggle is inescapable.

Somehow the self had to become others by speaking for them as an actual mass in history. Somehow the poem had to encompass the world by writing of it as a place in time.

Did Communism offer Neruda not only a way out of the solitude imposed on Latin America by its long military history but a way out of the claustrophobic genius of *Residencia* as well? Did it represent for him a weapon with which to fight the ultimately muting effects of poetic solipsism and the silence that rose with totalitarianism in Spain?

In *Canto general,* arguably his most political work, solidarity with the dead laborers of Machu Picchu is simultaneous with a great Whitmanian expansion of the poetic voice: "Hablad por mis palabras y mi sangre." "Speak through my speech and through my blood."

While it would be misguided to call *Canto general* the *Leaves of Grass* of Latin America, Neruda did indeed perform the (ironically very Borgesian) act of writing a single book which was himself. Unlike Whitman, Neruda did not consist of the grass nor was his poetic soul specifically the tally. Instead, he consisted of the Bio-Bio, of Valdivia the intruder, of the United Fruit Company and, as always, of the great Pacific itself. These are Neruda's leaves, these his eidolons. As if to prove definitively that his project was not only historical, not only tendentiously based upon a particular sociopolitical vision, Neruda ended *Canto general* with a section simply entitled "Yo soy" ("I Am"). The oblivion of faces, things, and beings that marked the poetic internalization of the world is not really gone despite the claim: "Por fin, soy libre adentro de los seres (At last, I am free within of other beings)." Instead, that oblivion is outside and part of the human earth. Neruda has come forth into the world: "Salgo a la multitud de los combates (I come out to the multitude of combatants)." It is in this way that "I" has become Others, that the poetic voice becomes the multiplicity.

It is in this way that it speaks in "una lengua llena de guerras y de cantos," the "language full of wars and songs" that *Veinte poemas* had promised some twenty years earlier.

VIII

> The life of man is a self-evolving circle, which, from a ring im-
> perceptibly small, rushes out on all sides outwards to new and
> larger circles, and that without end. The extent to which this
> generation of circles, wheel without wheel, will go, depends on
> the force or truth of the individual soul.
>
> (Ralph Waldo Emerson)

I can think of no more beautiful model for the ideal growth of the poetic self. A game of Chinese boxes played backwards: the walls collapse outward into larger walls into larger walls until the walls are invisible or simply do not exist at all. This must be how the poet encompasses the world.

Belatedness is annihilated and "men walk as prophecies of the next age." Suddenly it is early, suddenly dawn. Experience is primary. It recedes forever beyond, its trailing edge just barely brushing the self's outermost circumference and leaving whatever line of interface there is between the two as a space of discovery.

"Force" and "truth" are substitutable for one another and not at the expense of morality, either. What Peter Earle pointed out about Whitman's conception of Manifest Destiny holds for Emerson's circular expansion of the self in the world; James Polk, McKinley, and Theodore Roosevelt meant something totally different when they proclaimed all borders their own to expand toward. The poet's project is human-centered. Embracing the new is his or her opening gesture of an exchange, of a negotiation which does not demand the forfeiture of individual differences. Political expansionism only appropriates the term "Manifest Destiny" to conveniently mask its desire to descend upon, to swarm over, to strong-arm.

> In vain do we march with unprecedented strides to empire so
> colossal, outvying the antique, beyond Alexander's, beyond the
> proudest sway of Rome. In vain have we annex'd Texas, Cali-
> fornia, Alaska, and reach north for Canada and south for
> Cuba. It is as if we were somehow being endow'd with a vast
> and more and more thoroughly-appointed body, and then left
> with little or no soul.
>
> (Walt Whitman)

As if following his own metaphor for the motion of the self, Emerson's voice has spread infinitely outward through American poetry and continues to permeate its language. Even at the end of life, when only the past is real, Emerson's circles return to make memory fluid, expanding, a last instrument to discover what are perhaps the whispers out of time.

> Silence of water above the sunken tree:
> The pure serene of memory in one man,—
> A ripple widening from a single stone
> Winding around the waters of the world.
>
> (Theodore Roethke)

Yet how is one to understand this as a metaphor for the growth of the poet's self in 1988? Indeed, it might be better described now as the tiny dot in the center of the television screen, on the verge of winking out.

It is difficult to think of the growth of the great self or of its poeticization today. Perceiving reality, experiencing the world, is now inseparable from watching television. Gunmen attack a woman in her New York apartment. At least twenty people watch. Because the action is framed by windows they think it is an episode of "Miami Vice," perhaps, and continue watching. A colonel working for the United States Government breaks the law. At his televised hearing he looks so good, so earnest, so much the caring dad or husband from a situation comedy, that the viewing public not only spiritually acquits him, but commends him. If MTV [cable music channel] is indicative of anything (and I think it is), it shows that it is now so late in the day that it always feels like night and therefore time for a party. Perhaps the zest of the celebrants is due not so much to the music or the dancing but to a grim expectation of the final ka-boom that will put them all to bed.

I bring this up to suggest how strange the idea of "poetry of the great self" actually sounds. Certain problems of interpretation plague every generation of readers. This generation's seem particularly difficult.

IX

The circumferences of the circle that define the poetic self and its growth in Neruda are not the auras, not the rings of energy they are in Emerson. And no ripple dilates to enclose the waters of the world's surface.

At the beginning of the *Twenty Poems,* the circle that stands for the poet has only one circumference and does not move. It is part of the static geometry of the modern world, the end product of the process of history and the progress of industry:

Fui solo como un túnel.

(I was alone like a tunnel.)
(poem 1, tr. W. S. Merwin)

Although Neruda wrote *Veinte poemas de amor y una cancion desesperada* in Santiago, with this opening image of the poet he makes a gesture of response to European and modernist poetry after the First World War. The poet was no longer to derive his or her astonishment from the mountaintop of Mont Blanc. The massive collapsibility of political, social, and religious institutions and of the personality was to inspire a new kind of awe in a new species of poet: an awe before the sublimity of disintegration in a poet exiled within the native land.

The image places the poet in a setting which, one might imagine, is the only setting for such poetry: the city after the shelling has stopped. Fires are framed by first floor windows. Rubble tumbles down the pile. The sides and tops of apartment houses and factories have been ripped away and reveal how easily things fall apart. When they do, the poet, the tunnel, perhaps an empty drainpipe, is exposed, sitting among masses of smoking solitude. (And it is not that different for the contemporary reader, either. Imagine the abandoned urban construction site with its huge aluminum spindles looked at only by a far-off city skyline. Here the poet is the tunnel left behind with the poor and another breeding ground for solitude, slums.)

How does the empty, unexpandable ring grow? How does the poet become the vessel whose pliant, porous circumference encloses a vast shuttling of the world's objects and lives? How does the influence of European and Modernist poetry produce a cycle of poems which is radically Latin American and discontinuous with its own tradition?

Twenty Love Poems and A Song of Despair answers these questions by placing the poet in the vicinity of the beloved. Whoever she is, she is "hecha de todas las cosas (made of everything)," as Neruda describes her in poem 11. An original matrix, she not only encloses new life, she gives nourishment to the progeny outside of her as well: "Todo lo llenas, todo lo llenas (You fill everything)."

A thoroughly adolescent romanticism would depict her as a symbol of the pristine, pre-Columbian world, in one-dimensional representations of indigenous gods and mythologies. It is true that Neruda's tenor in this sequence runs along a kind of crack, a shadow-line between the deep resonances of the mature poet and the higher registers of the young poet awkwardly seeking his key. Yet nowhere does he wish the beloved to beckon him back only to an Indian state of innocence before the fall of Spanish swords. Like the worlds of *Residencia* and of *Canto general*, the world within the woman of *Veinte poemas* is not created by the poet's nostalgia. It is at one time the student's world in Santiago and the world between the wars in Europe. Ultimately, it makes intimations of the world Neruda's later poetry would embody and labor to bring forth—Latin America.

But beyond this, the world into which both poet and reader enter is, in Hart Crane's phrase, "the broken world" of modern civilization:

> Absorta, pálida doliente, así situada
> contra las viejas helices del crepúsculo
> que en torna a ti da vuelta.
>
> Muda, mi amiga,
> sola en lo solitario de esta hora de muertes
> y llena de las vidas del fuego,
> pura heredera del día destruido.
>
> (Abstracted pale mourner, standing that way
> against the old propellers of the twilight
> that revolves around you.
>
> Speechless, my friend,
> alone in the loneliness of this hour of the dead
> and filled with lives of fire,
> pure heir of the ruined day.)
>   (poem 2, tr. W. S. Merwin)

The world she inhabits, the world that inhabits her, gyrates in the slow circular motions of a world whose machinery has broken down. It is a universe on a downward, disintegrating spiral.

But a deep ambiguity becomes evident here. The poetry is subtly divided between entropic energy and kinetic energy. Dead bodies fill the cellars of *Residencia* and bones pour out of its hospital windows. Similarly, the world of the beloved is a world in which time itself is marked by death; it is a system in a state such that activity is no longer possible. Yet inaction bears within itself a form of energy. There are "lives of fire" in *Veinte poemas* just as there is an "aquello todo tan rápido, tan viviente (all that everything so fast, so living)," situated in *Residencia's* immobility.

"The greatest poverty," wrote Wallace Stevens, "is not to live in a physical world." And the beloved lives in enormous wealth. Not only does she live in the physical world but she embodies that world in its totality. She manifests creation and decay. In her all things run the full circle of their course. A presence mysterious and fluid, she can transform the hollow tunnel into the living vein, for she consists of the vital as well as mortal aspects. She can open the eye in the empty hole of the socket, and inspire the soundless throat. Consequently, the poet's contact with her effects a process of growth that exchanges tunnel walls for membrane, vision for darkness, voice for muteness.

The quest of *Veinte poemas de amor y una cancion desesperada* is for a poetic awakening. But Neruda was not a poet who lived only above his shoulders or in the darker, more abstracted space beyond that, the mind. The awakening of poetry in this poet takes place everywhere: "La sed eterna (the eternal thirst)" of the first poem refers not only to sexual desire, but to a longing for a means of expression and a poetic voice.

> y las miro lejanas mis palabras.
> más que mías son tuyas.

> (And I watch my words from a long way off.
> They are more yours than mine.)
> (poem 5, tr. W. S. Merwin)

Words are palpable and substantial. They are perceptible objects which can be watched as they pass in and out of the poet's domain. The poet himself is a word:

> el desesperado, la palabra sin ecos.

> (the one without hope, the word without echoes)
> (poem 8, tr. W. S. Merwin)

He is without echoes quite simply because he has never been sounded. The disconsolate poet has not yet written the poem. It lingers off somewhere in the distance, in the beloved.

The reversal described in poem 5 intimates the desire of the entire sequence. It is not a desire for Albertina Rosa Azocar, Marisol, Marisombra, or any other muse, shod or barefoot. Referring back to the words he glimpsed at a distance, he makes his reclamation:

> Ahora quiero que digan lo que quiero decirte
> para que tú me oigas como quiero que me oigas.

> (Now I want them to say what I want to say to you
> to make you hear as I want you to hear me.)
> (tr. W. S. Merwin)

It has all the elements of a sugar-coated machismo. (Although the sweetness is beginning to melt away.) But Neruda's desire is also exhibited through a machismo based more plausibly on fear than on swagger, on desperation than on elusive cool. He assumes the cock's stance when all other birds have fled his desolation. He wills control over a poetry and over a beloved which are too powerful to be mastered by him. He must affect the possessive stance because he has nothing to give.

Consequently in Poem 1, he attempts to turn the beloved into a kind of spoils, ready for the taking:

> Cuerpo de mujer, blancas colinas, muslos blancos
> tu pareces al mundo en tu actitud de entrega.
>
> (Body of a woman, white hills, white thighs,
> you look like a world lying in surrender.)
>
> (tr. W. S. Merwin)

He is aware of her as a world, as potential poetic voice which traffics in the things of a world, in "a language full of wars and songs." But his mistake comes in imagining her availability. No real world is ever simply given up to the poet. What lies in surrender must be what lies in miniature, a synechdoche for a greater, less accessible presence.

Nevertheless, in the second stanza of the same poem he writes:

> Para sobrevivirme te forjé como un arma,
> como una flecha en mi arco, como una piedra en mi honda.
>
> (To survive myself I forged you like a weapon,
> like an arrow in my bow, a stone in my sling.)
>
> (tr. W. S. Merwin)

"Forjar" carries the same connotations it does in English. The first that come to mind are those of the foundry and of the blacksmith's art of shaping. Certainly the verb is appropriate in that Neruda construes the beloved as a weapon, an arrow or stone pellet, which might be forged or shaped.

By casting the beloved in such a mold, however, he betrays her and all that she embodies, engaging in another kind of forgery. Neruda's falsification comes at the moment he believes the beloved has surrendered her world to him. Then not only does he attempt to possess her, but he attempts to transform his prisoner into his own means of defense.

But as a set of weapons the woman is unconvincing. By fashioning her and fabricating her as an arrow and a slingshot's ammunition, he fails to move beyond himself. He merely conjures the beloved up in images suggesting his own phallus and scrotum.

This first encounter with an all-inclusive poetic voice degenerated into a kind of masturbatory reverie of self-regard. As if aware of this himself, Neruda admits:

> Pero cae la hora de la venganza.
>
> (But the hour of vengeance falls).
> (tr. W. S. Merwin)

and the poem breaks down into a series of precious laments.

It is obvious that *Veinte poemas de amor y una cancion desesperada* are love poems with this essential difference: they are written by the poet to the poet. Neruda himself seemed to be aware of this:

> Así, de un drama intimo, del encuentro con mi
> propio ser y del amor nació aquel libro.
>
> (Thus, from an intimate drama, from an encounter
> with my own self and with love, this book was born.)
> (tr. Frank Menchaca)

This is part of their surprise, their careful and conscious destruction of the reader's expectations, their means of interrogation.

But only a small part. A deeper level of meaning opens up upon this purely autoerotic element surprising the reader even more and perhaps surprising the poet himself.

It is as if he knew on some intuitive level that the world-encompassing poetic voice he sought derived not only from himself, but from his negotiation with an other. Consequently, he wrote these poems aiming at himself in order to reach something or someone else. Like letters sucked backward into a despository and then run through an elaborate sorting system, these poems pass through the poet's self to arrive at the populous beloved, the world, the poetic voice. Their newness, their sense of wild originality, gives the impression that somehow they were partially erased en route, revised by the other, and sent back, collaborative efforts of a single poet. They return seemingly to catch the poet off-guard and there is no doubt that they surprise the reader.

Poem 9 is perhaps the sequence's best example:

> Ebrio de trementina y largos besos,
> estival, el velero de las rosas dirijo,
> torcido hacia la muerte del delgado día,
> cimentado en el sólido frenesi marino.

Pálido y amarrado a mi agua devorante
cruzo en el agrio olor del clima descubierto,
aún vestido de gris y sonidos amargos,
y una cimera triste de abandonada espuma.

Voy, duro de pasiones, montado en mi ola única,
lunar, solar, ardiente y frío, repentino,
dormido en la garganta de las afortunadas
islas blancas y dulces como caderas frescas.

Tiembla en la noche húmeda mi vestido de besos
locamente cargado de eléctricas gestiones,
de modo heroico dividido en sueños
y embriagadoras rosas practicándose en mí.

Aguas arriba, en medio de las olas externas,
tu paralelo cuerp se sujeta en mis brazos
como un pex infinitamente pegado a mi alma
rapido y lento en la energia subceleste.

(Drunk with pines and long kisses,
like summer I steer the fast sail of the roses,
bent towards the death of the thin day,
stuck into my solid marine madness.

Pale and lashed to my ravenous water,
I cruise in the sour smell of the naked climate,
still dressed in grey and bitter sounds
and a sad crest of abandoned spray.

Hardened by passions, I go mounted on my one wave,
lunar, solar, burning and cold, all at once,
becalmed in the throat of the fortunate isles
that are white and sweet as cool hips.

In the moist night my garment of kisses trembles
charged to insanity with electric currents,
heroically divided into dreams
and intoxicating roses practising on me.

Upstream, in the midst of the outer waves,
your parallel body yields to my arms
like a fish infinitely fastened to my soul,
quick and slow, in the energy under the sky.)

(tr. W. S. Merwin)

If "pine" has been understood thus far as a thing, a tree, whose context has been, most probably, the forest, now it is a source of inebriation when its resins couple with kisses. Its context has been removed.

On a ship with sails made of roses the poet is both pilot of his vessel and prisoner of the very water he steers. Hierarchy is dissolved.

The water itself is by turns ravenous, moving, wild and a solid block of delirium. Dynamism and stasis, activity and inertness alternate in the same system.

Sex has manifested itself in atmosphere and landscape. The "naked climate" is sour yet the isles are as "white and sweet" as hips. Pleasure coexists with disgust as sea with sky.

Things have become equal. Contexts dissolve. Yet what the poem enacts is not an instance of the poetic voice fusing or homogenizing the things of the world in order to encompass them. Objects and energies are loosed from the matrices and bodies which define them, yet mysteriously conserve their definition. What they exhibit is their own autonomous life. "Pine" does not stop being a tree, a thing, when removed from the forest, it does, however, find in the world of the poem another life, a sensual life, a set of fuctioning lips in its sap. It simultaneously becomes one thing and others.

The same thing has happened to the poet. "I" has also become others, an entire world of objects and energies. He has become the single wave embodying all principles of similitude and opposition. In this sense, he is an all-powerful being. Yet this moment of all-inclusiveness occurred when the hierarchy and specificity of context were removed. Power was got where power was denied.

Consequently, the poet most possesses the beloved, the poetic voice, when he most relinquishes control over it. That voice in turn liberates the world about which it speaks. The result is that subject and object, poet and beloved, are, for a moment, equal in the poem. What is created in the poem is a new kind of world: a world of original chaos in which all things remain differentiated. It is as if everyone and everything had been returned to a great crucible and fused to become one pure impure element by remaining themselves.

X

"Citizen Kane" is a great movie. At the very beginning, the RKO logo depicts a radio tower at the top of the globe sending out what I seem to remember are circles into space. At the very top of the tower was, of course, the point. It transmitted from its center a series of rings, presumably signals. Each of these rings had a circumference which expanded behind the previous one until, one by one, they expanded right off the screen. (I might have misremembered this; they could have been lightning bolts.)

What would happen if one took a second globe, with its own radio tower perched atop, set it next to the one in the RKO logo, then flicked the switch. I do not know much about radio signals and I wonder: Would the rings crash into one another? Would the signal from one be stronger than the other and overpower it? Or would they both transmit their circular messages out into space together, producing a new multivocal and discordant program that was difficult on the ears but nevertheless interesting since it was a broadcast from two wholly separate worlds?

A crude way of describing the poem I just quoted (and many of Neruda's poems, for that matter) could be as a poem taken down while the dial was stuck between stations. Yet it is, in a way, accurate. A poetic voice which was radically other produced the very original poems that make up some of *Veinte poemas*. It was one which had absorbed European, Modernist, and North American influences to the point where it could, in a sense, begin broadcasting through those traditions to lend its own voice to the populous airwaves.

There is also a sense in which Neruda was sending out his signals against those of his own voice and that his poems were created in space between the two, or, as he writes in "Galope muerto":

> desde el alto de los caminos
> cruzar las campandas en cruz
>
> (from the height of all roads
> the crossing of criss-crossed bells.)
> (tr. Frank Menchaca)

When one reads any kind of literature, one cannot help but appropriate it. It would be difficult to understand anything, especially literature, without, in some sense, embracing it, enclosing it, placing it within the vicinity of one's own body, at the tip of one's own touch.

One reads contemporary criticism, particularly of the new French species, and one feels one's body somehow dissolving in an oblivion of language. As the pencil's eraser obliterates a letter, so goes the face. Reading too becomes unbound from its physicality. The book comes to pieces (in what used to be the hands and now perhaps are figures of speech) and all the world is a space of lost pages and loose words, letters unhinged from one another.

Yet appropriation too is an abuse of art. It is like turning off the transmitter and allowing the receiver to remain on so that all of these new and wonderful signals may be recorded, hoarded, and stored for later study and use. This essay itself might be called into question as an appropriation for the poetry of Pablo Neruda for the author's own private collection.

Certainly, I am as guilty of having read Latin American literature like many North Americans: with the mentality of the tourist. It was fun, discovering the marvellous real. It was a little like going on vacation. Thrilling to the extraordinary adventures of, say, the Buendia family with their levitating women and pig-tailed offspring was like getting to wear a set of clothes that one would otherwise never wear, vacation clothes like brightly colored shorts, shirts with sea horses riding atop palm leaves, and strange mesh shoes.

Yet, clearly, behaving like a tourist when one was reading a novel about one's home is no longer an option.

> Through translation, Latin American literature has already filtered into the fiber of North American English, slowly but relentlessly modifying its canons, the reading of its classics, the writing of its authors, the inner search of its readers, the definition of its history.
>
> (Cesar Salgado)

Thus far, the relations between the Northern and Southern networks have worked like this: one broadcasts, the other receives, willingly or unwillingly. This has been the case for books as well as for bullets.

As more and more poets in the United States seem to sequester themselves in the museum, ranging around themselves paintings of great now-nonexistent gorges from the nineteenth century, or blurred watercolors of cab rides up Fifth Avenue at dusk, it would be unwise not to listen to news from the other side of the border. Similarly, since the concerns of Latin American writers are simply no longer extricable from the goings on up North, be they in publishing or politics, what is needed is an exchange.

This is not a call for dual takes on the American dream. Latin Americans, as Pablo Armando Fernandez points out, have their own dreams, and who can guess what the United States dreams about now? Perhaps a white rider appearing at the top of some cliff, one who could spin his pistols and pass a broad hand over the horizon and say that, yes, there was more out there and that soon is would all be ours.

It would be possible to put up with the occasional static, some noise, interference, and confusion, even if only two of the many means of communication were actually put to use. Like Neruda, one sends one's voice out into space. It is aimed at what appears to be a mere object. Upon reception, however, the object begins to unfold its multiple dimensions like a fan or a glove on an opening hand. It ceases to be an object. Exhibiting its own vitality and autonomy, it stretches into space like a dancer, like a baseball pitcher. It begins to sound its own song and somehow as the furthest circumferences of each signal pass through each other they are changed. They return no less one's own, but bearing a bit more of the dancer's art, of the pitcher's wind-up, and of the world.

A new adolescence is necessary. The old one just danced its way off the side of a cliff last night when the music was particularly good. This one might make better use of the peculiar ability of adolescence to spin the dial of selves and its willingness to assume the resultant combinations, whatever they may be. Perhaps that might provide at least some of the necessary elements of change for a generation that perhaps knows too well who and what it is. As the fireworks go out in the enormous evening sky, they are locked to their own self-definition, to their own place in history. Their position is fixed; their arms are too rigid to reach after an America, North or South, which has slipped palpably away from them.

A literature of foundation was what Neruda sought and he spent much time looking into Whitman for assistance. A new literature of foundation is necessary where Walt Whitman is conjured only by the mall that bears his name.

Chronology

<table>
<tr><td>1904</td><td>Neftalí Ricardo Reyes Basoalto is born in Parral, Chile, on July 12. His mother dies one month later.</td></tr>
<tr><td>1906</td><td>He moves with his father to Temuco, in the south of Chile.</td></tr>
<tr><td>1910–20</td><td>He attends the Liceo de Hombres where he studies with the poet Gabriela Mistral; publishes an article in La Mañana and poems in Corre-Vuela. He adopts the surname Neruda from a Czechoslovakian novelist.</td></tr>
<tr><td>1921</td><td>Neruda goes to the capital city, Santiago, to study French. He publishes "La canción de la fiesta" in Juventud and wins an award.</td></tr>
<tr><td>1923–24</td><td>Crepusculario, Neruda's first collection of poems, appears. Veinte poemas de amor y una canción desesperada is published and wins him instant fame throughout Latin America.</td></tr>
<tr><td>1925–27</td><td>Neruda publishes Tentativa del hombre infinito anonymously. Anillos and El habitante y su esperanza, a novel, appear. Appointed consul by the Chilean government, Neruda chooses (at random) to go to Rangoon, Burma. He begins to write the poems that will constitute the first volume of Residencia en la tierra.</td></tr>
<tr><td>1928–33</td><td>Serves as consul in Ceylon, Java, and Singapore. Meets Nehru. Marries María Antonieta Haagenar Vogelzanz. El hondero entusiasta. Residencia en la tierra, volume one. Neruda is named consul to Buenos Aires where he meets Federico García Lorca, with whom he becomes friends.</td></tr>
</table>

1934–37   Neruda travels to Barcelona as consul. A daughter, Malva
           Marina, is born. He meets Delia del Carril who will become
           his second wife. His reputation in Spain grows and he be-
           comes editor of *Caballo verde para la poesía.* The Spanish
           Civil War breaks out. García Lorca is killed. Neruda is re-
           lieved of his post as consul. He separates from María Anto-
           nieta. Founds and directs a number of political and cultural
           organizations to aid the Republican cause in Spain. *España
           en el corazón.*

1938–43   On the night of his father's death he begins *Canto general.*
           He joins the Communist Party. Once again named consul,
           he goes to Paris. *Las furias y las penas,* later incorporated
           into *Tercer Residencia,* is published. Appointed consul gen-
           eral in Mexico. Malva Marina dies. *Canto general de Chile.*

1944–47   Awarded the Premio Municipal de Poesía and the Premio
           Nacional de Literatura. His *Selected Poems* appears in En-
           glish. Neruda is elected senator to the Communist Party in
           Chile. Appointed Jefe de Propaganda for the campaign of
           González Videla, whom Neruda later denounces. *Tercer Re-
           sidencia.*

1948–49   Neruda is accused of disloyalty to the party and a warrant
           is issued for his detention. He goes into hiding throughout
           Chile, but is forced to flee into Argentina.

1950–55   *Canto general.* Neruda receives the Premio Internacional de
           la Paz. He travels to Italy, France, the Soviet Union, and
           Asia. *Los versos del capitán* is published anonymously and
           dedicated to Matilde Urrutia, who becomes his third wife.
           He is permitted to return to Chile. *Odas elementales. Las
           uvas y el viento.*

1956–60   *Nuevas odas elementales.* The first edition of *Obras Com-
           pletas* appears. In rapid succession *Tercer libro de odas, Es-
           travagario, Navegaciones y regresos, Cien sonetos de amor*
           and *Canción de gesta* are published.

1961–66   *Las piedras de Chile.Cantos ceremoniales.* Neruda is named
           a member of the department of philosophy and education at
           the University of Chile. Second edition of *Obras Completas.*
           Memorial de Isla Negra. His translation of *Romeo and Ju-*

liet is produced. Campaigns for the presidency of Salvador Allende. Oxford University awards Neruda an honorary doctorate. Travels to the United States. *Arte de pajaros.*

1967–70   Neruda's play *Fulgor y muerte de Joaquín Murieta* is produced. *Obras Completas* goes into its third edition. *Las manos del día. Fin de mundo. Aún.* Salvador Allende becomes president and Neruda is an active member of his administration. He is appointed ambassador to Paris. *La espada encendida. Las piedras del cielo.*

1971   *La rosa separada.* Neruda is awarded the Nobel Prize for Literature.

1972–73   He contracts cancer and, after two operations, resigns his post and retires to Isla Negra, Chile. *Geografía infructuosa. Obras Completas,* fourth edition. On September 11, 1973, Salvador Allende is assassinated. On September 23 Neruda dies in Santiago. His houses are ransacked. *El mar y las campanas.*

1974   *Jardín de invierno, El corazón amarillo, 2000, El libro de las preguntas, Elegía, Defectos escogidos,* and *Memorias* are published.

Contributors

HAROLD BLOOM, Sterling Professor of the Humanities at Yale University, is the author of *The Anxiety of Influence, Poetry and Repression,* and many other volumes of literary criticism. His forthcoming study, *Freud: Transference and Authority,* attempts a full-scale reading of all of Freud's major writings. A MacArthur Prize Fellow, he is general editor of five series of literary criticism published by Chelsea House. During 1987–88, he served as Charles Eliot Norton Professor of Poetry at Harvard University.

FEDERICO GARCÍA LORCA was one of Spain's major twentieth-century poets. He is best known for the poems which appear in *Romancero gitano* and *Poeta en Nueva York* and for his plays *Bodas de sangre, Yerma,* and *La casa de Bernarda Alba.*

WALTER HOLZINGER, a critic of Latin American literature, has taught at the University of Toronto.

FRANK RIESS is the author of *The Word and the Stone: Language and Imagery in Pablo Neruda's* Canto general.

FERNANDO ALEGRÍA is Professor of Spanish and Portuguese at Stanford University. His books include *Instructions for Undressing the Human Race, Nueva historia de la novela hispanoamericana,* and *Retratos Contemporáneos.*

AMADO ALONSO, the late Spanish critic, is the author of *Poesía y estilo de Pablo Neruda.*

ALEXANDER COLEMAN is the Chairman of the Department of Spanish and Portuguese Language and Literature at New York University. He is the author of *Eca De Queiros & European Realism* and editor of *Cinco Maestros*.

JULIO CORTÁZAR was one of Latin America's major novelists. He is best known for his experimental novel *Rayuela* (*Hopscotch*).

E. RODRÍGUEZ MONEGAL was Professor of Latin American Literature at Yale University. He is the author of the two major studies on the two major Latin American writers of this century: Borges (*Jorge Luis Borges: A Literary Biography*) and Neruda (*El viajero inmóvil*) as well as numerous articles on Latin Literature.

GORDON BROTHERSTON is the Reader in the Department of Literature at the University of Essex. He is the author of *The Emergence of the Latin American Novel, Image of the New World, Latin American Poetry,* and *Manuel Machado: A Revaluation*.

JAIME ALAZRAKI is Professor of Romance Languages and Literature at Harvard University. He is the author of *Jorge Luis Borges, Poética y Poesía de Pablo Neruda, La prosa narrativa de Jorge Luis Borges,* and *Versiones, Inversiones, Reversiones*.

BEN BELITT, poet and Professor of Literature at Bennington College, is one of Neruda's principal translators. His books include *Adam's Dream* (essays) and *The Enemy Joy: New and Selected Poems*.

RENÉ DE COSTA is the author of *The Poetry of Pablo Neruda* and *Vincente Huidobro: The Careers of a Poet*.

MANUEL DURÁN is Chairman of the Department of Spanish at Yale University. He has written widely on the Spanish Golden Age and is editor of *Lorca: A Collection of Critical Essays*.

JOHN FELSTINER is Professor of English at Stanford University. He is the author of *Translating Neruda: The Way to Macchu Picchu*.

ROBIN WARNER teaches at the University of Sheffield, England.

ENRICO MARIO SANTÍ teaches in the Department of Latin American Studies at Cornell University. He is the author of *Pablo Neruda: The Poetics of Prophecy*.

FLORENCE L. YUDIN teaches at Florida International University. She is the author of *The "Vibrant Silence" in Jorge Guillén's Aire Nuestro*.

ALFRED J. MacADAM is a professor of Spanish-American literature at Columbia University, and the author of *El individuo el otro,* a study of Julio Cortázar.

FRANK MENCHACA has translated numerous articles on Latin American literature as well as poems by Pablo Neruda, Lezama Lima, and Nicolás Guillén. His first collection of poems is forthcoming.

Bibliography

Agosin, Marjorie. *Pablo Neruda*. Translated by Lorraine Ross. Boston: Twayne, 1986.
———. "Pablo Neruda and Nicanor Parra: A Study in Similarities." *Poesis* 6 (1984): 51–60.
Alazraki, Jaime. "El surrealismo de *Tentativa del hombre infinito*." *Hispanic Review* 40 (1972): 31–39.
———. "Pablo Neruda: The Chronicler of All Things." *Books Abroad* 46 (1972): 49–54.
Alegría, Fernando. Introduction to *Pablo Neruda: A Basic Anthology*. Translated by Carlos Lozano. New York: Las Americas, 1961.
———. "Two Worlds in Conflict." *Berkeley Review* 1 (1957): 24–27.
Aligher, Margarita. "Don Pablo at Home." *Soviet Literature* 11 (1977): 88–100.
Alonso, Amado. *Poesía y estilo de Pablo Neruda*. 3d ed. Buenos Aires: Sudamerica, 1966.
———. "The Stylistic Interpretation of Literary Texts." In *Velocities of Change: Critical Essays from* MLN, edited by Richard Macksey. Baltimore: Johns Hopkins University Press, 1974.
Alonso, J. M. "Neftalí Ricardo Reyes Invents Pablo Neruda." *Review* 72 (Winter 1971–Spring 1972): 33–36.
Anderson, David Gaskill, Jr. *Intertextuality in the Odas of Pablo Neruda*. Ann Arbor, Mich.: Dissertation Abstracts International, 1986.
Barnstone, Willis. "Hispanic Chronicle." *Poetry* 111 (October 1967): 46–55.
Beckett, Bonnie A. *The Reception of Pablo Neruda's Works in the German Democratic Republic*. Frankfurt am Main: Peter Lang, 1981.
Belitt, Ben. *Adam's Dream: A Preface to Translation*. New York: Grove, 1978.
Bizzarro, Salvatore. *Pablo Neruda: All Poets the Poet*. Metuchen, N.J.: Scarecrow, 1979.
Bly, Robert. "On Pablo Neruda." *London Magazine* 8 (July 1968): 24–25.
———. "Refusing to Be Theocritus." *Neruda and Vallejo: Selected Poems*, edited by Robert Bly. Boston: Beacon Press, 1971.

————. "The Surprise of Neruda." *The Sixties* 7 (1964): 18–19.

Brotherston, Gordon. *Latin American Poetry: Origins and Presence.* Cambridge: Cambridge University Press, 1975.

Cano Ballesta, Juan. "Pablo Neruda and the Renewal of Spanish Poetry during the Thirties." In *Spanish Writers of 1936,* edited by Jaime Ferran and Daniel P. Testa, 94–106. London: Tamesis Books, 1973.

————. *La poesía española entre pureza y revolución.* Madrid: Gredos, 1972.

Christ, Ronald. "Poet Who Is Too Big for the Nobel Prize." *Commonweal,* 26 December 1969, 388–94.

Cohen, Jonathan. "Neruda in English: The Controversy over Translation Poetics." *Missouri Review* 6 (1983): 176–92.

Cortázar, Julio. "Carta abierta a Pablo Neruda." *Revista Iberoamericana* nos. 82–83 (January–June 1973): 21–26.

de Costa, René. "Pablo Neruda's *Tentativa del hombre infinito:* Notes for a Reappraisal." *Modern Philology* 73 (1975–76): 136–47.

————. *The Poetry of Pablo Neruda.* Cambridge, Mass.: Harvard University Press, 1979.

Durán, Manuel, and Margery Safir. *Earth Tones: The Poetry of Pablo Neruda.* Bloomington: Indiana University Press, 1981.

Earle, Peter. "Whitman and Neruda and Their Implicit Cultural Revolution." In *Actes du Xe Congrès de l'Association Internationale de Littérature Comparée,* edited by Anna Balakian, James J. Wilhelm, Douwe W. Fokkema, Claudio Guillén, and J. M. Valdes. 189–193. New York: Garland, 1985.

Engler, Kay. "Image and Structure in Neruda's *Las alturas de Macchu Picchu.*" *Symposium* 27 (1974): 130–45.

Eshleman, Clayton. "Neruda: An Elemental Response." *Tri-Quarterly* 15 (1969): 228–37.

Evtushenko, Evengi. "The Feast of Justice." *Soviet Literature* 11 (1977):104–9.

Felstiner, John. "Arauco Redivivus in Pablo Neruda." *Review* 25–26 (1980): 110–16.

————. "A Feminist Reading of Neruda." *Parnassus: Poetry in Review* 3 (1975): 90–112.

————. "Neruda in Translation." *Yale Review* 61 (1972): 226–51.

————. "Pablo Neruda, 1904–1973." *The New Republic,* 13 October 1973, 27.

————. "Pablo Neruda: Nobel Prize at Isla Negra." *The New Republic,* 25 December 1971, 29–30.

————. *Translating Neruda: The Way to Macchu Picchu.* Stanford: Stanford University Press, 1980.

————. "In Translation." *American Poetry Review* 5 (March–April 1976): 39–43.

Fiedler, Leslie. "A Second Life: The English Translations of Neruda." Paper presented at a symposium on Pablo Neruda, University of Illinois at Urbana-Champaign, May 1972.

Forster, Merlin H. "Pablo Neruda and the Avant-Garde." *Symposium* 32 (1978): 208–20.

Fraser, G. S. *News from South America.* London: Harvill, 1949.

Frawley, William. "Prolegomenon to a Theory of Translation." In *Translation:*

Literary, Linguistic, and Philosophical Perspectives, edited by William Frawley. Newark: University of Delaware Press, 1984.

Gallagher, D. P. *Modern Latin American Literature.* New York: Oxford, 1973.

Gugelberger, Georg M. "Blake, Neruda, Ngugi wa Thiong'o: Issues in Third World Literature." *Comparative Literature Studies* 21 (1984): 463–82.

Gullón, Agnes. "Pablo Neruda at Macchu Picchu." *Chicago Review* 27 (Autumn 1975): 136–45.

Halperin, Maurice. "Pablo Neruda in Mexico." *Books Abroad* 15 (1942): 164–68.

Hamburger, Michael. *The Truth of Poetry: Tensions in Modern Poetry from Baudelaire to the 1960s.* London: Methuen, 1982.

Hart, Francis. "Notes for an Anatomy of Modern Autobiography." *New Literary History* 1 (1970): 485–511.

Karsen, Sonja. "Neruda's *Canto general* in Historical Context." *Symposium* 32 (1978): 220–35.

Lazer, Hank. "The Letter Poem." *Northwest Review* 19 (1981): 235–45.

Lechner, J. *El compromiso en la poesía española del siglo XX.* Madrid: Leyden, 1963.

Lozada, Alfredo. *El monismo agónico de Pablo Neruda.* Mexico: Costa-Amic, 1971.

MacShane, Frank. "Neruda in New York." *New York Times Book Review,* 13 March 1977, 3, 20.

McGrath, Thomas. "The Poetry of Pablo Neruda." *Mainstream* 15 (1962): 43–47.

Modern Poetry Studies 5 (Spring 1974). Special Pablo Neruda issue.

Monguio, Luis. "Kingdom of This Earth: The Poetry of Pablo Neruda." *Latin American Literary Review* 1 (1972): 13–24.

Mundt, Tito. "Neruda Speaking." *Atlas,* 15 January 1968, 55.

Ortega, José. "Pablo Neruda: The Making of a Political Poet." *Perspectives on Contemporary Literature* 2 (1976): 3–11.

Paysero, Ricardo. "The Dead Word of Pablo Neruda." *Tri-Quarterly* 15 (1969): 203–27.

Paz, Octavio. "Pablo Neruda en el corazón." *Ruta* 4 (1938): 24–33.

———. "Repuesta a un cónsul." *Letras de Mexico,* 15 August 1943.

Peña, Alfredo Cardona. *Pablo Neruda y otros ensayos.* Mexico: Ediciones de Andrea, 1955.

Pring-Mill, Robert. Introduction to *Pablo Neruda: A Basic Anthology,* xv–lxxix. Oxford: Dolphin, 1975.

———. "A Poet and His Roots." *Times Literary Supplement,* 16 April 1970, 397–99.

———. Preface to *The Heights of Macchu Picchu,* translated by Nathaniel Tarn, vii–xix. New York: Farrar, Straus, & Giroux, 1967.

———. "The Winter of Pablo Neruda." *Times Literary Supplement,* 3 October 1975, 1154–56.

Reid, Alastair. "The Chilean Poet Pablo Neruda 1904–1973." *Listener,* 4 October 1973, 437–39.

———. "A Visit to Neruda." *Encounter* 25 (September 1965): 67–70.

Review 74 (Spring 1974). Special issue on *Residence on Earth.*

Riess, Frank. *The Word and the Stone: Language and Imagery in Neruda's* Canto general. Oxford: Oxford University Press, 1972.

Rodman, Selden. *South America of the Poets.* Carbondale: Southern Illinois University Press, 1972.

Rodríguez Monegal, Emir. "The Biographical Background." *Review* 74 (Spring 1974): 6–14.

———. *El viajero inmóvil: Introducción a Pablo Neruda.* Buenos Aires: Losada, 1966. Rev. ed. Caracas: Monte Avila, 1977.

Rosenthal, M. L. "Journey toward Rebirth." *Saturday Review,* 2 September 1967, 25.

———. "Voyage into Neruda." *Review* 74 (Spring 1974): 30–32.

Rumold, Inca. "Lorca and Neruda in Erich Arendt's Poetry." *Montashefte* 77 (1985): 143–50.

Saalmann, Dieter. "The Role of Time in Neruda's *Alturas de Macchu Picchu.*" *Romance Notes* 18 (1977): 169–77.

Salmon, Russel, and Julia Lesage. "Stones and Birds: Consistency and Change in the Poetry of Pablo Neruda." *Hispania* 60 (1977): 224–41.

Santí, Enrico Mario. *Pablo Neruda: The Poetics of Prophecy.* Ithaca: Cornell University Press, 1982.

Schade, George D. "Sight, Sense and Sound; Seaweed, Onions, and Oranges: Notes on Translating Neruda." *Symposium* 38 (1984): 158–73.

Shaw, Donald L. "Ebrio de Trementina . . . : Another View." In *Readings in Spanish and Portuguese for Geoffrey Connell,* edited by Nicholas G. Round and D. Gareth Walters, 235–40. Glasgow: University of Glasgow, Department of Hispanic Studies, 1985.

Spitzer, Leo. *La enumeración caótica en la poesía moderna.* Translated by Raimundo Lida. Buenos Aires: Coni, 1945.

Terry, Arthur. "Pablo Neruda: 'El fantasma del buque de carga.' " In *Readings in Spanish and Portuguese Poetry for Geoffrey Connell,* edited by Nicholas G. Round and D. Gareth Walters, 241–58. Glasgow: University of Glasgow, Department of Hispanic Studies, 1985.

Tolman, John M. "Death and Alien Environment in Pablo Neruda's *Residencia en la tierra.*" *Hispania* 5 (1968): 79–85.

Tomlinson, Charles. "Overdoing the Generosity." *Times Literary Supplement,* 24 March 1983, 286.

Walsh, Donald D. "Some Thoughts on Translation." *Review* 74 (Spring 1974): 20–22.

Willard, Nancy. *Testimony of the Invisible Man: William Carlos Williams, Francis Ponge, Rainer Maria Rilke, Pablo Neruda.* Columbia: University of Missouri Press, 1969.

Wood, Michael. "The Poetry of Pablo Neruda." *New York Review of Books,* 3 October 1974, 8–10.

Yglesias, Jose. "The Poet in New York." *The Nation,* 11 July 1966, 53–55.

Acknowledgments

"Introduction of Pablo Neruda to the School of Philosophy and Letters, Madrid" by Federico García Lorca, translated by Frank Menchaca, from *Ombras Completas*, Volume 1, © 1977 by Herederos de Federico García Lorca. Reprinted with permission.

"Poetic Subject and Form in the *Odas elementales*" by Walter Holzinger from *Revista Hispánica Moderna* 36, nos. 1 & 2 (1970–71), © 1971 by Hispanic Institute, Columbia University. Reprinted with permission.

"The Poet and the Collectivity" by Frank Riess from *The Word and the Stone: Language and Imagery in Neruda's* Canto general by Frank Riess, © 1972 by Oxford University Press. Reprinted with permission.

"Reminiscences and Critical Reflections" (originally entitled "Neruda: Reminiscences and Critical Reflections") by Fernando Alegría, translated by Deborah Bundy, from *Modern Poetry Studies* 5, no. 1 (Spring 1974), © 1974 by Jerome Mazzaro. Reprinted with permission of Media Study/Buffalo.

"From Melancholy to Anguish" by Amado Alonso from *Review* 74, no. 11 (Spring 1974), © 1974 by the Center for Inter-American Relations, Inc. Reprinted with permission.

"Neruda: Vox Dei" by Alexander Coleman from *Review* 74, no. 11 (Spring 1974), © 1974 by the Center for Inter-American Relations, Inc. Reprinted with permission.

"Neruda among Us" by Julio Cortázar, translated by Frank Menchaca, from *Plural* 30 (1974), © 1974 by Julio Cortázar. Reprinted with permission.

"A Personal Poetry" by E. Rodríguez Monegal, translated by Frank Menchaca, from *Neruda: El viajero inmóvil*, © 1977 by Monte Avila Editores, C.A. Reprinted with permission.

"Neruda's *Canto general* and the Great Song of America" (originally entitled "The Great Song of America") by Gordon Brotherston from *Latin American Poetry: Origins and Presence* by Gordon Brotherston, © 1975 by Cambridge University Press. Reprinted with permission of Cambridge University Press and the author.

"Music as Silence in Neruda's Eight Posthumous Books of Poetry" by Jaime Alazraki from *Books Abroad* 50, no. 1, © 1976 by the University of Oklahoma Press. Reprinted with permission.

"Pablo Neruda: A Revaluation" by Ben Belitt from *Adam's Dream: A Preface to Translation* by Ben Belitt, © 1978 by Ben Belitt. Reprinted with permission of Grove Press, Inc.

"The Vanguard Experiment: *Tentativa del hombre infinito*" (originally entitled "The Vanguard Experiment") by René de Costa from *The Poetry of Pablo Neruda*, © 1979 by the President and Fellows of Harvard College. Reprinted with permission of Harvard University Press.

"Pablo Neruda and the Romantic-Symbolist Tradition" by Manuel Durán from *Actes du VIIIᵉ Congrès de l'Association Internationale de Littérature Comparée*, edited by Bela Kapeczi and Gregory M. Vajda, © 1980 by Manuel Durán. Reprinted with permission.

"Translating *Alturas de Macchu Picchu*" by John Felstiner is taken from *Translating Neruda: The Way to Macchu Picchu* by John Felstiner, © 1980 by the Board of Trustees of the Leland Stanford Junior University. Reprinted with permission of the Stanford University Press.

"The Politics of Pablo Neruda's *España en el corazón*" by Robin Warner from *Hispanic Studies in Honour of Frank Pierce*, edited by John England, © 1980 by Robin Warner. Reprinted with permission.

"Vision and Time" by Enrico Mario Santí from *Pablo Neruda: The Poetics of Prophecy* by Enrico Mario Santí, © 1982 by Cornell University Press. Reprinted with permission.

"The Dialectical Failure in Neruda's 'Las furias y las penas' " by Florence L. Yudin from *Hispania* 68, no. 1 (March 1985), © 1985 by The American Association of Teachers of Spanish and Portuguese. Reprinted with permission.

"Neruda's *España en el corazón*: Genre and Historical Moment" (originally entitled "Genre and Historical Moment") by Alfred J. MacAdam from *Textual Confrontations* by Alfred J. MacAdam, © 1987 by The University of Chicago Press. Reprinted with permission of The University of Chicago Press and the author.

" 'A Language Full of Wars and Songs' " by Frank Menchaca, © 1988 by Frank Menchaca. Published for the first time in this volume. Printed with permission.

Index